Changing Identities in Modern Southeast Asia

World Anthropology

General Editor

SOL TAX

Patrons

CLAUDE LÉVI-STRAUSS
MARGARET MEAD
LAILA SHUKRY EL HAMAMSY
M. N. SRINIVAS

MOUTON PUBLISHERS · THE HAGUE · PARIS
DISTRIBUTED IN THE USA AND CANADA BY ALDINE, CHICAGO

Changing Identities
in Modern Southeast Asia

Editor
DAVID J. BANKS

MOUTON PUBLISHERS · THE HAGUE · PARIS
DISTRIBUTED IN THE USA AND CANADA BY ALDINE, CHICAGO

General Editor's Preface

Anthropology has traditionally taken the peoples and cultures of continental and large-subcontinental areas of the world as subject matter. One of these areas is Southeast Asia, including both the mainland and the islands. As the Editor of this book points out, however, anthropologists have more often than not viewed this region not on its own merits but as marginal to the Far East on one side and to South Asia on the other. In contrast, this volume presents a "peoples' perspective" from within and was not surprisingly inspired by a Congress of scholars from the whole variety of the world's cultures.

Like most contemporary sciences, anthropology is a product of the European tradition. Some argue that it is a product of colonialism, with one small and self-interested part of the species dominating the study of the whole. If we are to understand the species, our science needs substantial input from scholars who represent a variety of the world's cultures. It was a deliberate purpose of the IXth International Congress of Anthropological and Ethnological Sciences to provide impetus in this direction. The *World Anthropology* volumes, therefore, offer a first glimpse of a human science in which members from all societies have played an active role. Each of the books is designed to be self-contained; each is an attempt to update its particular sector of scientific knowledge and is written by specialists from all parts of the world. Each volume should be read and reviewed individually as a separate volume on its own given subject. The set as a whole will indicate what changes are in store for anthropology as scholars from the developing countries join in studying the species of which we are all a part.

The IXth Congress was planned from the beginning not only to include as many of the scholars from every part of the world as possible, but also with a view toward the eventual publication of the papers in high-quality volumes. At previous Congresses scholars were invited to bring papers which were then read out loud. They were necessarily limited in length; many were only summarized; there was little time for discussion; and the sparse discussion could only be in one language. The IXth Congress was an experiment aimed at changing this. Papers were written with the intention of exchanging them before the Congress, particularly in extensive pre-Congress sessions; they were not intended to be read aloud at the Congress, that time being devoted to discussions—discussions which were simultaneously and professionally translated into five languages. The method for eliciting the papers was structured to make as representative a sample as was allowable when scholarly creativity—hence self-selection— was critically important. Scholars were asked both to propose papers of their own and to suggest topics for sessions of the Congress which they might edit into volumes. All were then informed of the suggestions and encouraged to rethink their own papers and the topics. The process, therefore, was a continuous one of feedback and exchange and it has continued to be so even after the Congress. The some two thousand papers comprising *World Anthropology* certainly then offer a substantial sample of world anthropology. It has been said that anthropology is at a turning point; if this is so, these volumes will be the historical direction-markers.

As might have been foreseen in the first postcolonial generation, the large majority of the Congress papers (82 per cent) are the work of scholars identified with the industrialized world which fathered our traditional discipline and the institution of the Congress itself: Eastern Europe (15 percent); Western Europe (16 percent); North America (47 percent); Japan, South Africa, Australia, and New Zealand (4 percent). Only 18 percent of the papers are from developing areas: Africa (4 percent): Asia-Oceania (9 percent); Latin America (5 percent). Aside from the substantial representation from the U.S.S.R. and the nations of Eastern Europe, a significant difference between this corpus of written material and that of other Congresses is the addition of the large proportion of contributions from Africa, Asia, and Latin America. "Only 18 percent" is two to four times as great a proportion as that of other Congresses;

moreover, 18 percent of 2,000 papers is 360 papers, 10 times the number of "Third World" papers presented at previous Congresses. In fact, these 360 papers are more than the total of *all* papers published after the last International Congress of Anthropological and Ethnological Sciences which was held in the United States (Philadelphia, 1956).

The significance of the increase is not simply quantitative. The input of scholars from areas which have until recently been no more than subject matter for anthropology represents both feedback and also long-awaited theoretical contributions from the perspectives of very different cultural, social, and historical traditions. Many who attended the IXth Congress were convinced that anthropology would not be the same in the future. The fact that the next Congress (India, 1978) will be our first in the "Third World" may be symbolic of the change. Meanwhile, sober consideration of the present set of books will show how much, and just where and how, our discipline is being revolutionized.

In the series of which this book is a part, readers will find a score of other books dealing with peoples and cultures—and problems— of other large regions of the world. There are at least another score treating comparatively other subjects touched upon in this book such as ethnicity, identity, migration, urbanization, and cultural forms and symbols; and political, economic, and social processes and problems.

Chicago, Illinois   SOL TAX
October 29, 1976

Table of Contents

Introduction

DAVID J. BANKS

Studies of Southeast Asian peoples and cultures have faced two fundamental problems in recent decades. The first problem resulted from a scholarly heritage of excessive emphasis upon the unity and integration of the Great Civilizations of China and India on either side, to the neglect of Southeast Asia as an area of any but synthetic and assimilated culture traits, only rarely attaining, in specific regions, the degree of integration considered worthy of serious study by historians. In reaction to this implication of Southeast Asia's second-class status as an area of research interest, much of the work concerning its peoples consisted of systematic attempts to refute those who alleged a lack of creativity on the part of Southeast Asians or who minimized their contributions to world history. Scholars concentrated their efforts on searching for the uniquely Southeast Asian elements in local cultures and on unearthing ruins of previously unknown civilizations. Much of the social anthropology of the region consists of holistic descriptions of ways of life, accompanied by assertions of their uniqueness and attempts to convince the wider public of the intrinsic value and worth of studying a not-quite Indian or Chinese region.

The integration of Southeast Asian cultures thus became a weapon to wield against those who regarded them unworthy of serious attention. This response led to a second problem. Against the background of the academic "culturalism" of students of India and China (who spoke with excessive zeal and confidence about integration and variants within the Great Traditions), students of the so-called "marginal areas" of Southeast Asia developed reified models of their own. The bibliographies of ethnological literature of the area reveals the ahistorical quality of much of the work. In asserting the independence of Southeast Asia from the great civilizations to the east and west, many scholars took refuge in extreme application of the culture concept, divorcing their studies from change and history or incorporating history in culture through self-actualizing theories of development of micro-areas within the larger region. Certainly these statements about the ethnology of this area do not apply to all of the work in the field; lists of examples could be matched by exceptions. However, the tension has remained. One would either find a culture or a congery, and the latter possibility has been more disturbing to many than the former. For example, in formerly colonial areas, Europeans looked to custom, broadly defined, as a category from which bodies of legal insight were drawn, even when there was considerable behavioral deviation from ideal norms and differences of opinion concerning these norms.

The studies in this volume represent the harvest of a later perspective in Southeast Asian studies. Cultures are not simply studied as if they were independent entities, but are viewed instead as complex historical growths with consistent and persistent interchange between local groups. Ethnicity, in these often bi- or trilingual societies, is viewed as a series of ways of defining one's group or one's self-identity in contrast to those of other groups, in specific contexts. The writers emphasize the subtlety of the ethnic factors that produce distinctive forms of group and individual behavior, belief, and value. This emphasis is perhaps most apparent in the papers by Feingold, Hassan and Benjamin, and Kandre, and is addressed directly in the contributions of Dentan, who states the problem eloquently, and Banks, who discusses reification as an artifact of status and power variables in the field situation—but I think that all of the papers reveal a refreshing caution with respect to statements about whole cultures. Other contributions point to the crucial relevance of government policies in understanding social and cultural processes in Southeast Asia both within and between groups. The individual is not simply part of a unitary, ethnically defined category; rather, he may identify with any one of a series of sometimes conflicting sets of behaviors, beliefs, and values, and he may do so quite differently in different situations. Finally, and certainly not of least importance, the study of whole cultures has given place to an interest in the effects of cultural factors in specific local settings (see the articles by Banks and Zamora) and in the histories of areas (e.g. Wilder's article).

All in all, I would hope that this volume is not only a contribution to our knowledge about the peoples of Southeast Asia, but that it gives us some indication of where we are and where we might productively be going. It appears that in the new Southeast Asian studies, neither Asian nor Western scholars will possess an absolute advantage; rather, each will be able to view the contributions of himself and others as fruitful, much in the way that the Southeast Asian peoples under study have often viewed themselves and other groups: with caution and eclecticism.

The essays included in this volume were submitted to the IXth International Congress of Anthropological and Ethnological Sciences held in Chicago in September 1973 and were included in a panel of the same title. The panel was organized around several themes: aboriginal peoples in nation states; unity in diversity within the region as a whole and in subareas; on-going trends such as transmigration, population growth, frontiersmanship, rural-urban migration, and the effects of economic development and modernization on ethnicity in short- and long-term periods. Discussants at the panel were Professors Edward Bruner, F. K. Lehman, R. K. Dentan, Mario Zamora, and myself. Professor E. R. Leach offered helpful comments, joining the panel as a discussant of discussants. I also wish to express special thanks to Professors Kenneth David, Willis Sibley, Mario Zamora, R. K. Dentan, and F. K. Lehman, for useful suggestions at various stages of the preparation of the panel and its resultant volume, as well as to Professor Sol Tax, Ms. Gay Neuberger of the Congress staff, Ms. Karen Tkach of Mouton and, of course, my wife, Professor Ellen Banks. Finally, I wish to express my eternal gratitude to my father in Malaya, Md. Isa bin Hussin, to whose memory this volume is affectionately dedicated.

Political Functionaries in Rural Malaysia: Leaders or Middlemen?

SYED HUSIN ALI

This paper attempts to identify the significant categories of leading political functionaries in rural Malaya and to analyze their main roles within the context of their own society. The term "leading political functionaries" refers here particularly to those who occupy leading positions and play active parts in the branches of political parties at the village level. Of course there are others besides them who have political functions that are already institutionalized, as, for example, the *penghulu* [headman], but since the headman primarily serves as the smallest cog in the bureaucratic machinery (being head of the *mukim* [the administrative units into which the district is divided] and subordinate to the District Officer), his role may be viewed as being more administrative than political (cf. Husin Ali 1968:95–145; Burridge 1957). But some *penghulu* also participate in the activities of party politics, and, in the situation where this occurs, they will be referred to. The discussion in this paper is based upon data collected in the course of a number of field trips undertaken between 1962 and 1969 to three rural communities: Bagan in Johore, Kangkong in Kedah, and Kerdau in Pahang.

The concept of "middleman" or "broker" has been quite widely used to analyze the political relationship between smaller local communities and the wider structures they belong to. For instance, F. G. Bailey sees the middleman as the person who bridges the gap

The result of this study was presented as a Ph.D. thesis to the London School of Economics, and is now being published by Oxford University Press, Kuala Lumpur, under the title, *Malay peasants: Society and leadership.*

in communication between the smaller encapsulated structure and a bigger encapsulating one. The gap between the two structures may be the result of either a radical divergence in their cultural base or in their cultural values. Owing to these divergences, there exists between the smaller and bigger structures a state of discontinuity and conflict; thus, the success of the middleman lies in the ability to mediate between them, and this "can depend on his ability to deceive: to misrepresent the strength and intentions of both sides to each other" (Bailey 1970:168). On the other hand, A. C. Mayer does not stress the aspect of discontinuity and conflict very much, but, in fact, perceives the possibility of a middleman existing when central government or administration permeates and affects local level politics. Nevertheless, like Bailey, he also relates the success of the middleman with his ability to deceive, especially within the framework of political "action-sets." For him, the middleman carries out a kind of transactional relationship: ". . . the transaction is one in which he promises to obtain favours . . . [and] . . . the broker cannot maintain his reputation if too many of his efforts are unsuccessful" (Mayer 1966:114).

Perhaps, in the context of Malaya, those who most closely resemble the middlemen defined by Bailey and Mayer are the leading political functionaries. They have come into being as a result, particularly, of the postwar political development when several political parties were formed with the prime purpose of fighting for independence (*Merdeka*). These parties established branches in the rural areas in order to widen their support, and more often than not they are led by the people in the villages themselves. After *Merdeka* in 1957, some of the old parties continued to exist, together with some branches, but new ones were also formed. During the period under study, there were branches of four political parties in the communities studied: the United Malay National Organization (UMNO); the Pan-Malayan Islamic Party (PMIP); the Socialist Front (SF); and the Parti Negara (PN). At the time of the fieldwork for this paper, Bagan had branches of the UMNO and the PN; Kangkong had the UMNO and the PMIP; while Kerdau had the UMNO, the PMIP, and the SF.

The party branches in the three communities studied do not have large membership (they usually have from fifteen to forty members, although some of them have a larger following). Members are defined formally as those who have applied for membership and been accepted; they have at least paid membership fees, although most of them are irregular with their annual subscriptions. But there are also people in these areas who claim themselves members of one or the other party without having properly registered themselves. There are also those who are regarded as members of one or the other party because of their frequent appearance in the various functions held by that party. It is not unusual for some of them to claim to be, or to be regarded as, members of different parties at different times, depending on the company they are in at a particular time and what they hope to get. Only the "core" of a particular branch is fully committed to the branch, often showing their commitment by their willingness to do work for the party.

Generally, active people in the branches are small in number, confined mainly to a few leading members in the branch committees. They are often chosen either by consensus or by a show of hands during general meetings, and the same people seem generally to occupy the more important posts. They are the ones who normally initiate activities, discuss questions among themselves, and make decisions sometimes over the heads of the other committee members and the general membership. More often than not, these few people keep the branches alive and are regarded as the "strong men" of the branches. Through the branches, they organize welfare, cultural, social, sporting, and educational activities. Political activities seem to be confined mainly to the period before and during general elections.

Members of committees in the various branches come from a variety of backgrounds: among them are ex-officials, teachers, peasants, and laborers. But what seems to be significant is that most of the leading officeholders—the chairmen, secretaries, and treasurers—are mainly people who are respected, or in other words, who enjoy high status within their own communities. Two processes have led to this general arrangement. The first one is from above: quite often branches are first established through the initiative of organizers from the nearest district or state organizations. These organizers try initially to interest respected villagers to join the party and to start a local branch. The latter often prove to be efficient in drawing the support of their relatives, friends, and clients.

The second process is from below: with or without the initial push from above in the formation of the branches, these branches actually have a say in the choice of their leaders. The normal practice of the branch membership electing their own committee is often followed in a meeting. In the process of election, members tend to

2

choose the more respected among them for leading positions in the committee.

In the beginning, the UMNO especially was able to recruit its leaders from those who were in government service at the rural level. Later there was a ruling which restricted government servants from holding office in political parties, and this prevented many teachers and *penghulu* from being openly active. It did not, however, prevent them from being active behind the scenes, strongly influencing some of the branches. Some branches have had to turn to other people for their leading officeholders, since, arising from the government restriction, many of the serving teachers and *penghulu* are not readily available. One category of persons taking over the leading positions are the ex-government officials, particularly retired teachers, *penghulu*, and clerks. These ex-officials have several advantages. They are often quite advanced in age, and because of this they may be respected, as long as they are not considered senile. Of course, being ex-teachers and ex-*penghulu*, they enjoy high status. Furthermore, some of them are also owners of land (the tendency for some officials to become landlords is quite a common one). A second category consists of the relatively wealthy, especially landlords who are distinguished from those in the first category because they have never been in government service. Also, most of them may not have the advantage of education that those in the first category have. Although wealth as such may sometimes be despised as a source of evil, it is a great advantage if it is combined with other factors which give status, either ascribed or achieved. Another category is made up of the peasants themselves, especially those who are quite educated and who show the qualities of integrity, sincerity, eloquence, and an ability to organize, compensating for their lack of wealth and experience in government service. Finally, there are still some teachers who continue to be openly active. Most of them do not work with the government, but there are also a few who are able to ignore the government ruling, either because they are protected by important people, or because the implementation of the ruling is not so rigid in their areas.

Of the seven chairmen of the party branches in the three areas, three are ex-officials, two are landlords, and two are peasants; out of seven secretaries, one is an ex-official, two are landlords, and two are peasants; and out of the seven treasurers, three are landlords, one is an ex-official, one is a teacher, one is a peasant, and one is a laborer. Judging from these figures, it appears that the ex-officials serve mainly as chairmen, while the landlords act mainly as treasurers (although some of them are also chairmen). As for the secretaries, most of them are teachers, but there are also peasants among them. In terms of age, most of the chairmen are already rather old, usually around sixty, while the secretaries are relatively young—still within the thirties and forties. Most of the work in the branches is done by the secretaries. They are active and are often in effective control, with chairmen serving more as symbols. This pattern is common particularly in UMNO and PAS, while in the SF, most of the officeholders are peasants, with one laborer holding office.

Most of these leading officeholders are from high status categories in the village communities. Many of the ex-officials—and of course the landlords—have control over land, enabling them to be in good positions to mobilize and influence some of the villagers, especially those villagers who operate the land as tenants or laborers. To some extent, the nature of the influence that the landlords have over the tenants and laborers may be explained on the basis of what is often typified as the relationship between patrons and clients (cf. Blok 1969:365–378; Scott 1972; Wolf 1966:1–22). But it can also be more complex than that. Insofar as the landlords control the land and are free to choose who will operate the land, and insofar as the lives of the tenants and laborers depend on the "kindness" of the landlords, it can be said that the landlords are "patrons," and the tenants and laborers their "clients," at least in economic terms. Economically the clients are tied down to the patrons, because the amount of land available for operation is small compared to the supply of labor. So, for fear of offending the landlords and consequently losing the opportunity to work on their land, the tenants and laborers may sometimes have to—or at least appear to—support them. This is even more the case when the landlords are highly respected, and above all when they have kinship relationships with the tenants and laborers. For all these reasons, the landlords are able to determine some of the political behavior of the tenants and laborers.

There can be a certain amount of conflict of a class nature between the landlords, and the tenants and laborers. The peasants are often polite and seldom express their antagonisms against their landlords openly. Many of them consistently try to avoid direct confrontations, especially with landlords who are considered to have some status, because these can become unpleasant and can lead to the peasant being condemned as "ill-mannered" (*kurang ajar*). In such situations, the peasants may hide their true feelings, saying that they support the politics of their landlord, while they quietly oppose him, especially during the general elections. As some of them say, "wait till the election—we will see how." It appears that at a time when they are unable or not sufficiently organized to express their class conflicts or to show dissent with the landlords, they hope that the election, which ensures them some secrecy of their true feelings, will bring about changes for them.

In contrast to those who have control over land, there are those who have control over communication. They include ex-officials, teachers, and peasants elected to leading positions. They are often more literate than the others in the villages. They can talk fluently and persuasively during meetings; they know the art of writing letters to officials in the towns; and they also know how to keep minutes and records. Some of them do not feel ill at ease or afraid in the company of officials who may be associated with political parties or governmental departments. The teachers especially are quite close to the villages because their work concerns them with the village children, the parents, and education at the rural level in general. They are in more constant touch than the other villagers with news in their own communities and the outside world as well, because they read newspapers and frequently maintain contact with colleagues in the towns.

All these things give the teachers respect among the villagers. The villagers also go to them for help from time to time. When children pass the examinations to go to secondary schools, their parents often go to the headmaster or the teachers for advice as to what to expect and what preparations to make. These parents may also try to get help to recommend their children for some welfare aid or minor scholarships. Furthermore, some of the villagers may also ask help, not only from the teachers, but also from their more educated colleagues, to fill out forms or to write letters of application for land or financial aid for replanting rubber on their land. As a result of the help and favors that those who are educated can give, the peasants tend to feel obliged to them. Such feelings of obligation are often expressed as "kindness debts" (*hutang budi*), and according to a common Malay saying such a debt may be more difficult to repay than a debt of gold, and may even be remembered unto death (*Hutang emas boleh dibayar, hutang budi dibawa mati*). Even when this feeling of indebtedness does not really result in a strong relationship of obligation, it may at least strengthen the bond of friendship and respect, which can be very useful for mobilizing support.

Most of the leading personalities in party branches do not confine their activities to politics alone; they may also be involved in nonpolitical activities. In the three areas, there are various forms of associations. For example, in Kangkong there is a youth club and a cooperative society; in Kerdau there is a youth club and a welfare society; and in Bagan there is a youth club, a welfare society, and a cooperative society. All these associations are normally run by committees elected by their members. In addition, institutions like the schools and mosques also have their own committees. Although the headmasters and the "prayer leaders" (*imams*) are often the secretaries of the schools and the mosque committees respectively, other members of the committee are elected. In the case of the schools, committee members are elected by parents of students and ex-students, and in the case of the mosques, regular members of Friday congregations elect members.

In the committees of these associations and institutions, the teachers and the *penghulu* are not restricted from active participation. Many leading posts such as chairmanships and secretariats are taken by teachers, but there are also some ex-officials and landlords holding them. Some of the leading members in the party branches may compete for, or more often are persuaded to take, offices in the associations and institutions. In addition, there are also some who play leading roles within the belief systems too, either as magicians (*pawang*) or *imam* (cf. Taib Bin Osman 1972:219–231). When there are situations in which the same person holds different leading positions in different political and nonpolitical associations and institutions, or when he plays a leading role as religious functionary, there is a tendency to what may be called a "concentration of leadership" at the rural level. Such concentration, found in the three villages studied, is illustrated in Table 1.

Table 1 shows leading positions held outside their branches by seven chairmen and seven secretaries of the various party branches—those listed on the left column. "Leading positions" refers to positions such as chairman, secretary, and treasurer in committees of the various associations and institutions, and positions such as functionaries in the belief, and traditional political, systems. Most of these individuals hold two or three leading positions outside the party branches. This concentration of leadership does not result from deliberate attempts by the leaders in the various party branches to capture other associations in order to manipulate them for political advantage. Actually such deliberate attempts seldom take

Table 1.   Nonpolitical positions held by chairmen and secretaries of party branches

	Youth	Welfare	Co-op.	Mosque	School	Headman	Iman/Pawang
Kangkong:							
A1	—	—	—	—	—	—	—
A2	—	—	—	1	—	1	—
A5	—	—	1	—	1	—	—
A6	1	—	—	1	—	—	—
Kerdau:							
B1	1	1	—	—	1	—	—
B2	—	1	—	—	1	—	1
B3	1	—	—	—	—	—	—
B4	—	—	—	1	—	—	1
B5	—	1	—	1	—	—	—
B6	—	—	—	—	1	—	—
Bagan:							
C1	—	1	1	—	1	1	—
C2	—	—	—	—	1	—	—
C3	—	1	—	1	—	—	—
C4	—	—	—	1	—	—	1

Source: questionnaires.
Key: figures 1, 2, 3, in left column denote chairmen, and figures 4, 5, 6 denote secretaries of branches.

place. But what it really indicates is that there is a small number of people in rural areas who tend to be repeatedly chosen for positions of leadership because of their popularity, their ability, or their high status.

It is interesting to note that some of them hold positions within the traditional frameworks (e.g., two are headmen, two are *imams*, and one is a *pawang*). As a result of the respect these people enjoy through having traditional roles, they have been elected to take up leading positions in the party branches. This shows a continuity in leadership: leaders in traditional institutions, they are later elected leaders of modern associations. Some villagers still attach great importance to traditional factors in their choice of leaders, even for modern associations. For example, in Kerdau the local UMNO continuously persuaded an ex-*penghulu* to remain as their chairman, even though he repeatedly asked to be released of the post because of his age and general weakness of health. When he finally was released, his son succeeded him. Although the son was not well educated and did not display much ability either as speaker or organizer, he served as evidence to the villagers that the ex-*penghulu* was still associated with the UMNO.

In party politics, some people inside the party branches (like the leading committee members) and some outside them (like the *penghulu* and headmaster) have a great deal of influence. Serving, for their parties, as important links with the rural people, they ensure the support of these people to their parties, as, for instance, during the general elections to elect representatives to the State Legislative Council and the Federal Parliament. These elected representatives, whether they are State Council members or Federal Parliamentarians, are generally known as *wakil rakyat* [people's representatives]. Although there are branches of different parties in different states, most *penghulu*, as, for example, those in Kangkong and Bagan, tend to serve the party in power. These *penghulu* and the leading members of local branches, when the branches have party candidates who have been elected as representatives, often become middlemen between the representatives and their voters. The *penghulu*, as a government servant, is a subordinate to the District Officer within the framework of the administration, but he may also be a middleman for the elected representatives within the framework of party politics. As for the leading members of the party branches, they are middlemen for their respective parties only, or for the parties as well as the "people's representatives"—if their parties have succeeded in the election—without in any way being obliged to serve the District Officer.

As middlemen in party politics, the *penghulu* and some of the leading committee members in the party branches act as channels through which council members and parliamentarians can reach at least a segment of the villagers within their constituencies, and vice versa. The flow of influence and authority between the elected representatives and District Officer, and the rural people is shown in Figure 1. The District Officer, as head of the district administration, can reach the villagers through the *penghulu*, who in turn reaches the villagers either personally or through the headman supporting him, and through the leading members of the branches. The District Officer may even reach the villagers directly—in fact, personal and direct contact with their voters is one good way of ensuring popularity. But the *penghulu* and the leading members of the branches are not legally bound to serve the representatives in the way that the *penghulu* is obliged to serve the District Officer; instead they become middlemen on account of their allegiance to the representative and/or the party. Although a combination of many factors such as the personality of the representative, the standing of the party, and the policies of the party attract such allegiance, there is no doubt that the ability of the representative and the party to meet certain requests for the benefit of the middlemen or the villagers is also an important factor.

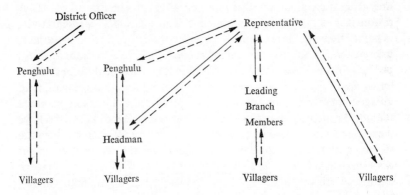

Figure 1. Flow of influence and authority between the District Officer and representatives and the villagers

The villagers make requests, for example, for land, mosques, or roads, from the government. There are two channels at the rural level which can normally be used for making such requests: villagers can work through the *penghulu* or through the leading members of the party branches. These people, as middlemen, may convey the requests either to the District Officer, to the elected representative, or both. While the *penghulu* can convey requests to both the representative and the District Officer, the leading branch members often go to their elected representative first. Of course, there are also villagers who ignore the middlemen and go straight to the elected representative or the District Officer. The District Officer is no more than an administrator, and the extent to which he can meet these requests is determined largely by the resources made available to him by the government and the plans of the government for that area. Subject to these factors, his decisions are made primarily on the basis of his administrative judgment, without taking into much consideration their possible effects on his personal popularity because his office does not depend upon popularity among voters.

What the District Officer can do is quite limited. There is a greater tendency now for villagers to make their requests through the elected representatives, who, after all, have made several promises during election campaigns. The villagers see that these representatives, as members of the policy-making bodies—the Legislative Council and/or Parliament—are the real sources of power. The members of Parliament especially are under pressure to do what they can to meet the requests of the villagers, who, with the voting power in their hands, have a great deal of control over their future.

It is not always the case that these representatives are able to meet the requests of the villagers. Promises made during elections and the publicity given to government programs to raise the standards of living, particularly in the rural areas, increase the expectations of the villagers. When these expectations are not realized, the villagers react in different ways. They may try to shift their support to another party to advance another person as the elected representative. The shifting of support from one party to another, even among those who are considered strong men of one party or other, is quite a common feature; it is often jocularly referred to as "leap-frogging" (*lompat-melompat*). But though this practice is quite common, it has not resulted in changes in the representatives from the constituencies affecting the three areas studied. In Kerdau and Bagan, the candidates from the UMNO have been successful in the three general elections that have been held. But in Kangkong, although the UMNO candidates were victorious in 1959 and 1964, they lost to the PMIP in 1969. The defeat of the UMNO in Kangkong cannot be attributed wholly to the dissatisfaction of the majority of voters in the constituency with the performance of the representative there. What was more important was that the persistence of the PAS propaganda finally convinced the majority of the voters that the UMNO (through the Alliance) had not been fighting for the interest of the Malays, and so ought to be replaced (Husin Ali 1968:51–60).

When people shift their party support or try to change their representatives, they are still acting within the framework of the law. However, dissatisfaction with the government and disappointment with the representatives for their inability to meet requests and demands may lead the villagers to adopt methods that are considered to be outside the framework of the law. For instance, many villagers in the three areas studied—as is quite common in the rest of the country—have been applying for land with no results, even after waiting for several years. They have tried to get the help of their elected representatives, but to no avail. As a last resort, many of them have organized themselves into small groups, have chosen their own leaders, and then have illegally opened land on their own. There is little chance to do this in Kangkong because most of the surrounding land has been cultivated. In Bagan, some villagers have gone further inland or to other areas, but in Kerdau, where there is still a lot of jungle available, many of them simply clear the land in or near the area. It is interesting that these activities have brought out leaders from among the peasants themselves. They have not had the support of the authorities for what they do, but they hope some pressure can be brought to bear on the government, so they will finally get the land that they have opened up illegally.

In the three areas studied, the movement by peasants to open land illegally has not been very sizeable or dramatic. One of the biggest such movements occurred in the state of Selangor and was led by one Hamid Tuah. Although he and the movement are outside the three areas, they will be examined here as an example of a new development in the nature of rural leadership.

Hamid Tuah was an auxiliary police constable. On leaving the service in 1955, he was given a piece of land which he worked and on which he built a house. He was often visited by a number of people from an area on the coast of Selangor. These people were mostly without land or regular jobs. They had made applications for land from the government through the local *penghulu* and political leaders but without success. They often discussed their plight with him. One day they agreed that the best thing to do was to go on their own and open new land without going through the normal government procedure. Led by Tuah, fifty of them occupied a piece of land in Sungai Sireh in 1960. Apparently it had already been planned that the land would be consigned to some villagers. So the *penghulu* and then the District Officer tried to persuade these "illegal squatters" to leave. They refused. Soon the Chief Minister stepped in, and when persuasion failed, a squad of policemen was finally sent to evict them. The leader was arrested and then sent to restricted residence. But meanwhile the vernacular newspapers gave wide publicity to the incident, and the public was sympathetic. The evicted peasants started a sit-down strike in front of the State Chief Minister's office, which lasted more than two weeks. It ended only when the Deputy Prime Minister of the country stepped in and promised that land would be given to them.

After a few years, Tuah was again approached by peasants to

lead them in another land-opening movement. Among them were some from the previous group, who said that the land promised after the first rebellion was never given. About 400 of them occupied an area of Telok Gong in 1967. There they erected small huts, and some of them brought their wives and children. Soon the authorities stepped in. Once again, much publicity was attracted, and the action of the peasants was supported vocally by university students and some academic staff. The students held a demonstration in front of the State Secretariat, which drew the attention of the country to the serious problem of land hunger among the rural people. Eventually, a group of lecturers and writers offered to mediate between the peasants and the state government. The government finally conceded to give land in Telok Gong, along with some other land, to these peasants.

In 1969, Tuah again led the same kind of movement, this time involving a larger group of people, estimated at about 1,500. They came from the coastal area of Selangor and neighboring Perak. Occupying a jungle area at Binjai Patah, they started clearing the forest. At that time the country was in a state of emergency, following the 13 May Incident,[1] and the government decided to move fast. A 24-hour curfew was imposed over the area, and police moved in to disperse the peasants. About 100 of them were arrested, while the others fled. Then, when the police withdrew, the peasants came back to the area. This time, the students and some politicians again came to their support, but the newspapers, under tighter control during the emergency, played the incident down. A number of local *penghulu* in the coastal area, backed by leading members of some UMNO branches, organized a campaign to condemn the "squatters" and tried to persuade the villagers in the area to support them. Once more, the security forces moved in to surround them, a curfew was declared, and workers from the public works department were mobilized by the government to destroy the temporary shelters built by the peasants and to confiscate their tools and utensils. Again many people were arrested, including Tuah. While the peasants arrested were charged in court, their leader was still in preventive detention. He was released in January 1970.

---

[1] The 13 May Incident refers to the outbreak of racial conflict, particularly in Kuala Lumpur, the capital of Malaysia, immediately following the country's general election. As a result of this incident, a state of emergency was declared, Parliament was suspended, and the country was ruled under a National Operations Council.

For the peasants involved, Hamid Tuah acted mainly as a symbolic leader. There were at least six group leaders during the Bijai Patah incident, and they were the ones who were present and directing the actions of the peasants. They consulted with one another; they supervized the movement of the peasants, the building of their sheds and shelters, and the forming of work teams to clear the jungle. These peasant leaders did not emerge through any formally instituted kind of association. They acted in defiance of authority and so were without the support and sympathy of the leaders from the bureaucracy and the governing party. In addition, they acted independently of any political party. They argued that the administration and the ruling party were not interested in their plight and that the other political parties were not willing to help them, beyond making verbal demands. Thus, they took matters into their own hands.

The movement did not support any particular political party. In fact, among those who participated in Telok Gong and Binjai Patah were several members of different political parties, from the government as well as the opposition. What brought them together was their common lot, that of peasants wanting land. In this type of movement the leadership came from among themselves rather than being fashioned by, or imposed upon them, from the top. Through their actions, they forced their problems and issues before the public. Some members of the public—in student or political bodies—acted in sympathy, and in this way the basis of support for the peasant movement was broadened. The pressure was brought to bear upon the government to act: it had either to concede to the peasants, as in the case of Telok Gong, or to smash them, for fear that they would grow into a large and powerful force, as in the case of Binjai Patah.

In these movements, leadership is exercised from the bottom upwards. The peasant leaders act as instruments of the peasants, to put their demands before the higher authorities. This is different from the *penghulu* and the main party functionaries at the rural level, who, while trying in limited ways to voice and meet the requests of the villagers, actually act mainly as instruments for the authorities above. Their actions are often consonant with the interests of the higher authorities, and most of the time their roles are to act as middlemen for the leaders at the top, to impose leadership downwards.

Although there are people who open up land illegally in the three areas, there has been nothing on the scale of the actions of Hamid Tuah and his followers. Most villagers in these areas express their support for what the peasants in Selangor have done. In fact, some villagers in Pahang who live quite near Kerdau apparently approached Hamid Tuah before he was placed under custody to lead a similar movement in the state. But nothing came of it after he was detained. The *penghulu* and the leading members of the party branches in the three areas still dominate, and, although they may occasionally serve to transmit upwards the wishes of the villagers, most of the time they serve the interests or wishes of the representatives and administrators above them. The *penghulu* do this because they have their jobs to look after. The leading members of the branches of the governing party have already gained something for themselves, by becoming teachers of adults or by receiving land. In this, they differ dramatically from the leaders who come from the ranks of the peasants themselves in the course of movements to open up land.

REFERENCES

BAILEY, F. G.
    1970   *Strategems and spoils.* Oxford: Blackwells.
BLOK, A.
    1969   Variations in patronage. *Sociologische Gids* no. 6 (November/ December): 365–378.
BURRIDGE, K. O. L.
    1957   Rural administration in Johore. *Journal of African Administration* 9(1).
HUSIN ALI, S.
    1968   Patterns of rural leadership in Malaya. *Journal of Malaysia Branch of the Royal Asiatic Society* 41 (1):95–145.
    1972   Some aspects of change, mobility, and conflict in post-Merdeka Malaysia. *Manusia dan Masharakat* 1:51–60.
MAYER, A. C.
    1966   "The significance of quasi-groups in the study of complex societies," in *The social anthropology of complex societies.* Edited by J. M. Banton, 97–122. London: Tavistock.
SCOTT, JAMES C.
    1972   The erosion of patron–client bonds and social change in rural Southeast Asia. *Journal of Asian Studies* 32 (1):5–37.

TAIB BIN OSMAN, MOHD.
1972   Patterns of supernatural promises underlying the institution of the Bomoh in Malay culture. *Bijdragen* 128 (203):219–231.
WOLF, ERIC R.
1966   "Kinship, friendship, and patron–client relations in complex societies," in *The social anthropology of complex societies*. Edited by J. M. Banton, 1–22. London: Tavistock.

Rivers' Tent in Southeast Asia: Ethnicity, Relative Status, and Empathy in Fieldwork

DAVID J. BANKS

It is said that W. H. R. Rivers, one of the founders of modern kinship studies and a major contributor to the tradition of intensive fieldwork in anthropology, gathered data by setting up a tent near Toda villagers' houses and inviting them in to talk about their quaint, strange way of life. This essay will discuss the problem of the role of the ethnicity of the anthropologist in his formulation of ethnic characterizations of peoples. Anthropologists may no longer, as Rivers did, assume that they are studying a way of life that is a positive reality, and that they, themselves, are neutral stimuli in the communities that they study. Instead, the writer will argue that the content of the data gathered, its emphases and biases, are always influenced by two closely interrelated factors present in the field situation, as in any other: relative status or prestige of the studier and the studied as defined in local terms, and a more subtle concept that is not less real—empathy. By empathy, the writer means the degree to which the anthropologist becomes entrapped in, and moulded by, the emotional concerns of the community in which he resides during the period of his residence and the extent to which he expresses this through use of local social forms. Some might argue that the degree of empathy, so defined, is inversely related to some factor of objectivity—that is, the more empathy, the less objectivity. However, the writer will suggest that although empathy does affect the content

This paper is an expanded version of a presentation made at the IXth ICAES in September 1973. I wish to thank Professors R. K. Dentan and E. R. Leach for comments on the earlier draft.

and quality of information gathered, one may not make absolute judgments concerning its worth.

Rivers' fieldwork methods appear to have produced the maximal status differential, he being the superordinate and his Toda informants wards of the Crown. Although one may only impute psychological motives to another with the greatest difficulty, it appears that establishing distance between himself and those he studied was part of Rivers' research strategy. Rivers distrusted information that he gained from any single informant and avoided the pitfalls of gathering false information from a single individual who could mislead him. Since the Todas were "inveterate beggars," he felt it wise to take an added precaution: to pay informants by the hour rather than for the information collected from them in terms of amount and quality. Rivers claims to have adhered to these rules save for rare exceptions when he would pay an individual for specific information. In difficult situations, when one informant appeared to be avoiding a subject, Rivers passed on to another topic and hired another person, asking him about the topic that the other was reluctant to speak about. Rivers did not regard empathy as a significant factor in anthropological methods or methodology. To be emotionally involved would have exposed him to the risk of being tricked.

In this essay I will contend that, just as Rivers' status relationship with Toda villagers and his lack of empathy with them (I shall call it "negempathy")[1] have called basic results of his work into question (see Yalman 1967:337–343), more recent fieldwork commonly regarded as "classic" has had an effect that is not far different than that of Rivers. While Rivers sought to control the quality of the data he later published through a series of precautions against attempts to sell fraudulent information, he may well simply have uncovered the kinds of information that Toda informants believed he would consider different from his own experience, and hence interesting. The effect of Rivers' work and of much of modern cultural anthropology has been to "bring to" the anthropologist a picture of a unique "way of life" presented in terms of core symbols of ethnic identities interesting enough to publish and sell monographs and articles, and to build careers—as if social scientists were physicists searching for new particles or waves. Furthermore, it appears that in the modern world, the creation of unique cultural

---

[1] I have chosen to use the term "negempathy" instead of "antipathy" since it simply implies the opposite pole in a continuum, rather than the positive implication of disdain the latter term might connote.

life-styles is more and more untenable as forces like urbanization, industrialization, education, and relocation of populations proceed around the globe. In such circumstances, cultural differences become quite subtle when one asks how peoples with unique histories will react to such forces. Rivers' cold exterior (perhaps a result of his medical training in neurology) created a kind of anthropology that was not unique either for his own time or for later periods in the discipline. It reified the cultures of peoples much as did the "configurationist school" of Benedict, Mead, Kardiner, and DuBois, who allowed only the most general traits of a common humanity to tie "them" together with "us" under one umbrella of a common humanity. In future decades, attempts to update these positions which postulate the discreteness of cultures even while allowing their ability to respond to new challenges will tell us less and less about the processes of change and development in new societies as years pass. This problem of meta-theory is acutely germane to Southeast Asian studies in the West, where the folk wisdom of area studies would suggest: should not peoples living halfway around the world have cultures very different from our own?

Some would say that Rivers' methods, symbolized by his tent, decomposed with his body and that his approach is irrelevant for the understanding of modern anthropological work. Others would deny that his work applies to modern anthropologists who are men of the people, often adding that Rivers' work was a great advance over the armchair theorizing about the long-term evolution of mankind that came before. Also, the argument might go, Rivers was living in a colonial situation in which he was a man apart from the people he studied; such conditions no longer exist with respect to most of the world's peoples studied in modern anthropology. I would suggest that, although the colonial situation is often a relic of past memories and remnants, much of modern anthropology recreates the old colonial situation, not only through the expenditure of huge sums of money in poor countries (which local scholars, let alone villagers, could not hope to see in an entire lifetime, much less the brief period for which many grants are funded), but also through the projection of attitudes, expressed in conscious and nonconscious behavior patterns that produce a colonial *type* of behavior pattern in local residents and anthropological fieldworkers. The anthropologist, under these circumstances, does not become part of the local system of dyadic interpersonal bonds which would at least modify his extremely superordinate economic position.

3

Fallers (1973) has recently posed the problem of the extension of anthropological attempts to impose external analytical constructs to the study of non-Western peoples into the realm of relations with informants in a real field situation, through an example from Uganda. He distributed a questionnaire concerning a layered concept of social class to informants and found that:

The questionnaire was virtually untranslatable into the local language. It was possible to translate the word "class" only with the most elaborate and tortured circumlocutions, unintelligible to most people. There was, however, a rich vocabulary for speaking about dyadic interpersonal relations of superiority and inferiority—words of the "master" and "servant" type. Africans conceptualized their relations with Europeans, as well as the internal structure of European society as they knew it, in much the same way; although they perceived Europeans . . . as a superordinate category . . . they continually probed that category in an effort to establish personal patron–client ties—with some success, thereby imposing, to a degree, their own definition of the situation (1973:4).

In this excerpt, one may observe the anthropologist being regarded as simply another European administering a new kind of questionnaire, coming to his informants with his own conceptual social system intact, and the Africans trying somehow to adjust their own to incorporate him. As a result of the realization of this basic problem, Fallers attempted to adjust his methodology and methods to the unexpectedly different situation and is gratifyingly apologetic about his initial naïveté. The events that Fallers describes might easily have taken place in Southeast Asia.

Unfortunately, however, anthropologists have not always been aware of their unique Western social systems and how alien these systems are to the social expectations of their informants. The very act of thinking in terms of constructs such as villages, temple communities, etc., are often quite alien to non-Western peoples save in extremely circumscribed and clearly defined contexts. In most situations, one may expect dyads to be crucially important in the understanding of the social vocabularies of these peoples and other constructs transcending the dyad to have a much more subtle influence on behavior and thought (much to the chagrin of colonial administrators and modern nation builders). For an anthropologist to enter a community and move from group to dyad rather than from dyad to group appears to illustrate a point that Max Weber makes in an essay on "Castes, estates, classes and religion," in which he suggests that premodern peoples do not normally become parts of congregations save through the most unusual circumstances, generally those that would threaten their very survival. More commonly, premodern people fall back on their stronger ties to nature and upon "peasant traditionalism," Weber's term for the normal form of documented descriptions of the behavior of non-Western peoples living outside of the dynamic urban sectors of society (Weber 1963:80–94). This is not to suggest that individual bonds are more important than group membership in any ultimate sense, only to indicate that the traditionalism or conservativism of premodern peoples expresses itself through the idiom of the dyad even when that dyad appears to preserve or strengthen a group. This traditionalism also explains the extreme difficulty with which new conceptions of group identity emerge in such societies.

In these respects, Southeast Asian peasantries are wholly typical. One learns about the power of supradyadic groups through often complex chains of personal relations leading around them and finally, hopefully, to their centers, always moving one step, one person at a time, and never forgetting how difficult it is for Southeast Asian villagers, as ultimately it is for oneself, to consider groups as apart from dyadic relations. Movement in the other direction is invariably interpreted as indicative of great power, much as that power which existed in the colonial situation. Before a dyadic connection can be made within a given community, there can be no assumption by its members that the attempt to gather information concerning group charters is not itself the embodiment of social extraterritoriality. Nonetheless, one must distinguish between two kinds of powerful outsiders: those with responsibility for the collectivity to a higher power, and those without such responsibility. In the first case, the outsider is not a completely external force; usually his source of power is known and there are some sanctions on his own behavior. In the second case, the individual is free of the constraint which I have above called empathy; he is, in fact, at the other extreme, having negative empathy or negempathy and high social status—which translates in this instance as wealth and power. I will return to this point and its consequences shortly.

As an example of the result of power and negempathy in a field situation, one may cite a recent article by a well-known anthropologist in the Southeast Asia field, C. Geertz, on "Deep play: notes on the Balinese cockfight," in which the author moved from "the center" or "centers" of a community to make statements about the psychosociology of Balinese people in general, with implications for the understanding of dyadic behavior (see also Geertz 1959); he concludes that:

Drawing upon almost every level of Balinese experience, it [the cockfight] brings together themes—animal savagery, male narcissism, opponent gambling, status rivalry, mass excitement, blood sacrifice—whose main connection is their involvement with rage and the fear of rage, and binding them into a set of rules which at once contains and allows them play, builds a symbolic structure in which, over and over again, the reality of their inner affiliation can be intelligibly felt (1972:27).

These various elements present in the cockfight, vividly described in the article, are part of a uniquely Balinese "temperament" (1972: 23) lying beneath the poised quality of "awayness" that Jane Belo called the basis of the "Balinese temper." While I will not attempt to question the extreme conclusions of Geertz' work as a commentary on Balinese ethnicity directly, Geertz' laudably frank summary of his first ten days in Bali, which saw an entire village opened to him, raises certain questions concerning these conclusions and the quality of the data from which they were derived, making use of the concepts of relative status and empathy developed above.

Upon arrival in Bali in April of 1958, Geertz and his wife moved into a compound in a village community. This arrangement was made by the provincial government, but it was not a happy one. He and his wife were treated as "nonpersons" and, somewhat more suggestively, as "invisible men" (Geertz 1972:1). Geertz found this strange since everywhere else that he had done fieldwork—in Java and Morocco—he had been a center of local attention. To be anonymous in a distant village appears to have been an uncomfortable experience which, Geertz implied, would also have been counterproductive for the entire purpose of the field stay. Ten days later, however, an event occurred which changed all of that and the Geertzes were back at the center of village attention. In the article the event is presented as a marvelous chance happening which salvaged an otherwise potentially depressing period. The event in question was a large, illegal cockfight which was being held to raise money for a new local school. It was thought that there would not be any legal intervention during the course of the event, but there was. A convoy of police with guns arrived at the scene of the fight causing a panic among spectators. The spectators ran, hiding not only themselves but also any evidence that there had been a cockfight. The scene appears to have been one of complete confusion and disarray. The Geertzes ran too, to avoid personal injury as well as to avoid the police. They ducked into the yard of the compound of an apparently important local villager, whose wife quickly prepared a table, chairs, and tea for them.

Soon the police arrived, asking for the village headman, who was responsible for the illegal behavior from the point of view of the higher level administration. The host of the compound met the police and explained the presence of these "white men" in his compound, indicating that he was simply being hospitable to them. He then went into a strong defense of their presence in the village, demonstrating that he knew more than a small amount about their purpose for being in the village, their place of origin, and the government's role in arranging their accommodations. The host also said that they had not been at the cockfight, even though he clearly knew that they had. The police then left, and thereafter the villagers' apparent lack of interest was transformed into a situation similar to those experienced by the Geertzes in Java and Morocco. Villagers inquired again and again about their attendance at the cockfight and how they escaped from it without, as many had thought they would do, simply showing their papers to the police and explaining that they were from America, had been granted special status in the village, were naïve concerning the details, were not betting or participating in any way but simply observing, etc.

As a result of the event and the general change in attitude in the village, Geertz argues that he was "accepted" and now had "rapport" with the village which he had not had before. This occurred because he had identified with the villagers in opposing the police—primarily, he concedes, a development of the "sheer extraordinariness" of the entire sequence. This "complete acceptance" gave him an inside view of a " 'peasant mentality' that anthropologists not fortunate enough to flee headlong with their subjects from armed authorities normally do not get."

One might question this conclusion on a number of grounds, but it did produce a considerable number of talkative informants who provided, presumably, the bulk of the information upon which the article is based—although, I think, surely not its analyses. Further, it is clear from the article that entry into a Balinese village involved sponsorship by government agencies and that this sponsorship had been obtained. Were not the Balinese justified in being suspicious of outsiders sponsored by their superiors, especially before they thoroughly knew the nature of the information sought and the means

which the anthropologists would use to obtain it? After the cockfight, the villagers' suspicion abated: the Americans had shown that
they could remain silent while a powerful villager committed himself
to a falsehood, without saying that they were distinguished visitors
and that they had simply availed themselves of hospitality after a
confusing escape amid unfamiliar faces. In short, in the eyes of the
villagers, they could have taken the position that they were above the
law, much as the Dutch had been before them, not liable to arrest
by a "Javanese upstart" (1973:3).

One might well ask whether the Balinese concept of acceptance is
in any way similar to the notion as Geertz uses it, or whether the
Balinese even think in the same terms of the kind of rapport with
whole villages that the Geertzes gained after their abortive brush
with the law. There can be no doubt that their cultural extraterritoriality filled the anthropologists' field notebooks with information and brought many distinguished visitors to their door (rather
than the reverse). But might not one also ask if there was not an
element of fear in the Balinese attitudes toward the villagers who,
through an act of silent, perhaps unintended, deception committed
an entire village to assist a pair of researchers who could, if they broke
ranks, "crow like cocks" and "sing a song" on the village? Is not
rapport a two-way street? The Geertzes ran one way; the police
pursued. The villagers were afraid individually and collectively.
It is difficult to conceive of anyone but an outsider, with immunity
to the very problems and pressures which (according to Weber 1963)
shape peasant traditionalism, being the recipients of a multi-
directional barrage of information. And was the kind of information
gathered not information of a special kind? Was it not intended, as
the village host suggested, to produce a book about Bali for
American consumption? Did it not tend somewhat toward exag-
geration when compared with the kind of information that would
have been obtained through questioning about the same topics
within the umbrella of the guarded personalistic style of relationships
on the island? I would argue that the author did not learn more about
the Balinese character or temperament from within this newer version
of Rivers' proverbial tent—and perhaps learned a good deal less—
than he would have learned if he were not simply regarded as
another temporarily unconnected visitor with a job to do.

The danger of this kind of negempathy goes well beyond exaggera-
tion, for it may lead to the kind of distortion that brings to the

anthropologist's door the very information that people think that he wants to hear: great detail about the extraordinary, exciting events that are either outside of, or enliven, their agricultural round. Rapport on Balinese terms might well have lead to an intensive study of the cockfight, but I hardly think that the cockfight would have been proposed as a cultural cynosure, except for the bored urbanite, the gambling addict, the villager with nothing better to do, or, and probably most rarely, when social obligation demands that a bet be made for a communal project.[2]

The power a great volume of information collected by extra-territorial outsiders holds over the anthropological profession should not be underestimated. Yalman (1967:336–343) has offered a spirited defense of Rivers' interpretation of the Toda system of marriage rules, contending that the arguments of later writers (e.g. M. B. Emaneau 1937 and Prince Peter 1963) that Rivers failed to recognize a matrilineal principle of relationship among them cannot be correct. While Yalman's argument is interesting and his treatise on Ceylonese and South Indian caste, kinship, and marriage is a very important contribution to its field, his defense of Rivers tends to exaggerate the statements of Rivers' critics concerning the matrilineal principle (see Emaneau 1937; Prince Peter 1963:240–298) and to brush aside Rivers' own suspicions, expressed in a later article, that he might possibly have missed something. Yalman's appeal for his own theoretical credibility is basically through *ad hominem* adulation of the sheer volume of Rivers' material, even when its content lends support to the assertions of Emaneau and Prince Peter! He asks:

Was Rivers wrong? Against the deep insight demonstrated in Rivers' 700-page work, the brevity of Emeneau's few articles make such radical "correction" dubious, especially since Rivers himself inclined toward the view that the confrontation of patrilineal and matrilineal features was responsible for the South Indian patterns; and he would most certainly have detected the matrilineal groups in the course of his meticulous work (Yalman 1967:336).

In light of present evidence, this writer finds Yalman's brushing aside the possibility of a matrilineal consanguineal principle as part of an explanation of Toda marriage rules, in favor of an explanation in

---

[2] Similarly, New York State winked at the playing of the game of chance bingo, periodically cracking down on games sponsored by Roman Catholic parishes, but eventually granted it full, if grudging, legal status when arguments were made in its favor on grounds of its support for projects in behalf of the public good,

terms of the rules as independent and sole explanatory principles, unconvincing.

I do not, of course, mean to suggest that one should be suspicious of an anthropologist's work as it becomes more voluminous and rich—rather, that the structure of the situation in which the data are gathered, defined in terms of relative status and empathy, will determine much about its content and about the kind of questions that one might reasonably expect the data to answer. Viewing the possibilities of interaction patterns from the perspective of the observer produces a simple matrix diagram, with empathy to negempathy representing one dimension, and superordination to subordination the other, with a middle category—equality—producing three categories in the second, vertical dimension (see Table 1).

Table 1.   Relative status—empathy matrix

	Negempathy	Empathy
Subordinate	Displaced person, adventurer, vagabond: disdain and/or fear by local residents.	Anthropologist as client of villager and/or local researcher: requires building a data corpus by moving through a series of dyads with the patron's sponsorship.
Equal	Outsider imposing unilateral definition of equality: movement about in a social vacuum, derision from local residents.	Insider or accepted outsider: complementarity of skills and resources, gratitude, mutual respect, affection.
Superordinate	High-level Western colonial administrator: extraterritoriality, mutual exploitation, local resentment, status defined as power.	Insider, local patron, government bureaucrat, local researcher, anthropologist as patron to assistants: requires attachment to a government or research agency and working through its procedures.

The first and easiest case to consider is that of superordinate status and negempathy. I have argued above that this case applies to both Rivers and Geertz, neither of whom had any specific responsibility for the community in which they resided, and both of whom enjoyed extraterritorial status in their villages. This led to a pattern of exploitation of the anthropologists by the villagers, and vice versa. In return for information, Rivers and Geertz were sources of money and gifts on the one hand and a different kind of money on the other

—status, through the ability to associate with those who could flaunt the constituted authorities, or at least to be listened to by someone who had been able to flaunt them (that is, to gain status through association with "white men" long after the Indonesian government had announced that they had ceased to be powerful). However, one can equally well envision this situation leading to harsh resentment, since wealth, in its old and new forms, is virtually universally understood, and there is a common Southeast Asian folk saying that kings are generous to strangers, stingy toward their own. Geertz appears to have recognized that some problem existed in an article on the ethics of fieldwork (1968), but in his analysis of a case in which he attempted to establish empathy with one Javanese informant, he demonstrates his complete misunderstanding of the interpersonal dynamics of the situation, consigning his failure and subsequent "bitterness" to the inevitable irony of the anthropological situation and its professional ethic of cold concern necessary for a "scientific attitude" (Geertz 1968:147–157).[3]

In contrast to this case in which the interaction between villagers and outsiders is defined by the ability of each party to exploit the situation of interaction through gaining some form of status (trading identification with the alien on one side, data gathering on the other), the best example of superordinate empathy is found in the relationship between the wealthy or prestigious insider; that is, village member and the rest of the village, or between the local prince or government officer and villagers. In this situation, there is considerable pressure on the superordinate party to prove his fitness in accomplishing tasks defined for him, or in handling relationships with individuals of lower status in the village system through the management of dyadic relationships defined in terms of patronage: the ability to distribute objects of value to inferiors. Anthropologists are rarely insiders in this sense. Although there has recently been an apparent rise in the number of anthropologists studying their natal

---

[3]   In this case, Geertz lent a typewriter to an important informant who was also a writer. One day he refused to loan the machine, considering the informant's demands excessive within a relationship chartered, as Geertz viewed it, on equality, respect and mutual acceptance. This young clerk became furious and refused to cooperate further with Geertz' work or to use his machine. Geertz argues that the disappointing failure of the relationship had to do with the clerk's desire to be respected as a writer entitled to share the typewriter as a token of a shared esteem. It would appear more likely that the informant was asserting exactly what he denied publicly to Geertz: that the typewriter was, or should be, *his*, the informant's, and that the gift of it had long been overdue considering the prodigious wealth of one party *vis-à-vis* the other (Geertz 1968: 147–155).

communities, it is doubtful that any social scientist could be part of a non-Western social network in the way that a continuous, prestigious resident could. More commonly, elements of the insider and the outsider are present, of empathy and negempathy, and this is what makes such social situations painful, not only for the Western anthropologist, but also for the government employee posted to an "outstation" to do anthropological fieldwork or to perform any of a variety of other tasks. The outsider both belongs and does not belong; he is both a part of, and at the same time disturbing to, the local status system. To alleviate some of the personal problems that inhere in this structure, Southeast Asian governments have attempted to completely bureaucratize positions in rural administration through frequent transfers and other means, so that the civil servant or anthropologist does not have to become involved in the problematical dyads of the local status system. However, it appears that, short of extreme changes in the structure of rural society, these government workers must make some compromises by finding out who can get whom to do what and at what price, for the external hierarchies to which they answer can only bend so much before they interpret lack of performance as inefficiency and ineffectiveness. At the local level, the civil servant often feels that his peasant charges have an infinite ability to stall, procrastinate, and even sabotage his best-laid plans.

Wertheim (1965) and others have argued that working through local status systems acts to make differences in status more pronounced through channelling scarce resources to those villagers most able to benefit from their use, these villagers tending also to be the most articulate and wealthy. Implicit in his argument is that outsiders and quasi-outsiders incorporated into a peasant social system get a distorted picture of society; and whole series of works have been written on the perils of the unwary anthropologist who becomes involved in factional disputes, hearing only one side of the story. The history of these critiques probably goes back at least as far as Oscar Lewis' attacks on Redfield's idyllic picture of the Mexican village of Tepotzlan, which Lewis found riven with strife and dissension (Lewis 1951). I have no way of testing that a nonwhite or non-Western anthropologist is more susceptible to the role of "duped fieldworker," due to a closer identification of him by the people he studies as an "inside superordinate," since the number of works by nonwhite or non-Western anthropologists has been lamentably low (see, for example, Koentjaraningrat 1964, for a Southeast Asian anthropologist's perspectives), but I suspect that this risk has been greatly exaggerated. For even if the anthropologist is asked to take sides in local political disputes, this does not necessarily imply that he is unaware of the existence of the other point of view, or unable to report concerning it, or unable to separate his personal feelings of loyalty to those who have been helpful to him from his balanced assessment of rival positions. Nonetheless, being part of any factionalized status system (and most village systems are factionalized) does make certain doors more open to him than to others, even though in many cases the doors are neither completely open nor completely closed. In contrast to the situation of the complete outsider working with all members of the village *en masse*, there are severe limits upon the exploitation of the "inside superordinate," for it is understood that he may simply terminate a relationship. While this would lead to some loss of face to himself, the loss of face would be greater for the local person, since the outsider has chosen to play the game by local rules and is, in most anthropological cases, a transient. He has, therefore, a powerful lever to work with, which may enable him to hear all sides of any story that he chooses to investigate. In any event, the role of anthropologist as superordinate insider seems to be a new one, and one which will probably become commoner as governments co-opt more and more anthropological talent to work on problems of nation building, particularly in rural settings.

More often, the anthropologist becomes a client of a local powerful villager with whom he interacts through a relationship defined in the kinship idiom. In this situation, the anthropological observer is, or becomes, a dependent or subordinate of his host family. Commonly, this host family may have considerable wealth compared with the median income figures for the local area. This situation is usually possible only when the local patron can test the state of finances of the visitor and can establish the special transient nature of his wealth, implying too that the fieldworker accept a style of life not markedly different from, and certainly not more expensive than, the style of life of his host. In the initial phases of research, the establishment of this kind of relationship may be painful for both sides since it involves demonstrations of good faith from both parties and usually requires a patron who has little to gain from the association, if anything at all. It also implies that there be some early personal rapport between local patron and anthropological client.

Recently, local patronage for anthropological fieldworkers has been extended to include the patronage of local scholars and frequent consultation with them. As with village dyadic bonds, relationships with local scholars discourage the incredible displays of affluence characteristic of some Western anthropological research grants in recent years. Extra funds that would place the fieldworker from outside in a life-style markedly superior to that of a local scholar may have to be placed in bank accounts for use in emergencies or for support of local assistants working under the aegis of the local scholar where this is legally permissible through a grant to a local university. In both of these cases of patronage, in village and urban university settings, the outsider must often accustom himself to much harsher life-styles than he has previously known, and to life-styles harsher than those known by some members of the society that he is entering. As in the case of the anthropologist as patron, the anthropologist as client may be accused of being "fed" information through local status systems and is liable to the perceptual difficulties implicit in membership in local factions. The same arguments against the negative effects of this in the former case apply in the latter.

There are anthropologists of non-Western origin, but it would be extremely rare and unlikely to find a village patron and sponsor who is also an anthropologist; hence, although the life-style of the anthropologist in his village may not differ significantly from that of a wealthy member of the community, the host will generally recognize that their various kinds of affluence do not impinge upon each other. The villager may have a larger house and more productive land than the anthropologist and may be his patron with respect to matters of general know-how and survival techniques in the area, covering everything from daily nutritional requirements to statements about the general level of expectation that he may have with respect to informant responsiveness. However, the villager may also recognize that his client in this area may be his patron in another, by articulating the villager's problems to local officials in language that those familiar with bureaucratic procedures may easily comprehend, or by using a Western language to iron out problems in situations where this is discreetly possible. The anthropologist may also have other kinds of knowledge concerning health care, availability of local resources, and may have "extra funds" set aside for travel or his own health that may be used to provide ready cash in emergencies, with the understanding that both villager and anthropologist are subject equally to the guidelines of the researcher's grant. Similarly, in the case of the urban scholar, initial patronage from the local scholar may be repaid in the form of support for local research, or provision of new kinds of expertise not previously present. As scholar and researcher recognize the complementarity of each other's skills and knowledge of procedures, university patronage becomes a matter of food and shelter while in the urban center and provision of access to scholarly resources. In both the village and university contexts, the initial subordinate dependence translates itself into symmetrical reciprocity and partnership, tending toward equality between internal and external scholar, and, in a quite different way, between village patron and fieldworker. Mannoni has expressed this movement well in his brilliant analysis of sociopsychological aspects of relationships between foreigners and Malagasies:

... the feeling of gratitude presupposes a loosening of the bonds of dependence. ... The common idea that gratitude is primarily a matter of an exchange of services against expressions of thanks is clearly unacceptable, for it would soon lead to a feeling that there was no indebtedness where no real gratitude was felt. True gratitude seems to be an attempt to preserve a balance between two feelings which at first sight seem quite contradictory: on the one hand the feeling that one is very much indebted, and on the other the feeling that one is not indebted at all. It implies a rejection of dependence and yet at the same time the preservation of an image of dependence based on free will. It is perhaps the prototype of the obligations assumed by the independent individual outside the framework of group behavior. That is why gratitude cannot be demanded, even though in a way it is obligatory, and why, in spite of appearances, it can exist only where persons are equal (1956:47).

Having a patron in a local community or in a university in a country other than one's own will have considerable liabilities for a Westerner who is used to efficiency or to a society skilled in creating the impression of efficiency. He may be told that he must wait considerable periods in order to obtain certain kinds of information, since it will be assumed that he is equally subject to the problems of the host country as is his local contact. His behavior will be thought to reflect upon the ethical standards of his host. Commonly, this will mean moving through networks of interpersonal connections in which he is expected to do small favors in return for cooperation as a minimal show of good faith, or simply to meet people who at first seem to be completely irrelevant to the purposes of his project. In short, the Westerner, used to taking the short cut and to getting to the point quickly, may be told that to do so would be improper and that he would not really be welcome in the homes of certain individuals for a variety of reasons. He may also find that, even after the aims and purposes of his research are comprehended, his sponsors may find them difficult to take seriously or may argue that the data would be of doubtful value. I am reminded of one informant who would not grant a genealogical interview because he thought that the field method used was embarrassing, excessively structured, and not at all to the point. The same man later volunteered much useful information about how people "felt" about each other and how they spoke about their feelings, going into great detail on one occasion about his several marriages and the causes, from his point of view, of their successes or failures. He would help, but he would not be manipulated. This individual liked to send information indirectly through third parties when he thought that the topic involved was embarrassing or improper for me to discuss directly with him. The contacts through which I had met him, his position as the father of a marriageable daughter, as well as his personality, all contributed to his reticence.

Bearing Mannoni's statement in mind, it is not difficult to understand the apparent ingratitude of villagers in non-Western countries for services rendered to them. When an outsider lacking a specific patron in a village community moves freely and rapidly between households, imposing a general definition of equality in his analysis of social situations without taking into account the elements of dyadic reciprocity, he commonly finds himself ignored or the object of derision. I have observed, with some amusement, the anger of American rural development workers toward Asian villagers who did not take the projects seriously because of the simple failure of the American workers to work through local status systems. My amusement was shared by Asian rural development workers as well, although both a considerable amount of pity was accorded to those individuals who had not learned that the social mores of an advanced industrial society are quite unique, and must be compromised to some degree in most situations in underdeveloped rural areas.

In a series of writings, Francis Hsu has shown that the understanding of Western man and the psycho-social equipment that he takes with him wherever he goes is basic to the understanding of the Western outsider. Hsu argues that the "psycho-social homeostasis" of Westerners is extremely problematic for them since they must seek intimacy among peers known for a limited amount of time or in wider associational groups (Hsu 1971:31–32). Commenting specifically on Americans, whom he appears to regard as the epitome of "Westernness," Hsu states:

The lack of permanent human relations, the idea of complete equality among men, the contract principle, and the need for definite affiliation to achieve sociability, security and status combine and generate a situation in which club life is of the essence of existence (1963:208).

In an article on prejudice in American anthropology, Hsu discusses the consequences of these factors for theory formation and concludes that:

Having been reared in an individual-centered culture in which men do not form lasting and close ties with each other, American anthropologists seem to avoid delving deeply into the question of how human beings relate to each other. Instead, they resort to what I describe as theoretical escapism. They have not improved on Durkheim's distinction between mechanical and organic solidarity. They repeat Linton's concepts, status and role. They excel in componential analysis of kinship terms. But they leave the entire area of affect—how human beings feel about each other—untouched . . . (1973:9–10).

"White" or "Western" ethnicity in the fieldwork situation often determines more than not only the methodology used in gathering data, furthermore, as in the case of Rivers, the content of the data will be determined to some degree by the nature of the interaction situation. This commonly leads to a circular, delusional system in which the anthropologist ignores the very social system he pretends to study, much as does the rural development worker who is dedicated to a naïve operational utilitarianism, with the added difficulty that the anthropologist, rather than being a self-defined "man of the people," is more commonly a man apart from and above them.

I will conclude here with a series of highly personal comments about my own experiences as a Western but nonwhite anthropologist in Asia. I feel that, despite my Western identity, I could not but be absorbed, if imperfectly, by the local social systems with which I dealt. At first the experience of this process of absorption was a source of considerable frustration, but after a time, I came to learn that I was being accorded a chance for respect and esteem that I would probably never receive at home. I further suggest that although the number of non-Western, nonwhite anthropologists is small, and the number of Western, nonwhite anthropologists smaller still, my experiences are quite typical of both groups. I also venture that this position as the "inside outsider" will produce serious theoretical tensions between Western, white anthropologists and their nonwhite colleagues (see Hsu 1973:5; Committee on Minorities 1973).[4]

My experiences doing fieldwork formally in Malaya and informally in Hawaii and other areas of the United States would suggest that a non-European anthropologist simply does not have the option of residing in a metaphorical Rivers' tent. He cannot opt to be the wealthy outsider living outside local status systems. It appears that the unique effects of the era of colonialism in wide areas of the world have created in the minds of even relatively isolated populations the impression that white men live by a set of laws which is completely alien to their own and which generates a series of interests that do not necessarily have any relevance for their own lives. By contrast, I found it extremely difficult to convince informants that I did not understand many things about them of which I knew nothing or very little.

From the very beginning of my stay in Malaya, villagers assumed that I was more closely related to themselves culturally than to the white rural development workers in the area. This was, at first, an extremely disturbing insight because I felt that it would be impossible to learn something new if it were assumed that I possessed prior knowledge. Villagers exacted much higher linguistic standards of me, often asking me to translate for other foreigners. Some of my experiences bordered on the absurdly humorous. Once I was offered a ride by a wealthy Thai after being stranded without transport. During the half-hour journey, I read a section of Nathanael West's novel, *Miss Lonely Hearts*. Meanwhile, the other riders conversed freely in English, at one point, somewhat to my surprise, singing a chorus of the song, "Getting to Know You." Venturing one word in English and being answered in Malay, I politely returned to proper

---

[4] It is worthwhile to note that, as far as I and a number of other minority anthropologists are aware, the findings of this most extraordinary *Report of the Committee on Minorities and Anthropology* have not been the basis of any reforms within the American Anthropological Association. Instead, ethnic problems in the profession have been merged with the quite different issue of feminism. There are, as of this writing, no minority members on the editorial boards of the two most important journals of the Association: The *American Anthropologist* and the *American Ethnologist*, although women are represented on both boards. The preannounced, topical, solicited article format of a substantial portion of the second journal hardly seems to be a step in the direction of incorporation of minority viewpoints. The editorial boards are, of course, the primary patronage-granting bodies of the Association.

urban Malay in the refined Penang dialect (as best I could) and thanked my patron in Malay when he informed me that he would be ashamed to accept any payment for the favor.

Gradually, I learned that my Malay village patron became curious about my situation at home, and, learning more about it, he began to see that I was both like and unlike my fellow countrymen. He became extremely protective for a time, providing large amounts of information on presumably hostile, dangerous, or improper situations and advice on how to deal with them when they arose. Essentially, I received a course in how *not* to act like an American. My patron found it hard to believe that my countrymen thought that I was an American anyway, and he asked why I should suffer the liabilities of being American, for I certainly was not, from his point of view, getting many of the benefits (this was the period of the assassination of Martin Luther King and of the ascendancy of Muhammad Ali, two extremely popular figures in rural Malaya). I was urged to take my time, to move slowly, to be discreet about resources, to leave the village whenever I became bored, and to learn some things about the local religion, for sooner or later, it was argued, I would find out that only Muslims would accept me as one of them. In churches, I was told, floors creak, and people know who comes and goes, but anyone is welcome in a mosque if he knows the forms of ablutions, the method of prostration, and a few Arabic phrases. The mosque should always be open serving as a cool place to pray to God for deliverance, to meditate, and to be alone. Furthermore, if one has a friend of the same age, one may go to pray in the local village *madrasah*, for who would care? Accompanying the assumption that I would convert to Islam eventually was the assumption that I would eventually marry a local girl, and, as a man with some prospects, I received various hints about marriageable girls considered to be appropriate mates. At the same time, I was warned against liaisons with women in the local community on the grounds that Malay society is one in which sex and marriage should coincide. Being like and unlike my countrymen, like and (initially) unlike the local people, I was pushed in the direction of empathy and subordination, gradually moving in the direction of a relationship of the kind of equality that develops between a father and a son as the son comes of age.

These remarks have not been meant to suggest that European fieldworkers have not had similar experiences in the same and other areas of the non-Western world—but where this has happened, it is
4

likely that incorporation into an unfamiliar society has taken Europeans much longer, since local people simply make different assumptions about them, about what Europeans expect, and about how they will respond. I would also suggest that the possibility of carrying out research projects as an independent and powerful foreigner in Southeast Asia, as in other parts of the world, is rapidly diminishing.[5] This should not be viewed with distress by any but those who believe in the myth of the completely objective outside observer who can see things that no one with prior primary exposure to the culture can, or by those who would apply unmodified research schedules uncritically everywhere, assuming that an outsider is a bland stimulus (see Lewis 1973). One would also hope that more attempts would be made to consider the contribution of the observer's ethnicity to the content of his data, under the specific conditions of his field study period.

REFERENCES

COMMITTEE ON MINORITIES
  1973   *Report of the Committee on Minorities and Anthropology.* Washington, D.C.: Committee on Minorities and Anthropology of the American Anthropological Association.

EMENEAU, M. B.
  1937   Toda marriage regulations and taboos. *American Anthropologist* 39:103–112.

FALLERS, L. A.
  1973   *Inequality: social stratification reconsidered.* Chicago: University of Chicago Press.

GEERTZ, CLIFFORD
  1959   Form and variation in Balinese village structure. *American Anthropologist* 61:991–1012.
  1968   Thinking as a moral act: ethical directions of anthropological fieldwork in the United States. *Antioch Review* 28:138–158.
  1972   Deep play: notes on the Balinese cockfight. *Daedalus* (Winter): 1–37.

HSU, FRANCIS L. K.
  1963   *Clan, caste and club.* New York: Van Nostrand.

[5]   Anthropologists have only recently begun to realize that failure to take account of and work through local social systems may prevent them from doing field research of any kind outside of their home countries.

1971 Psychosocial homeostasis and Jen: conceptual tools for advancing psychological anthropology. *American Anthropologist* 73 (1): 23–44.

1973 Prejudice and its intellectual effect in American anthropology: an ethnographic report. *American Anthropologist* 75 (1):1–19.

KOENTJARANINGRAT
1964 "Anthropology and non-European anthropologists: the situation in Indonesia," in *Explorations in cultural anthropology.* Edited by Ward Goodenough. New York: McGraw-Hill.

LEWIS, DIANE, *et al.*
1973 Anthropology and colonialism. *Current Anthropology* 14 (5): 581–602.

LEWIS, OSCAR
1951 *Life in a Mexican village: Tepotzlan revisited.* Urbana: University of Illinois Press.

MANNONI, O.
1956 *Prospero and Caliban: the psychology of colonization.* New York: Praeger.

PRINCE PETER
1963 *A study of polyandry.* The Hague: Mouton.

RIVERS, W. H. R.
1906 *The Todas.* London: Macmillan.

WEBER, MAX
1963 *The sociology of religion.* Boston: Beacon Press.

WERTHEIM, W. F.
1965 *East-West parallels.* Chicago: Quadrangle Books.

YALMAN, NUR
1967 *Under the Bo tree.* Berkeley: University of California Press.

The Administration of the Aboriginal Tribes of Western Malaysia

ISKANDAR CAREY

According to the last census of the aboriginal population, carried out by the Department for Aboriginal Affairs in 1969, there are now about 53,000 aborigines in Western Malaysia.[1] This represents only a tiny fraction, some 0.5 percent, of the total population, but the administration of these people presents special problems. The aborigines[2] live in small groups, varying from about 20 to 200 people, spread all over the country in nine of the eleven states of Western Malaysia. Moreover, some 60 percent of the aboriginal population still live in the deep jungle in almost inaccessible mountain country, with no roads or other forms of communication. Some aborigine villages are located near rivers, but the majority of the rivers are really mountain streams and cannot be navigated except sometimes by small bamboo rafts. In many cases it still takes several days of walking and climbing to reach an aborigine village. It is therefore not surprising that the aborigines have for many centuries been a neglected and underprivileged minority group. Effective administration of the aborigines is of quite recent date, having been started as

---

[1] Malaysia is of course divided into two parts. Eastern Malaysia, separated from the rest by hundreds of miles of sea, consists of the Borneo territories, i.e. Sabah and Sarawak. This paper concerns only Western Malaysia, the country formerly known as Malaya.
[2] The term "aborigines" has now been abandoned in Malaya because the word was thought to have certain pejorative connotations. Instead, the Malay words "*Orang Asli*" are now used, even in English official correspondence. But because the new terms have not found general acceptance outside Malaysia, I have kept to the old usage in this paper.

the result of a political and military "emergency" in what was then called Malaya.

THE EMERGENCY

The insurgency in Malaya started early in 1948 with the assassination of two European planters in Sungei Siput, a small town in the state of Perak. At this stage the insurgents, members and supporters of the Malayan Communist Party of mainly Chinese origin, had no intention of living in the jungles; accordingly, the aborigines were of little importance to them. The insurgents attacked isolated police stations, fought in the more remote villages, slashed trees in Western-owned rubber estates, and concentrated especially on influencing the Chinese squatter communities. During the Japanese occupation of Malaya in World War II, small Chinese communities had settled on unused parts of land, some owned by the government and some by individuals. There they planted vegetable crops and made a precarious living. They had no title to the land they occupied, but, under the confused conditions of war, most of them were allowed to stay. During the war, also, the communist guerrillas fighting the Japanese had obtained food supplies and other forms of help from these squatters. This policy was revived, and the insurgents put strong pressure on the squatter communities to obtain food, so the insurgents could carry on their struggle against the British colonial government.

In 1951, according to the so-called "Briggs Plan," these dispersed squatter communities were collected together and put into a large number of "new villages." These villages consisted of newly constructed dwellings, together with sanitary and other elementary facilities. Each village was surrounded by a barbed wire fence and was guarded at night by soldiers or police. The villagers had to carry identity cards at all times. The basic aim of this policy was, of course, to deny food supplies and other help to the insurgents and, in general, this policy was successful. As food supplies became more and more difficult to obtain, the insurgents tried to get food from the more accessible groups of aborigines, and also from certain deep jungle groups.

The spotlight of war thus switched to the aborigines, and the colonial government then tried to apply the same policy of resettlement to the jungle peoples. This, as it was to turn out, was a grave mistake, and the attempt to resettle the aborigines showed lack of imagination and great stupidity. Moreover, the way in which the aborigines were resettled clearly shows that the colonial government looked down upon them; the government did not consider it necessary to provide for them the same facilities, such as adequate housing, as had been given to the Chinese squatters.[3] On the contrary, thousands of aborigines were brought out of the jungle and resettled —that is to say, put behind barbed wire, without adequate facilities. Most of the people concerned had been brutally rounded up by the military or the police, put into trucks without any explanation, and transported in long convoys to the various centers of resettlement. Before leaving their villages, the aborigines watched the destruction of their houses and the killing of their livestock. Now they suddenly found themselves surrounded by barbed wire, guarded day and night, and without proper shelter. Unlike the Chinese new villages, these little villages hastily established for the aborigines resembled miniature concentration camps, although there was no overt cruelty —just ignorance and folly. Apparently some of the officers organizing this resettlement just did not realize that the aborigines had the same needs for shelter and food as had other human beings. Instead, they appear to have regarded them as wild jungle animals who could survive without further help.

The results of this policy were disastrous. The aborigines were used to living in the cool and healthy climate of the hills. They did not like the heat of the plains, and, more important, being accustomed to complete freedom all their lives, they could not get used to the idea of living behind barbed wire. The food rations they got were usually inadequate, and in any case they did not like a diet consisting almost exclusively of rice and salt fish. Worst of all, perhaps, was the enforced idleness. The Chinese squatters, at least, were able to continue in their old occupations, tending of vegetable gardens, etc. Some of them were also skilled craftsmen of one kind or another, and these people were able to carry on with their accustomed work. This was not at all the case with the aborigines. In their natural environment, the normal occupation of the men was hunting, fishing, and clearing hills for shifting cultivation; the women collected wild jungle roots and vegetables. All of this was impossible in the

---

[3] Housing was the greatest need. Many colonial and also many local officials thought that the aborigines were nomads, with little need for shelter. (In fact, only about two percent of the aborigines are true nomads. Most of the others follow a system of shifting cultivation.)

resettlement camps. Day after day was spent in futile idleness and black depression.

It has been impossible to obtain any accurate statistics on this point, but all concerned agree that hundreds of aborigines died in these squalid little camps, some from various illnesses, others from mental and psychological shock, yet others because they simply had ceased to want to live. Luckily, not all shared this fate. The more intelligent and active of the aborigines simply refused to take part in this tragic farce. The camps were not particularly well guarded, and hundreds of people escaped, mostly by cutting the barbed wire at night; these fled back to the deep jungle.[4]

The resettlement policy of the colonial government was not only a failure, but actually worked against the interests of the established authorities. The many hundreds of aborigines who escaped contacted their kinsmen in the deep jungle and naturally told their friends and relatives all about the squalid conditions in the camps. This caused great fear and alarm, and many groups of aborigines who had not been affected by resettlement as yet decided not to risk a similar fate. They abandoned their villages and moved further back into the deep jungle. There they sought the protection of the insurgents, deciding to collaborate with them more closely than they had done before. In short, the ill-considered and ill-advised policy of resettlement had exactly the opposite effect to what had been intended: the aborigines now supported the insurgents more fully and more strongly than ever before.

However, as has already been explained, the policy of resettlement had largely succeeded as far as the Chinese squatters were concerned. The insurgents found that they could no longer obtain food supplies freely, and this caused them to withdraw from the densely settled areas into the deep jungle. Their general policy now began to change. Acts of terrorism in the towns and villages became increasingly difficult, so the insurgents decided to regroup and to establish secure bases in the deep jungles. This immediately raised the question of how to get sufficient food supplies; for the solution to this problem the insurgents again looked to the aborigines. This was not difficult— first, because the great majority of the aborigines had become hostile to the colonial government, and second, because the insurgents already had firmly established ties with the deep jungle communities.[5]

[4]   The fact that the majority of the resettled aborigines did not escape is undoubtedly the result of a lack of leadership and organization.

[5]   Some of the Chinese insurgents also married aborigine women, thus establishing ties of affinity and kinship.

The insurgents were already familiar with the deep jungle and its inhabitants. During the Japanese occupation, the communists formed the only effective resistance group in Malaya, the Malayan Peoples' Anti-Japanese Army (MPAJA). The insurgents now re-established their former contacts, and considerable thought and care was given to the problem of maintaining excellent relations with the aborigines. The Politburo of the Malayan Communist Party issued a number of directives on this point. These directives explained that a gentle approach must be used on all occasions in encounters with the aborigines, with coercion or violence specifically condemned. Further, it was stated that the aborigines must be given the greatest possible help, and that they should be taught elementary hygiene and simple medical remedies. The insurgents were also advised to help improve agricultural methods, not only to assist the aborigines, but also to ensure sufficient food for themselves.[6] Finally, great stress was laid on indoctrination, that is, on teaching the principles of Marxism-Leninism to the aboriginal population.

These various directives had a limited success. The aborigines naturally welcomed Chinese medicines and similar help, but the plan of indoctrination did not really succeed. This is not surprising. The social structure of the tribes concerned was highly democratic and egalitarian; nobody went hungry and nobody was rich. In jungle conditions, there was no opportunity for the acquisition of wealth or for exploitation and none for the development of social and economic classes. In such circumstances, abstract arguments against capitalism and the like fell upon infertile ground. But the insurgents did succeed in winning the personal friendship of many aborigines.

The insurgents enlisted the assistance of the aborigines in a highly methodical way. There were two main objectives. The first aim of the insurgents was to get help from the aboriginal population as a whole, mostly to obtain food supplies, but also to obtain intelligence about the movement of troops and so on. The second, and more limited objective, was to enlist armed help. For this purpose, a special organization was set up, called by the Malay word *Asal*, meaning "original" or "aboriginal." The choice of this word was clever, because at this time both the government and the population in general still referred to the aborigines by the derogatory term *Sakai*, meaning "slave." Each river valley was to have its own Asal organization, comprising insurgents together with a small number of

---

[6] The insurgents succeeded in bringing about an expansion of land under cultivation. Chinese agricultural techniques were of little use in jungle conditions.

young and intelligent aborigines especially trained for this purpose.[7] It was hoped that these small but efficient Asal groups would control the aboriginal population as a whole. In Marxist terminology, the aborigines were the masses, while the Asal groups were the spearhead of the proletariat.

To a great extent, although for other than ideological reasons, this policy succeeded, and by 1953 almost the entire hill population was under effective control. Each river valley had its own Asal group or committee, usually under the chairmanship of a prominent headman or chief. Although nominally independent, these committees always functioned under the guidance of various Chinese Asal organizers. These Asal groups had a number of tasks. Most important was the provision of food and shelter for the insurgents; to ensure this, the general aboriginal population was directed to cultivate as many additional fields as possible. In addition, the Asal committees ensured a steady supply of guides and porters, and the population as a whole was directed to obtain information about troop movements and similar matters. Selected aborigines were armed and asked to join the insurgents in their struggle in a more active manner. Finally, it was the task of the Asal group to make sure that all the surrounding aborigine villages and settlements were under effective control and that they remained sympathetic to the cause of the insurgents.

In this way, the insurgents succeeded in erecting a kind of screen around their movements and their bases. Whenever government forces ventured into the deep jungle areas, their movements would at once be reported to the insurgents, who would then take action to avoid or ambush them. This was all the easier because the Malayan jungle is heavily wooded, and it is comparatively easy to take shelter. It often happened that groups of insurgents would be within a few yards of patrolling soldiers and yet remain unseen and undetected.

By the end of 1953, it had become obvious that the policy of resettling the aborigines outside the jungle was a complete failure, and the colonial government reversed its stand. It decided to gain control of the aboriginal population, not by taking them out of the jungle, but instead by advancing government control into the deep jungle itself. This was to be done principally by establishing "jungle forts" in a few key areas where there were thought to be appreciable numbers of aborigines and insurgents. These forts were to be manned

[7]   This arrangement closely followed aboriginal social and territorial organization in the deep jungle.

by the Police Field Force, a kind of paramilitary body especially trained in jungle warfare.

By early 1954, a total of five jungle forts had been constructed at strategic points. At this stage, however, the new policy was not very successful, partly because the aboriginal population was still under the effective control of the insurgents, and also partly because normal police methods did not work well when applied to the aborigines. On the whole, the aborigine population remained frightened of the police and avoided contact with them. The aborigines at this time had little use for the jungle forts, which provided no effective help; they rarely came to visit them.

Gradually it became clear that something more was needed. It was not enough to try to control the aborigines by negative methods such as interrogations by the police; on the contrary, the only hope of enlisting the help of the jungle dwellers was by providing some more effective forms of assistance. A very small Department for Aboriginal Affairs was already in existence by 1953, but it had purely advisory functions and was largely ineffective. The government decided to regenerate this department, to enlarge it, and to make it an effective force in trying to enlist the help of the aborigines. There was no philanthropic reason behind this decision. The only purpose for reorganizing the Department for Aboriginal Affairs was simply to ensure control of the aborigines and to win them away from their support of the insurgents. Thus the department, at least in theory, became responsible for all matters concerning the aborigines, including their administration and welfare, medical treatment, and a limited amount of education.

The urgency of the situation was such that the department now saw a very rapid expansion. Within two months, the number of officers employed by the department increased from 10 to over 200, and by the end of that period it had become a reasonably effective force. The department unfortunately was organized on a state basis, the aboriginal administration in each state being headed by a Protector of Aborigines. This created a great many difficulties and weaknesses which were not remedied until several years later, after Malaya had obtained its independence and the department was centralized.

As time went by, the number of jungle forts was expanded and, more important, the forts gradually came to offer some real attractions to the surrounding aboriginal population. A male nurse was stationed at each fort, along with an adequate supply of medicines.

The aborigines gradually came to visit the forts in order to obtain treatment for minor ailments. In addition, each fort had an airstrip suitable for light planes, and really sick aborigines were flown out to a hospital. Another attraction was that each fort had a small shop which sold such basic goods as salt, tobacco, and various tools and implements; this again was a service much appreciated by the aborigines. In the course of time, the establishment of the jungle forts played an important part in winning over the aboriginal population—within certain limits—to the side of government.

The new policy, the establishment of jungle forts, was undoubtedly a great improvement upon resettlement, but of course there were some setbacks and difficulties. Mistakes continued to be made, and as late as 1957, for example, it was decided to remove a group of about 200 Temiar aborigines from their natural environment on the Kelantan-Perak watershed. These people had been helping the insurgents, and it was decided, despite strong protests from the Department for Aboriginal Affairs, to bring them nearer the settled areas of Kelantan. Luckily this move was not "resettlement" in the old sense, as the people concerned were left in a jungle environment, although far away from their hereditary areas. Because adequate food rations and good medical facilities were also provided, this move happily had no tragic results and there was no loss of life. On the other hand, there were no positive results either. The aborigines in question had left behind huge cultivated fields, so that the insurgents merely continued living there, and actually had more food than ever before.

The military next decided, at great cost, to destroy the cultivation in the original area, but this in fact proved to be physically impossible. The limited resettlement just described served, therefore, no purpose at all, and, after tens of thousands of dollars had been wasted, the group concerned was quietly allowed to slip away and to resume living in its original area.

However, this piece of stupidity was an exception to the rule, and, after the establishment of the jungle forts, attempts at resettlement were largely abandoned.

The policy of establishing jungle forts had a definite, although limited, success. This limitation was inevitable. The aborigines liked the amenities provided in the forts and many of them established friendly relations with the police. The fact remained, however, that the great majority of the aborigine villages were not in the immediate vicinity of the forts, and these groups naturally remained open to the insurgents' domination. At night the insurgents would visit the more outlying settlements, and at such times the aborigines were quite defenseless. There were at the time strong military and police units all over the country, but their presence gave little comfort to the most isolated groups, who had to rely on their own wits and diplomacy in order to survive. Although the establishment of the jungle forts was clearly a vast improvement upon the tragic stupidities of resettlement, it also put strong and painful pressures upon the aboriginal population. The outlying groups were, so to speak, caught between two fires. From time to time, their villages would be visited by patrols of police stationed in the forts, and these would put strong pressure on the villagers, especially upon the headmen, to give information about enemy movements. The next day, or perhaps even the same night, a group of insurgents would visit the village, and similarly demand information and other help.

These competing demands put a great stress upon the aboriginal population in the more remote areas, whose first and main concern was to lead a quiet life. The aborigines reacted to this situation in a characteristic and intelligent way, although their attitude had a somewhat synical aspect. Typically, two influential and neighboring headmen would get together and discuss the situation. The two headmen, with the full agreement of the villagers, would then conclude a pact. One village would help the insurgents, while the other would assist the government. In this way it was hoped that, whoever would win, the aborigines would not lose. In addition, it was agreed that both sides, whether nominally supporting the government or the insurgents, would in fact do everything in their power to avoid any conflict that would endanger the aborigines. For example, it was acceptable to give information about the movements of the insurgents to the police—but the aborigines always made sure that the information was a few days old, so that in fact it was of little use to the police. Similar considerations applied to information given to the insurgents about the police or the military. Some information clearly had to be given; this was unavoidable, because the aborigines were under strong pressure both from the police and from the insurgents. Their typical reaction to this situation was to give a minimum of information and to make sure that this was stale and out of date. In this way actual violence could usually be minimized or altogether avoided. A final feature of the pact was an agreement that all neighboring aboriginal communities not directly concerned would remain entirely neutral.

Thus the situation brought about by the establishment of the jungle forts was far from ideal from the government point of view. Nevertheless, it was undoubtedly an improvement on the previous position, in which a majority of the aborigines had been actively hostile. It would be fair to sum up by saying that the general result of the establishment of jungle forts was to move the deep jungle dwellers from a position of hostility to one of benevolent neutrality.

PRESENT-DAY ADMINISTRATION

The most important result of the insurgency as far as the aborigines were concerned was the establishment of a special department to look after their affairs. But to understand the present situation more fully, it is necessary to briefly recall some historical facts.

Malaysian historians often say that Western scholars regard the history of their country merely as a story of European settlement. There is much justice in this complaint, but, on the other hand, little is known about life in the Malay peninsula in ancient times, and historical accounts of this period tend to blend with mythology. If this is true of the (numerically) most important race of Malaysia, the Malays, it is doubly true of the aborigines. Until about ten or fifteen years ago, all the aborigines were illiterate. They had no written history, only a number of myths concerning their origin.

In these circumstances it is not surprising that we have very little information about the political position of the aborigines and their administration before the beginning of European settlement. Only a few facts can be gleaned from the oral accounts of the aborigines themselves and from what we know in general about conditions in Malaya before the advent of colonialism.

Before the coming of the Europeans, political power in Malaya was largely in the hands of the Malays, who formed by far the most numerous and the most important segment of the population. Malaya at that time was not a unified country, but a collection of petty states.

In the course of time, the spread of Malay settlement into the more remote areas of the country brought them into contact with the aboriginal population. These initial contacts were characterized by cruelty and mutual hostility. In Pahang especially, the aborigines were often hunted and captured as slaves, to be sold to the ruling sultan as curiosities, in the same spirit as some people nowadays keep wild animals as pets. Gradually, there developed a considerable trade in aborigine slaves, and unfortunately some of the aborigines themselves took part in this commerce. But the traders did not primarily concentrate on the capture of adult aborigines. They preferred small children, who were sold for about 30 to 40 Malayan dollars, a fairly large sum at the time. Regrettable and cruel as this was, it should in fairness be stated that these children were then brought up as Malays. As they grew up, they were no longer regarded as slaves, but were treated by their owners much the same as their own children. Nevertheless, traces of these cruel acts still remain in the folk memory of the aborigines; during the insurgency, for example, the guerrillas often frightened the more remote aboriginal groups by claiming that Malay villagers would come to steal their children.

These facts no doubt explain why even now many aborigines have suspicious, and even hostile, attitudes towards the Malays, although this is much less evident today than it was a few years ago. Hunts for aborigine slaves in the old days were often carried out with great cruelty, and they are wholly to be condemned. But in fairness, we must remember that this was an age when small and supposedly savage minority groups were not regarded as human. It was an age when the American Indians were decimated, when the Tasmanian aborigines were totally wiped out, and when millions of African slaves were transported to America and to the islands of the West Indies. Compared to tragic events such as these, slavery in Malaya was a small-scale and comparatively humane affair. Nevertheless, it is important to realize these facts, as they, to some extent, explain the ambiguous attitude of the aborigines towards the Malays even in recent years, and the aborigines' remarkable refusal, in view of their wide-spread knowledge of Malay customs and language, to assimilate into the majority community.

The coming of the British to Malaya did not significantly effect the aborigines during the early years of settlement. This is not surprising because the early colonialists were undoubtedly more concerned with the majority communities of Malaya, while the aborigines, then termed *Sakai*, were numerically small and lived in virtually inaccessible areas.[8] Little or no effort was made concerning administration of the aborigines, although many of the earlier British

---

[8] The term *Sakai* [dependents or slaves], used until quite recently, is undesirable because of its meaning; it has now been abandoned.

colonial officers did valuable work in describing their encounters with aboriginal groups and the like. While these people were not trained anthropologists, some of their earlier accounts are interesting and revealing.

Attempts at administration of the aborigines came at a much later date, and even then they were of a rather sporadic and ineffective kind. The Perak government, for example, pioneered in appointing an Italian as a kind of liaison officer with the aborigines. This was G. B. Cerutti, who in 1908 published a book called *My friends the savages*. The title of the book is significant, for it reveals the general and official attitude of the authorities in those days. It was taken for granted that the aborigines were wild; often they were referred to as "savage Malays," a title flattering neither to the aborigines nor to the Malay element of the population.

But in fact, the general attitude of British colonial officials towards the aborigines was rather ambiguous. On the one hand, the typical British colonial officer felt that the aborigines were uncivilized, that they were savages; on the other hand, he thought that the British had a special kind of intuitive rapport with them and that it was therefore their task to guide and to protect the aboriginal population. The simple and comparatively uncomplicated lives of the aborigines appealed greatly to these British officials and in their attitude was undoubtedly a very romantic and unrealistic element. In brief, the attitude of the British colonial government from its early days until the coming of independence was one of somewhat unrealistic and patronizing benevolence towards the aboriginal tribes. The aborigines were regarded as noble savages, leading an idealized and romantic form of existence, and the task of government was to protect them from the ravages of modern life. It is significant that until twenty or so years ago, the concern of the administration with the aborigines, such as it was, consisted entirely of sporadic attempts at research, which was always closely connected with museums, particularly the museum at Taiping in the state of Perak. The aborigines, in other words, were regarded as museum pieces, and it was taken for granted that the proper task of the government was to protect and preserve them.

This attitude was still current as late as the years immediately preceding World War II. There was no specific administration of the aborigines as such, but it came to be regarded as part of the task of the curator of the Taiping museum to concern himself with some research among the aboriginal tribes. The curator of the Taiping

Plate 1. The aboriginal construction corps at work in the jungle

Plate 2. New homes being constructed for Malaysian Negritos

Plate 3. The aboriginal hospital at Gombak near Kuala Lumpur

Plate 4. A community hall for patients at the Gombak hospital

Plate 5.   Aboriginal dwelling: the old style

Plate 6.   Aboriginal dwelling: the new style

Plate 7.   Aboriginal medical assistants hearing a lecture at the Gombak hospital

museum at that time, I. H. N. Evans, did some valuable work among the northern Negritos, and he was succeeded by a brilliant young British anthropologist, H. D. Noone.

Pat Noone, as he was popularly called, graduated with a first class honors degree at Cambridge and in 1931 was offered the post of field ethnographer to the Perak museum in Taiping. He rapidly acquired local fame as an expert on the Senoi-speaking aborigines, particularly the Temiar. He identified very closely with these people himself, learned their language and their customs, and finally took a pretty young Temiar girl as his wife. Noone carried out several field trips in the deep jungle, but unfortunately most of his notes and ethnographic materials were lost during the Japanese occupation. Noone himself was murdered by a young Temiar during the occupation, apparently as the result of sexual jealousy and despite Noone's great popularity among the Temiar people (for a biography of Noone, see Holman 1958).

Noone's enduring contribution to the administration of the aborigines, as well as to our knowledge of them, is a brief work published in 1936 called "A report on the settlement and welfare of the Ple-Temiar Senoi of the Perak-Kelantan watershed." This report, although a little old-fashioned by present standards, is highly readable and contains a concise and most valuable preliminary account of the social organization of the Temiar. More important from our point of view is that it also includes a section called "Proposed aboriginal policy," which made concrete suggestions to the government regarding the administration of the aboriginal tribes. Although primarily concerned with the Temiar, some of these suggestions were later adopted by the government to deal with the aborigines as a whole.

Noone's proposals called primarily for the creation of a large aboriginal reserve in parts of Perak and Kelantan, where the aborigines would be left free to live according to their own traditions and customs. But although the emphasis of the report was therefore on preservation, there were also proposals of a more positive kind, such as the creation of pattern settlements in the more accessible areas where the aborigines would be taught modern agricultural skills. The report also called for the encouragement and the development of aboriginal arts and crafts, and for the creation of other forms of employment among the aboriginal population. In addition, various measures of a protective—if somewhat paternalistic—nature were also proposed. For example, the introduction of alcohol

5

into aborigine reserves was to be totally banned. These proposals were not adopted at the time, perhaps because the British colonial government had more urgent business to attend to in view of the growing Japanese menace, but some of the suggestions were put into effect after the end of World War II.

During the Japanese occupation, there was no effective administration of any kind of the aborigines. Contrary to widespread opinion, the Japanese forces were not really jungle experts, and throughout the war they failed to reach even comparatively accessible areas of the jungle. The deep jungle aborigines thus had no contact of any kind with the Japanese forces, although rumors of cruelty and the like had reached many of these groups. On the other hand, the aborigines, particularly in the deep jungle areas, had close and intimate relations with the Malayan Peoples Anti-Japanese Army (MPAJA), a force of largely Chinese Communist guerrillas who were in reality the only effective form of resistance to the Japanese imperialists in Malaya, the great majority of the population having settled for a quiet life.

After the end of World War II, the British military administration which succeeded the Japanese tried to reimpose an old-style colonial administration, but in view of worldwide policies of liberating colonies, this could not succeed. In the meantime, the insurgents staged a full-scale revolt against the British military administration, and when this did not succeed, large numbers of them returned to the jungle in order to resume their guerrilla activities, this time not against the Japanese but against the British. This development has already been described.

The British colonial government gradually came to realize the importance of the aborigines as a security factor and so decided to establish a special Department for Aborigines; Major P. D. R. Williams-Hunt was appointed as Adviser on Aborigines to the Federation of Malaya. This was the first time that anyone had been appointed to an administrative capacity for the aborigines, rather than to conduct researches among them.

But in fact the new department was extremely small, consisting of a staff of only three or four persons, and its powers were very limited. This was partly because of a lack of money, but, even more so, it was a result of regarding the administration of the aborigines as a state and not as a federal matter. One or two states, such as Pahang, had a very limited organization concerned with the aborigines, but the other states had none. The powers of the Adviser on Aborigines were therefore strictly circumscribed.

So little was known about the aborigines at the time that the first tasks facing Williams-Hunt were to find out where they lived and to get some idea of their total numbers. Because such a very small staff was available to him, Williams-Hunt tried to speed up this task by means of aerial surveys. He used to fly over the Malayan jungles in a light aircraft looking at aborigine clearings and estimating from the extent of their cultivations the number of people likely to be living there. This was not altogether satisfactory, because inevitably a great many old clearings were believed to be still inhabited. As a result Williams-Hunt produced a vast overestimate of the total number of aborigines in Malaya.

Apart from his aerial surveys, Williams-Hunt spent most of his time in making field trips to jungle areas in Perak, where he made brief studies of the Semai tribe. He was especially interested in these people and was more or less adopted by them; he finally married a young Semai girl. Unfortunately, this work was cut short by the tragic death of Williams-Hunt as the result of an accident in the jungle in early 1953.[9]

For a few months following the death of Williams-Hunt, the small Department for Aborigines was without a leader and remained dormant. This situation could not be allowed to go on, especially because the aborigines had by now become a factor of considerable importance in the "emergency."

General (as he then was) Sir Gerald Templer, the governor of Malaya, solved this problem by appointing R. O. D. Noone as Adviser on Aborigines. Dick Noone, as he was generally called, was a Cambridge-educated anthropologist with considerable experience of Malaya. Moreover, he already had some standing among the aborigines, as he was the younger brother of Pat Noone, whose work we have discussed above. Dick Noone was a man of considerable intellect and enormous energy, living almost entirely for his work and seeming to have a special affinity for the Malayan jungles and the people who lived there.

This period also saw the first important attempt at legislation to protect the aborigines, and this work again was largely pioneered by Noone. The result was the publication by the government in 1954

---

[9] Williams-Hunt stumbled and fell on to a sharp piece of bamboo. The wound turned septic and, although help was speedily obtained, it was impossible to save his life.

of an "Aboriginal peoples ordinance," a document that was amended in 1967 to conform to changing conditions. This ordinance was a milestone in the administration of the aborigines, for at long last the government had officially admitted its responsibility towards them, as well as the right of the aboriginal tribes to follow their own ways of life.

Here it is only possible to summarize this document very briefly. The ordinance starts by defining who is an aborigine, and this is very sensibly done, not by race, but in terms of a person's culture and his way of life. For example, Chinese and Indian children adopted by the aborigines are rightly regarded as aborigines and are thus entitled to special protection. The ordinance provides for the establishment of aboriginal reserves, the general intention being to ensure that the aborigines would be able to continue living in their traditional and hereditary areas. In later years, a great many places were declared aboriginal reserves, although in general it must be said that this procedure has been much easier in the deep jungle than in the more accessible areas where the Department for Aboriginal Affairs has had to face counterclaims from more numerous and therefore politically more powerful ethnic groups. The ordinance also provides for the eviction of undesirable persons from aboriginal areas and goes some way to protect the aborigines from economic exploitation. It establishes that the aborigines have the same civic rights as all other citizens. For example, it clearly states that aborigine children cannot be excluded from national schools.[10] It also gives the aborigines additional protection on several points. For example, aborigine children cannot now be adopted by outsiders without the consent, not only of their parents, but also of the government; similarly, religious instruction to aborigine children can only be given with the written consent of their parents. The general purpose of this provision was to help preserve the traditional way of life of the aboriginal communities. Various fines and other penalties are prescribed against persons who break these rules.

Another important document affecting the aborigines was published by the new independent Malayan government much later, in 1961, under the title *Statement of policy regarding the administration of the aborigine peoples of the Federation of Malaya.* This document starts by saying that "the aborigines, being one of the

---

[10]   There have been some cases where Malays objected to the presence of aborigine children in national schools.

ethnic minorities of the Federation, must be allowed to benefit on an equal footing from the rights and opportunities which the law grants to the other sections of the community." The document goes on to say that because of their present economic backwardness the aborigines need special help, especially in such fields as medical treatment and in raising their standard of living. It also states that the aborigines should be encouraged to integrate with the more advanced sections of the population, but that "recourse to force or coercion ... shall be excluded." Another important paragraph of this document recognizes the rights of the aborigines over their traditional areas and states that "aborigines will not be moved [from these areas] without their full consent." The rest of the statement deals more specifically with questions of how the aborigines may be helped, especially in the fields of education and rural development. But the importance of this document lies not so much in its detailed provisions, but in the fact that the government of independent Malaysia clearly set out its firm intention to assist the aborigines, while at the same time recognizing their right to their own traditional way of life.

It should be said here that, just before the coming of Malayan Independence in 1957, many British colonial servants (in private conversation) predicted that the new Malayan government would at best totally ignore the aborigines and at worst would try to "civilize" them, change their religions by force, and so on. It is pleasant to report that nothing of this kind has happened. On the contrary, since the Independence, help to the aborigines has been increased on a most impressive scale, and—despite the fact that there is no longer an "emergency,"—this assistance is now given for wholly altruistic reasons.

After the Independence Dick Noone retired, and the present author became Commissioner for Aboriginal Affairs, a post he held until 1969. The department was reorganized and the staff was increased to some 800 persons, most of whom were themselves aborigines. At present the department has six different sections or divisions, covering all the states, with a headquarters in Kuala Lumpur. These divisions include a general administrative section; a medical section; a signals section, responsible for communications in the jungle areas; a rural development section, primarily responsible for raising standards of living among the aborigines; an educational section, responsible for aborigine schools; and an anthropological research section. The three main tasks of the department essentially remain the same: medical treatment, education, and rural development.

As regards the first, the department now administers a very useful and attractive hospital at Gombak, some eleven miles from Kuala Lumpur, which has about 450 beds. There are five full-time doctors and a great many nurses, both male and female, the great majority of whom are themselves aborigines. Still more important, there are more than 140 medical posts in the deep jungle. Each post consists of two small, prefabricated huts (one for patients and one for a nurse) and a helicopter landing zone.[11] Each post also has a radio, and seriously ill patients are flown out by helicopter to the Gombak hospital. In this way, even the most remote groups of aborigines nowadays enjoy the benefits of modern medical treatment. It has been estimated that there is now no aboriginal group, no matter how remote, that cannot be reached by helicopter from Gombak within sixty minutes or less.[12] The medical section has perhaps expanded a little too rapidly, and in some medical posts there has been insufficient control in regard to standards of cleanliness and hygiene. Yet it cannot be denied that this work has been of inestimable value to the aborigines, a fact clearly seen by their greatly decreased infant mortality rate.

Another important area in which the department has helped the aborigines is the field of education. Until about fifteen years ago, nearly all the aborigines were illiterate. This is no longer the case. The department has established nearly eighty special schools in the deep jungle. Although the standard of education is far from high, mainly because of a lack of qualified teachers, nevertheless the existence of these schools is a great improvement over the past. In the more accessible areas, the aborigines are encouraged to attend Malay or English schools. Thus the majority of aborigine children nowadays learn to read and write, and this has of course produced important changes in their way of life. Many young aborigines are now employed as nurses, teachers, drivers, clerks, and stenographers; there are also some aborigine taxi drivers. The comparative success of education was recently shown, unfortunately in a negative way, by the discovery of the first aborigine to forge a check. More seriously, it is pleasant to report that there are now several aborigines studying subjects such as business administration, and there is no

[11]   The helicopters are provided by the Royal Malaysian Air Force.
[12]   This probably makes it safer to live in the deep jungle than in ordinary rural areas.

doubt that within the next few years there will be aborigine boys and girls entering the universities.

The third important task of the department is to improve the living standards of the aborigines. This has primarily affected the groups living outside the deep jungle, in the more accessible areas.

To encourage economic development, the Department for Aboriginal Affairs has constructed a large number of "pattern settlements." The construction of a typical pattern settlement includes building new dwellings, providing a water supply, planting land with rubber and fruit trees, and constructing a school, a community hall, and various other facilities, including sanitation.

A special feature of these pattern settlements is that most of the work is done by the aborigines themselves on a cooperative basis. To encourage such cooperation, the department, some years ago, established a special Aborigine Construction Corps comprised of carpenters and other similarly skilled workers. The construction corps has its own transport and tools and is thus able to move quickly from one place to another and to give help where this is most needed.

It would be idle to pretend that all these schemes have been a success, and indeed there has been some stupidity, some corruption, and much idleness. In view of low educational standards, low salaries, and low motivation, this was inevitable. But on the whole, the work of the department has indeed succeeded to a remarkable extent. It has changed the infrastructure of the aboriginal economy; it has raised standards of education; and above all, it has succeeded in introducing standards of health and hygiene unheard of as recently as fifteen years ago. Since the Independence, the history of the Department for Aboriginal Affairs has largely been a story of success.

SOCIAL AND CULTURAL CHANGE

The extent to which the aborigines have been affected by social and economic changes depends, not upon their ethnic affiliations or upon their languages, but upon their geographical distribution. This is only natural. The closer aborigine villages are to the settled areas, the more they have been affected by change. As much as 40 percent of the aboriginal population now lives outside the deep jungle in relatively accessible areas. Some groups, in fact, live just a few miles away from fairly large towns and many aborigine villages can nowadays be reached by car. It is important to realize that this situation is not the result of aborigine immigration into urban or into rural but accessible areas. On the contrary, the aborigines in question remain in their traditional areas; it is civilization that has caught up with them. They have not been driven out, but now they find themselves surrounded by huge numbers of Chinese, Malay, and Indian fellow-citizens, and in addition, of course, by all the usual paraphernalia of modern life.

From this point of view, it may be useful to divide the aborigines, irrespective of their tribal or ethnic affiliations, into four main categories. First, we have the jungle communities, that is, the people who still live in the deep jungle, perhaps several days' walk from the nearest Malay village. These people have of course been least affected by change. They are geographically isolated and have comparatively few contacts with the outside world. But even these people have been affected by social changes to some extent. For example, we have already seen that the Malaysian government now offers medical treatment to these jungle dwellers, and that in many places special schools, even in the most remote areas, have also been provided. In addition, many of the jungle dwellers now own inexpensive transistor radio sets and are in general well aware of main events taking place in the outside world. But apart from these changes, the contact of the deep jungle communities with the rest of the country is still very limited, and on the whole the aborigines in these areas still follow their traditional way of life.

Second, we must mention the border communities, that is, aborigine villages that are only a few hours' walk from the nearest road. These people naturally have more contacts with outsiders, especially as regards trade and economic activities in general. In particular, they sell their jungle produce to outsiders, especially to Chinese middlemen.[13] The aborigines in these areas accordingly have more cash, and they buy consumer goods such as Malay or Western clothes, radio sets, bicycles, canned goods, and similar articles.

Third, we find groups of aborigines who live outside the jungle in areas accessible by car and usually near Malay villages or Chinese rubber estates. These people have been greatly affected by social change, and it is of course in these areas that the Department for

---

[13] There is less trade with the Malays, as compared with the Chinese, as village Malays nearly always lack capital.

Aboriginal Affairs has been able to implement most of its rural development schemes.[14]

Fourth, there are groups of aborigines, especially in the south, that may be regarded as virtually assimilated into the Malay population. These people are Muslims, have close contact with their Malay neighbors, and lead an almost completely Malay way of life. Nevertheless, they have not become Malays. These aborigines still cherish most of their traditional customs and in the great majority of cases marry only within their own tribe.

Social and economic changes introduced by outside agencies, such as the government, have already been discussed in previous sections of this paper. Here I would like to discuss two other factors: changes in the realm of ideas, such as religion; and some unintended consequences of social change.

The great majority of the 53,000 aborigines in Western Malaysia still hold fast to their own religions. They are animists, who believe that natural forces such as thunder, lightning, and rain, and also physical features such as unusual rock formations and large trees have living within them one or more spirits, deities, or other supernatural beings. There are now also several thousand aborigines who practice either Islam or other world religions.

As might be expected, missionary activities have had almost no effect on the deep jungle groups, who are isolated and who in addition are strongly attached to their own traditional beliefs. Instead, missionary activities have concentrated almost entirely upon the more accessible groups. According to information obtained in January 1968, a total of 1,600 aborigines have embraced Islam and about 700 have adopted Christianity.[15] Of the Christians, about 50 are Catholics; about 230 are Methodists; 360 are Lutherans; and about 20 people belong to a sect known as the Church of the Gospel. In addition, there are also about 350 aborigines who have become members of the Bahá'í faith. It will be seen from these figures that some 2,600 aborigines now follow world religions of various kinds, while the rest, some 50,000 persons, still cling to their traditional religious beliefs.

The figures I have quoted show that some 1,600 aborigines have embraced Islam, as compared to some 700 Christians and about 350 Bahá'ís. It would therefore seem that the Muslim missionary

[14] Absence of roads makes it, for all practical purposes, impossible to implement rural development schemes. The only alternative, dropping equipment and tools by air, is far too costly.

[15] I am indebted to the Department for Aboriginal Affairs for this information.

effort has been the most successful. But in reality this is not the case, for the figures paint a misleading picture. Of the 1,600 Muslim aborigines, no fewer than 1,400 are members of the Orang Kuala tribe. These people have been Muslims for a long time, probably for more than 100 years. They are comparatively recent arrivals in Malaya. Their home was in Sumatra, and all of them still have relations in Indonesia. These people were already Muslims before their arrival in Malaya.

When these considerations are taken into account, it will be seen that only some 200 aborigines have in fact been converted to Islam during the last 100 years or so; this is a small figure when compared with that for Christian and even Bahá'í converts and is surprising in view of the fact that Islam is the state religion.

The comparative failure of Muslim missionary efforts has a variety of reasons. One important problem arises from the organization of the Malaysian religious departments. These are organized entirely on a statewide, rather than a nationwide, basis, which means that there cannot be any coordinated effort in the teaching of Islam.

Another important reason for the lack of success of the Muslim missionaries lies in their lack of financial resources. The state religious departments have very little money, and they have not been able to offer the aborigines any help in such fields as welfare, education, or medical treatment. The religious teachers are paid very low salaries, which means in fact that there are no educated persons engaged in this type of work. The religious teachers know little or nothing about the way of life of the aborigines; they accordingly do not know how to approach them in the best way. They also often know little about the positive aspects of Islam such as its emphasis on social justice and its stress on human brotherhood, and as a result they are unable to make the religion appealing and attractive to the aborigines.

The policy of the Malaysian government, at least in theory, is to encourage the aborigines to become part of the Malay community. This would seem to imply eventual conversion to Islam. But unless the Muslim missionary effort among the aborigines is completely reorganized and brought up to date, it is very unlikely that this policy will ever succeed. Furthermore, a successful Muslim missionary effort would depend on a complete reorganization of religious departments. It is very unlikely that this will take place in the foreseeable future.

One of the earliest Christian missionary efforts took place in Perak before World War II. This was carried out by a Batak Lutheran missionary, a man called Napitoepoloe. He married an aborigine woman and succeeded in converting no less than six aborigine villages to Christianity. He also started the first primary school for aborigine children and produced three books on Christianity in the Semai language.[16] These are still widely circulated among the aborigines today.

After the death of Napitoepoloe, Christian missionary work among the aborigines was mainly carried out by European missionaries. For a number of reasons, this policy has been changed in recent years, and now the missions appoint educated aborigines to do this work. These posts carry a reasonably attractive salary. The appointment of aborigines as missionaries has made the work of propagating Christianity more successful, because the aborigines are naturally more likely to be persuaded by their own people than by outsiders. In addition, the Christian missionaries continue to offer help in educating aborigine children, and they provide other assistance of various kinds. There is today a special church for the aborigines in Perak and another in Negri Sembilan.

Although no doubt well intentioned, these Christian missionary efforts have created some serious problems. For example, in Negri Sembilan there is a small Temuan village where about half of the population has been converted to Christianity, while the rest of the villagers still follow their traditional religious beliefs. A church has been built in this village, and religious services are held every Sunday. The Catholic villagers look down upon their animist kinsmen, and the whole village has been split into two different and largely hostile segments. Conversion to Catholicism has also created difficulties in such areas of the traditional culture as marriage customs. Among the Temuan, little value is placed upon premarital chastity, and the premarital period is in fact regarded as one of trial and error, resulting eventually in a stable marriage. This is of course contradictory to Catholic values. Divorce, formerly not difficult, is now for all practical purposes impossible, and a married couple who cannot get on with each other are, at least in theory, condemned to stay together for life.

Similar difficulties are also common among the Methodist and Lutheran converts of Perak. Here again, conversion to Christianity has resulted in intertribal conflicts and quarrels without, of course,

[16] Semai and Temiar are the two most widely spoken languages of the aborigines.

facilitating a compensatory integration of the aborigines with their Malay neighbors. These problems are multiplied when it comes to small and obscure Christian sects with very limited financial resources. Missionaries of this kind are not able to offer any concrete benefits, concentrating entirely on matters of theology. In other words, all help offered is strictly on a "pie-in-the-sky" basis. In recent years, there has also been an energetic effort by Bahá'í missionaries to convert the aborigines, especially in Perak, and about 350 of them have embraced this religion. Most of the Bahá'í missionaries have been Americans.

The various missionary efforts described have created some serious problems, but their impact has been limited. The great majority of the aborigines still follow the traditional religions, and this position is likely to remain so. Government policy, and I think very rightly, has been to concentrate upon improving the social and economic conditions of the aborigines, without worrying too much about their spiritual life.

As regards the introduction of new ideas, missionary efforts have been completely overshadowed by the availability of transistor radio sets and similar facilities. Until the invention of the transistor radio set, the aborigines were unaffected by the existence of modern means of communication, since almost without exception, they live in areas where there is no electricity. But this has changed very rapidly in recent years. It is now possible to buy inexpensive, small transistor radio sets, mostly of Japanese manufacture: these are light, easy to carry, and work on ordinary flashlight batteries. Furthermore, there has in recent years been a considerable increase in the amount of cash available to the aborigines, partly as the result of the sale of jungle produce, but mostly because many of the younger aborigines have found jobs in government and, to a much lesser extent, in the private sector of the economy. The result of all this has been that the aborigines now own many hundreds of small transistor radio sets; this is true of the deep jungle groups as well as of aborigine villages in the more accessible areas. It is now almost impossible to find a village, no matter how remote, that does not have at least one radio set. Probably the only exception to this are the nomadic Negritos, but they comprise only a very small percentage of the total aboriginal population.

Radios are not only a very popular form of entertainment, especially appreciated in the evenings in deep jungle villages, where previously life tended to be dull, but they have also become a sign of social prestige. Most aborigines, after obtaining some kind of employment, devote their first month's wages to the purchase of a radio set. The aborigines are consequently very much more aware than previously of developments in the modern world, especially what is happening in Malaysia. Radio Kuala Lumpur is especially popular, because during the last few years special programs for the aborigines have been introduced. There are at present four hours a week set aside for aborigine programs, and two of their main languages (Temiar and Semai) are used. These special programs are extremely popular among the aborigines, who find in them a source of pride and a sign that the government is really interested in them. It is quite usual for an entire village to gather in one house in order to hear the special transmissions. It is also interesting to note that these broadcasts, although primarily designed for Temiar and Semai, are listened to by most other groups of aborigines as well. Indeed it may be said that all the aborigines feel that these are their own special programs. This is true to such an extent that many aborigines who previously had no knowledge at all of these two languages have now acquired a good working knowledge of Temiar and Semai merely by listening to these special radio programs.[17] A few aborigines with more sophisticated sets also listen to foreign stations broadcasting in Malay, such as various Indonesian stations.

I now turn to another type of social change: the unforeseen and unintended consequences of human actions, the original purpose of which were not necessarily connected with social change as such. The analysis of this type of social and cultural change is both interesting and important, but it is also difficult, mainly because it requires an intimate knowledge of the social structure of the people concerned. Among the aborigines few such detailed studies have as yet been made, and I can accordingly only give a few examples of this type of change.

One example concerns modern medical treatment. The Department for Aboriginal Affairs, in an effort to obtain the cooperation of aborigine medicine men, has issued them medicines of various kinds, mostly simple but highly effective drugs against illnesses such as malaria and dysentery. An unintended, although not necessarily undesirable, consequence of this has been that in some areas the prestige and the powers of these medicine men have greatly increased. This is of course because their ministrations have now become much

---

[17] Most aborigines appear to be excellent linguists, usually speaking two or three languages without much effort.

more effective than before.[18] Another important result of the provision of modern medical treatment has been a fairly sharp numerical rise in the aboriginal population. It is of course completely desirable that infant mortality and illness in general should be reduced, but we should also be aware that the rise in population may eventually result in a shortage of land and various other problems unless effective methods of birth control can be introduced.

The provision of educational facilities, while equally desirable, has similarly had some unintended and unwanted consequences. There are now large numbers of young aborigines who are not educated enough to obtain jobs in the modern economy of Western Malaysia, but who at the same time are no longer willing to live in isolated places in the jungle and have lost all taste for agricultural work.

Perhaps the most important consequence of social actions as they affect the aborigines has been the creation and the continued existence of the Department for Aboriginal Affairs itself. As has already been mentioned, the department employs aborigines in large numbers from all tribes and all areas, and this has undoubtedly given the aborigines a new feeling of community, of belonging to one particular ethnic group. This is not altogether true, of course, because in fact the tribes differ widely from both a racial and a cultural point of view. Nevertheless, this community feeling has been established and it has had important consequences. Typically, an aborigine now thinks of himself first as a member of a particular tribe, second as a member of a general aboriginal community, and third as a Malaysian. The implication of this for the future, in my opinion, is that it is extremely unlikely that the aborigines will be absorbed by any larger ethnic group such as the Malays. Not only, in most cases, do religious and linguistic factors prevent this, but even tribes which are already Muslims and which only speak Malay still retain their own identities. The long-term future of the aborigines lies therefore not with assimilation into any particular ethnic group but rather with an increased adaptation to the Malaysian nation and to the modern world as a whole.

---

[18]   In serious illness, the medicine men refer their patients to the aboriginal hospital at Gombak.

REFERENCES

CAREY, ISKANDAR
    1961a Tenglek Kui Serok: an introduction to the Temiar language, with an ethnographical summary. Kuala Lumpur: Dewan Bahasa dan Pustaka.
    1961b The aborigines in the five year plan. *Seed* 1 (5).
    1961c The Orang Asli in Malaya. *Seed* 2 (1).
    1970a The Orang Asli and social change. *Federation Museums Journal* 13.
    1970b The religious problem among the Orang Asli. *Journal of the Malayan Branch, Royal Asiatic Society* 43 (2).
    1971a A brief account of the Mah Meri. *Journal of the Malayan Branch, Royal Asiatic Society* 44.
    1971b Some notes on the sea nomads of Johore. *Federation Museums Journal* 14.

CERUTTI, G. B.
    1908   *My friends the savages.* Como, Italy.

FEDERATION OF MALAYA
    1954   "The aboriginal peoples ordinance." Number 3 of 1954. Kuala Lumpur: Government Printer.

HOLMAN, DENNIS
    1958   *Noone of the Ulu.* London: William Heinemann.

MINISTRY OF THE INTERIOR
    1961   *Statement of policy regarding the administration of the aborigine peoples of the Federation of Malaya.* Kuala Lumpur.

NOONE, H. D.
    1936   A report on the settlement and welfare of the Ple-Temiar Senoi of the Perak-Kelatan watershed. *Journal of the Federated Malay States Museum* 19 (1).

SKEAT, W. W., C. O. BLAGDEN
    1906   *Pagan races of the Malay Peninsula.* London: Macmillan.

WILLIAMS-HUNT, P. D. R.
    1952   *An introduction to the Malayan aborigines.* Kuala Lumpur: Government Printer.

Ethnics and Ethics in Southeast Asia

R. K. DENTAN

This paper poses two questions that seem critical to any discussion of ethnicity in Southeast Asia. The first is whether the concept of ethnicity, historically conditioned as it is by specifically Euro-American racism and nationalism, can be fruitfully applied to cultural variations in Southeast Asia. The other is whether, even if this concept is fruitful, it is socially responsible to introduce a concept so historically weighted into discussions of an area which already has ample political and social problems of its own. To stimulate discussion, I am going to answer both questions negatively, although obviously no philosophically adequate, historically documented justification for such simple-minded answers could fit within the length of this paper. In the interest of economy, this paper distinguishes between ethnicity (the concept a set of Southeast Asians may have of their culturally belonging together; i.e. if you will, "ethnoethnicity"), and "ethnicity" (a concept by which Euro-Americans classify sets of Southeast Asians).

THE UTILITY OF "ETHNICITY"

Like "ethnicity" itself, any critique of the concept has historical and social roots. It may therefore be relevant to point out that the arguments in this paper are conditioned by the fact that the author is American. The peculiarly American condition relevant here is our ambivalent and pervasive racism, which the American experience of

6

slavery makes historically unique. Europeans unfamiliar with this American dilemma about racism (Myrdal 1964) are often bemused by the degree to which the "racial problem" obsesses and traumatizes Americans of every political complexion, including, as Hsu (1973) properly points out, American anthropologists. Yet, of course, a race in the American folk sense is just an ethnic stratum whose position is rationalized and justified by American ethnozoology. The relevance of this point should be clear shortly.

The question of the utility of the concept "ethnicity" as applied to studies of Southeast Asia falls into two parts. First, how fruitful is the idea of "ethnicity" as imposed on Southeast Asian peoples; that is, how useful is it as part of the anthropologist's tool kit? Second, how relevant are Southeast Asian concepts which resemble Euro-American "ethnicity" to understanding how Southeast Asians live together; that is, how important are Southeast Asian notions of ethnicity to understanding their lives?

"Ethnicity" as a Tool

Feingold lays out the first question in his meticulous and scholarly study of Akha subgroupings elsewhere in this volume:

One of the singularly important and complex theoretical questions to emerge from the ethnology of mainland Southeast Asia [is] . . . how does one identify, designate, and classify significant ethnic units in an area where the ethnolinguistic and cultural complexity of many groups, intermingled in the same or similar ecological settings, virtually forces upon the investigator recognition of the lack of congruence among linguistic, cultural, and societal boundaries?

Setting up the problem this way may, in fact, generate the problem. It seems conceivable that rather than the data forcing recognition of the problem on the investigator, the investigator is forcing the problem on the data by making assumptions which are not *a priori* necessary. The reasoning is as follows: "Ethnic" characteristics are covariants, not independent variables; therefore a person must belong to one, and only one, "ethnic" unit. Other authors suggest that: Ethnic units occupy defined ecological niches (e.g. Barth 1969); they should then occupy a definable common territory (Deutsch 1966: 17–19). It seems to be the inadmissibility of this last assumption that leads to the problem of "ethnicity" in Southeast Asia (Leach 1960). The difficulty noted by Feingold may thus be the product of the fact that the data do not admit a static, monolithic notion of "ethnicity," that, indeed, they need Procrustean treatment to make them mesh at all. The last sentence is not mere polemic. Suppose that none of the assumptions listed above are true. To that degree, cultural anthropologists working in Southeast Asia might model their world on that of those physical anthropologists who have discarded the notion of covariant parameters implicit in the folk concept of race, and who pursue the frequencies of various isolable characteristics ("clines": see Livingstone 1961). Wilder's work, reported in this volume, suggests how such an approach might work. Olsen's study, also in this volume, might be amenable to rephrasing in clinal terms, with the "ethnic" names serving primarily as geographical locatives.

A piecemeal, clinal approach to real life differences between Southeast Asian peoples seems emotionally or aesthetically unsatisfactory to Euro-American cultural anthropologists. Since 1848, we have been tempted by the idea that for some unearthly reason, race, language, geographical area, and culture should be covariant: *ein Land, ein Volk, ein Führer* (cf. Izikowitz 1969: 136). I can only briefly sketch here what I think the roots of this American predilection are.

Shortly after World War I, American anthropology split into warring camps: those who thought that variations in the way people lived were biologically explicable, and those who preferred cultural explanations. This was no mere academic piffling. Feelings ran high and jobs were at stake. Each side made grandiose claims for the power of its central ideas: biology and race, culture and "ethnic" unit. Never precisely differentiated previously, and then becoming competing ways of explaining the same phenomena, anthropological notions of race and "ethnic" group became very similar (cf. Stocking 1968:270–340; Valentine 1971). Fifty years ago, human races were thought to be readily identifiable entities defined by covariant parameters. It did not matter that no such entities existed in the phenomenal world. To supersede race, "ethnicity" needed similarly precise definition. The cultural anthropologists won the battle, although its echoes still linger. Convinced that they had fought the good fight against racism, many cultural anthropologists were shocked when Hsu (1973) accused them of racism. Yet it seems retrospectively obvious that when one notion ("ethnicity") purports to have the same explanatory power as another (race) to which it is structurally similar, then the former can substitute for the latter in the rationalization of any social institution. In brief, I am suggesting that Southeast Asian "ethnicity" presents a problem because the data do not meet utterly arbitrary criteria derived from fossilized cultural racism.

Again, this conclusion is not to be construed as polemical. My own admittedly evasive attempt to define the Semai of Malaysia as a people (Dentan 1968:3–4) rested on Deutsch's (1966) discussion of "ethnicity." Wallace (1971:23) has expanded that timid definition far beyond what it was intended to cover. I was primarily trying to specify a set of people to whom my observations more or less applied and to avoid problems posed by less specific accounts (e.g. Appell, et al. 1966). In fact, "Semai" is primarily a linguistic category of some (but not much) significance to Semai speakers. As such, it meets the criteria set up by Hymes (1968), Naroll (1971), Naroll et al. (i.p.). I would be hard pressed indeed, to call it an ethnic group.

Suppose, however, that "ethnicity" does apply to Southeast Asians. Surely then, we want a directly observable objective correlative. A minimal definition of race requires a breeding population (e.g. Buettner-Janusch 1966:612–620). For a similarly objective notion of "ethnicity," there should be an equally explicit set of observations on, for example, interaction frequencies (cf. Birdsell 1973). For example, Fix (1971), a physical anthropologist, provides demographic data, particularly on migration patterns, that are crucial to any understanding of Semai life. Failing such studies, "ethnicity" seems far too fancy and global a concept to be useful in Southeast Asia.

"Ethnicity" as a Folk Concept

Of course, if Southeast Asians had a similar notion of "ethnicity," one which guided their lives significantly, then ethnicity would be a datum to deal with. *A priori*, it is hard to imagine why such a concept would be as obsessive as "ethnicity" is for Euro-Americans. Empirically, the case is gnarly since each instance presents its own peculiar problems.

Many Southeast Asian lexicons include a few words (like Vietnamese *Moi*, Malay *Sakai*), often derogatory, with which speakers label neighbors who are in some sense alien. Appell's remarks (1968:2) about the Bornean situation apply to many parts of Southeast Asia:

Such classification does not recognize the ethnic distinctions that the members included in these populations make themselves. These categories thus include a conglomeration of . . . societies, some of which have no historical relationship and, therefore, share few, if any, cultural traits. The problem of ethnic terminology and the ascription of relevant cultural behavior to the specific, self-conscious, named, social systems where it occurs is a bugaboo. . . .

Such terms are of ethnographic interest to the degree that they reflect the speakers' conception of a heterogeneous set of people as an undifferentiated mass, a conception that relieves the speakers of any imagined need to adapt their responses to the needs of the various peoples lumped together. Such terms, in other words, are useful clues to the ways in which the speakers conceptually organize their social universe. In dealing with interactions between different peoples, a topic discussed below, such terms are of considerable importance, but they tell us little about the people they label.

As Barth (1969) emphasizes, self-identification seems, at least at first, to be a more reliable guide to folk ideas about ethnicity. Elsewhere in this volume, Ichikawa describes the relationship between native Thais and sojourning Japanese businessmen in a way which strongly suggests that each party conceives its ethnicity as discrete from, even opposed to, the ethnicity of the other. The anti-Japanese demonstrations and editorials which greeted the Japanese prime minister's visit to Thailand in January 1974 seems to confirm this inference (Halloran 1974; Shaplen 1974:67). Yet there is some reason to think that this antagonism stems from a conscious and deliberate Japanese policy of self-alienation from Thai society, an exclusiveness exacerbated by Japanese control of over a third of Thailand's imports and foreign investments.

For Thai ethnic identity is scarcely hermetic. Even when Thai hostility to local Chinese businessmen was at its height, the offspring of Thai-Chinese marriages were considered Thai and there was great difficulty deciding who was Chinese (Steinberg 1971:243–244). Nor is this permeability one way. Banks (i.p.) gives evidence of Thai "becoming Malay," although many British observers characterize the Malays as xenophobic.

The situation of the Chinese in Southeast Asia merits special attention since the Chinese are often supposed to be particularly clannish and socially problematic. Nevertheless, as Steinberg (1971:395) notes:

Of all the alien or supposedly alien influences at work in Southeast Asian economies, none has been more heavily canvassed academically or more strongly suspected politically than that of the overseas Chinese. Yet to be a "Chinese" in Southeast Asia is largely a matter of self-identification, the preservation of a surname inherited patrilineally from a Chinese ancestor or retention of the ability to speak some form of the Chinese language. Numerous Southeast Asians of Chinese origin can neither speak nor understand Chinese, and widespread assimilation, contrary to popular belief, has taken place in the past.

As the supposedly unassimilable Chinese seem not to constitute an impregnable, impermeable, and monolithic ethnic unit, the other Southeast Asian "nationalities" seem even more labile (cf. Leach 1954). In fact, as Leach (e.g. 1954, 1960) has long argued, the Western model of a nation state is far too rigid for the Southeast Asian situation, even when the notion of ethnic unit substitutes for that of nationality.

Now, besides arguing that "the characteristic of self-ascription and ascription by others" is the "critical feature" of ethnicity, Barth (1969:13, 17) insists that: "regarded as a status, ethnic identity is superordinate to most other statuses and defines the permissible ... statuses ... which an individual with that identity may assume." I know Malays and Semai, one hundred percent Chinese by blood, who simply manipulate their "ethnicity" as the occasion and their desires suggest (cf. Williams-Hunt 1952:6). This ability to switch identities does not seem to be rare in Southeast Asia, particularly among the hill peoples. In such cases, ethnicity becomes a fleeting, Goffmanesque persona, more or less manipulative, and not a trap. For instance, if a man is adept at handling both Thai and Chinese situations, and if Thai and Chinese audiences accept him as legitimately Thai or Chinese on occasions when he properly asserts one or the other identity, then he is both Thai and Chinese. The question of whether he is or is not *really* Chinese borders on the metaphysical and is of no social consequence. In West Malaysia, very similar relationships seem to occur between Thai peasants and some segments of the aboriginal population on the one hand and the local Malays on the other (Banks i.p.; Dentan i.p.). Under such circumstances the appropriate model would not be one that postulates two mutually exclusive cultures and two sorts of enculturation. In other words, it would be inappropriate to use what Valentine (1971) calls "difference models." Rather, following Polgar's work with American Indians (1960) and Valentine's development of the bicultural model for Afro-Americans (1971), anthropologists working in Southeast

Asia might recognize the possibility that one person or set of persons might have two ethnic identities, describable by situationally appropriate models of biculturism and biculturation, which can account for the often conscious manipulation of their own ethnic identities by Southeast Asians fluent in two cultures.

To allege that in parts of Southeast Asia a person may present characteristics that legitimate his membership in ethnic unit A at time A, and later present others that validate his membership in a coordinate contrastive ethnic unit B at time B, does not exhaust the possibilities which abandonment of a unicultural notion of ethnicity offers anthropologists. P. Kunstadter has a photograph of a Luo nuclear family. By dress and posture alone, an outsider would immediately infer that the father was a montagnard, one boy Chinese, and the other Thai. As far as I know, there seems to be nothing in the phenomenal world or in Luo ideology to prevent this family from being simultaneously, serially, or piecemeal Luo, Thai, *and* Chinese. Once a monolithic notion of ethnicity is discarded, there is no theoretical reason why a person should not participate so fully in a variety of cultures that he becomes a member of each. Cultural anthropologists, for example, are expected to do that. But what for a white Euro-American anthropologist may be an exotic exercise undertaken for allegedly intellectual reasons may be for many Southeast Asians a necessity of everyday life. In short, to understand ethnicity in parts of this region, multicultural models may be necessary.

To conclude this discussion of the theoretical utility of concepts of ethnicity in Southeast Asia, I would like to draw an example from my own field experience. The Semai, an aboriginal people of West Malaysia, stress language as one of the three or four crucial criteria for being a Semai. Similarly, Malaysian law makes speaking Malay one of the three or four basic criteria for being a Malay. Thus, under most circumstances, speaking the appropriate language is a necessary denotation or identity feature of being Semai or Malay (cf. Sorensen 1967). Talking to the local Malays, Semai speak the local dialect. Talking to the local Chinese, they speak Malay with a thick Chinese accent. Talking to Malays from out of state, canny Semai use the national language. Finally, when a spirit seems unresponsive to requests made in Semai, the Semai try out various Malay dialects until they find a mode of discourse that yields the desired results. Obviously the Semai are not, to an anthropologist's way of thinking, shifting linguistic affiliation whenever they accommodate their verbal behavior to their audience. But the category "linguistic affiliation" does not seem salient in Semai ideology. I wonder whether behavior, which to an anthropologist would seem to mark a shift in ethnic identity, would be any more significant to a Semai than speaking the language with which one's interlocutor is comfortable. Good manners, after all, are just good manners, and one adjusts them to the situation one finds oneself in. I know several Semai who belong each to two or more mutually exclusive religions; they manifest no existential difficulty.

In brief, what the foregoing discussion suggests is this: multi-culturation in Southeast Asia provides many people with a series of identities which they can don and doff as particular interactions dictate. Goffmanesque models of self-presentation and interaction ritual are adequate to describe this behavior, often with only tangential reference to notions of ethnicity. To the degree that, in parts of Southeast Asia, "ethnicity" is thus sometimes a matter of manners and masks appropriate to particular times and places, we need not be as surprised as Webb that ethnic identities "are unstable from generation to generation, the racial [*sic*] designation of a community sometimes changing so rapidly that its elders consider themselves as belonging to one race while their descendants claim to belong to another" (see Feingold, this volume).

THE ETHIC OF "ETHNIC"

The attitudes of many anthropologists have changed drastically since "the early 1960's, in those palmy days of research in the behavioral sciences when pretty much anything went" (Marcus 1974:2). What follows is not intended to be *ex cathedra*, but simply an account of what I think may be potential dangers in doing ethnically oriented research in Southeast Asia at the present time.

First, where real ethnic tensions do exist, the potential for communal conflict is also real. The mere presence of an outside investigator may exacerbate these tensions. What he publishes about one faction may serve the hostile intentions of the other. Furthermore, that same information is open to other outsiders who may want to meddle in the situation. Thus, socially significant results are potentially useable for the most depraved ends, and insignificant results are not worth the perils of the investigation upon which they rest.

Where ethnicity is not currently a source of conflict, research with a misguidedly "ethnic" bias may actually create tensions. Moreover, as Hassan points out elsewhere in this volume, "respectable" (educated) stress on ethnicity" tends to lead people who had not previously thought in those terms to explain their own behavior "ethnically," and perhaps even to start seeing their "ethnic" difference from their neighbors. The European experience with "ethnicity" has brought so much suffering to the whole world that the concept seems scarcely a desirable import.

Finally, appeals to folk concepts like ethnicity often serve to mystify problems and to divide people so that they fail to deal directly with more serious but less oretic problems that crosscut ethnic boundaries—problems like illiteracy or disease. To risk making respectable or in other ways seeming to rationalize or justify such divisive appeals is, I think, less than socially responsible. The current Malaysian laws that severely limit public discussions of ethnicity seem to me entirely progressive, and I see no reason for anthropologists, like so many Procrustes, to try to mangle Southeast Asian data into a Euro-American conceptual scheme whose roots are inextricably intertwined with those of a particularly vicious racism.

In fact, like Leach (1960; 1954) I prefer the Southeast Asian notion of nation to the Euro-American one. I like the idea of an ethnic identity that depends on the situation one finds oneself in better than one assigned at birth. The Southeast Asian notions seem more those of free men than do the absolutist Euro-American ones.

REFERENCES

APPELL, G. N.
  1968 A survey of the social and medical anthropology of Sabah: retrospect and prospect. *Behavior Science Notes* 3:1–54.

APPELL, G. N., P. R. GOETHALS, R. HARRISON, C. SATHER
  1966 North Borneo ethnography—a protest. *American Anthropologist* 68:1505.

BANKS, D. J.
  i.p. "Assimilation to Malayness: tolerance or chauvinism?" in *Ethnic relations in Asian countries*. Edited by T. Kang. New York: Praeger.

BARTH, F., *editor*
1969   *Ethnic groups and boundaries.* Boston: Little, Brown.

BIRDSELL, J. B.
1973   A basic demographic unit. *Current Anthropology* 14:337–356.

BUETTNER-JANUSCH, J.
1966   *Origins of man.* New York: John Wiley.

DENTAN, R. K.
i.p.   "Ethnic relations in Perak, West Malaysia (1963)," in *Ethnic relations in Asian countries.* Edited by T. Kang. New York: Praeger.
1968   *The Semai.* New York: Holt, Rinehart and Winston.

DEUTSCH, K. W.
1966   *Nationalism and social communication* (second edition). Cambridge, Mass.: M.I.T. Press.

FIX, A. G.
1971   "Semai Senoi population structure and genetic microdifferentiation." Unpublished Ph.D. thesis, University of Michigan.

HALLORAN, R.
1974   "Rich man in a poor community." *New York Times*, 13 January 1974, page E3.

HSU, F. L. K.
1973   Prejudice and its intellectual effect in American anthropology: an ethnographic report. *American Anthropologist* 75:1–19.

HYMES, D.
1968   "Linguistic problems in defining the problem of 'tribe'," in *Essays on the problem of tribe.* Edited by J. Helm. Proceedings of the 1967 Annual Spring Meeting, American Ethnological Society. Seattle: University of Washington Press.

IZIKOWITZ, K. G.
1969   "Neighbors in Laos," in *Ethnic groups and boundaries.* Edited by F. Barth. Boston: Little, Brown.

LEACH, E. R.
1954   *Political systems of highland Burma.* London: London School of Economics.
1960   The frontiers of Burma. *Comparative Studies in Society and History* 3.

LIVINGSTONE, F.
1961   On the nonexistence of human races. *Current Anthropology* 3:279.

MARCUS, S.
1974   "Review of S. Milgram, 'Obedience to authority'." *The New York Times Book Review*, 13 January 1974, pages 1–2.

MYRDAL, G.
1964   *An American dilemma.* New York: McGraw-Hill.

NAROLL, R.
1971   The double language boundary in cross-cultural surveys. *Behavior Science Notes* 6:95–102.

NAROLL, R., G. L. MICHIK, F. NAROLL
i.p.   "Hologeistic theory testing," in *Harold Driver Festschrift*. Edited by J. G. Jorgensen.

POLGAR, S.
1960   Biculturation of Mesquakie teenage boys. *American Anthropologist* 62:217–235.

SHAPLEN, R.
1974   Letter from Thailand. *New Yorker* 49 (47):67–93.

SORENSEN, A. P., JR.
1967   Multilingualism in the northwest Amazon. *American Anthropologist* 69:670–684.

STEINBERG, D. J., *editor*
1971   *In search of Southeast Asia.* New York: Praeger.

STOCKING, G. W.
1968   *Race, culture and evolution.* New York: Free Press.

VALENTINE, C. A.
1971   Deficit, difference and bicultural models of Afro-American behavior. *Harvard Educational Review* 41:137–157.

WALLACE, B. J.
1971   *Village life in island Southeast Asia.* Boston: Little, Brown.

WILLIAMS-HUNT, P. D. R.
1952   *An introduction to the Malayan aborigines.* Kuala Lumpur: Government Printer.

On Knowing Who You Are:
Intraethnic Distinctions Among the
Akha of Northern Thailand

DAVID A. FEINGOLD

Forty-two years prior to the publication of Leach's influential discussion of ethnicity in *Political systems of highland Burma* (Leach
1954), that careful British imperial enumerator, C. Morgan Webb,
inserted a brief caveat into the *Census of India, 1911*:

An accurate estimate of the numerous tribes and races found within the
province of Burma is a matter of extreme difficulty. The physical characteristics of the Northern portion of the country have induced innumerable
differences in customs, languages and tribal distinctions. But it is not only
in the number of categories to be considered that the difficulty lies. The
distinction between them are neither definite, nor logical, nor permanent,
nor easy to detect. They frequently depart from the lines of linguistic
differences and are subject to local variations impossible to estimate. They
are unstable from generation to generation, the racial designation of a
community sometimes changing so rapidly that its elders consider themselves as belonging to one race while their descendents claim to belong
to another (Webb 1912:247–248).

The research upon which this paper is based was carried out primarily from
October, 1967, through March, 1969, in an Akha village on the Burmese border in
northern Chiengrai Province, Thailand. I had conducted research in the same
region in 1964. The village, which I shall refer to as *Akha Pu*, consisted of 204
persons composing 30 households.

My research was made possible by a National Institute of Mental Health
Fellowship, an NIMH research grant (#1–RO4–MH–13626–01), and a supplementary grant from the East Asian Institute, Columbia University. I wish to
express my gratitude to the Fellows and Associates of the Institute for the Study
of Human Interaction for their encouragement and assistance, and to acknowledge the support of ISHI during the preparation of this paper. Finally, and most
especially, I wish to thank Karen Kerner for her cogent and erudite comments.

In doing so, he isolated what has since become one of the singularly important and complex theoretical questions to emerge from the ethnology of mainland Southeast Asia: how does one identify, designate, and classify significant ethnic units in an area where the ethnolinguistic and cultural complexity of many groups, intermingled in the same or similar ecological settings, virtually forces upon the investigator recognition of the lack of congruence among linguistic, cultural, and societal boundaries? Conversely, how is one to understand the meaning and significance of the large variety of local designative terms, the semantic boundaries of which seem so evanescent?

Nadel's work (1942:12–26) clearly indicated that such problems were not limited to Southeast Asia, but few anthropologists appeared willing or able to follow his early lead and discuss the range of variation within the group or groups which they studied. However, early work by Leach (1954; 1960) and more recent articles by Naroll (1964, 1968), Moerman (1965, 1968), Lehman (1967a, 1967b), Fried (1968), Hackenberg (1967), and Barth (1968) have drawn attention to various aspects of the problems of boundary phenomena and group identification relevant to the delimitation of ethnic groupings.

Ethnicity can no longer be dismissed as a simple, consistent, and constant co-occurrence of a given set of linguistic and nonlinguistic cultural traits. It is clear that there is no simple one-to-one correspondence between linguistic affiliation and ethnic unit designation (Hymes 1968). Moreover, it has become obvious that there are significant situational and aspectual determinants of group identification.

Nevertheless, if these cultural and linguistic incongruities have been recognized to present some major obstacles to the delineation of *gross* ethnic groups, the difficulties which they pose for the demarcation of certain ethnic subgroupings are greatly exacerbated. In considerations of the complex ethnic distributions to be found among the hill peoples of northern Thailand, these problems of intraethnic subcategorization have, surprisingly enough, rarely been touched upon. Unfortunately, the model for the discussion of hill tribe groupings has been drawn all too often from those groups among whom custom, costume, language, and social structure are alleged to vary only in harmonious correspondence (e.g. Young 1962). I found such a limited conceptual outlook and the investigative approaches deriving from it to be less than useless in my studies among the Akha of Chiangrai Province, Thailand.

THE AKHA: BACKGROUND

The Akha are traditionally a non-Buddhist, mountain dwelling people who speak a Tibeto-Burman language and who presently inhabit a discontinuous belt extending from southwestern Yunnan through the northeastern Shan states, across northern Thailand and Laos to North Vietnam. In common with other people of the hill regions, they are generally dependent upon a system of shifting cultivation for their economic base. The primary agricultural emphasis is on the production of rice and opium, with chili peppers displacing opium in some areas. Crops of secondary and tertiary importance include maize and chili, as well as tea, tobacco, and a variety of less significant vegetable crops. This system of swidden agricultural production is supplemented by the practice of forest horticulture which provides a variety of seasonal fruit and other tree products.

Animal husbandry occupies a position second only to agriculture in the village economies of the Akha. Moreover, the various types of livestock raised are essential for the sacrifices which form a central part of the Akha ritual system. Edible livestock includes chickens, goats, pigs, dogs, cows, and water buffalo. In addition, some few horses are kept as pack animals by those who can afford them, and cats are valued as pets. Hunting and poison fishing provide intermittent and supplementary sources of high-quality animal protein, the relative importance of which varies from region to region.

Almost all Akha reside in autonomous villages; the village is the basic political and governmental unit in Akha life, and little political organization exists beyond the village level. Within the village, the basic unit of production is the ritually independent household. Such a household may be composed of a nuclear, stem, or joint family. It is almost exclusively within the village arena that economic and political cooperation takes place among these basic productive units.

In the course of my investigation into the structuring of Akha political behavior, it became apparent that it was necessary to understand how an Akha places another Akha, as well as non-Akha, within a social context (Feingold 1968). To do so, it was necessary to determine what internal groupings the Akha distinguish among themselves; on what basis the significant differentiations are made; and, finally, what is the significance of these groupings (Feingold 1969). It was also of interest to discover how—if at all—these related to the so-called "subtribes" mentioned in the literature.

When we turn to the literature on the Akha, we find numerous divergences and inconsistencies. *The gazetteer of upper Burma and the Shan states* (Scott and Hardiman 1900:590) cites the information collected in Chinese by Warry and quotes him as follows:

> There are seven main divisions of the tribe, said to be named after seven brothers, from whom all Akha are descended. These are Suli, Chi-cho, Sat-do, Chi-ma, Mota, Luwei, and Puchet. . . . I met and conversed with members of the first four divisions. The people are further subdivided into many different clans, the names of which it is not worth setting down here. The dialect of each division of the tribe varies, but not so much as to make communication difficult. There is also considerable difference in the costume affected by the women (Scott and Hardiman 1900:590).

Telford (1937:90), also speaking of Burma, however, lists nine subgroups: Lehleubo, Jeu G'we, Jeujaw, Jo Byawn, Leh Nyi, Che Mui, Hpyo Hso, Zeu Zi, and Hteu La, Roux and Chu (1954: 154), on the other hand, list seven: Nu Quay, O Ma, Pu Li, Muc Chi, P'u Sang, O'Pa, and La Ma. It will be noted that the three lists are not comparable, even allowing for radical differences in the systems of transliteration employed in notation. This fact alone, however, does not necessarily represent any insuperable difficulty; that is, according to the Lebar, Hickey, and Musgrave compendium (1964:34), there are always seven or nine groups (having mythological origin explanations), and any variances are explicable in terms of local naming patterns.

Bernatzik (1947:456) goes further, grouping seven subdivisions into three tribal divisions: Akha Tyitso, Akha Puli, and Akha Akho. He cites Telford (1937:90) in support of such a grouping. However, I was unable to locate any mention of these larger divisions by Telford, either on the page cited, or elsewhere in his work. Bernatzik (1947:458) also maintains that marriage restrictions—nonexistent between the first two groups—proscribe marriage between members of these and the Akha Akho. This assertion appears to be predicated upon Bernatzik's position that the Akha exhibit strict prescriptive, and actual tribal, endogamy—a situation dissimilar from that which I found to prevail among the Akha of Chiengrai Province at present.

In order to clarify this confused situation, it was necessary to turn from attempts at extrinsic bases for categorization to behaviorally validated classifications. From the observation of encounters between Akha previously unknown to one another, it was learned that, "What kind of Akha are you?" represents a significant, culturally appropriate question for initial encounters. (It should be noted, however, that this question was most likely to occur in male/male encounters and least likely—apparently—in female/female encounters.)

To the question, "What kind of Akha are you?," there are three responses possible within an Akha context: an Akha may give his sib surname (*nga yemo akha* or *yemo agu*); he may give a geographical reference (*nga pu akha*: an Akha of Pu village); or he may give a sub-cluster name (*nga Johgwo akha*). His choice will be situationally determined by his location, the perceived identity of the questioner, his expectation of the content of the conversation, and its social setting.

The subtribe names referred to in the literature on the Akha (for example, Bernatzik 1947; Roux 1924; Roux and Chu 1954; Telford 1937) are a mixture of all three possibilities. A good example of the problem is the term, "Puli Akha," the Akha group most mentioned in the limited literature on the Akha. Puli is a Shan place name— it is not an Akha word—which some peoples use to refer to Johgwo groups.

All Akha are members of named, unranked patrisibs called *agu*. Recruitment into these groups is via three channels: birth, marriage, and to a limited extent, adoption. At birth, a child is a member of the *agu* of his father. For males, this remains so forever. Girls, however, become members of their husband's *agu* upon marriage. Although adoption (*pa do do-ö*) into an *agu* is possible, it is generally limited to a non-Akha, who will sometimes be taken into the *agu* of his father-in-law at the time of marriage to an Akha woman. The names cited in the literature as subtribe are most often, in reality, *agu* names. According to my informants, although the number of these groups is clearly finite and limited, it is a large number and not known; one is told that "there are more than 100," "there are so many that you can't count," and that "no one can know them all." In Pu, five of these groups are represented by one or more households. Other villages in the area, however, show even greater variety.

The Akha define their *agu* geneologically and, therefore, it would be good to have some understanding of the nature and significance of Akha geneologies and their role in Akha life. One is often told, "All Akha must be able to count their generations." This does not mean that everyone can, although many are able to, or that mistakes are not often made, particularly by the younger men. Nevertheless, geneological competence is widely admired, and it is a source of pride to the man who possesses it.

7

In geneological naming, the Akha follow a typical Tibeto-Burman pattern of patronymic linkages. The last syllable of an ancestor's name is used as the first syllable of the name of his immediate descendant. It should be noted, however, that geneological names are rarely used outside of the context of counting generations, since it is often considered unlucky to use them. A separate name or version of the geneological name is used for ordinary circumstances. For example, a Pu villager, Apai, of *yemo agu*, has the geneological name Tu Pa. The last eight generations of his generation geneology are as follows: Ya Tu, Tu Sa, Sa Hge, Hge Dzaw, Dzaw Te, Te Dja, Dja Tu, Tu Pa.

Apai's sib, *yemo agu*, includes all those persons, regardless of their dwelling place, who can trace their geneologies back to a common ancestor, Ye I. In Apai's case, this represents a span of 17 generations of a total of 47 generations for his entire geneology.

The Akha geneological system is a universalistic one, which can include not only all Akha, but all mankind. When an outsider is brought into the system, his name appears in the geneology at generation 15, a syllable of his name being appended to Ton Pon. For example, the son of a Lahu, living in Pu, married an Akha and was taken into the *agu* of his wife's father; he is called Acha. His geneological name is Ton Pon Cha, and this is placed in the fifteenth position in his geneology. It will be seen, therefore, that a short geneology is indicative of recent recognized non-Akha ancestry. It should be noted here, however, that these comments apply only to the geneologies of men; women's are reckoned quite differently. They include only the three previous generations of patrilineally related males, but include Mo, FaMo, and FaMoMo as well. The male geneologies exclude all females.

Agu are not effective corporate groups: they do not have a leader; they do not possess exclusive economic or ritual rights; they do not come together for purposes of warfare or trade. They do not even regulate marriage. Marriage within the *agu* is perfectly acceptable, as is marriage outside it. The exogamous grouping within Akha society is the smaller division of the *agu*, the lineage or *lõn do*. All named sibs (*agu*) are divided into one or more unnamed *lõn do*. In theory, the boundaries of the *lõn do* may be coterminous with those of the *agu*. In practice, *agu* are composed of many different *lõn do*. Marriage within the *lõn do* is prohibited, but sexual relations are not. If a girl becomes pregnant under these circumstances, however, the boy must pay a fine of 200 rupees (about 100 dollars). A ceremony (*lon do hgwo*) is held which splits the *lõn do* and the couple may then marry. In addition to the preceding instance of marriage, it is not rare for a boy to decide that he wishes to marry a girl within his own lineage, despite the prohibition on such unions. If he cannot be dissuaded, a *lõn do hgwo* ceremony will be held and the lineage split, thereby legitimizing the proposed marriage. This is considerably less expensive if the girl has already become pregnant. As the Akha themselves point out, no one can control young people in love.

While marriage is the primary cause of lineage splits, conflicts between male siblings and those between fathers and sons contribute a significant number of splits, although the former are considerably more common than the latter. Nevertheless, recently in the village of Ba Kwe Mai, a split took place between a father and an eldest son who had stolen money and silver. The father, after killing a pig, declared that "... he ... didn't need ..." his son; that is, that they were no longer related. As a result, when the son counts his geneology, he leaves out his father, but includes his grandfather.

Besides the above, fear of a mistaken marriage is an additional cause of fission. In theory, there is no limit to the potential size of the *lõn do*. Although there is some indication that local practices may vary, there is no automatic splitting of the lineage among the Akha in my region. I have been told, "even after 100 generations, we could not marry without *lõn do hgwo*"; that is, without splitting the lineage. When a lineage grows beyond the point where its members can easily keep track of it, they fear that a "wrong" marriage will be made. If a wrong marriage is made, and it is discovered, a man must pay a fine of 1500 baht or divorce his wife. If the mistake is not discovered, the Akha believe that the woman and any children will become sick.

It will be noted that, as a result of the various sorts of fissions discussed previously, the size, composition, and depth of one's lineage is liable to considerable variation in the course of one's life. Similarly, the overall internal composition of a sib is in a continual state of flux. (In this regard, it is interesting to note that when an outsider is taken into an *agu*, he is not included in any of the pre-existing lineages (*lõn do*), but constitutes a separate new one.)

SEMANTIC PROBLEMS

The analysis of Akha kin groupings and their relation to problems of group differentiation is complicated by a basic lexical problem: the term *agu* has three major semantic referents. First, it designates a patrilineally surnamed group, as discussed above (e.g. *yemo agu, yeshaw agu, jope agu*, etc.). This is its primary referent, and hence its most common usage.

Second, it can refer to a ritually defined occupational group. For example, all blacksmiths (the position of blacksmith has considerable ritual significance in Akha society, and the importance is more than economic) are said to be *baji agu*. This does not mean that all Akha blacksmiths are related, as, for example, are all Akha who belong to *yemo agu*. A *yemo* man who went through the ceremony to become a blacksmith (*baji*) would remain a member of *yemo agu*, yet still be included in the term *baji agu*.

Third, the term *agu* is used to designate named clusters of patrisibs (such as Johgwö *agu*, Adjo *agu*, Sa-du *agu*, Akho *agu*, etc.). For example, the five *agu* (patrisibs) represented in Pu (*yemo, yeshaw, jelu, cho-mü*, and *boche*) are part of a large number of *agu* which are referred to collectively as Johgwö *agu* (patrisib cluster), or Johgwö Akha. There is no terminological distinction made between the usages of the term at these two very distinct levels.

It is possible to establish contrasts and differentiations based on partially synonymous substitutions, that is, testing through the use of terms with similar but not congruent semantic ranges. To cite a brief and, of necessity, underdeveloped example, the word *pa* is a rather diffuse Akha term, sometimes glossed "extended family." In the seven villages in the immediate research area, it is sometimes used as a synonym for *agu*, but never for *lõn do*. The word *pa* seems to be capable of substituting for the first usage of the term *agu* (sib) in most semantic environments, but not for the second or third usages. That is, it appears that *yemo pa* is acceptable, but *baji pa* or Johgwö *pa* most certainly are not.

In theory, the Akha sib clusters are geneologically determined: all the Adjo sibs have Je *djo* at generation 28 in their geneologies. In practice, the situation is considerably more complex. In Pu, for example, all the people of *boche agu* (sib) say that they are Johgwö Akha, as does everyone else in the village. Regrettably for the anthropologist, they are geneologically much closer to several non-Johgwö groups.

Let us return, however, to the problem of the Akha who is asked what kind of Akha he is. Among the villagers of Pu and among most of the Johgwö Akha in that area of northern Thailand, the most frequent response to a request for identification is to give the surname (e.g. *yemo agu*). In fact, in some 500 recorded encounters, this response was given in over 70 percent of cases. The geographical identification response occurred in virtually all the remaining cases. In no naturally occurring setting was the sib cluster designation used. In the case of Adjo Akha, however, the situation was quite the reverse. While the percentage of geographical references remained approximately constant, the other two responses were reversed. An Adjo would say that he was an Adjo Akha or Adjo *agu*. Only a second or third response could yield his sib designation.

The Akha account for this by saying that the sib cluster names are only used by groups who do not know the correct surnames of another group. My informants have said that if they were in an area with a heavy concentration of Adjo or Sa-dü people, they would refer to themselves as Johgwö *agu* instead of giving their surnames, which no one would know.

If dialect complexes, ritual patterns, and costume are correlated with the distribution of sib cluster groups, numerous incongruities appear. The dialectology of Akha is extremely complex and far too little information is available to make any meaningful generalizations; it is clear, however, that the demarcation of linguistic boundaries is not consistently coterminous with that of the sib cluster groupings. While the speech of some of the groups in some geographical areas is characterized by certain distinct phonological and morphological features, the range of variation within and across groups is such as to preclude their productive designation as dialect groups. Sib clusters clearly cross-cut speech communities, and vice versa.

To date, this has not been clearly understood. A case in point may be found in the discussion of dialect in the otherwise extremely valuable *Akha-English dictionary* compiled by the Rev. Paul Lewis (1968:viii).

This dictionary is of the Jeu g'oe (Puli) dialect, as it is spoken in Central and Central-eastern Kengtung State. This is the dialect which all Akhas I have met recognize as the "standard" dialect of Akha. Other Akhas usually know enough of the Jeu g'oe dialect so that they can communicate without any special trouble with the Jeu g'oe speaker, although they may speak with an accent.

Various features of the Akha language as spoken in Thailand may be different from the Akha in this dictionary. But for the most part words included in this dictionary represent, with some predictable phonetic changes, their speech as well.

In fact, however, the Jeu g'oe (Johgwö) dialect presented does not correspond to the dialect spoken by the Johgwö Aka in Akha Pu, nor does it correspond to the speech found in a number of other Akha villages in northern Thailand, the residents of which are Johgwö Akha. In so stating, I am not maintaining that Lewis was "wrong" in his description of the "Jeu g'oe dialect"; his description fits quite nicely with the speech of some other villagers in the region who are identified as Johgwö Akha. What I am maintaining is that there is no Jeu g'oe (Johgwö) dialect to describe, and consequently, it is hardly surprising that the correspondences apply equally as well to some of the non-Johgwö Akha in the same area.

The named intraethnic distinctions in Akha society constitute not so much groups as they do categories. They provide an initial frame-work within which an Akha may begin—at its most basic level—the process by which he locates another Akha within a social context. Furthermore, this system of internal categorizations articulates with the process of external categorization by which the Akha desig-nate and account for non-Akha. To the extent that intraethnic dis-tinctions fulfil a locator function, they provide a bridge between the outer boundaries of Akha social space. Moreover, they represent the latent potential, however dormant, for the rationalization of extra-village political organization.[1] It should be emphasized, however, that this is hardly the case in Thailand at the present time.

REFERENCES

BARTH, F.
   1969   *Ethnic groups and boundaries*. Boston: Little, Brown.

BERNATZIK, H.
   1947   *Akha and Meau*. Innsbruck: Wagnerische Universitäts Buch-drukerei.

FEINGOLD, D. A.
   1968   "Networks of identity: ethnic designations and kin groupings among the Johgwo Akha of northern Thailand." Paper pre-sented at the Eighth International Congress of Anthropological and Ethnological Sciences, Tokyo and Kyoto, Japan.

[1]   This may have been the case among the allegedly hierarchically organized Akha in Laos (see Roux and Chu 1954).

1969 "What kind of Akha are you? Subgroup differentiation among the Akha of northern Thailand." Paper presented at the American Anthropological Association meetings, New Orleans, November.

FRIED, M. H.
1968 "On the concepts of 'tribe' and 'tribal society'," in *Essays on the problem of tribe*. Edited by J. Helm. Proceedings of the 1967 Annual Spring Meeting, American Ethnological Society. Seattle: University of Washington Press.

HACKENBERG, R.
1967 The parameters of an ethnic group: a method for studying the total tribe. *American Anthropologist* 69:478–492.

HYMES, D.
1968 "Linguistic problems in defining the concept of 'tribe'," in *Essays on the problem of tribe*. Edited by J. Helm. Proceedings of the 1967 Annual Spring Meeting, American Ethnological Society. Seattle: University of Washington Press.

LEACH, E. R.
1954 *Political systems of highland Burma*. Cambridge: Harvard University Press.
1960 The "frontiers" of Burma. *Comparative Studies in Society and History* 3 (1):49–68.

LEBAR, F., G. HICKEY, J. MUSGRAVE
1964 *Ethnic groups of mainland Southeast Asia*. New Haven: HRAF Press.

LEHMAN, F. K.
1967a "Ethnic categories in Burma and the theory of social systems," in *Southeast Asian tribes, minorities, and nations*. Edited by P. Kunstader, 93–124. Princeton: Princeton University Press.
1967b "Burma: Kayah society as a function of the Shan–Burma–Karen context," in *Contemporary change in traditional societies*. Edited by J. H. Steward, 2–25. Chicago: University of Illinois Press.

LEWIS, P.
1968 *Akha-English dictionary*. Linguistics Series III, Data Paper 70. Ithaca: Southeast Asia Program, Department of Asian Studies. Cornell University.

MOERMAN, M.
1965 Ethnic identification in a complex society: who are the Lue? *American Anthropologist* 67:1215–1230.
1968 "Being Lue: uses and abuses of ethnic identification," in *Essays on the problem of tribe*. Edited by J. Helm. Proceedings of the 1967 Annual Spring Meeting, American Ethnological Society. Seattle: University of Washington Press.

NAROLL, R.
1964 On ethnic unit classification. *Current Anthropol* 5:283–291, 306–312.

1968   "Who the Lue are," in *Essays on the problem of tribe*. Edited by J. Helm. Proceedings of the 1967 Annual Spring Meeting, American Ethnological Society. Seattle: University of Washington Press.

ROUX, H.
1924   Deux tribes de la region de Phongsaly (Laos septentrional), I: A-Khas ou Khas Kos; II: P'u Noi. *BEFEO* 24:373–500.

ROUX, H., TRAN VAN CHU
1954   Quelques minorities ethniques du Nord-Indochine. *France-Asie* 10:135–419.

SCOTT, J. G., J. P. HARDIMAN
1900   *Gazetteer of upper Burma and the Shan states*. Part 1, volume I. Rangoon.

TELFORD, J. H.
1937   Animism in Kengtung State. *Journal of the Burma Research Society* 27:85–238.

WEBB, C. M.
1912   *Census of India, 1911*, volume nine, part one: *Burma report*. Rangoon: Office of the Superintendent, Government Printing, Burma.

YOUNG, G.
1962   *The hill tribes of northern Thailand*, Siam Society, Monograph no. 1: Bangkok.

Structure, Function, and Ideology of a Karen Funeral in Northern Thailand

JAMES W. HAMILTON

Over the years there has been a great deal of discussion, theorizing, and speculation in social anthropology concerning the symbolism and behavior surrounding a set of related factors called religion, sacred ritual, magic, death rites, etc. (Some of the more recent works have been Leach 1961; Lévi-Strauss 1963, 1966; Turner 1969; Lessa and Vogt 1965; Rappaport 1971; Malinowski 1939.) Of all the variability found in human societies concerning these issues, one thing is certain: some type of ceremony and ritual have surrounded the fact of death in all societies for a very long time. It does, therefore, provide a cross-cultural regularity that is amenable to comparison, and it demands explanation.

I will not attempt here to deal with all the issues, nor will I be so bold as to try to resolve major theoretical points. Rather, my intent is to consider the funeral as an empirical "event" (Bohannan 1963: 367) to be described and analyzed as a methodological technique for discovering and interpreting characteristics of Karen society and culture. The underlying theoretical orientation is structural, cognitive and systemic.[1]

This is a revised version of a paper originally presented at the Annual Meeting of the American Anthropological Association in 1964. It is based on data gathered during two years of field research among the Pwo Karen in northern Thailand from October, 1959, to October, 1961.
[1] The term "structural" may have various interpretations. By it, I mean to indicate that the funeral has a series of clearly definable, related parts that follow one another (Leach 1961: 132ff.; Bohannan 1963: 358ff.). The term "cognitive" is also in vogue today and may have different connotations as well. I use it here to

The death and funeral of a Karen, presumably killed by magic, is described and analyzed in terms of the structure of the ritual event and the purposes (mostly latent functions) it serves in Karen culture. In this case of the Pwo Karen in northern Thailand, in addition to disposing ritually of a dead body, the funeral is an occasion for courting and for economic distribution; it is a time when authority must be expressed, decisions made, and social control maintained; it is a time for meeting old friends and fulfilling kinship obligations; it is a dangerous time during which strict procedures must be followed in carrying out rites; and it is thus a time for manifesting the belief system through behavior which strengthens psychological sets in the culture.

We begin with an empirical event—the funeral—rather than with a scientific construct such as economic, religious, or political organization and attempt to show that much of the entire socio-cultural system is reflected in the event. Or, if one prefers, constructs concerning the parts of culture may be abstracted from behavior at the funeral. On the basis of describing and analyzing an episode such as a funeral, what can be said, quoting Malinowski (1961:xvi), about the "totality of all social, cultural and psychological aspects of the community . . ."?

The funeral as a specific rite would seem to have a definite beginning and end, but there is always a series of events leading up to and trailing off after the rite. And the funeral itself can be subdivided into a series of connected rituals.[2]

THE FUNERAL

Pre-Funeral Events

A nineteen-year-old boy from Ban Hong, whom I will call Jai, borrowed twenty baht (about one dollar) from a friend from another

---

indicate that my interpretation is based on what I "know" the Karen to believe, from their own statements (Tyler 1969: 1ff.), at the same time recognizing that variation may be crucial to analysis. By using the term "systemic," I assume that the culture may be analyzed into a number of interrelated sets of variables (subsystems) that inter-influence one another (Harris 1968: 521). These subsystems are sometimes called "institutions."

[2] This paper discusses one specific funeral. However, the description and analysis are based on approximately ten funerals observed during the course of fieldwork.

village so that the two boys could go to Lampoon together.[3] A short time after reaching this northern Thai town, the two friends began to quarrel because Jai wanted to return home early. They parted with bitter words. By the time Jai reached home he was feeling ill and had a slight fever. He did not appear to be very ill and it seemed to be a case of malaria, but Jai and his kinsmen were adamant that it was not malaria. The condition began to worsen very rapidly, but there were no overt signs of a serious illness. The villagers believed that Jai was sick because of the argument with his friend—black magic was suspected as retaliation for coming home after money had been borrowed, and because of the open argument between the two boys. Among the Karen, face-to-face argumentation is considered very improper behavior and may provoke the use of black magic.

Jai stopped eating and drinking, and would not take the medicine I offered. He became delirious, but still had no great rise in temperature; his pulse rate was normal. Jai's father went to a Karen fortune-teller with the hope of finding a cure, but to no avail. In the meantime, Jai said that he must die and that no one could help him. He began to act hysterical, and people, regarding his behavior as inappropriate, laughed at him. His father next went to a Thai "spirit doctor" and was told that in order to be cured, the boy must make an offering to his lineage spirit in a nearby village. Instead, however, the father offered two baht (ten cents)—which was to represent two pigs—to the local village spirit to protect the boy. Later a real offering of two pigs was promised whether the boy recovered or not (the offering was never made, however). The victim went into a coma and died the next morning at 5 A.M. The total time from onset of "illness" until death was three days.

Funeral Ritual

The word was passed and preparations for the funeral began almost immediately. The body was cleaned, clothes were put on it backwards, and it was wrapped in a mat and tied. The adult married men of Jai's village and a few surrounding villages began to arrive and to build a small structure to house the body during the funeral proceedings. When they finished work, the raised platform was swept with burning bamboo by the head elder of the village, who was

[3] Ban Hong is the name of the village in which I concentrated my field research. It no longer exists as an identifiable entity because of the building of the Yanhee Dam. However, I have kept track of the village members.

directing operations. This was to disassociate the builders from the structure, and as it was being done, each worker called his *lae* [personal spirit] ("soul" is a poor translation).

The ladder to the family house was turned around, and the body was removed and placed on the platform in the small structure. The house ladder was then turned right again. As soon as the ladder had been turned in the first place and the body removed, the women of the family began a stylized wailing for a short time. Next, a man stood at each end of the body with a piece of curled and burning bamboo. They pointed out and loudly proclaimed the cardinal directions for the *lae* of the dead boy. However, north was said to be south, and east was said to be west, trees grew upside down, and the river flow was reversed. A baby chick was then killed and put on the ground under the body.

These initial preparations finished, the core of the ceremony could begin. This involved a twenty-four-hour cycle repeated on three days. First, two sets of married men sang. One group marched around the body in pairs, and the other sat on the ground nearby and sang a different song, while playing a kind of game. On the first notes of these songs, the family of the boy again began a loud wailing. Next, the unmarried boys marched around the body in pairs and sang. When they stopped, the unmarried girls, also in pairs, marched and sang. The boys and girls alternated their singing throughout the rest of the twenty-four-hour period until the last round, when one boy marched with a pair of girls, and they sang together. The cycle was then repeated.

The songs of the marching married men were for, and to, the *lae* of the dead boy, and the content of the songs conveyed the general idea of "rest in peace," "go on your trip to the spirit world," and "do not stay in this world." The group playing the game sang a different song and moved "fruit" up a tree for the *lae* to eat on the trip. The unmarried boys and girls sang courting songs to each other, and sometimes these were very suggestive. During the singing, people would come and go, bringing gifts of rice, tobacco, betel, money, and so forth. These goods were presented to the body by a member of the family, but they were to be used by the guests. The tobacco and betel were put out for the adult spectators who chatted, joked, and watched on a porch; the rice was taken inside and cooked. Also during each period, the reverse directions were loudly pointed out for the *lae* of the dead boy, and cigarettes were offered to it from time to time.

On the morning of the fourth day, as each group of young singers finished, they left immediately for their homes without looking back. The adult men tore down the structure housing the body and the material was burned on the spot. Next, a long bamboo carrying pole was attached to the wrapped body and the whole group of men from several villages left for the cemetery. A short distance from the cremation area, the body was touched to the ground three times. On reaching the cemetery, two base logs were chosen for the pyre and were held by two men facing each other. Again directions were pointed out for the *lae* to hear, and presumably see. When the pyre was finished, the head elder (who had been directing operations) swept it, and each man called his own *lae*.

The *lae* of the boy was offered a cup of whisky by his father; this was poured over the body. The head elder drank a cup, and finally so did each man. The body and some personal effects were put on the pyre, which was then lighted at the four corners. While the pyre was thus being lighted and fanned, the head elder ritually spilled some water from a bamboo vessel a few feet from each end of the body, to represent the tears of the living, and to provide drink for the *lae* on its journey.

After the body had burned for a time, a long pole was used to jab and poke it. Some men joked and laughed, but all watched attentively. Finally, some finger bones were retrieved to be used a little later. In this instance, the body was not burning well—which is an indication of magic—so it was further poked and moved, and there was some attempt to knock off the skull.

After a time, when the body was nearly consumed, it was abandoned and the men retreated a short distance for the final rite for the *lae* of the boy. The men gathered around a tiny structure on the ground made of bamboo in which were placed the following items: the dead chick killed on the first day, the boy's flashlight, his tobacco container, and some cooked rice. A cup of liquor was then poured over it all. This was to represent a final feast for the *lae* before it began its journey. Next, the boy's father touched the pieces of finger bone first to water and said, "If you are cold, take a cool bath." Then he touched them to hot charcoal and said, "If you are hot, sit by the fire." Each man then stuck two pieces of long thin bamboo into the ground and called his own *lae*.

The men immediately began to leave the cemetery without looking back, again calling their *lae* to follow. When the group reached the spot where the body had been touched to the ground on the way to the cemetery, the head elder chopped into a tree three times and each man took a thorny twig from a bush and carried it back to the village, where it was discarded.

When the party reached the village, taboo signs had been erected at each path leading into the village. Anyone who had not gone to the cemetery could not enter the village until the final ceremony was completed.

At the home of the dead boy, each person who had gone to the cemetery had his wrists tied by an elder who had not gone and who was not a member of the boy's matrilineage. This rite involved holding a small amount of rice and chicken in each hand, one at a time, while the elder called the person's *lae* and then tied a piece of black cotton thread around the wrist. When all participants had had their wrists tied, there was general feasting (this usually includes either chicken or pork curry and [glutinous] rice, and sometimes a considerable amount of liquor). This ended the funeral ceremony, and gradually people straggled away.

Post-Funeral Events

There is, however, a postscript to this particular funeral. That night Jai's father put a bowl of rice on the porch along with some cigarettes for the boy's *lae* in case it returned. During the night the family heard the rice pan rattle, and they detected the odors of cigarette smoke and Jai's hair oil. The next morning, there was a "foul odor" in the rice pan. That day the father returned to the cemetery and found signs of black magic. The most important of these was the fact that the skull had two layers, which meant that an invisible pot had been placed over Jai's head. This was interpreted as the cause of death. The villagers were now convinced that Jai had died from black magic, and they strongly suspected the friend with whom Jai had argued.

FUNERAL ANALYSIS AND INTERPRETATION

Magic, Religion, Symbolism

From the description of the death itself, it is obvious that magic plays a powerful role in Karen culture in terms of social control and as a sanction against certain kinds of behavior, one of which is open argument. I will not go into the details of magic as a social control here. I merely wish to stress that magic, and the ideological system surrounding it, actually "caused" the death of a seemingly healthy nineteen-year-old boy. He was literally frightened to death because of his belief in the efficacy of magic. Magic is part and parcel of Karen personality and life. The world may be manipulated by it, and magic must be taken into account constantly.

One might argue, of course, that Jai had a real and fatal disease, which is possible. However, at the very least belief in magic hastened the death, and all individuals were thinking and reacting in terms of magic rather than disease. There is also an additional bit of data that validates the contention that the ideology (of magic) has a strong influence on behavior and the senses: Jai's family actually perceived him with the senses of sound and smell, and they felt the porch move.[4]

Turning to the religious and ideological aspects of the funeral, one can construct a complete picture of the world of the dead and its relationship to the world of the living. The afterworld may be said to be in complementary distribution with the world of the living. It may be described as inside out, upside down, and backwards to this world. Or, to use a term from science fiction, it is an antiworld. In fact, it may be in the same geographical location as this world: the afterworld is said to be "over there," but no specific direction can be given. (The cemetery is, however, a dangerous place.)

There is an obvious religious aura surrounding the whole funeral rite: the pageantry and dramatic effect are striking. The courting young people are dressed in all their finery. The marching girls walk one in front of the other, a taller, older girl in black with her arms around the waist of the younger one. Thus their bodies are touching and they must be in perfect step. The girls are covered from head to toe with long, thin, colorful cloth. The unrelated but simultaneous singing presents a counterpoint effect that leaves no one untouched, and the singing between boys and girls is a challenge and response. The Karen funeral is truly exotic—even to the local Thai. It is an emotionally charged and dangerous period for all, because it is a time when the two worlds are in closest contact, and there is the

[4] During another funeral that I observed, that of a Thai boy in a nearby community, the dead boy was actually "seen" in several places by various individuals.

possibility that they may become confused with disastrous results: the *lae* of the living may wander into the world of the dead.

At any rate, the spirit or *lae* of the dead person must be dealt with properly and sent on its way to the spirit world. Much of the funeral, therefore, revolves around teaching the spirit how it should act in its new state of being. The dead chick leads the way. Food, drink, and other goods are supplied, but the *lae* is concerned with the essence of these items (the inside), while the living need the material part. At a final feast, provided after the material body is cremated, the *lae* eats and drinks with other lineage spirits before it starts the journey. This is what the rite involving the finger bones, which takes place just before the men leave the cemetery, is all about.

Aspects of the other world are inculcated. Directions are in reverse; trees grow upside down; clothes are worn backwards; rivers flow in the opposite direction; the inside of the house ladder is out; the human body may be treated irreverently because it is of no use to a *lae* of the dead. When it is hot, a *lae* sits by the fire; when it is cold, a *lae* should go in the water. The *lae* is socialized anew.

Because of the possibility that the two worlds may become confused, boundaries are formed. These are indicated by sweeping the platform and pyre on which the body is to rest. When the living call their *lae*, it is to keep a separation between the worlds. There are also several other boundary-forming activities: the bamboo sticks that are jabbed into the ground at the last rite at the cemetery; touching the body to the ground on the way to the cemetery; the thorny twig that is carried back to the village; chopping into a tree three times. All of these are to separate the two worlds, and the purpose is to keep the *lae* of the two worlds from seeing each other. They are to be kept in their separate "states of being," not merely separate geographic domains.

Much could be said in terms of the relationship of the individual to the funeral (i.e. what he feels and thinks during the ceremony), but I will restrict myself to three examples:

First, the stylized, ritual crying is very specific and appears to be turned on and off at will. However, there are two emotion-charged signals that bring it on—the family is deeply affected, but others are too. The first signal is the turning of the ladder and removing of the body from the house. The second signal is the first notes of singing by the married men around the body. People should not cry at a funeral (for reasons to be mentioned in a moment), but these are two times when crying bursts out and then is quickly controlled.

The second example concerns the apparently irreverent attitude in the teasing and courting that goes on, and in the way the body is treated at cremation. On closer examination, this behavior is seen as a psychological set determined by ideological conceptions. There is a myth among the Karen that a large venomous serpent enjoyed killing Karen until they fooled it by being elated at funerals. Thus the attitudes and behavior *seem* unconcerned. Courting goes on among the unmarried (but this is only among individuals who are not members of the lineage of the dead); the adults have a good time, feast, and joke; and the body is treated in a most irreverent manner at the cremation. However, the body is no longer of significance because the *lae* is gone. The *lae* itself, on the other hand, is treated with respect throughout the proceedings, and at the final rite it is feasted and taught, and then sent on its way.

This brings up the final example of individual concern, that for the personal *lae* of the living. As was pointed out, a funeral is a dangerous time, particularly for the individual *per se*. His *lae* may be tempted by, or accidentally pass into, the world of the dead. There is, therefore, constant care and concern for the personal *lae* of each individual. Only when safely back in the village, after the *lae* has finally been enticed into the body with food and is secured at the final wrist-tying rite, can one relax. These psychological concerns characterize the behavior of all individuals participating in a funeral.

Social Organization

I will present here only the barest outlines of social organization, to give at least a flavor of what can be gleaned from analyzing the funeral proceedings.

SOCIAL STRUCTURE. By analyzing behavior at the funeral in structural terms, the following social units or corporate groups emerge:
1. The household-family unit is the focus of the proceedings. Household members are set off, since they do not actually participate in the rites, except in minor ways—they cook food, care for guests, see that tobacco and betel are available, and so forth.
2. The village is reinforced as a social unit because it is closed off, and all work stops while all villagers participate to a greater or lesser degree in the funeral. The corporateness of the village is manifest in

8

that a funeral is a village affair as much as a family affair, and the village functions as a unit.

3. The village complex, which is a group of related villages, unites at a funeral. People from all the villages attend, and it is the elders from the village complex that are important.

4. In addition to these strictly residential units of Karen society, there is a fourth unit that cross-cuts all of these and extends beyond them to connect groups of village complexes. This is the matrilineage. Members of the lineage from villages far and near attend. They help the family in various ways during the proceedings but do not participate in the singing, and thus are set apart.

If we look at the behavior at the funeral in terms of functional categories, the following may be abstracted concerning economy and polity.

ECONOMIC ORGANIZATION. An economy may be analyzed in terms of the categories of production, distribution, and consumption (Hamilton 1965). Using these categories, distribution and consumption become important aspects of the funeral. A great deal of pooling and redistribution take place. Goods of various types are channelled into the household of the deceased on the basis of kinship, village, and lineage connections. These are then redistributed to a wide area.

Redistribution and consumption are almost simultaneous at the funeral, but consumption as an aspect of the economy is a very important element of the funeral. The Karen cannot afford much meat, so ceremonial occasions are virtually the only times when chicken or pork is consumed. Therefore, a funeral is an important time for protein consumption. Chicken and/or pork are always supplied, as are liquor, tobacco, betel, fermented tea, rice, peppers, and so on.

Other types of consumption are carried on, too. There is a "cost" in terms of the various materials, goods, and money consumed. All these values, however, cannot be calculated in terms of money because the Karen are not yet entirely within a money economy. The money actually spent by the family, though (and this is not figuring a money value for other contributed items), was roughly five dollars —which is one-tenth of the maximum annual income in money. Some funerals cost as much as thirty dollars, which means that the economic aspects of the funeral are considerable. But more significantly, the organization of the economy, in terms of distribution and consumption at least, is manifest in this episode; that is, the important mechanisms or the means of distribution show up as well as consumption patterns.

POLITICAL ORGANIZATION. The political aspects of the funeral include decision making, social control, and the power and/or authority involved in organizing, controlling, and directing the various activities. The important functionaries are the headman, the head elder, and the body of elders which, in the case of a funeral, includes more than merely those in one village. Tradition, strong kinship ties, and face-to-face relations take much of the burden off those with authority—and this shows up clearly in the funeral. There are, of course, the sanctions of religion and magic as aspects of social control which are strongly manifest in the funeral.

The men in authority positions are given deferential treatment, and they are said to have some supernatural powers that justify their positions. They are the ones who see to it that everything gets done, in the proper order and according to tradition. In other words, general Karen political behavior is manifest in the direction of funeral activities in terms of organization, authority, and in moral control of all present.

SOCIAL RELATIONS. An analysis of the behavior in terms of social relations reveals other aspects of general social organization. First, important status distinctions show up between male and female. Women are very important in the society—kinship is traced through them and residence is matrilocal—but males fill nearly all specialist positions and men are given differential treatment. At the same time, status distinctions based on their specialist positions are manifest throughout the proceedings. Second, in terms of the organization and division of labor, important distinctions are based on membership in the various social units, and this in turn tends to define the social units. One example of both status and social unit differentiation may suffice: *elders* who are *nonlineage* members tie the wrists of participants in the cremation.

Another aspect of social relations and a most important element of the funeral is that of courting. The unmarried boys and girls come to a funeral openly and overtly to meet, court, and begin more permanent alliances, often leading to premarital sexual relationships, and finally resulting in marriage. The structural and interpersonal social aspects of the funeral ideally assure that the "proper" unmarried individuals do meet. Marriageable individuals have been heard to hope for a death in order that they may meet and participate in courting.

Some aspects of Karen patterns of socialization also show up in the proceedings. Except in cases of extreme infractions, Karen parents do not apply corporal punishment to children. They do, however, whip them if some act may offend the spirits. Furthermore, children are frightened by parents' stories about spirit attacks.

In the marching and singing at the funeral, the very young children learn a great deal about proper courting behavior from watching and listening. Also, the younger of the two girls in the courting pairs is acting as a chaperon for the older girl, as well as learning the songs from her.

The funeral, then, serves the functions of ritualizing the breaking of social relations with the dead, reaffirming ties between the living in terms of structural and social relations, and ritualizing the establishment of new alliances for perpetuating the society. The symbolism here is obvious: out of death comes life. This is not left to chance. Sexual alliances and marriages always follow a funeral.

DISCUSSION

In conclusion, I would like to discuss a few things concerning method, theory, and application. I should point out, first of all, that this analysis is not based entirely on one Karen funeral. I observed, participated in, and asked questions about many. Other kinds of events, ceremonies, and activities were also analyzed during the course of field research. Although I cannot demonstrate, therefore, that all of the above analysis did come from observation of the funeral, it is at least probable that it could have come from careful analysis of the funeral alone. In fact, many other aspects of social structure, relations, politics, and economy were not discussed here because they could not have been gathered from merely dealing with the funeral. It would, of course, be foolish to arbitrarily limit oneself to studying only a funeral. My methodological intent in this paper was to indicate how much one *can* glean from careful, detailed analysis of empirical events like the funeral. Validation can only come from other types of analysis as well.

The underlying theoretical assumption was that events such as funerals, marriages, and village spirit ceremonies do, in fact, manifest structural and cognitive aspects of the sociocultural system. Or one could put it the other way around: structural and cognitive aspects of the sociocultural system constrain or regulate the events. Either way (thus implying no particular direction of causation), such an analysis allows one to get at the structural, cognitive, and systemic features of interest. And by starting with empirical events, there is less chance that the analyst is imposing Western or culturally biased categories on the data (Tyler 1969:3). There is still the general issue, of course, that *any* analysis is abstractive and categorizing. But if we insist on avoiding these features of analysis, then we give up the work of science.

It was on the basis of another assumption that I chose the funeral, in particular, for analysis. I assumed that the funeral would probably allow me to draw out information on many more aspects of social organization and beliefs than would some other ritual events.[5] I must admit, however, that this assumption was based on some general observations made on Karen cultural activities before starting systematic analysis.

It is not the case that one can only do a synchronic analysis with this approach. It may provide an explicit way of analyzing aspects of change by attention to differences between funerals. That is, I would assume that observations of a series of funerals would reveal slight variations in the behaviors manifested. This might not indicate change, but merely variability within the system. However, if change is occurring in the sociocultural system, then it ought to manifest itself in empirical events such as the funeral. In this Karen situation, I began to perceive rather dramatic changes in economy, polity, social relations, and ideology which manifested themselves in a few funerals where Thai Buddhist elements were incorporated. In the analysis, I asked myself what difference, if any, this made concerning traditional aspects of Karen culture apart from the funeral (as discussed above). These will not be detailed here as I have discussed them elsewhere (Hamilton 1963). I merely wish to stress that one can deal efficiently and empirically with change using this type of analysis.

Another cultural distinction that can be analyzed through attention to variation is that of status distinctions and differences. As one might guess, there are not many status positions in Karen culture (compared to more complex societies), and the distinctions are often very subtle. However, by noting variations in the rituals for different individuals and by asking questions about them, I was able to

[5]   I would not like to generalize, however, that this is true of all cultures.

determine that at least some of the variation was not random, but rather highly significant. Funerals for the unmarried, or male, or young, or nonlineage head, etc., have different elements than those for their opposites. Analysis of funerals for different "types" of people will tell one something of the characteristics of the statuses, as well as provide additional information about the functional categories of culture.[6] And one does not have to make a culturally biased prejudgment about what or how many statuses there are, nor about the cultural categories. This will emerge from the analysis. The point here is that when anthropologists have "smoothed out" the variations from raw data in their analyses, they have thus lost vital information.

REFERENCES

BOHANNAN, PAUL
   1963   *Social anthropology*. New York: Holt, Rinehart and Winston.

HAMILTON, JAMES W.
   1963   Effects of the Thai market on Karen life. *Practical Anthropology* 10:209–215.
   1965   "Kinship, bazaar, market: the Karen development of a dual economy as an aspect of modernization." Paper presented at the Annual Meeting of the Association for Asian Studies, San Francisco, California, 1965.

HARRIS, MARVIN
   1968   *The rise of anthropological theory*. New York: Thomas Y. Crowell.

LEACH, E. R.
   1961   *Rethinking anthropology*. London: Athlone Press.

LESSA, WILLIAM A., EVON Z. VOGT
   1965   *Reader in comparative religion* (second edition). New York: Harper and Row.

LÉVI-STRAUSS, CLAUDE
   1963   *Structural anthropology*. New York: Basic Books.
   1966   *The savage mind*. London: Weidenfeld and Nicolson.

[6] In one case of variation, an old woman died. Her house was torn down; a duck, instead of a chick, was killed and put under the body; a small wooden "boat" was constructed and burned with the body; a small "spirit house" was broken and discarded on the route to the cemetery. Questioning elicited the facts that this woman was a lineage head—the last in the line, as there were no more females to hold the position; that she would travel to the spirit world by boat with a flying duck to lead the way; that no one can occupy the house of a dead lineage head; and that the lineage spirit house, kept well back in one's home, is of no use to a lineage with no women.

MALINOWSKI, BRONISLAW
  1939   The group and the individual in functional analysis. *American Journal of Sociology* 44:938–964.
  1961   *Argonauts of the Western Pacific.* New York: E. P. Dutton.

RAPPAPORT, R. A.
  1971   The sacred in human evolution. *Annual Review of Ecology and Systematics* 2:23–44.

TURNER, VICTOR W.
  1969   *The ritual process.* Chicago: Aldine.

TYLER, STEPHEN A., *editor*
  1969   *Cognitive anthropology.* New York: Holt, Rinehart and Winston.

Ethnic Outmarriage Rates in Singapore: The Influence of Traditional Sociocultural Organization

RIAZ HASSAN and GEOFFREY BENJAMIN

A recent study of ethnic intermarriage in Singapore (Hassan 1971) found that intermarriage between members of the major ethnic groups takes place far more frequently than previous studies had indicated. In the present follow-up study, we report the extent to which members of the various ethnic groups marry out, and attempt to explain the different outmarriage rates of these groups in terms of their sociocultural characteristics.

As in most Southeast Asian countries, the population of Singapore is marked by considerable ethnic heterogeneity. Table 1 summarizes the ethnic constitution of Singapore in 1967 and demonstrates that, though the sex ratio for the population as a whole is about normal, the Indian-Pakistanis, Europeans, and Eurasians show rather unbalanced sex ratios. Outmarriage rates for the different ethnic groups were obtained by examining the records of all marriages registered and solemnized in Singapore between January 1962 and December 1968. Two sources were used: the *Report on the registration of births*

The authors gratefully acknowledge the assistance and cooperation of the Department of Statistics, Singapore, in the collection of data for this paper. Thanks are also due to Dr. R. Suntharalingam and Miss Linbert Chiu for relevant information, and to Professor Hans-Dieter Evers for his comments on an earlier draft of the paper. The authors are solely responsible for the presentation and interpretation of the data in this paper.

and deaths, marriages and persons published annually by the Singapore government; and unpublished figures kept by the Department of Statistics, Singapore, which compiles marriage statistics annually from the reports on the registration of marriages furnished by the Registrar of Marriages and the Registrar of Muslim Marriages. We omit reference here to the legal and other aspects of marriage in Singapore and to the methods of data collection employed in this study, as they have already been described in the earlier paper (Hassan 1971).

Table 1. Population of Singapore in 1967, by ethnic affiliation, sex, and sex ratio

Ethnic affiliation	Male	Female	Total	Percent	Sex ratio (males per 1,000 females)
Chinese	734,600	719,900	1,454,500	74.4	1,020
Malays[1]	144,900	138,600	283,500	14.5	1,045
Indian– Pakistani	100,000	59,400	159,400	8.1	1,684
Eurasian	10,100	8,100	18,200	0.93	1,247
European	11,000	7,900	18,900	0.96	1,392
Others[2]	12,300	8,800	21,100	1.1	1,398
Total	1,012,900	942,700	1,955,600	100.0	1,074

[1] "Malays" includes Indonesians.
[2] "Others" includes Ceylonese, Arabs, Filipinos, Thais, Vietnamese, Japanese, Jews, and other smaller nationality and minority groups.
Source: Computed from the *Report on the registration of births and marriages* (Registrar-General of Births and Deaths, Singapore 1967: 22–23).

Table 2 summarizes the data on interethnic marriages for the period under study, while Tables 3a and 3b provide a breakdown of these data by ethnic group for grooms and brides respectively.

In Singapore, official figures are usually based on the informants' own declaration of their ethnicity. In cases of doubt the informant is almost always regarded as belonging to his or her father's ethnic group, even in cases where traditional criteria would have regarded the mother's ethnicity as more important. It is thus not possible to produce separate figures relating to the marital behavior of the offspring of mixed marriages. The figures in the tables, therefore, include an unspecifiable proportion of persons of "mixed" ethnicity, but since it is cultural allegiance rather than genetic make-up that concerns us here, this slight confusion has no significant effect on our argument.

It is important to note that in Singapore "Eurasian" does not count as a "mixed" group: it is regarded simply as one of the Republic's constituent ethnic groups, both informally and officially. The above comments, then, apply as much to Eurasians as they do, say, to Chinese. Nowadays the child of a Chinese father and European mother would in most cases be treated as Chinese for census purposes, and the child of a European father and an Indian mother as a European. However, it remains possible for the child of a Malay mother and a European father to become a Malay by entering the Muslim religion.

In general, polygamy is too rare in Singapore to have any significant effect on the figures in the Tables.

Table 2. Interethnic marriage in Singapore, 1962–1968

Year	Total marriages	Interethnic marriages	Percent interethnic marriages
1962	6,044	359	5.93
1963	7,056	450	6.37
1964	7,810	423	5.41
1965	8,993	507	5.63
1966	10,226	500	4.88
1967	10,960	529	4.82
1968	11,552	527	4.56
Total	62,647	3,295	5.25

Source: Computed from the *Reports on the registration of births and deaths and marriages* (Registrar-General of Births and Deaths, Singapore: 1962–1968).

Table 3a reveals a wide variation in the rates of groom outmarriage, but the general tendency is clear: the proportion of grooms marrying outside their ethnic group varies inversely with the relative size of that ethnic group in the population. Thus the Chinese, the largest group, show the lowest rate of groom outmarriage while the Eurasians, the smallest group, married out the most. That the same general tendency holds true for brides is demonstrated by Table 3b. Similar findings have been reported in other parts of the world (Simpson and Yinger 1965:371–372; Rodman 1965:54–55), and the

Table 3a.   Numbers and percentages of grooms marrying out by ethnic affiliation in Singapore, 1962–1968

| | Ethnic affiliation | | | | | | | | | | | | | | | | | |
| | Chinese | | | Malay | | | Indian–Pakistani | | | Eurasian | | | European | | | "Others" | | |
Year	Total	Mar-ried out	Percent married out	Total	Mar-ried out	Percent married out	Total	Mar-ried out	Percent married out	Total	Mar-ried out	Percent married out	Total	Mar-ried out	Percent married out	Total	Mar-ried out	Percent married out
1962	3,971	31	0.78	1,303	92	7.06	350	76	21.71	71	37	52.10	254	66	25.98	95	57	60.00
1963	4,758	44	0.93	1,466	142	9.68	396	112	28.28	69	42	60.86	281	63	22.41	86	47	54.65
1964	5,441	37	0.68	1,498	144	9.61	422	105	24.88	70	35	50.00	296	65	21.95	85	39	45.88
1965	6,309	49	0.78	1,716	170	9.90	432	104	24.07	80	48	60.00	335	79	23.58	121	57	47.10
1966	7,494	39	0.52	1,707	160	9.37	506	119	23.51	73	38	52.05	348	98	28.16	99	47	47.47
1967	8,182	45	0.55	1,692	163	9.63	556	114	20.50	75	39	52.00	359	101	28.13	96	57	59.37
1968	8,684	64	0.70	1,689	105	6.21	663	143	21.56	71	43	60.56	355	108	30.42	90	64	71.11
Total	44,839	309	0.68	11,071	976	8.82	3,325	773	23.24	509	282	55.40	2,228	580	26.03	672	368	54.76

Source: The Department of Statistics, Singapore.

Table 3b. Numbers and percentages of brides marrying out by ethnic affiliation in Singapore, 1962–1968

Year	Chinese			Malay			Indian–Pakistani			Eurasian			European			"Others"		
	Total	Married out	Percent married out	Total	Married out	Percent married out	Total	Married out	Percent married out	Total	Married out	Percent married out	Total	Married out	Percent married out	Total	Married out	Percent married out
1962	4,100	160	3.90	1,282	71	5.54	319	45	14.10	72	38	52.77	195	7	3.58	76	38	30.00
1963	4,904	190	3.90	1,425	101	7.08	355	71	20.00	73	46	63.01	225	7	3.11	74	35	47.29
1964	5,594	190	3.39	1,438	84	5.84	378	61	16.13	69	34	49.27	242	11	4.54	89	43	48.34
1965	6,494	234	3.60	1,634	88	5.38	422	94	22.27	65	33	50.76	273	17	6.22	105	41	39.04
1966	7,687	232	3.01	1,637	90	5.49	459	72	15.68	78	43	55.12	263	13	4.94	102	50	49.01
1967	8,379	242	2.88	1,616	87	5.38	529	87	16.44	63	27	42.85	277	19	6.85	96	57	59.37
1968	8,807	187	2.12	1,695	111	6.54	606	86	14.19	82	54	65.85	264	17	6.43	97	71	73.19
Total	45,965	1,435	3.12	10,727	632	5.89	3,068	516	16.81	502	275	54.78	1,739	91	5.23	639	335	52.42

Source: The Department of Statistics, Singapore.

meaning of the Singapore figures has already been discussed in an earlier paper (Hassan 1971) in the light of those findings.

The only discrepancy here is the relatively low proportion of out-marrying European brides, especially when compared to the much larger proportion of European grooms who married out. This is probably due to the fact that the majority of Europeans in Singapore during the period under study consisted of male British Armed Services personnel and male employees of various European business firms. Most Europeans in Singapore at that time were thus not "indigenous" in the manner of the other ethnic groups. Further-more, most of these Europeans were accompanied by their families, so there was a relatively low number of European females in the marriageable age range. One must assume that those European women who were of marriageable age came into contact with Euro-pean men much more frequently than they did with men of other ethnic groups, and hence were more likely to marry the former than the latter.

The second thing to note about these figures is the apparently irregularly placed peaks in the outmarriage rates of the major "indigenous" ethnic groups for the years 1963 and (less markedly) 1965. In Singapore's recent history, these are important dates, mark-ing events that had great effects on all levels of life: the state's entry into the newly formed Federation of Malaysia in 1963, and its seces-sion from the Federation in 1965 to form an independent sovereign republic. This was also the period of threat from Indonesia's policy of "confrontation" against Malaysia, when Singapore too had to steel itself against the possibility of external aggression. It may well be that these events had the effect of strengthening the sense of solidarity between the main ethnic groups in Singapore. If so, this could well have led to the marked increase in the rate of interethnic marriage that we have noted for the two years when Singapore was most faced with the problem of defining itself as a supraethic entity. We admit that this effect is not entirely uniform for all ethnic groups and sexes, but the general tendency is sufficient to suggest that future investigations into interethnic marriage could fruitfully pay attention to the effects of larger social and political events at the national level.

From a comparative point of view, the outmarriage rates for Singapore fall somewhere into the middle of the range of worldwide figures (cf. Hassan 1971:312). This suggests that the figures we have presented betoken a moderate degree of social integration among

Table 4. Occupation and ethnic affiliation of brides and grooms who married out between December 1966 and January 1969

Occupation of groom and bride:	Mean years of education[1]	Total Nos.	Total %	Chinese Groom	Chinese Bride	Malay Groom	Malay Bride	Indian-Pakistani Groom	Indian-Pakistani Bride	Eurasian Groom	Eurasian Bride	European Groom	European Bride	Others Groom	Others Bride
Professional and technical workers	11.8	339	15.2	40	77	19	12	32	14	20	21	48	10	31	15
Administrative, executive and managerial workers	9.2	74	3.3	10	6	2	–	9	–	2	3	31	2	8	1
Clerical workers	8.6	243	10.9	15	59	44	4	34	10	21	20	7	6	13	10
Sales workers	4.5	43	1.9	7	8	4	2	5	2	6	2	4	–	2	1
Craftsman, production process workers	3.8	203	9.1	11	10	76	–	69	–	12	–	17	–	7	1
Workers in transport and communication	3.7	137	6.2	11	5	37	2	29	1	6	7	22	1	11	5
Workers in service sports and recreation	3.4	363	16.3	20	31	66	2	61	6	29	8	113	2	23	2
Agriculture workers	2.5	–	–	–	–	–	–	–	–	–	–	–	–	–	–
Occupation N.A.	–	802	36.0	11	286	17	196	25	143	3	41	10	13	6	51
Students	–	22	0.9	5	4	1	–	2	1	–	4	–	4	–	1
Total	–	2,226	–	130	486	266	218	266	177	99	106	252	38	101	87
%	–	–	100.0	5.8	21.8	11.9	9.8	11.9	7.9	4.4	4.8	11.3	1.7	4.6	3.9

[1] For further details about the computation of mean educational years for each principal occupational group see Hassan (1970: Table 3).

Source: The Department of Statistics, Singapore.

the ethnic groups in Singapore. This conclusion is confirmed by studies that have been made of other aspects of this problem (Chiew 1971; Hassan 1970).

There is no significant relationship between class status and inter-marriage rates. As Table 4 shows, the ranking of Singapore's population, either in terms of occupational status or in terms of educational standing, does not correspond in any regular way with a propensity for intermarriage. Nor do Singaporeans generally express informally the belief that intermarriage is more typical of one class rather than another. The point here is that in Singapore there is no support for the argument that greater interethnic accommodation (as measured by intermarriage) is facilitated by longer education.

As for religious factors, Hassan (1971) has shown that Muslims and Christians in Singapore are far more likely to override ethnic considerations than are the adherents of other religions, and that these two religions serve as channels of ethnic assimilation.

The most interesting thing about these figures, however, is the way in which the proportion of men to women marrying out varies con-siderably between the ethnic groups. Although this fact has been commented on before (see, for example, Freedman 1957:125–126), there has been to our knowledge no satisfactory attempt to explain these differences. It is our belief that the major factor influencing these differences lies in the cultural characteristics of the groups concerned, and what follows is our attempt to demonstrate this. (In the ensuing discussion, we have excluded the category "other" from consideration as constituting not one cultural entity, but many.)

An examination of the relative position of the sexes within the traditional Malay, Chinese, Indian, and Eurasian social structures leads to the conclusion that traditional social ethics have long con-tinued to influence marital behavior, even in Singapore's forcing-house of cultural change. In particular, the pattern of authority relationships within the family and household would seem to hold the key to the differences in behavior that we are seeking to explain.

The aggregated and properly weighted figures for the years 1962–1968 (Table 5) show that: among Eurasians, there was no significant difference in the extent to which males and females married out; among Indian–Pakistanis and Malays, nearly one-and-a-half times as many males married out as females; among Chinese, nearly five times as many females married out as males; and among Europeans, nearly five times as many males married out as females.

Table 5. Sex differences in outmarriage rates, by ethnic affiliation, 1962–1968

Ethnic affiliation	Sex	Outmarriage rates	Ratio m/f
Chinese	m	0.68	=0.22
	f	3.12	
Malay	m	8.82	=1.49
	f	5.89	
Indian–Pakistani	m	23.24	=1.38
	f	16.81	
Eurasian	m	55.40	=1.01
	f	54.78	
European	m	26.03	=4.98
	f	5.23	

Source: Computed from Tables 3a and 3b.

Europeans. The figures for European outmarriage probably do not relate to any deep-seated feature of European sociocultural organization. Most of the marriages involved were between British servicemen and Chinese women—a situation that, from the point of view of the present investigation, is purely fortuitous. We shall therefore not discuss the European figures any further.

Eurasians. In Singapore, Eurasians are not regarded as merely a residual category in which to place the offspring of mixed marriages. As pointed out earlier, children of European and Asian parents today are usually assimilated to the ethnic group of the father (cf. Freedman 1957:126); they would not be classed as Eurasian, a term which now denotes a closed cultural unit with its own corporate organizations and its own recognizable life-style. Unfortunately there has been no significant research into the sociology of the Eurasian community of Singapore, and what follows is only a guess at the reasons for the marked equality in their rates of bride and groom outmarriage.

If one assumes that the present-day cultural pattern of Singapore Eurasians reflects conditions obtaining several generations ago when the first marriages between Asians and Europeans took place, one would expect that among them nuclear family relationships would claim precedence over extended family relationships. In the early days, the families of the marrying couple would have been of decidedly different cultures, and hence would be unlikely to have had much to do with each other. Furthermore, ostracism, or even a simple lack of ease in social relationships, would have restricted

9

contact between each partner and his or her spouse's family. Thus one might expect any "Eurasian culture" that developed later to throw more emphasis on to individual status and choice, leaving little room for influence by other family members in the mate selection process. Such a society should have no need of differential sexual status as a structural element, and its men and women members should be equally unconstrained in their choice of marital partner. The almost exactly equal rate of outmarriage reported for Eurasian males and females provides considerable support for this argument.

Malays. Like the majority of Peninsular Malays, Singapore Malays have a cognatic kinship system, treating relationships through the father as formally equivalent to those through the mother. They do not (again, as in most of the Malay Peninsula) use their kinship system to form extended corporate descent groups. The normal pattern is for a marriage to lead to the setting up of a new nuclear family household.

However, ethnographic studies in Singapore and elsewhere (Djamour 1954; Wilder 1970) have shown that, in extra familial contexts, the Malays do place differential stress on sexual status. They are Muslims and consequently give heed to the notion of male precedence in public life—indeed their cognatic kinship organization does not prevent them from making token acknowledgment of male precedence in those aspects of family life, such as inheritance and divorce, which should be run according to Muslim law. On the other hand, a statistical examination of their actual family organization (Djamour 1954:79–81, 142) leaves no doubt that there is a strong matri- and uxori-focal bias in the way Malays organize such things as residence and child rearing. Married or divorced daughters (the Malay divorce rate has until recently been one of the world's highest, by any standard) tend to live near their mothers—though not usually in the same household—in a pattern similar to that of the matrifocal family that Young and Wilmott (1957) have described for working-class London.

Wilder's recent study has shown how (at least in village society) Malay socialization practices fit with this pattern. Whereas girls tend to be secluded at home, the circumcised but unmarried boys are expected to put on a display of conspicuous nonactivity outside the home. The result is that the intergenerational solidarity of the females contrasts strongly with the marginality of the unmarried boys and the resulting intergenerational disjunction of the males. The men are expected to "move," the women to "stay" (Wilder 1970:238–239). In Malay theory, the father has the absolute right to arrange his children's marriages, but in practice, his hold over his sons will be somewhat less complete than over his daughters. This factor, coupled with the wish of the daughter to stay close to her mother even after marriage, would ensure that Malay women marry out less often than Malay men. This is what the figures show to be the case in Singapore.

Indian–Pakistanis. Although the proportions of males to females outmarrying are very similar in the Malay and Indian–Pakistani cases, the great differences in social organization between the two groups force us to look for different explanations of these figures. Moreover, in spite of the usual statistical practice in Singapore, it is necessary for the purposes of this paper to divide the Indian–Pakistani community into Hindus and Muslims, as the differences in socio-cultural organization between these two religious groups are just as great as those between the other ethnic groups (see Table 6).

Table 6. Indian–Pakistani outmarriage by sex and religion, 1962–1968

Religion	Sex	Total	Outmarriages	Percent outmarriage	Ratio m/f outmarriage
		marriages		rate	rates
Muslim	m	1,159	499	43.15	1.16
	f	1,051	391	37.30	
Hindus	m	1,547	126	8.17	1.93
	f	1,483	62	4.23	

Source: The Department of Statistics.

Hindus. There has unfortunately been no thorough study of social organization among Singapore's Indian–Pakistanis. (Some good partial studies exist in manuscript, however; see, for example, Schooling 1960.) But casual inquiry, coupled with incidental remarks in publications (e.g. Arasaratnam 1970:66), suggests that caste is still the major element affecting marital choice in local Hindu Indian society.

In traditional Indian society, the basic unit of the caste system is the subcaste, or *jati.* Subcastes are localized or regional social groups, arranged hierarchically in terms of an overall purity-pollution continuum (see Stevenson 1954 for a comprehensive account), which is operated by ensuring that the women of the subcaste—but not necessarily the men—do not have sexual contact with persons of lower rank in the caste hierarchy. In practice, this means that the subcaste and its constituent families take pains to ensure that their women marry men of the same subcaste, or occasionally of a higher subcaste. In Hindu–Indian belief, then, it is maternity, and not paternity, that determines a person's ritual (and hence social) standing. Consequently, Indians expend much effort in ensuring that their daughters marry properly, in Singapore as elsewhere. The clearest sign of their concern is their willingness to pay quite large sums of money as dowries to attract the right man. Current rates in Singapore are said to range from a few thousand dollars to over 100,000 dollars (S\$3 = approximately US\$1), sometimes placing a considerable strain on family finances. Bride price payments from the groom's side play no significant part among Singapore's Indian–Pakistanis. Singapore Hindus still regard it as a major preoccupation of the family to organize the marriage of their daughters, and the pressures against a girl making her own choice of husband are very strong indeed. The fact that (approximately) only one Hindu woman marries out for every two Hindu men who marry out clearly supports our view that caste affiliation is still a major determinant of marital choice among Singapore Hindus.

Muslims. Among Muslim Indian–Pakistanis, who constitute about 30 percent of the Indian–Pakistanis in Singapore, the picture is markedly different. The outmarriage figures in this case show only a slight preponderance of outmarrying men over women, which suggests that, though caste may still have some residual influence, Islamic allegiance in itself has an overriding and equalizing effect. Almost all such marriages are with Malays, the major Muslim community in Singapore. Indeed, this particular pattern of inter-marriage is so favored that about 70 percent of all outmarrying Indian–Pakistanis (not just the Muslim ones) in Singapore marry Malays (Hassan 1971:313). There is nothing new in this: it is an ethnological commonplace that the Peninsular Malay population has, for many centuries past, continued to absorb a large Indian element. It would seem that at present this process involves men and women in equal proportions.

Chinese. Chinese traditional social organization, at least ideally, was based on a system of highly corporate exogamous patrilineages of great generational depth, reinforced by a formal yet domestic worship of the lineage ancestors. (The standard study is Freedman 1958; a good summary account may be found in Fox 1967:116–119.) As a perpetual corporation, the patrilineage has the problem of ensuring that its male members produce a steady supply of (male) offspring— children of female members are by definition not members of the lineage. Since the lineage is exogamous, it cannot reproduce itself except by importing women from other lineages, and ensuring, through a highly formalized marriage system, that they remain under the control of the lineage long enough at least to raise their children to maturity. The result, for societies (like traditional China) that take their patrilineality seriously, is that paternity, legitimated by the lineage's continuing control over the inmarrying wives, is the crucial determinant of a person's social status. As a corollary, the lineage's own female members are from a structural point of view expendable: they are of interest only to other lineages as possible wives for their sons. A traditional Chinese view (still often expressed in Singapore) is that daughters are goods on which a father loses (Freedman 1957: 132). The contrast with the Hindu case is striking, and one would expect that, to the extent that patrilineal ideology still holds among Singapore Chinese, their pattern of outmarriage would be the reverse of the Hindu pattern.

In Singapore, Chinese lineages have ceased to be landholding corporations, and it is increasingly the case that patrilineally extended families are ceasing to be the typical household group (Yeh 1967: 97–115). But as Freedman makes clear in his study of kinship in Singapore Chinese society, the patrilineal emphasis persists firmly enough, in that children take the surname of their father and look upon their agnatic kin as more closely related than their matrilateral kin (1957: cap. 3). It is still not unusual, even among third- or fourth-generation Singapore Chinese, for children of sons to be much more favored in inheritance than children of daughters, or indeed for daughters-in-law to be treated more favorably in family relationships than daughters.

The fact that at present approximately five times as many Chinese women marry out as Chinese men suggests that patrilineal ideology is still a potent cultural force among Singapore Chinese, and that their sons' behavior as regards marriage is still more circumscribed by family control than that of their daughters. It will be interesting to see what changes occur in this respect as the next generation of

Chinese parents, who will have been exposed to ideas of romantic love as a basis for marriage, come to see their own children married.

DISCUSSION

The comparison of Malay, Indian, and Chinese family organization that we have just undertaken has received some indirect confirmation from a recent sociological study of family organization made in neighboring West Malaysia, where the only major difference from Singapore is the larger proportion of rural dwellers in the population (Palmore et al. 1970). Although the Malaysian study had very different aims from our own, it provides quite clear evidence that in various aspects of family organization, a patri-virilateral bias is still significant among the Chinese, and an uxori-matrilateral bias among the Malays. Among Indians, the bias, at least as regards extended household residence, is only slightly virilocal (cf. Palmore et al. 1970: Table 1, p. 383). This is precisely the distribution that would be expected on the basis of the familial-organization theory of differential interethnic marriage rates that we have put forward in this paper.

Although at the present time the official policy of multiracialism probably reinforces the tendency of Singaporeans to explain their social behavior in ethnic terms to a greater degree than the facts warrant, our data on interethnic marriage suggest that, for a large section of the population, there is indeed a meaningful fit, within the domestic domain, between contemporary patterns of behavior and traditional, ethnically based ideals. However, we are not entitled to make suppositions about behavior in the extrafamiliar domain— "society at large"—on the basis of this result, as there is every reason to expect a fair degree of disjunction between the two domains in a rapidly changing society, whether or not the people involved are themselves aware of it. In any case, the figures for the Muslim section of the population show such a degree of convergence as would suggest that nonethnic factors outweigh ethnic factors in influencing the behavior of a sizeable minority section of the population (cf. Hassan 1971:318).

We make no advanced claims for the study we have just presented. We hope only that it might serve as an example of how the apparently recondite problem of *measuring* (rather than just describing) certain elements of sociocultural change might be undertaken in a manner that does not do injustice to the cultural features of the situation. Of course, even as regards the problem we have discussed here, this is only a tentative beginning. Until detailed comparative figures and full cultural data are made available for a wide range of societies, we can achieve only some kind of scale measure; it is not yet possible to deal with the equally interesting problem of the absolute values of the figures. We are not yet in a position to suggest why, for example, five times as many, rather than, say, twice as many, Chinese women marry out as Chinese men in Singapore.

REFERENCES

ARASARATNAM, S.
  1970 *Indians in Malaysia and Singapore.* London: Oxford University Press.

CHIEW, SEEN KONG
  1971 "Singapore national identity." Unpublished master's thesis, University of Singapore.

DJAMOUR, J.
  1954 *Malay kinship and marriage in Singapore.* London: Athlone Press.

FOX, R.
  1967 *Kinship and marriage.* Harmondsworth: Penguin Books.

FREEDMAN, M.
  1957 *Chinese family and marriage in Singapore.* London: HMSO.
  1958 *Lineage organization in southeastern China.* London: Athlone Press.

HASSAN, R.
  1970 Class, ethnicity and occupational structure in Singapore. *Civilisations* 20:496–515.
  1971 Interethnic marriage in Singapore: a sociological analysis. *Sociology and Social Research* 55:305–323.

PALMORE, J. A., R. E. KLEIN, ARIFFIN BIN MARZUKI
  1970 Class and family in a modernizing society. *American Journal of Sociology* 76:375–398.

REGISTRAR-GENERAL OF BIRTHS AND DEATHS
  1962–1968 *Report on the registration of births and deaths, marriages and persons.* Singapore: Government Printing Office.

RODMAN, H.
  1965 *Marriage, family and society.* New York: Random House.

SCHOOLING, NALINI
    1960   "A study of caste practices and attitudes towards caste among
           Tamil Hindu labourers in Singapore." Unpublished dissertation,
           University of Singapore, Department of Social Work and Social
           Administration.

SIMPSON, G. E., J. M. YINGER
    1965   *Racial and cultural minorities.* New York: Harper and Row.

STEVENSON, H. N.
    1954   Status and evaluation in the Hindu caste system. *Journal of the
           Royal Anthropological Institute* 84:45–65.

WILDER, W.
    1970   "Socialization and social structure in a Malay village," in
           Socialization: the approach from social anthropology. Edited by
           P. Mayer, 215–268. London: Tavistock.

YEH, STEPHEN H. K.
    1967   The size and structure of households in Singapore, 1957–1966.
           The Malayan Economic Review 12 (2):97–115.

YOUNG, M., P. WILLMOT
    1957   *Family and kinship in east London.* London: Routledge and
           Kegan Paul.

Vietnamese Women:
Their Roles and Their Options

MARILYN W. HOSKINS

How can the conflict between the mystique of the oppressed female described in Vietnamese literature and verbalized by Vietnamese women be understood in light of the equally common belief that they are the real power in the country? How can traditionally demure wives adjust to a rapidly changing society without apparent redefinition of roles? How is it possible that women are becoming more active in Vietnamese society and are profiting by an improved status within the political and economic systems in both the North and South without meeting the prejudice and resentment of males so frequently found in the Western world? Raising instead of answering these important questions are many generalizations about the roles and options of the Vietnamese women. These generalizations frequently conflict, are often inconsistent in themselves, and are seldom based on research.

My interest in Vietnamese women began in 1963 when I worked with a UNESCO project studying goals and values of Vietnamese in rural communities. It grew during the next several years as I lived in Saigon and did an ethnographic study of a lower socioeconomic Saigon urban quarter (Hoskins and Shepherd 1970; M. Hoskins 1971). I studied women—but not apart from the rest of the family. In reviewing the research, including my own, it became apparent that the role Vietnamese women play in mediating and reacting to culture change must be understood if we were to answer the above questions. I therefore isolated some of these frequently raised questions, looked into some reasons for the inconsistent conclusions, and attempted to evaluate the available material.

One major reason for the inconsistent conclusions by authors is a confusion between actual behavior and cultural values which are imposed from outside. The Vietnamese have been the repository of forces from other civilizations for centuries as far back as the India-influenced Cham and Khmer people who occupied much of Viet Nam before the Vietnamese. An even more important influence came from the Chinese who ruled Viet Nam for approximately 1,000 years (111 B.C. to A.D. 939) and who established the first legal code and national governmental structure. Eighty years of French rule, ending in 1954, with its Westernizing influence, have also had a great effect. Conflicts between the indigenous practices and the imposed patterns create confusion in evaluation if these historical perspectives are not kept in mind.

Another major source of confusion comes from making generalizations based on behavior appropriate in specific situations. For instance, a Vietnamese wife will often use formal respectful language and an attitude of deference towards her husband, but she may run the family business, handle the money for the family, and refuse to give him the extra spending money he requests. One author may describe the subservient role of a woman from her demeanor and another sees only her dominance in economic affairs. Neither realizes that both behavioral complexes are part of the total female role and that all roles are actually a composite of a variety of roles (Gross, McEachern, and Mason 1958; Linton 1936), even when, as in Viet Nam, the domestic family roles of daughter, wife and mother, and the public societal roles including occupational activity and social leadership have developed somewhat differently.

Confusion comes also from the lack of attention during the last several decades to the role and status of women in this rapidly changing society. Even books specifically about women and change hardly mention the Vietnamese woman, e.g. Ward (1963) and Boserup (1970). An attempt has been made to fill this gap by using historical records and legal codes to establish the setting, selected folk stories for information on indigenous patterns, social science research done during the French occupation up to the present, and comments in the local press and national journals by Vietnamese women about their current roles and role options.

HISTORICAL AND LEGAL SETTING

Anthropologists and historians report that up to the last century before the Christian era, Vietnamese practiced slash-and-burn rice agriculture and had a matriarchal or bilateral kinship system (Huard and Durand 1954; Le Thanh Kkoi 1955; Buttinger 1962). About the beginning of the Christian era the Chinese overwhelmed Viet Nam and incorporated it into China. There followed a deliberate and thorough program of sinicization which included the introduction of the plow and buffalo and with it a sedentary agrarian life (Buttinger 1962). The Chinese supported by Confucian ideology created laws which permitted male domination of women. These laws allowed women no power over their dowry and no access to inheritance or other property. A woman was also bound to her husband for life and upon his death was not permitted to remarry (Cadière 1958; Lusteguy 1953). These concepts were codified in China during the Ch'in Dynasty (259–219 B.C.) and later imposed on the Vietnamese by their Chinese administrators.[1] This era came to an end when the Vietnamese gained their independence in A.D. 939 after 1,000 years of Chinese domination.

The next recorded legal code was initiated by Emperor Le Thanh Ton (1459–1497). It was more humanitarian and progressive than the previous Chinese Code, combining more equalitarian and local customs with some of the Chinese legal precepts (Nghiem Xuan Viet 1963). It declared women equal to men in almost every respect, including inheritance of family property and freedom to marry without parental consent. It also placed a time limitation on engagement periods that protected girls from being engaged by their families in infancy (Le Thanh Khoi 1955).

After Le Thanh Ton's reign, the country fell into intermittent periods of war and civil strife and was only restored to peaceful unity by Emperor Gia Long in the early 1800's. He established the Gia Long Code of 1812 which again incorporated Chinese patterns, withdrawing women's rights to make contracts or control property (Philastre 1909). However, where the Gia Long Code contravened well-established customs, especially in family matters, it was ignored. For example, parents left their daughters property in wills, and if the matter happened to come to court the presiding mandarin usually

---

[1] In practice, however, they were frequently modified to fit the Vietnamese family pattern whereby most family problems were settled within the family councils where women traditionally had a more equal voice (J. Hoskins 1971).

decided the case by local custom (Nghiem Xuan Viet 1963). The Gia Long Code was the structure, but not necessarily the practice, in Viet Nam when the French began to exert increasing control over the country in the mid-1800's. They annexed South Viet Nam as a colony, made North and Central Viet Nam protectorates and ruled the country for approximately eighty years.

At first, the French were confused by the Chinese-patterned Code and sought to enforce it, not realizing its violation of established Vietnamese custom (Nghiem Xuan Viet 1963). This had the temporary effect of strengthening male legal dominance, especially of men in the upper classes. Later French efforts to eliminate some practices which they believed were unjust to women, such as divorce and child marriage, were unsuccessful (Pham Huy Ty 1957).

When the Vietnamese again regained the opportunity to make laws for themselves, the ruling powers in both the North and the South declared men and women equal. The first constitution enacted by the South Vietnamese government in 1956 declared men and women equal in dignity, rights, duties, pay, and ability to vote and hold public office. In 1967, the South Vietnamese government established a new constitution retaining these rights. It also emphasizes the importance of the family:

The State recognizes the family as the foundation of society. The State encourages and supports the formation of families, and assists expectant mothers and infants. Marriage must be based on mutual consent, equality, and cooperation. The State encourages the unity of the family (*Constitution of the Republic of Viet-Nam 1967*).

The government of North Viet Nam promulgated its current constitution in 1960. It also gave women equal rights with men in political, economic, cultural, social, and domestic areas, and stressed the importance of the family. It sanctioned equal pay for women, paid leave before and after childbirth, and supported the development of maternity hospitals, day-care centers, and pre-schools (Fall 1965).

Although the ideals expressed in these constitutions are not always fulfilled, the governments have gone a long way towards giving women legal equality. This is often represented as a revolutionary departure from past practices, but the earlier codes which gave women no legal rights were reflections of pressures from the Chinese and French, not the indigenous practices that tended towards more equality (J. Hoskins 1971).

FAMILY ROLES

Traditional folk tales and contemporary anthropological studies describe Vietnamese women as the power within the family structure. This is the case in all the twenty-six stories that mention women from four well-known collections of folk tales (Le Huy Hap 1963; Pham Duy Khiem 1959; Sun 1967; Schultz 1965). It is also true of descriptions written in the early 1900's by French anthropologists and oriental scholars (Huard and Durand 1954; Cadière 1958; Lusteguy 1953). More recent rural studies (Hickey 1969; Hendry 1964; Donoghue 1961a, 1961b), and urban studies (Hoskins and Shepherd 1970; Slusser 1965; Slote 1966; Bourne 1970) bear this out. In all these sources there is, with only minor variations, a picture of the powerful roles of women in the family. When a woman fulfils her part in the family, she strengthens that group which is her source of power as well. In this setting, it is the group welfare that is most important, not the individual. The individual does not ask herself if others make her happy, rather if she and others are fulfilling their roles within the family structure. As long as she lives up to her role, she can count on the power and support from the family. If she fails to do so, power and support are withdrawn.

The Role of Daughter

Both the traditional and contemporary source materials emphasize the daughter's value as a member of the family. Although sons are essential for carrying on the family line, daughters are also desired and their actions can enhance or ruin the family name.

The role of daughter, both in myth and in present-day descriptions, is to be virtuous, marry well, and have children. The concept includes both "shyness" and "chastity." Shyness describes a quiet calmness, an indirectness, an avoidance of conflict, a polite formal respect shown elders and authorities as well as ancestors, and the control of aggressive feelings. This is well illustrated in the folk story, "The girl from Lim village."

More than ten generations ago, there dwelt in Lim village a very beautiful girl. Orphaned of her mother as a small baby, she lived with her old father in a tiny house at the end of the village. She was betrothed to a young man in the next hamlet, and the wedding was to take place in the near future. One day on the way home from the market a man came toward her and started to speak. His presence embarrassed her for she was a proper and shy girl from a very traditional family and had never been in such close contact with any man other than her father and her fiancé.

The father coming upon the couple standing together misunderstood the situation and severely reprimanded the girl and the man. The girl stood respectfully in front of her father. Her shyness prevented her from defending herself. Unfortunately, the man was a roguish mandarin who then arrested the father and daughter.

The mandarin tried in vain to seduce the imprisoned girl, often resorting to violence. Each time she attempted to end her life, rather than give herself to the man who had caused misfortunes to her family. The king, hearing of the situation, demoted the mandarin and impressed by the girl's virtue, presented her and her father with gold and precious embroideries. The father and daughter returned to the village with honor and wealth (Le Huy Hap 1963).

This story also illustrates a second aspect of virtue, that of chastity. In this case, chastity precludes even speaking to men outside the family. Chastity is related to virginity but may also mean keeping one's "heart pure" so that if a demand of loyalty to the family impels even the sacrifice of virginity, it can be done without the loss of honor. This is vividly illustrated in the most famous Vietnamese epic poem.

. . . This story concerns a young maiden endowed with all spiritual and bodily graces; an elite, who when placed between love and filial devotion, deliberately chose the harder way; she sold herself to save her father, a victim of an unjust calamity. And from that day, she passed from one misfortune to another until she sank into the most abject depravity. But, like the lotus, in the midst of this mire, she always preserved the pure perfume of her original nobility . . . (Nguyen Du in Le Huy Hap 1963:iii).

To benefit the family, a daughter is expected to marry a man with the highest possible status. The uniting of families in marriage includes uniting the ancestors in heaven and tends to combine the power and wealth of the two families.

In a study of the role of the family in transmitting culture, Leichty (1963) studied attitudes towards their families of a number of Vietnamese school children. She found Vietnamese children oriented towards family expectations, their main concerns being their future roles as adult members of the family group. Families retain their cohesiveness and their emphasis on traditional family roles by fostering the attitude that the family gives life and sustenance and one can only repay one's debt by assuming an expected role in the family structure. In rural areas, one frequently hears Vietnamese telling toddlers that they must not nurse for too many years or they will build a debt they cannot repay.

The Role of Wife

A wife is the center of the household. It is she who is constantly caring for the family, influencing the husband, caring for the finances, and doing whatever benefits the family group. Her role is to pay formal respect to her husband, to his family and ancestors as well as her own, to continue her virtuous way of life so that she brings no shame to either family, and to produce children, especially sons. A husband has great freedom to come and go at will. This leaves the woman major authority within the family. Like daughters, wives use indirect persuasion and exert "gentle pressure" to control their husbands, and this can sometimes include threatened or real attempts at self-destruction.

The folk story, "A woman's wit," shows correct behavior on the part of the wife who finds an unusual way to prove her point.

An elder brother is married to a wise woman. She is aware that her husband is generous to friends but stingy to his family, especially his younger brother. Several times she quietly and politely points out to her husband that his brother is loyal and the friends are "fair-weather" friends, but her husband does not listen. One day this wise woman tells her husband she accidently killed a beggar who surprised her, and has hidden the body in a cloth sack. She urges her husband to get some friends to help bury the sack where officials will not find it and arrest them, bringing shame to the family name. The husband goes to "friend" after "friend" but finds only his brother willing to help. The "friends" actually report the case to the authorities in hope of a reward. When the authorities come and dig up the sack, they find the carcass of a dog. The wife explains to the judge how she planned this incident to prove to her husband that friends may come and go, but brothers cannot be replaced. The judge commends the wife's virtue and cleverness and dismisses the case. The husband sees his error and the family is united (Le Huy Hap 1963).

In a newspaper interview Tran Thi Hoai Tran (1971), assistant professor of law at the University of Saigon, explains that Vietnamese women have never needed a woman's liberation movement. Dr. Tran says that Vietnamese women have always been trained to capitalize on their "femininity," using the soft approach to get their way in the family. She states that the soft approach is very effective and claims that although a Vietnamese woman would not ask her husband to do housework and although she shows her husband formal respect, she still manages to get what she wants. Although the Vietnamese woman's overt behavior is formally submissive, she is frequently called "the general of the interior" because she makes most of the family decisions. Researchers have noted that the Vietnamese woman also has the ability to operate independently of her husband to a degree that would amaze many American women (Bourne 1970).

The Role of Mother

The role of mother is the least described of all. In the twenty-six folk tales, mothers play a part in only seven and never as the main character. The mother-daughter dyad is never a major element of the stories as is the father-daughter dyad. Parent worship and role idealization operate in such a way that even Vietnamese themselves have a difficult time characterizing mothers as having human personalities and characteristics (Bourne 1970; Slote 1966).

While the traditional ideal for the man points to the scholar-poet or the warrior-politician as the road to honor, wealth, and power, women have a family-centered road to similar honor, wealth, and power. This role is a continuing one for the women, with the goal for the daughter to become a successful wife, so that she can repay her family for what they have done for her by increasing their wealth and power through the combined family status. The goal for the wife is to have a strong family and to become a mother. Once she is a mother, she has helped fulfill her obligations as daughter and strengthened her position as wife.

OCCUPATIONS

Throughout Vietnamese folk literature, women have pursued gainful occupations to support their families. Women in folk tales worked with their husbands or ran the family farm or business when the husbands were away meditating or studying for the mandarin examinations, fighting bravely in some war, or attending to a political assignment in a province far away. When women took up medicine or trade, it was usually in connection with a family business. Historical studies show women working to support their families in a wide variety of occupations, but these were not always the most prestigious. The Chinese gave the highest position to scholar-mandarins, a middle status to warriors, and gave merchants a low position. During the time of Chinese control, women were frequently merchants, seldom warriors, and were forbidden to participate in the scholastic mandarin exams. However, there are historical heroines famous for military or literary skill.

The French undermined the power of the mandarin-scholar by establishing French schools, many of which were open to girls, and by introducing alternative paths to power and wealth formerly monopolized by the mandarins. In South Viet Nam the positions of high governmental officials are still considered very prestigious, but so is teaching, owning a business, and practicing a profession—all open to women. Wealth is an important determinant of class though it can only give a "grade B" status at the highest levels if not accompanied by education and familial qualifications. Money itself can give a family upward mobility as well as opportunity for its children to get the education necessary for a more stable place in the higher class (Slusser 1965). This new evaluation of status away from the mandarin system does not indicate the society is any more materialistic and less intellectual. It is merely a change in the path to wealth and power, and this change has made the path more available to women.

French colonial rule had different effects on families of different economic classes, and it increased inequality between the sexes in certain sectors of the population. New rules allowing larger land holdings created more foreclosures on small farms. In the rural context men and women had worked more or less equally, but when workers were forced from their own land, they went into the newly established factories and plantations where wages were not equal. In 1931 average daily wages in some areas of Viet Nam were nearly twice as much for men as for women (Turley 1972). Although the constitutions of both the North and South declare wages are ideally the same, women of both areas complain that this is not the actual situation. In 1971 in South Viet Nam, average daily wages paid to skilled women workers were still approximately two-thirds those paid to men and for unskilled work women received from three-fourths to four-fifths the wages of unskilled men laborers (*Viet Nam statistical yearbook, 1971* [1972]). These averages do not reflect different wages for identical work for the most part, but the fact that more advanced and skilled positions are held by the men. Although equivalent statistics are not available for the North, women in both areas stress the difference in wages is frequently tied to lack of education and training for women.

When the French left in 1945, they vacated a number of higher level jobs in commerce, in the professions, and in the civil service.

10

Due to the manpower shortage and the availability of educated women, many women had the opportunity to enter higher level jobs.

Within one generation Vietnamese women, passive and subservient at home, have entered business, politics, and the professions in larger numbers and with great success. Vietnamese husbands expect docile wives, yet they work on a basis of equality with professional women. Francis Hsu reports that this has also been true among Chinese women. About Chinese in contrast to American attitudes Hsu-says:

In the Chinese pattern, sex being relegated to particular areas of life, does not pervade every aspect of life . . . The American woman is, in male eyes, never separated from the qualities of her sex . . . and he is resentful because she brings with her the advantage of her sex in addition to her professional abilities. The Chinese woman's sexual attractions belong to her husband or fiancé alone . . . Once she has achieved a new occupational or professional status, the Chinese woman tends to be judged in male eyes by her ability and not by her sex (Hsu 1972:56–57).

Hsu goes on to point out that China has never known the concept of "chivalry" through which psychological distances between males and females are accentuated. This same result occurs in Viet Nam with situation-centered, formalistic roles taking precedence over individual interests.

Most rural South Vietnamese women help with the rice production and retain well-understood and valued economic roles working along with their husbands. In a study of one rural village, approximately a third of the women held part-time jobs, usually in rice production or commerce, but only wives with no financial support from their husbands held full-time jobs (Hickey 1969; Hendry 1964). Inflation has made it difficult for urban South Vietnamese families who depend solely on a salary income to retain their standard of living, and women of all classes have felt pressure to get jobs. Urbanization has been rapid in South Viet Nam partially due to the pressures of war, and many families have moved to the urban areas without the extended kin group. Even when family groups have moved from the rural to urban areas, they have frequently had to find housing in separated areas and live in nuclear households. This has had the dual effect of relieving wives from much of the daily responsibility for service to the extended kin group and yet taking away the many hands that helped with housework and babysitting. Women complain that servants are becoming more difficult to find and many solve this problem by taking a niece or other young girl from the country. Others have "adopted" older homeless women who work for room and board (Hoskins and Shepherd 1970). The government has recognized this problem and has made an effort to establish day-care centers and pre-schools though there are waiting lists for all such facilities.

Newspaper articles written by women in the South in the 1960's and 1970's stress the desire to work and to justify this employment in family terms (*The Vietnam Observer*; *Miet-My*; *Viet Nam magazine*; Chiem T. Keim 1967). Some reasons these women give for working are that it makes one a more mature, interesting, and understanding wife; it keeps women from acquiring vices caused by idleness; it helps dutiful daughters-in-law get away from nagging mothers-in-law; and, it helps families in this time of inflation keep up or improve their standards of living. One article ends, "So we can see why working not only makes a woman's life independent but also effectively preserves her family's happiness" (Chiem T. Keim 1967:69).

In the North there has been strong governmental pressure towards getting women educated especially for technical and paraprofessional jobs. In articles translated from the Northern press during the 1960's and 1970's, women write that their status in the working world has improved though employers are not living up fully to their legal obligations to give lighter work loads to pregnant women and to provide baby-care centers, etc. (*Women of Viet Nam* 1972; Mai Thi Tu 1963; Chiem T. Keim 1967). In these articles, women urge other women to fight for their occupational rights, to get better training for higher jobs, and to work hard to help other women, other workers, and the nation's economy. They too are urged to justify their employment in family terms, but differently than the terms stressed in the South. They too are urged not to disregard the family, but unlike the South Vietnamese women, they are urged to expand the definition of the family to include the community. One article, for example, entitled "On the way in the fight for women's equality with men" concludes, "On the road to socialism, not only is our life —the women's life—better, but our interests are also wider. At the present time a number among us regard co-op and factory work as their own family's tasks" (Chiem T. Keim 1967:41).

The development of incongruent values and the effects of Westernization probably created the most stress on girls in the elite families who bridged the gap between Confucian tradition and French education and have since entered the professions. Mme. Le Kwang Kim, a well-known pharmacist in Saigon, describes vividly what it was like in 1940 to be an eighteen-year-old traditional upper-class girl, and some of the changes that happened to her and to many girls in this situation. In 1940 like other higher-class Vietnamese, she had a great deal of contact with the ruling French, she attended the only available school, a French-run boy's college. Coming from a Confucian background, she and her small group of co-ed friends rarely spoke to their male classmates. The girls were chaperoned to and from school. The classwork, all in the French language, dealt with French subjects. One evening, while writing an essay on Voltaire, her father came into her room and announced that the following day she would return her books to the school. Her father continued:

"Your mother and I, with the approval of your grandparents, have arranged a marriage for you with the sixteenth son of Madame H. The young man is one of the most eligible *partis* in the country. They are Catholics and have asked that you should become one, and therefore you will do so. It is of no importance since, as a girl, you would not have to be responsible for the cult of the ancestors. Your brother will undertake this honorable duty. The day after tomorrow you will attend instruction at the Cathedral of Saigon" (Le Kwang Kim 1963:463–464).

Le Kwang Kim describes how she accepted these decisions which had been made for her. As she had seen the "Great Family" care for and support its members, she trusted its system would take care of her.

At that time I was not an independent person responsible for my own future. I was only the grand-daughter of the Great Nobleman of Binh-y, daughter of his second son, existing not on my own account but in relation to my family (Le Kwang Kim 1963:464).

Le Kwang Kim was caught up in the confusion caused by the violence beginning in 1945. Many of her friends who had led secure lives found them shattered with the disappearance of prosperity. Her "Great Family" and that of many others had shrunk to the nuclear family due to death, loss of land, and enforced mobility caused by war. Mme. Kim found herself a widow with a two-year-old son and younger brother to raise, a mother to support, and an inadequate education. She describes this as a time when many young women saw an alternative to living solely within the family—that of becoming more independent in newly opening jobs and occupations as the country began to organize itself without the French.

To marry again was out of the question; it was not considered fitting for a woman to marry twice. Was my reluctance to marry due to a desire to show myself worthy of my mother-in-law, that indomitable woman who, though widowed, was bringing up her children alone? No, I think rather, though I was unaware of it at the time, that the fact of being able at last to take my life and my future into my own hands, having no longer either father or husband in authority over me, liberated me from my bonds, so that I intended to preserve my new-found freedom at all costs (Le Kwang Kim 1963:468).

Selling her jewellery, she traveled to France where she studied pharmacy. Returning to Viet Nam seven years later, she found the changes amazing. There was a two-way pull. Not only had things become "Westernized," but at the same time people were returning to traditions of the past, as if conscious of a need to rediscover themselves. Writing in 1963, she said that times were still changing rapidly and that the adjustment had not been altogether comfortable. She felt it would be some time before the Vietnamese would become integrated again and know, as they had known in the past, what their roles and options were and what to expect of those around them.

LEADERSHIP

Vietnamese women have exerted leadership throughout history, but almost always through their family role and the men around them. The most famous folk heroines in both the North and South are the Trung sisters or the *Hai Ba Trung*. In A.D. 34 Viet Nam, then called Giao Chi, was ruled by a Chinese governor noted for his tyranny and for forcing the proud Vietnamese to assimilate Chinese culture. This governor executed Tri Sach, an influential Vietnamese landowner and literary man of the time. His widow, Trung Trac and her sister Trung Nhi, sought to avenge his death, raised an army, and, riding elephants at its head, fought the Chinese. Exercising great military skill, they defeated the Chinese. Though their reign was short, they have remained enduring national heroines of the Vietnamese.

The occasional examples of female leadership in descriptive studies show women are almost invariably leaders due to the positions held by their husbands. For example, in one rural community the wife of the village chief organized a women's militia, but she did not serve in a leadership capacity (Donoghue 1961b). In looking at leadership in an urban community, I found that when women had no men in the family they would work through other women whose husbands could take the recognized leadership for a project, while the women designed, organized, and saw that their project was completed (Hoskins and Shepherd 1970).

Only recently have women begun to conceive of a leadership role apart from the family role. Women have traditionally had equal votes with men in family councils and the current governments of both the North and South have recognized their potential leadership and have given women equal votes in national elections. For almost twenty years, women have been declared politically and socially equal to men and for that length of time they have held elective and appointed leadership positions in both governments. Articles from the South indicate, however, some ambivalence on the part of women to define leadership roles outside of their relationship with their family or the strengthening of their husband's political role. A group of interviews of prominent women by the journal *Xa Hoi Moi* [Modern Society] shows a range of opinions from those who said women were too emotional and sentimental to be good politicians to those who believe that from long practice in getting along with their mothers-in-law women had a gift for diplomacy which would be crucial in politics. One female professor said women needed to participate actively in politics to protect their own interests, while a female mayor said that most women should stay home and become better informed voters (Chiem T. Keim 1967). In an article entitled "Women and their new responsibility," the author summarizes a theme common in the newspapers, that women's first duty is to their family and if they become active in society they must guard against "libertinism" or losing their traditional virtue of shyness and chastity. ". . . If the family is no longer firm and respectable, then women will be the ones to suffer most... If a woman fails to be a deserving wife and mother, then she cannot possibly perform any valuable work" (Chiem T. Keim 1967:26).

Articles from the Northern press also indicate the ambivalence of women towards leadership positions. A number of females were nominated for the national assembly, but, despite pressure from the party, women lost seats in the 1971 election. The party has also appointed a number of female vice-chairmen of cooperatives, many of whom have resigned. The newspaper articles discussing these failures to take leadership say that the old system taught women they were inferior and that women must gain confidence. They urge women to get better educations and urge husbands to take pride in wives who show community leadership. As in the articles on occupations, women are urged to extend their attitude of responsibility from the family to the community and country.

CONCLUSIONS

The most important conclusion from this wide variety of material deals with the relationship between the domestic and societal roles of women. Well-defined and relatively stable domestic roles have been the power base for Vietnamese women, while traditionally loosely circumscribed societal roles offer them flexibility and options to take advantage of current changes in society. In addition, this conclusion gives insight into the three questions asked at the beginning of this article. For example, we can now see the roots of the conflict between the mystique of the oppressed female described in Vietnamese literature and verbalized by Vietnamese women and the equally common belief that they are the real power in the country. The "powerless Vietnamese woman" was an ideal imposed by other cultures, particularly the Chinese; it was not the indigenous pattern. Closer evaluation of historical and legal documents reveals that in actual practice women always had a strong position in the family. The roles women play in Viet Nam are predetermined, with positions and behavior closely prescribed. Women continued to play a powerful role within the family, while maintaining the stance of outwardly submissive behavior at the appropriate times. Women emphasize the family but are free to participate in any outside activity that furthers it as long as she brings no embarrassment to the kin group.

In practice, this freedom, along with the feeling that commerce is a natural field for women, has given her great opportunities to participate in the economic structure of the country. The French developed an economic structure which made new positions available for women at various levels, but they also encouraged the concept of unequal wages for men and women. Though women now own many commercial enterprises, other women still work for wages and incomes lower than men. The laws in both the North and South, however, are encouraging more sexual equality. Women are also filling some leadership positions in the North and the South and though not yet any top positions, they are being encouraged to work towards assuming these roles.

This type of analysis had shed light on our second question of how traditionally demure wives adjust to a rapidly changing society without apparent redefinition of roles. The answer includes an awareness that wives are not challenging domestic roles, for the most part, and as a matter of fact their roles have always included the mandate to do whatever was necessary to support the family unit. Dr. Bourne, a psychiatrist studying values of Vietnamese says:

The Vietnamese man is facing increasing difficulty in adapting his traditional role to the rapid changes in this society. Disintegration of the old culture, which began under the French, has accelerated precipitously under American influence. The Western emphasis on productivity, materialism, and personal security based on emotional dependence on the nuclear family is much closer to the traditional expectations of the Vietnamese woman than the Vietnamese man (Bourne 1970:220).

In other words, traditional values put women in a very good position to function within the changing Vietnamese society.

Our final question asked how it was possible for women to become more active in Vietnamese society and profit by an improved status within the political and economic systems in both the North and South without meeting the prejudice and resentment of males so frequently found in the Western world. Historical developments and wartime conditions have created openings for women which they can fill without changing their domestic role regarding the separation of sexual behavior and of aspects of life concepts. The previous quote by Francis Hsu offers further insight into the answer. Sex is limited to specific situations and does not dominate other aspects of daily male-female relations outside of these situations. Therefore, educated females do not challenge the male ego when working with them on a professional basis. And, traditionally women are expected to be concerned about the material well-being of the family, so for a wife to bring an income into the family funds is not a challenge to males.

As to the future, the material raises a number of questions. With legal rights in marriage, property, voting, education and economic opportunity assured in both North and South Viet Nam, what role will the Vietnamese woman play in the future? Throughout history the women of Viet Nam have participated in wars, commerce, music, arts, teaching, and medicine, whenever family position and obligations permitted or required it. However, there is only so far that a woman can go, especially in leadership positions if her activities are tied to her husband's position. The traditional role, which includes strengthening the family, offers women the rationale for participating in the political and economic systems, especially for the educated middle and upper classes. However, new opportunities for leadership are unrelated to the position of the woman's husband and many would require a commitment beyond that of supporting the husband's status.

There are other important questions to raise such as what will happen to the forces in society which have been pushing women to take a more active role in the economic and leadership positions in their country when the crisis of war lessens? Will men returning to the labor market create a surplus which will reverse the trend that presently encourages women to participate actively? Will the lessening of nationalistic fervor also lessen the desire to have women participate actively in politics? What effect would the possible future reductions of inflationary and urbanization pressures have on the woman's role? And finally, if there is a partial return to extended family living, will the women affected be asked again to spend most of their time fulfilling roles within the extended kin group?

The future of women in Viet Nam appears to depend on whether or not they wish to or can redefine their power base. In the North the government is encouraging women to make the "duty of the family" ideal include "duty to the community." In the South the path may be through an emphasis on individual achievement within the social structure. Currently many women are participating in the socio-economic systems of their country but still primarily to improve or solidify the position of their family. Much of the future of Vietnamese society will depend on whether this element of consistency continues to underlie women's perception of their external roles, or whether they will exercise their options to redefine their power base as they participate more fully in the power and economic structures of their country.

REFERENCES

BOSERUP, ESTER
  1970 *Women's role in economic development.* New York: St. Martin's Press.
BOURNE, PETER G.
  1970 *Men, stress and Vietnam.* Boston: Little, Brown.

BUTTINGER, JOSEPH
 1962   *The smaller dragon: a political history of Vietnam.* New York:
        Frederick A. Praeger.

CADIÈRE, LEOPOLD
 1958   *Croyances et pratiques religieuses vietnamiens* (second edition).
        Saigon: Imprimerie Nouvelle d'Extrême Orient. (Originally pub-
        lished 1905.)

CHIEM T. KEIM, *translator*
 1967   *Women in Vietnam; selected articles from Vietnamese periodicals,
        Saigon, Hanoi, 1957–1966.* Honolulu: East-West Center.
Constitution
 1967   *Constitution of the Republic of Viet-Nam.*

DONOGHUE, JOHN D.
 1961a *Cam An: a fishing village in central Vietnam.* Saigon: Michigan
        State University Press.
 1961b *My Thuan: the study of a delta village in South Vietnam.* Saigon:
        Michigan State University Press.

FALL, BERNARD B.
 1965   *The two Viet-Nams: a political and military analysis.* New York:
        Frederick A. Praeger.

GROSS, N., A. W. MC EACHERN, A. W. MASON
 1958   "Role conflict and its resolution," in *Readings in social psychology*
        (third edition). Edited by Eleanor E. Maccoby, T. M. Newcomb,
        and E. L. Hartley, 447–459. New York: Holt.

HENDRY, JAMES B.
 1964   *The small world of Khanh Hau.* Chicago: Aldine.

HICKEY, GERALD C.
 1969   *Village in Vietnam.* New Haven: Yale University Press.

HOSKINS, JOHN A.
 1971   "The Vietnamese legal system." Lecture presented to the Viet
        Nam Training Center of the Foreign Service Institute.

HOSKINS, MARILYN W.
 1971   *Building rapport with the Vietnamese.* Washington, D.C.: U.S.
        Government (AGDA-A M OPS-IA-SO).

HOSKINS, MARILYN W., ELEANOR SHEPHERD
 1970   *Life in a Vietnamese urban quarter* (second edition). Carbondale,
        Illinois: Southern Illinois University.

HSU, FRANCIS L. K.
 1972   *Americans and Chinese* (second edition). Garden City, New York:
        Doubleday Natural History Press.

HUARD, PIERRE, MAURICE DURAND
 1954   *Connaissance du Viet-Nam* (second edition). Hanoi: Ecole Fran-
        çaise d'Extrême-Orient. (Originally published 1908.)

LE HUY HAP
 1963   *Vietnamese legends.* Saigon: Khai-Tri.

LE KWANG KIM
1963   "A woman of Viet-Nam in a changing world," in *Women in the new Asia*. Edited by Barbara B. Ward. The Netherlands: UNESCO.

LE THANH KHOI
1955   *Le Viet-Nam: historie et civilisation*. Paris: Editions de Minuit.

LEICHTY, MARY M.
1963   The role of the family in transmitting culture. *Viet-My* (83).

LINTON, R.
1936   *The study of man*. New York: Appleton-Century.

LUSTEGUY, PIERRE
1953   *The role of women in Tonkinese religion and property* (second edition). Translated by C. A. Messner. Yale Human Relations Area File Press. (Originally published 1935.)

MAI THI TU
1963   "The Vietnamese woman, yesterday and today," in *Vietnamese women*. Hanoi: Democratic Republic of Viet Nam.

NGHIEM XUAN VIET
1963   "La technique juridique du credit immobilier en droit." Unpublished thesis for the Doctoral en Droit, University of Saigon.

PHAM HUY TY
1957   Law and society in Vietnam. *Studies in the Law in Far and Southeast Asia*. Washington: The Washington Foreign Law Society and George Washington University Law School.

PHILASTRE, P. L. F.
1909   *Le code annamite*. Paris: Ernest Leroux.

SCHULTZ, GEORGE
1965   *Vietnamese legends*. Rutland, Vermont: Charles E. Tuttle.

SLOTE, WALTER H.
1966   *Observations on psychodynamic structures in Vietnamese personality*. Arlington, Virginia: Advanced Research Projects Agency.

SLUSSER, MARY
1965   *Characteristics of the people of Indochina*. Washington, D.C.: External Research Division, Department of State.

SPINDLER, LOUISE, GEORGE SPINDLER
1958   Male and female adaptations in culture change. *American Anthropologist* 60:217–33.

SUN, RUTH A.
1967   *Folk tales of Vietnam: land of seagull and fox*. Rutland, Vermont: Charles E. Tuttle.

TRAN THI HOAI TRAN
1971   "Quiet persuasion used; Viet women use femininity for liberation." *Daily Egyptian*, Southern Illinois University, August 6.

TURLEY, WILLIAM S.
  1972   "Women in the Vietnamese revolution." Paper presented to Panel
         on Vietnamese Communism, Convention of the Association for
         Asian Studies, New York, March 27–29.

Viet Nam government organization manual, 1957–1958
  1958   Saigon: National Institute of Administration.

Viet Nam magazine
  1970–1972   Volumes three, four, and five. Saigon: Vietnam Council on
              Foreign Relations.

Viet Nam statistical yearbook, 1971
  1972   Saigon: National Institute of Statistics.

VO HONG PHUC
  1960   The role of women in Vietnamese society. *Viet-My* 4 (winter).

WARD, BARBARA, *editor*
  1963   *Women in the new Asia: the changing social roles of men and
         women in South and South-East Asia*. The Netherlands: UNESCO.

Women of Viet Nam
  1972   Hanoi: Viet Nam Women's Union I–IV.

Social and Cultural Change of Japanese and Chinese in Thailand

KENJIRO ICHIKAWA

With the expansion of economic and technical cooperation between Japan and Thailand since the 1960's, the population of Japanese residents in Thailand, including advisers and technicians serving the Thailand government, civil entrepreneurs, and office workers for industrial companies, increased to almost 5,000 by the end of 1971. The increasing Japanese economic activity in the land caused the Thai people to fear domination of their domestic economy by the highly industrialized power of Japan. In a spirit of economic nationalism *vis-à-vis* the neocolonialism of developed societies, many Thais seek to assert their own economic independence. Few Japanese residents in Thailand today are permanent settlers. Most visit Thailand for only a short time as partners for economic and technical cooperation, although large numbers of Japanese and Chinese immigrants in the developing societies of South America before World War II were agricultural laborers.

There are three ways that Japanese should operate in Thailand:

1. Japanese managers or technical advisers in Thailand should provide Thais with executive training for managers and superintendents of industrial factories.

2. As an increasing number of Thais complete these modern training courses for company supervisors, Japanese managers and advisers should go back to Japan, transferring power to the native people.

3. Following such Japanese withdrawal, future Japanese aid to

Thailand should be limited to providing capital and technical aid and importing large amounts of agricultural products from Thailand for maintaining a trade balance between the two countries.

HISTORICAL BACKGROUND

The Chinese in Thailand have a much longer history of immigration and a much larger number of immigrants than the Japanese in Thailand. Long before the southward movements of the Thai race from border provinces of southern China, Chinese merchants navigated the Gulf of Siam and settled in villages along the coast. The Chinese population in Thailand was probably about 10,000 in the 1660's and increased several times by the end of the eighteenth century. By 1825, the Chinese population in the whole country had probably reached 230,000 and by 1850, it was approximately 300,000 (Skinner 1957: 68–72). After Thailand opened the door to foreigners in the middle of the nineteenth century, the number of Chinese immigrants from mainland China increased greatly until the end of the century and again after the fall of the Chin Dynasty of China in 1912. It decreased during the years of World War II and again after 1949 when the People's Government was established in mainland China. Since then, the Chinese in Thailand have gradually merged with the native society under Prime Minister Phibul's policy of assimilation. Nowadays, there are probably two and one-half million native-born Chinese with Thai nationality, in addition to the estimated one million of Chinese nationality claimed by the Chinese newspapers; the actual number of Chinese nationals, however, may be less than 400,000 (Chinese Chamber of Commerce 1965: D-159).

In contrast to the steady growth of Chinese population, the history of Japanese immigration has been intermittent. In the seventeenth century when Nagamasa Yamada, Japanese commander for the Thai king, was at Ayuthaya, then the capital city of the Thai kingdom, the Japanese residential village near the capital had a population of several hundred. After the ban on Japanese travel abroad under the Tokugawa regime, however, Japanese travelling in Southeast Asia were permanently cut off from their homeland and assimilated into the native societies.

During the period of World War II when the Japanese army spread into the Malay Peninsula and Burma from Thailand, the Japanese population in that land increased greatly. After 1946, when about

3,000 Japanese prisoners under the supervision of the United Nations were sent back to their homeland, the Japanese population in Thailand declined to almost zero. In April 1953, the Japanese Association in Thailand started again with only 130 members, but gradually increased to 634 by 1963; to 1,323 by 1968; and to 2,140 by June 1971 (Japanese Association in Thailand June 1971:28). The present total population of the Japanese in the land is almost 5,000, twice the number of regular members of the Japanese Association in Thailand but still only a small fraction of the Chinese population.

CHINESE SOCIETY

Because of the assimilation policy of the Thai government during and after the war and of declining communication with mainland China since 1949, a large number of Chinese in Thailand have assimilated rapidly into the native society. Consequently, the native-born Chinese who usually obtain Thai nationality have been educated as Thais at Thai schools, in the Thai language, and by Thai teachers. With the development of the economic and social structure towards modernization and urbanization, the generation gap between older and younger members of Chinese society in Thailand has widened in recent years. Many older people (over fifty) who are first-generation Chinese prefer to speak their Chinese dialects, to write Chinese characters, and to join speech group meetings such as the Teochiu Association or the Cantonese Association. They are also willing to work for guilds such as the Rice Merchants Association or the Rice Millers Association, in which relatives and friends of the same dialect group help each other. They are also members of same-surname associations, such as Mr. Huang's Association or Mr. Ma's Association, in which they preserve tradition cults for common ancestor spirits.

While most young people (under thirty) are native-born, they have Thai nationality, Thai ways of thinking, and can speak Thai as their native tongue, but they usually write a little Chinese. It is a natural consequence that these younger people have less interest in speech groups than their parents do and prefer to live in Thai society as Thai people. In one small-scale guild society, for example, the young people plan to modernize and rationalize the old guild structure maintained by the older generation and to move from older downtown Bangkok to eastern areas of the city where the wealthy people live. They also engage in price and quality competition with their friends who are members of the same guild and the same speech group.

The age distribution of the Chinese society today is almost the same as in the Thai society and has little imbalance in the sex ratio by years, although there are some refugees who have come from mainland China since 1949. The upper-class people who speak Thai freely confine themselves to the nuclear family structure and assimilate into Thai society through international marriages. The lower-class Chinese, such as laborers, do not have enough money to send their children to school and tend to speak only Chinese dialects within their own speech group. They have therefore assimilated into the native society much less and have less opportunity to marry Thais, mainly because of their poor economic situation. Families are large, as they live together with their relatives in one house. Houses are small by upper-class standards, so families accumulate enough capital to build new houses for their young couples (Punyodyana 1971:47).

Chinese merchants in rural districts usually work for rice mills or transport agricultural products. However, in Bangkok in recent years, merchants have tended to invest capital in suburban land or industrial factories, so that they become owners of land or companies.

JAPANESE SOCIETY

Most Japanese in Thailand are temporary residents who enter the country on nonimmigrant visas, staying there usually only one or two years. Company workers are concerned with affairs in their own homeland rather than in Thai society; for example, although Thailand is a hot and humid tropical country, employees work hard until midnight to show loyalty to their company in competition with other companies in Southeast Asia so they may be promoted after going back to Japan. Although they are in Thailand, their prime concerns remain the promotions or movements of their colleagues at their main offices in Japan, better jobs at other companies in Japan, and so on.

Japanese company wives' clubs in Thailand provide welfare services for company workers and their families, especially when they are newcomers in Thailand. For friendship and solidarity for Japanese university graduates, branch meetings of alumni associations are often held at Japanese restaurants in Bangkok where alumni sing college songs in chorus. Provincial associations of Japanese in Thailand are not so active as Chinese speech groups there, because local traditions in Japan have become very much urbanized in recent years.

On New Year's Day and the emperor's birthday, many Japanese residents in Bangkok attend ceremonies at the Japanese Embassy, cheering *"banzai"* three times in the traditional manner. The Japanese Association in Thailand provides a variety of cultural and sports activities for members and the Japanese Travel Agency in Bangkok offers several sightseeing tours for the Japanese. Thus, even if the Japanese are in a group tour to Angkor Wat, for example, they can keep to their way of life.

As for the age distribution, probably half the total population of the Japanese society in Thailand are office workers, 30 to 40 years old, who are Japanese university or college graduates, usually accompanied by their wives and children of school age. However, men over 50 who are administrators or managers of companies generally leave their wives and children in Japan, mainly because of the high school or university education of their children there. For the education of Japanese children in Bangkok, the Japanese school, known as the Japanese Language Class and attached to the Japanese Embassy, brings 17 full-time teachers from Tokyo in addition to 20 part-time teachers and secretaries selected from among members of the Japanese Association. They teach primary and junior high school courses in a total of 23 classes for 500 Japanese pupils, plus 120 kindergarteners. Japanese parents in Bangkok are very concerned for their children about entrance examinations to secondary school courses in Japan.

In the summer of 1972, the Thai government asked the Japanese school in Thailand to follow the private school law of the land. According to this law, only Thai people may be school managers or masters and the Thai language is a required subject for language training. However, this met with some opposition since Japanese children in Bangkok are very close to their parents and the generation gap is very small compared with that of Chinese parents and children in Bangkok.

As for social stratification, professionals such as United Nations officials, Japanese government diplomats, technical advisers to the Thailand government, as well as private company managers and plant superintendents, are apt to live within small isolated Japanese societies and not to speak the Thai language. Consequently, it is very hard for them to understand and adjust to the native society. In contrast, lower-class Japanese, such as workers in Japanese restaurants, bars, hotels, apartment houses, and Turkish baths, and construction workers, have to associate with the native people and to speak Thai. However, these people also usually stay only a limited time and do not assimilate into the native society as do the Chinese. Japanese technological advisers for agriculture or fisheries, too, stay only briefly in rural districts, generally leaving quickly to resume their own professions in Japan.

In short, Japanese professional and business people in Thailand, who rarely assimilate into the native society and prefer to live in their own isolated society, sharply contrast with upper-class Chinese who have assimilated very much into political and economic society in Thailand.

ASSIMILATION AND ISOLATION

Although there are different patterns of behavior between Japanese and Chinese in Thailand, we cannot generalize immediately that overseas Chinese assimilate into native societies much more readily than overseas Japanese do. Japanese agricultural immigrants in North and South America, for example, often moved from rural to urban societies where second- or third-generation Japanese-Americans have gradually assimilated into the native society and have given up the traditional value system preserved by the first-generation Japanese.

Furthermore, the Chinese in Thailand today are regarded as Thai people, although their ancestors who came to Bangkok 100 years ago lived together in small Chinese towns, and some of them organized secret societies by speech groups for illegal activities. This means that many Chinese residents in Bangkok 100 years ago were only strangers there and did not assimilate into the native culture. Their history since the middle of the nineteenth century, however, has changed their society to amalgamate to the Thai, and mixed-blood Chinese-Thai people gradually have begun to assume a leading role in political and economic circles.

Today, Thailand is on her way towards industrialization and is imbued with a strong sense of economic nationalism reflecting the wish of Thai people to gain economic independence and to be free of colonial invasion by foreign powers. Meanwhile, Japanese immigrants have transformed their image from that of agricultural workers to a new image of partners in economic and technical cooperation for developing societies. As a highly industrialized power in Asia, Japan in recent years has expanded economically to the Far East and Southeast Asia and is regarded as a big power of neocolonialism in the region. Under these international circumstances of economic nationalism, the Japanese assimilation into Asian societies is not to be expected.

For the development of their own society towards industrialization, Thai leaders of political and economic circles seek to obtain foreign capital and the technical assistance of developed countries. Rapid expansion of Japanese enterprises to Thailand, however, is regarded by Thai nationalists as conquest over their domestic economy, a foreign invasion which could defeat the economic independence of their land. For these nationalists, all Japanese people in Thailand are looked upon as forerunners of neocolonialism, a revival of prewar Western colonialism. In early 1971, Thai university students in Bangkok made plans for an anti-Japanese movement, and young office workers demanded that Thai-Japanese joint companies give Thais the same treatment in positions and payment as Japanese workers. Such demands for equality could escalate to demands for positions such as company manager or plant superintendent. If the situation takes a bad turn, all Japanese could be asked to leave Thailand. Social structure in Thailand today is quite different from that of the last century, when large numbers of Chinese immigrated to that land.

Viewing the matter from the Japanese side, prewar immigrants to North and South America were called "unwanted, abandoned people," cast offs from a society which shipped them out and tried to forget them. Even today, many Japanese office workers in Thailand feel that they are abandoned people, and their present home felt to be an abandoned land. Most of them are anxious to get back to Japan as soon as they can.

REFERENCES

CHINESE CHAMBER OF COMMERCE IN THAILAND
  1965   *Annual report*, 29. Bangkok.

JAPANESE ASSOCIATION IN THAILAND
1971   *Kulungtep* (monthly magazine), June 1971, Bangkok.

PUNYODYANA, B.
1971   *Chinese-Thai differential assimilation in Bangkok: an exploratory study*. Ithaca, N.Y.: Cornell University, Southeast Asia Program.

SKINNER, G. W.
1957   *Chinese society in Thailand: an analytical history*. Ithaca, N.Y.: Cornell University Press.

Monastic Education, Social Mobility, and Village Structure in Cambodia

M. KALAB

The hypothesis I present here is that the Cambodian village structure is dependent on the existence of Buddhist monasteries. During the last decades fewer and fewer young men were becoming monks and this was partly related to the availability of modern secular education. But when the situation became critical in the late fifties, the availability of improved higher monastic education reversed the trend.

My own statistical data come from only one monastery and one small hamlet which form part of a village situated on the left bank of the Mekong River, halfway between Phnom Penh and Kompong Cham town. The Cambodian government had kindly given me permission to copy data from the completed questionnaires of the 1961 census and I was also allowed to make use of the cadastral records of the village. When, however, in 1967, I wished to augment my incomplete information, I was refused a Cambodian visa. Therefore, if I make tentative generalizations about the whole country on the basis of scanty information about one hamlet, it is not because I am unaware of the limitations of such a procedure, but because I was unable to get more data.

Under the circumstances it might be useful to consider to what

This paper is based on unfinished fieldwork conducted in Cambodia in 1966 and financed by research grants from the Royal Geographical Society and the International Federation of University Women. If I speak about Cambodia rather than about the Khmer Republic, that is because many new factors have entered the field during the last few years and my conclusions might not be quite applicable today. To that extent this is a historical study.

extent the village is typical and representative of the state as a whole. Cambodia is not one of the overpopulated countries of Asia. There are about seven million Cambodians living on 70,000 square miles, giving a density of about 100 persons per square mile; but about 90 percent of the inhabitants live in about one-third of the area, in the plains, along the river and lakes. Though at least 80 percent of the people are agriculturists, only about 25 percent of all cultivable land, which is about 10 percent of all land, is actually under cultivation. In Cambodia nobody needs to die of hunger; to be poor means simply to be short of cash.

The village of Prek Por Suosdey (see Maps 1 and 2) lies in the district of Srey Santhor in the province of Kompong Cham, one of the most fertile areas of Cambodia. There is very little virgin land

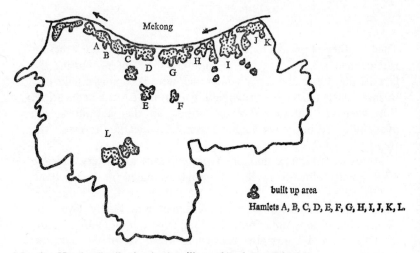

Map 1.   Hamlet distribution in the village of Prek Por Suosdey.

left in the village but serious pressure on land has not yet started. The village area covers almost 2,000 hectares, and of these about 1,600 are cultivated; the inland crops are mainly paddy and maize and on the riverbank there are diverse cash crops. About 1 percent of this land belonged to the crown, 1 percent to monasteries, 1 percent to the village community, and 12 percent to the state, while 83 percent was privately owned. This privately owned land was divided about equally between men and women.

The relatively slow and quiet pace of life probably came from the poor transport facilities. Though a jeep could travel along the river-

bank and on a few tracks inland, it was most unusual to see one. No
bus service existed there; transport was mostly by boat or by bicycle
or motorcycle. One could go by the steamer to Phnom Penh in four
or five hours and in about the same time to the provincial capital,
Kompong Cham. There were at least half a dozen runs a day and the
fare was very cheap. But the passengers on a steamer never get off
before their final destination, so there was no mixing of strangers in
the village tea shops as there would have been if a bus service passed
through the village.

Though most villagers seemed to be reasonably well off,
modernization had not made any great impact on the traditional
way of life, and the monastery was usually the first to enjoy any
innovation. An electricity generator and loudspeakers were in use

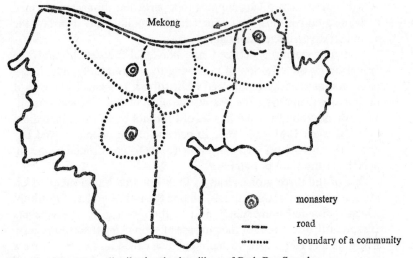

Map 2.   Monastery distribution in the village of Prek Por Suosdey

during festivals, bottled drinks were common, but almost the only
sophisticated gadgets anybody owned were a transistor radio or a
motorcycle. Everybody still supported the monastery according to
his ability and even the construction of the medical center was
organized largely by the monastery. Only a French-educated teacher
from outside the village expressed doubts about the usefulness of
Buddhist monks. The same informant told me that in villages on
important motorways boys are no longer interested in becoming
novices. This change most likely affects the richer areas rather than

the poorer ones where people cannot afford to imitate urban styles of life and thus remain traditional out of necessity. But in Prek Por monastery support seemed to be a voluntary choice, a situation likely to apply to the majority of Khmer villages.

Prek Por had about 4,500 inhabitants living in 1,500 houses, and the village was subdivided into twelve hamlets. But the boundaries between these communities as understood by the inhabitants themselves are not always identical with those on government maps. This applies even to individual hamlets in areas of dispersed settlement.

A true community is formed by the households supporting the same monastery, and in this sense Prek Por had three monasteries and therefore consisted of three communities. Though in theory any person may support any monastery, in practice—at any rate in this village—the houses giving support to a particular monastery formed a distinct contiguous area. Such a community may overlap the administrative village boundary.

A dyadic relation between an individual household and the monastery is the criterion of belonging to a community, and it is a relation that is easily established or dissolved. It seems to be one of the factors facilitating the spatial mobility of the Khmer peasant. The rate of mobility in the hamlet of Prathnol was almost incredibly high. Between 1961 and 1966, 30 percent of the people moved out and new immigrants arrived who, by 1966, constituted some 40 percent of the total population.

One of the three monasteries in Prek Por was Vatt Prakal which was supported by seven hamlets, among them the hamlet of Prathnol which is situated immediately next to the monastery. The villagers are specially organized for the purpose of supporting their monastery. Every hamlet elects its own representative called an *achar*, always a respected man who knows all the Pali formulae and the details of ceremonies, usually somebody who was a monk for a period of time and, moreover, a man who can be trusted with money. The seven *achars* then elect from among themselves a chairman, the big *achar*. They keep in touch with the monastic dignitaries, organize ceremonies and festivals, and address the monks on behalf of the congregation in the temple; they lead recitation and chanting by the lay people. They also collect contributions from the villagers in cash and in grain, and they keep all the accounts.

As in other Theravada countries, only older people attend the weekly services on Buddhist holy days and attempt to keep the precepts. The young and the householders, who contribute most of the offerings and labor, attend services only on special occasions, and though they then repeat the eight precepts after the monks, they make little effort at observing them. Very young boys may become pagoda boys, doing minor services for some particular monk and either living in the monastery or spending only the day there. Older boys may become ordained novices. Only older people attend meditation retreats during the rainy season, and, of the nineteen people in Prathnol who did so, sixteen were women. Of course men interested in the contemplative life can become monks, and some do so later in life, especially widowers.

I mentioned the committee of *achars* which acts as the liaison between the lay community and its monks. The inhabitants are connected through a quite different system with the administration of the country. An elected headman acts as the representative of the villagers to the administration and he also represents the administration to the village. He is responsible to the district officer, who is responsible to the governor of the province, who is responsible to the central government. The headman is the only member of this hierarchy who has any grasp of the local affairs; all other officials are members of the civil service, bureaucrats moved every few years to other locations. The headman is a local man and he is elected.

The other elected person who represents the people directly at the center is their member of parliament. A third link with the administration center is their member of parliament. Under Prince Sihanouk, a third link with the administration was the National Congress, a public meeting attended by all the ministers and other officials. It was held twice a year in the capital and any citizen had the right to attend and bring up a question or a complaint to which the officer responsible for the matter had to answer in public.

The secular administrative hierarchy is paralleled by a monastic hierarchy. As in Thailand, there are two monastic orders in Cambodia, the Thommayut and the Mohanikay, but unlike Thailand, in Cambodia each of these orders has a separate hierarchy of dignitaries with a *sanghanayaka* at the top of each order. The Thommayut monasteries are virtually limited to towns, with a very few exceptions (Ebihara 1966:176), and their supporters are the royal family and most officials. Out of about 3,000 monasteries, only about 110 were Thommayut. There were none in Prek Por.

On the village level, every monastery is headed by an abbot and his two deputies. Only some abbots are permitted by the central

organization of the *sangha* to act as preceptors at ordination ceremonies. In every district there is an *anukon*, a monastic position
corresponding to the district officer of the secular hierarchy. In the
district of Srey Santhor this official resided in a different village than
did the district officer. On the provincial level there is the provincial
monastic head called a *mekon* who resides in the provincial capital.
There is a council of monastic dignitaries at the center, and there are
also councils on the provincial and district levels. The provincial
and higher dignitaries were nominated by the king, the lower ones
by the head of the order (Chau-Seng 1962).

In most matters concerning the *sangha* both the secular official
and the monastic official cooperated; for instance, teachers in the
monastic schools had their nominations countersigned by the
governor and the *mekon*. In theory, this harmonious cooperation
was essential for the life of the Khmer nation, which was likened to a
chariot with two wheels, one of them being the state and the other,
religion. But sometimes there appeared to be a slight tension between
the two hierarchies.

Though the main aim of a monk's life is the attainment of Nirvana
and the villagers support him materially to gain religious merit, the
monasteries always provided many more immediate services. The
monks were the most trusted advisers of the people, who discussed
their agricultural work with them, borrowed money from them, and
sometimes received medical advice. Today if a monk takes charge
of a community project, people do cooperate with him and the project
is likely to succeed. Though monks are supposed to keep aloof from
politics and have no right to vote in a general election, during the last
electoral campaign in 1966, all four candidates in Prek Por's electoral
district, instead of holding public meetings and delivering speeches,
spent their time visiting the abbots in all the local monasteries.
Grass-roots politics were in the hands of the influential monks in the
villages, and this was one of the reasons why Prince Sihanouk and
other politicians, even when followers of the Thommayut order, paid
more and more attention to the Mohanikay hierarchy. But while the
head of state showered special favors on the late *sangharaja* of the
Mohanikay order, tensions occasionally developed on a lower level.

For instance, the district officer at Srey Santhor and his family
were supporters of the Thommayut order. When attending a
Mohanikay service in the village, they complained to me that the
Mohanikay pronunciation of Pali was quite unintelligible to them.
Later I witnessed a clash during the funeral of the *anukon* of the

district. Cremations of important personalities are always accompanied by a series of ceremonies and entertainments lasting for several days. These are planned well ahead to avoid any conflicts. This time one of these special events was the distribution of gifts to poor people by the district officer, but he was delayed by some family matter and missed the fixed time in the morning. He then decided to hold the distribution at the time when the *mekon* was giving his sermon. It would have been quite easy to postpone the occasion for an hour, but as neither dignitary would give way, both ceremonies proceeded at the same time, about one hundred yards from each other, and both used loudspeakers to their fullest advantage. The appointed bureaucrat had obviously much less reason than the elected politician to be polite to a monk. Even so, the *mekon* had a larger audience than the district officer.

The introduction of compulsory secular primary education was a more serious blow to the power of the *sangha* than such personal skirmishes. Education was always one of the traditional functions of the Buddhist monastery. Various monastic institutions founded by the kings of Funan were seats of learning and places for the education of the young. Their inscriptions mention not only how much food and incense each resident was to receive every day, but also the number of blank leaves, ink, and chalk needed for students (Chatterji 1964:115). Among the servants who were attached to these institutions were preparers of leaves for writing (Chatterji 1964:123).

As it was the practice until recently for every boy to become a novice or monk for a period of time before marriage, and as every monk must be able to read sermons, almost all Khmer men were literate and all women were illiterate. The term "literate" meant in this context a man who could read, but not necessarily one who could also write. This distinction is so important that the census questionnaires make a distinction between those who can read and write and those who can read only. More significantly, the census taker questioning monks in Vatt Prakal indicated that all the monks could read only, though I know that at least some of them were good at writing.

When King Chulalongkorn in Thailand decided to modernize the Thai educational system, he continued to use the monasteries for the purpose (Wyatt 1969:116), gradually training more and more teachers, both monks and laymen. This system started in 1884, and it was introduced into the Cambodian provinces of Thailand in 1900. When Battambang and Siemreap were returned to Cambodia in 1908, the people there wished to continue the modern pagoda schools, so the French adopted the idea in 1911. Thus for some time the traditional function of the monastery continued in a modernized version. Later, however, more and more secular primary schools were founded, and this happened at a time when the other functions of the monasteries, such as giving medical help, banking facilities, and architectural assistance, started to fade away as well.

Education was always one of the means of social mobility. Now education not only could be had without monastic training, but the certificates from the secular schools were more useful in getting employment. So fewer and fewer boys became novices. This was the situation in the middle of this century, and it seemed at one stage that the monasteries might die out, which in turn would necessitate drastic changes in the village structure.

Meanwhile the level of literacy was constantly improving. The primary school sector has been enormously expanded during the last dozen years, so that illiteracy has ceased to be a problem for the younger generation. In 1964 an adult education campaign was started with the target of teaching every Khmer person how to read and write within one year and every foreigner within two years. In Prathnol this effort was very successful, partly due to the fact that the district office was in the neighboring hamlet, but also due to the genuine enthusiasm of several local teachers, Except for some very old ladies, everybody could soon read and some people actually did read books; middle-aged ladies read tracts on religion, young girls love stories and manuals on writing love letters, men preferred historical novels, and everybody read the election manifestoes of parliamentary candidates. In 1966 nobody was interested in reading newspapers. Though at this time there were only three adults below the age of forty at Prathnol who were illiterate (Kalab 1968:533), only three persons had some secondary education: one man and one woman in their twenties, and one man in his thirties who had had monastic secondary education.

It was at the stage, when the monopoly of primary education was passing away from the monasteries to secular schools, that the *sangha* started paying more attention to higher education. They had always had some Pali schools in the capital. From 1933 on they had introduced a system of elementary Pali schools into village monasteries. In 1962 there were 570 primary Buddhist schools in the country. Apart from Pali and elements of the Buddhist doctrine, the students also learned mathematics, science, history, geography, civics, and administration. If after three years they passed the state examination, they received the title of *Maha* and could take part in the entrance examination to a Buddhist lycée.

In 1962, there was only one Buddhist lycée in Phnom Penh which admitted 150 new students every year (Vajirappano 1962). Later a Buddhist lycée was opened also at Battambang. There the students study Pali, physics, chemistry, mathematics, religion, history, geography, hygiene, Sanskrit, French, English and Khmer. Later, as more monks were able to go for higher education to India rather than to France, there was a tendency to choose English rather than French as their European language. After four years at the lycée there is another state examination and successful candidates are allowed to sit for the entrance examination to the Buddhist university. Each year 40 new students are admitted. The study at the university lasts ten years and is divided into three parts. During the first three years the student has to master 14 different subjects. After the first degree he specializes, choosing one of six courses. After four years he can obtain a master's degree. After three more years and a thesis he may receive a doctorate.

The Buddhist secondary schools and the university were started with the intention of creating an up-to-date Buddhist intellectual elite, because the monks were losing their intellectual leadership to the French-educated scholars. But the effect of this new network of schools was much wider. The decisive move was the recognition of the certificates issued by monastic institutions as equivalent to those issued by secular institutions. This happened (according to Choan and Sarin 1970:139) in 1963. According to the Cambodian secular system, a child starts school at the age of seven in class 12, and the first grade of the Pali elementary school corresponds to class 9, the third grade to class 7. The Buddhist lycée corresponds to classes 6, 5, 4, and 3 of the French lycée.

There was one schoolteacher resident at Prathnol who had a diploma from what was known in his time as the Higher Pali school. According to him it should have been recognized as equal to a certificate from class 3 of a French lycée, and he should have been paid as a full teacher; actually it was recognized as only a certificate from class 6 and he was employed as an assistant teacher. He believed that this situation would be amended soon by yet another new law. But whether these certificates are recognized completely or only in part, the main thing is that they are recognized.

Despite the success of primary education and the literacy drive, poor children still found it difficult to get secondary education. The schools might be far away and the student would have to reside near it and pay for his board and lodging. It might be a little cheaper if he lived in a monastery, but even then he had to pay for his books and uniforms. According to Choan and Sarin (1970:140), most of these schools were new and expected the students to contribute between 1,000 and 4,000 riel to the cost of construction. I was also told that some teachers demanded bribes. Girls are helpless here, but poor boys who desire an education can become ordained novices and join one of those monasteries which have Pali schools.

Rich people in Phnom Penh have complained about this development, which deprived their Paris-educated children of a complete monopoly of certain jobs. This development also may not be true in all areas of Cambodia. In cities and on the main roads monkhood presumably continued to decline in popularity among the young. But the situation at Vatt Prakal seemed to confirm the renewed interest in the novitiate. According to the census of 1961 there were eighteen monks and eighteen novices in this monastery. In 1966 there were fourteen monks and thirty-eight novices there.

Though I have no information about the number of monks in Vatt Prakal before 1961, one can deduce indirectly that in the past their number must have been higher in relation to village population. I have the statistics for men from the hamlet of Prathnol who were or were not monks (Table 1).

Table 1.   Men of the hamlet of Prathnol

Age group	Number of males	Number who are or were monks	Number who never were monks
11–15	17	3	14
16–20	11	5	6
21–25	9	1	8
26–30	10	6	4
31–35	11	7	4
36–40	10	8	2
41–45	5	4	1
46–50	4	3	1
51–55	5	4	1
56–85	9	9	0

We may disregard the 11 to 15 age group, because few boys join before they are 14 or 15 years old. In the 16 to 20 age group almost half the boys are novices. This contrasts with the 21 to 25 age group where only 10 percent became ordained.

From this table it appears that before 1930 or so everybody became ordained. Later the numbers slowly declined. For the 36 to 55 group it is still 80 percent, for the 26 to 35 group 60 percent, then suddenly the lowest point is reached at 10 percent, which happened probably around 1960. It seems that the recognition of the monastic certificates around 1963 had considerable effect, bringing the figure of boys becoming monks to 50 percent.

Most of the new novices stay as long as they can continue their studies. After two or three unsuccessful attempts at an entry examination either to the lycée or to the university, they are likely to leave and to seek government employment with the help of the last certificate they were able to obtain. According to Choan and Sarin, most stated they wished to return to agriculture when they left the monastery. This is a rather surprising wish, even though most of them might have to do so in the end. I remained in correspondence with a few monks, of whom two have left the monastery. One of them had attended only an elementary Pali school and also studied some English. Then he worked as a mason at the Angkor conservation project and later as a cycler, taking tourists around to the monuments. His aim was to become a tourist guide. The other monk had completed the Buddhist lycée, but was not admitted to the university. After two years as a Pali teacher he left the monkhood and became a clerk in a government office.

Obviously, the monastic system of education does offer a channel of upward mobility to the poor boy, but it is not a soft option. There are good reasons why some sons of well-to-do parents do not choose this path, except when they genuinely wish to become monks for life. The novices are kept under strict discipline by their teachers and by the abbot. At Vatt Prakal, in addition to their studies, daily alms rounds, and chores within the monastery, they also worked daily on the construction of the medical center, carrying stones, mixing cement, and the like.

Attendance at a monastic school is also no guarantee of a final certificate. Places in the higher institutions are very few and the competition is intense. There were about 10,000 students in the elementary Pali schools in 1961 (about 3,500 in each grade), and about 3,500 appear for the final examination each year. Of these only about 2,000 are successful, or approximately 57 percent. Of these 2,000, only a fraction can be admitted to a Buddhist lycée—

150 students in 1961, maybe 500 today. Of these again about 60 percent pass the final examination, though the statistics are not very clear on this point. But whatever the number of successful candidates, only 40 can be admitted to the university each year. Only the very best get that far.

Having worked so hard for so many years, what have they learned? Much of their study is still done by rote rather than by understanding, and though some secular subjects are taught, this is probably on a very elementary level. Most of their time is spent, understandably enough, on the Pali language and Buddhist doctrine. Tambiah (1968:101) mentions that the monks in northeast Thailand often do not understand what they recite. This does not happen in Cambodia, because, since 1926, Pali recitations by both monks and laymen are followed by a Khmer translation of the texts, except the precepts. This, however, does not mean that the person knows which word means what. Some monks have a very vague idea about the grammar even after several years of Pali studies. But no doubt the Pali schools have made some improvement here.

In the secular sector the government wisely encouraged technical education—science, medicine, and agriculture—so that Cambodia probably does not have the surplus of lawyers and economists that India used to have. A Buddhist education is of necessity geared towards the humanities, so that the most useful forms of employment, like agriculture and engineering, are closed to the poor student with monastic training who is obliged to indulge in such luxuries as philosophy, linguistics, or archaeology. Of course this paradox applies only to the few at the top; the majority probably end up as teachers. As monks study all subjects through the medium of Khmer and not French, they may be specially well-qualified to help with the Khmerization of instruction (Vann Molyrann 1967).

This whole development was disrupted in Cambodia in April, 1970. In 1952, the Khmer branch of the Viet Cong claimed to be following the tradition of revolutionary Buddhist monks, and it was proud of having several Buddhist monks of repute on its committee. They also wrote that "the schools opened in liberated areas taught people how to read and write Pali" (Khmer Peace Committee 1952:21). Now it seems, at least according to the official *Cambodian News*, that the communists are concentrating on liquidating the *sangha*. They destroyed 208 pagodas and after a year of war only one-half of the original 70,000 monks were still in the monkhood and alive (*Cambodian News* 1971). Monks who did not leave the monkhood under pressure or were not killed are said to be concentrated in the towns where army protection is available. As all higher schools have always been in towns, many more monks may be using this unfortunate situation to study—or at least the number of students should not diminish. But the elementary Pali schools are bound to be affected.

According to information received in July, 1972,[1] the interest in monkhood is indeed increasing, at least in areas under government control.

While the Khmer-Reds do not persecute monks in the same way as the North Vietnamese, they do not support them. They do not allow members of the *sangha* hierarchy to attend their annual congress in Phnom Penh, they nominate their own monastic dignitaries with a *sanghadhipati* at the top of the hierarchy, and they hold their own monastic congresses every six months in the forest. They also stop young men from becoming monks.

In the Khmer Republic parents now encourage their sons to enter the *sangha*, partly in the hope that in this way they will not get involved in fighting. On the other hand the qualifications gained through monastic education are recognized by the Khmer government, and in the army a bachelor's degree leads to the rank of sublieutenant, a master's degree to that of lieutenant. Though until now military service has not been compulsory, there is no shortage of volunteers, and especially in the military police there are fewer places than applicants.

The increased interest in ordination is best seen in peaceful Battambang province where the number of monks doubled. In July, 1972, it was proposed to increase the salary of Pali school teachers from 1,500 riel to more than 3,000 riel per month. The Buddhist lycée in Battambang prepares students only for their diploma; at the lycée in Phnom Penh they study only for the bachelor's degree while the university has now only master's students. Apart from the two Buddhist lycées, three Dhammaduta colleges were started, two in Phnom Penh and one in Battambang. In these colleges teaching is done by unpaid volunteers, mainly university students.

The number of students admitted to the Buddhist University each year has also been raised. In 1971, sixty new students were admitted,

[1] Personal communication from the Venerable Tor-Ann Aggarato, lecturer at the Buddhist University in Phnom Penh (to whom I am also obliged for several corrections in this text).

12

and, in 1972, there were 200 first year students, divided into four classes. As of 1972 the entrance examination to the Buddhist University has been abolished. All students now receive scholarships which are fixed at 300 riel per month for a bachelor's degree and 600 riel for a master's degree. (A lay master's student in the Arts University in Phnom Penh receives 900 riel per month.)

These developments seem to confirm my hypothesis at least for the government-held areas. Whatever may be happening now in other parts of Cambodia, in 1966 it seemed that the improved system of higher monastic education saved at least some monasteries from extinction and so preserved the traditional focus of village life and the traditional village structure. Social change initiated by modernization in the secular education field was cancelled out by modernization in the monastic system.

REFERENCES

CHATTERJI, BIJAN RAJ
   1964   *Indian cultural influence in Cambodia*. (Reprint of 1928 edition.) Calcutta: University of Calcutta.

CHAU-SENG
   1962   *L'organisation buddhique au Cambodge*. Phnom Penh: Université Buddhique Preah Sihanouk Raj.

CHOAN; SARIN
   1970   Le vénérable chef de la pagode de Tep Pranam. Bulletin de l'École Française d'Extrême-Orient 57:127-54.

EBIHARA, MAY
   1966   "Interrelations between Buddhism and social systems in Cambodian peasant cultures," in *Anthropological studies in Theravada Buddhism*. By Manning Nash et al., 175-196. New Haven: Yale University Southeast Asian Studies.

EMBASSY OF THE KHMER REPUBLIC IN LONDON
   1971   *Cambodian News*. August 19th.

ÉTUDIANTS DE LA FACULTÉ ROYALE D'ARCHÉOLOGIE DE PHNOM PENH
   1969   Le monastère buddhique de Tep Pranam à Oudong. *Bulletin de l'École Française d'Extrême-Orient* 56:29-56.

KALAB, MILADA
   1968   Study of a Cambodian village. *The Geographical Journal* 134: 521-537.

KHMER PEACE COMMITTEE
   1952   *Khmer armed resistance*. Cambodia: Khmer Peace Committee.

L'ÉDUCATION
1964   Cambodge d'aujourd'hui. *L'Éducation* 3:23–25.

TAMBIAH, S. J.
1968   "Literacy in a Buddhist village in northeast Thailand," in *Literacy in traditional societies.* Edited by Jack Goody, 85–131. Cambridge: Cambridge University Press.

VAJIRAPPANO, HUOT TATH
1962   *L'enseignement du buddhisme des origines a nos jours.* Phnom Penh: Université Buddhique Preah Sihanouk Raj.

VANN JOLYVANN
1967   La khmérisation de l'enseignement. *Le Sangkum* 26:54–59.

WYATT, DAVID K.
1969   *The politics of reform in Thailand.* New Haven and London: Yale University Press.

Yao (Iu Mien) Supernaturalism, Language, and Ethnicity

PETER K. KANDRE

The magical Taoists and ancestor worshippers of the present study, who use a Yao dialect as domestic language and who call themselves Iu Mien (or simply Mien) are mobile agrarians employing slash-and-burn, shifting cultivation. They have a long history of cultural and political interaction with South China and adjacent areas of North Indochina.[1] It seems that due consideration in regard to the supernaturalistic basis of their internal and external linkages and boundaries can elucidate the long-debated problem of ethnic and linguistic persistence in complex cultural and residential interpenetration. The manifest and latent function[2] analysis used in this paper will be focused first on the rules and idioms of ceremonies in which identities are ascribed, supernatural power is delegated, statuses and values are articulated and roles are performed in accordance with: (a) the

For administrative and financial support I am indebted to the National Research Council and the Public Welfare Department of Thailand, UNESCO, the Swedish Councils for Humanistic and Social Science Research, and the Carl-Bertel Nathorst Foundation. I am grateful to the Rector of the University of Uppsala, Torgny Segerstedt, and to the Kurt and Alice Wallenberg Foundation for a grant to support my participation at the IXth International Congress of Anthropological and Ethnological Sciences, Chicago 1973.

[1] An impressive documentation on the ethnohistory of the Yao can be found in the Ph.d. dissertation of Richard Cushman (1970), who also provides a meticulous scholarly bibliography on the Yao.

[2] By "latent function" is meant, following Merton (1957), the "unintended and unrecognized consequences ... for a specified unit (person, subgroup, social or cultural system) which contribute to its adjustment and adaptation." The paired counterpart of this concept is the "manifest function," which refers to intended and recognized relationships.

Confucian concept of a ceremony as the correct expression of sentiments, appropriate in a social situation; and (b) the quasipolitical
concepts of hierarchies of supernatural rulers, dispensers of magical
power.

These native tenets are then made ethnoecologically relevant for
the group's adaptations in a concrete region. Finally, Mien self-
identification will be related to concepts of purity and pollution.

The themes of the paper closely relate to the author's earlier statements concerning the cultural ecology of the Mien of Thailand,
Laos, and Burma (Kandre 1967; 1970) and the dynamics of their
domestic group (Kandre and Lei 1965; Kandre 1971). The 1967
article (delivered for publication during ongoing fieldwork in 1965)
stresses—and I believe quite correctly—the crucial significance of
believed-in transcendent frameworks of powers that combine temporal and supernatural elements for Mein choice and action. The
ethnospecific cultural subsystem is called by native informants "The
Custom" (*lĕi nyèi*), which corresponds to the Chinese concept of *Li*
[good customs, rites and ceremonies, natural law, in human society]
(Needham 1956:519, 521–522, 530–532, 544ff.). In native Mien
theory it encompasses the properties of social life that have to be
maintained (in the interest of long-term survival) in the ongoing
process of opportunistic, situation-specific adaptations (in the
interest of short-term viability) to local supernatural and temporal
powers. Short-term, situation-specific adaptations are suggested by
the native term *lei fĭng*, and they are viewed as necessary complements to "The Custom."

The data were mainly collected (1964–1966) among the approximately one thousand Yao speakers (Iu Mien) of the Mae Chan region
of northern Chiang Rai Province of Thailand. The ethnography of
this extended case category relates, however, to a wider setting than
Mae Chan in the 1960's. With few exceptions, the senior members of
the group were born in adjacent parts of northwest Laos or northeast Burma, where in many cases they had essentially built their
careers before they came to Mae Chan approximately between 1948
and 1963. This somewhat vaguely defined zone of narrow alluvial
plains and vast areas of broken hill terrain (originally covered with
monsoon forest) in the lower foothills of the Himalaya range (alti-
tudes usually below 2,000 meters) is drained by the Mekong and its
tributaries. It will be referred to in this paper as the Upper Mekong.

MIEN LANGUAGE AND IDENTITY

According to G. Downer the Mien dialect of Yao (*mîen wàa*) contains, like the related Meo dialects, many loanwords from various
Chinese dialects, giving evidence of a great variety of contacts with
Chinese culture. Many men among the Mien of Thailand, Laos, and
Burma speak modern southeast Mandarin dialects and are semiliterate in Chinese script. What is known about Yao dialects suggests
that Mien probably has the widest geographical distribution—from
northern Kwangtung down to Laos and Thailand (Downer 1961;
1973). The same general distribution has been independently established by the writer for the residence/graves of the ancestors of the
Mien of Thailand, Laos, and Burma on the basis of genealogical and
other native literary documentation (Kandre 1967:631–636; unpublished field notes 1964–1966).

If Mien dialect is coextensive with a specific ethnic identity—
which I consider possible—one might expect to encounter it among
native criteria for classifying people as Mien. This is, however, not
the case. My informants distinguish between definition of identity/
status and the actual performance in the corresponding role. Of
course, the skills and resources that can in fact be necessary for
adequate performance in a role (e.g. linguistic competence and
wealth) do not necessarily appear in a stipulation of the rights and
obligations of a status. Among the Mien identity is ascribed as a
combination of name and rank, to which graded doses of supernatural power, blessing, and purity are usually attached. Obviously,
linguistic competence cannot be ascribed; it must be achieved.

In the process of ascription/delegation the receptor remains silent.
The talking is done by a mediator who introduces the person to
higher authorities. The mediator usually also serves as a link in the
downward flow of power. For example, a baby introduced to the
family ancestors is lifted up by the mother. A male individual being
initiated to adult status through Taoist merit making remains pas-
sively seated and is "lifted up" by "teachers." The prospective
parents-in-law use intermediaries (matchmakers) and the couple is
"put together" and their married rank established in a wedding
ceremony. The couple's contribution is to remain silent and to show
deference to their social seniors.

Ethnic identity is ascribed (indirectly) as a consequence of the
individual's ritual incorporation into some of the patrilineal sub-
units of a superclan defined in terms of assumed descent from the

creator-god mythological ruler Pien Hung, sometimes also referred
to as Pien Kòu (Chinese *Pan Ku*). Among the Mien of Thailand,
Laos, and Burma, many individuals of alien ethnic origins—not only
babies, but children and even youths—are assimilated, and always
before they have acquired competence in Mien language. I do not
know any case where Mien ethnic identity has been ascribed after
the person has learned to speak Mien. However, the member's initial
skills are irrelevant for inclusion or exclusion. One is Mien by virtue
of his belonging to certain temporal or supernatural masters who in
turn belong to other masters. Membership thus adheres to a chain
of control/ownership relationships.

Ceremonial Communication

Ascription of ethnic identity among the Mien involves the establishment of a relationship of belonging—in the sense of being controlled
and protected by a parental couple with affiliated ancestor spirits (the
supernatural owners of the family). Ideally the latter are the father's
patrilineal ascendants and their spouses. The inclusion of a new
member into the ethnic category amounts to the formation of a new
parent-child relationship, which among the profoundly sinicized
Mien is the very obvious locus of the norms and values of Confucian
filial piety (*khyao*, derived from the Chinese *hsiao*).[3] For an individual who subscribes to Confucian ethics, filial piety takes precedence over other norms and values, prevailing even against state
law (Needham 1956:208, 245). It is culturally defined as the individual's reciprocation for the gift of life, nourishment, and protection
(Hsu 1969:2, 29–30; Kandre and Lei 1965; Kandre 1967:590, 607).
Although informants agree that Mien identity is ascribed independently from performance, they also agree that some people are
more filial than others and that some are better Mien than others.
Certain criteria, on which ethnic excellence is judged, are ritually
articulated on various ceremonial occasions of the *rite de passage*
type, when the basic meanings of social grouping and reciprocity are
particularly and clearly emphasized.

[3]   To denote the particular respect due to parents my informants gave the terms
tăai [to care for; to serve] and *thŭng nìm tĭe màa* [to revere father and mother],
which are also reported by S. J. Lombard in her very useful Yao-English
dictionary (Lombard 1968), which I did not have access to during my fieldwork.
According to Professor G. Downer of Leeds University, the Mien usage in the
Upper Mekong also includes the well-known Chinese term.

Erving Goffman (1956) coined the term "presentational rituals" for prescribed patterns of polite communication of messages serving to promote people's involvement in social interaction; he reserved the term "avoidance rituals" for the equally formalized paired counterpart referring to communication of information which serves to maintain social distance between, and autonomy of, the participants in the situation. These complementary behavior patterns are involved in a kind of dialectic give-and-take of "deference behavior" that "attests to ideal guidelines to which the actual activity between actor and recipient can now and then be referred" (Goffman 1956: 479). To avoid anarchy, individuals must be reminded, at least symbolically, of the underlying order (Leach 1954:16).

Marriage and Ethnicity

Traditionally, the native document in Chinese script, from which translated extracts will be offered, has been used in the wedding ceremony (I have not seen it used in Mae Chan), from which it also has received its name: the *Book of the marriage custom (tsîng kjaa lēi sòu)*. It is recited (sung) aloud in Mien "song language," while simultaneously held by representatives of the bride-givers and bride-receivers (see Plate 1). Its idioms are explicit and unsophisticated:

. . . Pien Kou, Sing Hung, opened the sky, raised the earth and made the ten countries in the four directions. Kuu Hung made the heaven. Paeng Hung made the soil, created the forests and the water-sources, made the rice and the rice-fields, made the *yin* and the *yang* principles, created the hundred surnames [the patrilineal surname categories, i.e. the *hsing* of the Chinese and the *fing* of the Mien] . . . Sing Hung [bisexual] gave birth to six men and six women and married them with each other . . . Confucius made schools and books and the rulers among men . . . The Ming dynasty was born and destroyed everything, killing a multitude of people. Afterwards the heavenly father Pien Hung sent the Five Banners Cavalry [*mkêe peeng mãa*; i.e. tutelary spirits] to save life . . . Sing Hung died after 1,754 years. Six men/sons received six surnames and six women/daughters received six surnames . . . They were given passports for moving through the wilderness . . . When everything was ruined Heaven changed the ruler . . . Iu Mien moved the twelve surnames to Kwangtung, where they settled to plant and to sow. Then we come to the year of the Tiger, when Heaven sent three years of great drought . . . The multitude of men drifted away. Everything was eaten up and everybody was impoverished. The lords ate lords and the multitude of common people ate common people. The twelve Iu Mien surnames floated across the sea. For three months they could not reach the shore . . . The Mien were at a loss. There was no ladder to the heaven and no gate into the earth. They feared that storm would blow them down into the open door of the Dragon. Only Pien Hung, the divine father, could help. The twelve Iu Mien surnames in the boats appealed to the Flag Soldier of Pien Hung. They made a covenant for the protection of the people [the Mien promised subsequent sacrifices of pigs in return for their rescue from distress]. After three days the boats reached the shore . . . They stayed in Saa-tsiu Fuu, Loo-tshiang Shien [in North Kwangtung Province] and then raised hands for greeting before going where each of them desired. Some are in Kwangtung, some in Kwangsi, some in Huu Kwang [Hupeh-Hunan], some in Yunnan and some in Vietnam. You are staying in the east. I am staying in the west. And we do not meet yet. We move back and forth and meet again, because you have raised a son who needs a wife and I have raised a daughter, who needs a husband . . .

The document also emphasizes that "a man must have a cap and a woman must carry even boards." The Iu Mien of the Upper Mekong represent the same category of people whom the Chinese called variously Paan [Board] Yao (Wist 1938:80); Taa-Paan [Big-Board] Yao (Bonifacy 1908:879); or Ting-Paan [Mortar-Board] Yao (Warry in Scott and Hardiman 1900:602).[4] These "boards" of the female headgear have been a conspicuous distinction from the external observer's point of view.

"Big boards" refer particularly to the large supporting frame of the ceremonial wedding coiffure, still used in the Upper Mekong (see Plate 1). Today the Mien females in the area do not use boards in their everyday attire. They wear instead small turbans. Approximately in the last decade of the last century, the daily use of boards was abandoned, possibly under the influence of Tai-Lue fashion. However, the symbolism of the big boards in weddings persists. It

---

[4]   Warry met the Mien of the Upper Mekong in the end of the last century: "The men all wear the queue and dress like Chinamen, but the women retain the tribal costume—a short jacket with richly embroidered edges folded across the breast in what milliners call cross-over blouse fashion, and a short skirt, open in front like that of the Burmese. But the chief characteristic is the exaggerated mortar-board, a sort of 'cart-wheel' college cap. This is a square framework of bamboo covered with leather and supported by struts at the height of some inches above the head. The hair is carried up in a rope or column through this and fastened down with gum or stick lac on the leather, and then the whole is covered with red cloth with pendent tassels. Such a headdress cannot be done up every day, and the misery of learning to sleep with this roof projecting over the head can only be equalled by that of the Padaung women of Möng Pai with their foot-wide brass tube collars, or of a fashionable Chinese lady with her hair gummed into the semblance of butterflies or flowers. The head covering is so striking that it monopolizes all attention and has prevented any one from passing an opinion on the personal appearance of the wearers" (Scott and Hardiman 1900).

suggests the importance of affinity for ethnic solidarity, which the *Book of the marriage custom* defines through idioms that, along with the concept of a common source of supernatural power, emphasizes complementary relationships (organic solidarity) between parents-in-law.

What evidence there is from the Upper Mekong attests to the critical function of ethnic endogamy for males; i.e. Mien males are expected to marry only females who have been previously incorporated into, and socialized in, Mien domestic units. The only other Yao speakers in the area are the so-called Lantien [Indigo] Yao of Laos, and also with regard to them, the big boards constitute a clear ethnic marker. The Lantien brides do not carry big boards and the Taa-Paan males do not marry Lantien. Various elaborations of this theme are possible, but they fall outside the scope of the paper.

CATEGORIES OF MIEN SOCIAL ORDER

The ordering of social life among the Mien proceeds through the ideally uninterrupted succession of interlocking dyadic relationships, which, through the principle of the precedence of the donator over the receptor define grouping and status.[5] The largely coincidental idioms of Mien socioethical discourse and ceremonialism, relating to descent and marriage, actualize the analytical distinctions of compartmentalization and linkage, variety and similarity, and, very importantly, reciprocity.

The organizational framework of the domestic situation is provided by the coresidential lineage segment. The terms by which it is designated (*kjaa, hŏu* or *tšòu*) are derived from the Chinese terms for family (*kia*), household (*ho*), and patrilineage (*tsu*). The coresidential segment is ideally recruited—a significant proportion of its members may consist of adopted aliens—through patrilineal descent, patrilocal marriage, and assimilation of wives. In reality, an initial period of residence may be with the wife's parents for settlement of part of the quite important bride price in work instead of in cash. More rarely, the whole of the bride price is paid in work. When this happens, uxorilocal residence may extend over twelve years, which is the amount of time normally considered equivalent to full bride price.

---

[5] This is a fundamental premise of Chinese culture which establishes the *donator* (father, heaven, king . . .) above the *receptor* (mother, earth, people . . .) (Needham 1956:313).

Men very rarely permit themselves to be adopted by their fathers-in-law, although it happens that when the wife is her parents' only child, the marriage contract includes a clause according to which, for example, half of the offspring will be adopted by the parents-in-law. No case of neolocal marriage has been recorded. The developmental cycle of the coresidential segment normally involves the older sons leaving home in succession and establishing their own residences. Despite the Chinese-inspired concept of the precedence of the oldest brother, there are proverbial expressions concerning the relative excellence of the last-born.

The coresidential segment is the effective unit of the ancestor cult, which follows a written list. This has a spine of nine generations of direct patrilineal ascendants and their spouses. To these are often added childless or unmarried patrilateral descendents (if they reached adulthood). Also barren inmarried women and adult spinsters of the lineage are included. As a regular complementary element, the lists contain postmortem titles of the purified souls of the dead parents of the women assimilated through marriage. This ritualization of complementary filiation continues through the inmarried women's lifetimes—or permanently if it has been stipulated in the marriage contract. The underlying postulate is that the identification between parent and child is so close that not even the child's marriage can obliterate it. Sometimes first husbands of remarried widows appear among the ancestors of the wife's second husband, i.e. when the first marriage remained childless.[6] In both cases, it is believed that ritual neglect will lead to physical weakening of the daughter/wife.

The Mien pattern of the ancestor cult suggests that certain norms and values of filial piety and Chinese-type marriage are accentuated more, in terms of the implications of the general postulates (for these, see Hsu 1969:65–71), than they are among ethnic Chinese—to judge on the basis of available literature on Chinese religion and kinship. The serious possibility remains, however, that similar complementary cults have also been maintained by ethnic Chinese (e.g. by peasants) but that the ethnographical documentation is simply incomplete.

The ancestor lists contain information about the original surnames of the ancestors, Taoist titles (obtained in feasts of merit), and often, but not always, information about the topographical location of the

---

[6]   Being childless is a major individual and social problem, which one always attempts to solve by adopting children, mostly from alien ethnic groups. However, such adoptions are not always successful.

ancestral graves and about the political landlord (*tii-tsu*) in whose domain the grave lies. The document sometimes also contains instructions for the performance of rituals: e.g. the amounts of ritual paper money and "horses" that are due to the family ancestors and to the ultimate ancestor, Pien Hung.

The coresidential segment is the core of the operational household, "one-house people" (*yèt péao mîen*), which may possibly include sons-in-law, parents of inmarried women or of adopted children, and sometimes (though very seldom) nonkin like hired hands, for example. The house is the main forum for social activities and the household is the focal unit of everyday life. The other organizational forms seem to serve—if the abundant ethnographical evidence is taken into consideration—as props for the ongoing adaptations of the coresidential segment/household; sociologically, they may be relatively unimportant.

The large majority of the Mien of Upper Mekong (approximately 85 percent) have been born in Mien homes and an even larger proportion are socialized from early childhood in Mien homes. A certain number of aliens are adopted after they have reached puberty to spend their adult lives in Mien homes. Most of the time that is not allocated to subsistence activities is used for participation in exchanges, politics, feasting, and ceremonialism in which Mien domestic groups, singly or in multiple combinations, are involved.

When they die, most of the Mien die in their own homes. It is considered a great misfortune to die elsewhere. People who do not belong to the coresidential segment are not permitted to die in the house. Exceptions are those people who have contractually secured for themselves places among the household ancestors.

The coresidential segment is the strictly exogamous unit among the Mien and the effective unit for establishment of affinal relationships. Coresidential segments which are linked by genealogically identified common ancestors, particularly when these are close, or which are related through marriages of actual or earlier members, tend to combine as village neighbors and as sponsors of the expensive Taoist feasts of merit. The important distinctions from the individual male actor's point of view are those between: (a) relatives of the same (his own) lineage (*tŭng tsŏu tshien*); (b) relatives of lineages/segments from which his mother and wife originated (*ngooi tsŏu tshien* [outer-lineage relatives]); and (c) relatives on his outmarried female relatives' side (*sía?pung njei tshien* or *tse mùi tshien*).

After those in category (a), people in category (b) are relatively privileged by comparison with those of category (c), since one has to show special respect and regard to "givers." The underlying cultural postulate seems to be close to that of the Kachin *mayu–dama* relationship, where the bride-givers (*mayu*) enjoy a certain precedence over bride-takers (*dama*) (Leach 1954; Lehman 1970). In the Mien system the donator-receptor relationship is, however, not as neatly maintained in terms of prescribed asymmetry of marriage exchanges. In terms of ceremonial rank, parents-in-law face each other as equals. They are viewed as parties in a complementary relationship.

The nonlocalized lineage (*tsŏu*, from Chinese *tsu*) is not a group, but a category of people who do not necessarily know about each other's existence, but who may, when they meet, identify each other through pedigrees.

The patrilineally defined networks are contained in named clans (*fīng*), which, through the assumption of common ancestry, are understood to be the maximal units of "real" kin, as contrasted to the more general concept of kinship (*tshien*), which also involves affines. The term used for the clan grouping is the same as that used for the surname category. Clan relatives are referred to by the same term (*tung tsŏu tshien*) as are the relatives of the coresidential segment and lineage.

Clan names sometimes suggest special functions in the ceremonies addressed to the ultimate progenitor Pien Hung. Clans also have differentiated rituals, within the wider context of supernaturalism, which involves the annual cycles of ceremonies, incumbency in the role of a Taoist priest, and rules for the acquisition of magical power and titles. Clan membership may in some cases affect matchmaking for marriage. Certain clans are supposed not to marry women from certain other clans. Mien clans are not ranked according to principles reported from adjacent regions in Burma (Leach 1954; Lehman 1970).

The surnames (*fīng*), already mentioned in the myth of origin, assemble clans under labels that are meaningful for the mythological and genealogical discourse with the concept of the ultimate patriarch and his twelve children constituting the primordial locus of filial piety. The surname enters as an element in the personal names both of males and females. However, people of different clans who have the same surname do not refer to each other as relatives (*tshien*).

Piety for the Ethnic Progenitor

Pien Hung's position in the Mien world view has been described by Lei Tsan Kuei in the following terms (extracts from field notes 1965).

. . . Pien Hung is on a level with or above the gods of the "celestial government," that have no connections with Mien ancestors. He did not create the world alone, but was helped by others, probably his brothers. Some people say that he had no wife, for, when he lived, there was no sexual intercourse. Some say that he had many wives. It is impossible now to know exactly. Pien Hung resides in the highest of heavens and helps and protects those who present him offerings and show him respect. When a man has become wealthy and prosperous, having many sons and sons' sons, it has been the custom to invite Pien Hung, in gratitude. There is no rule how often the ceremony must be made. Everybody follows his own heart and judgment, making it once in every two, three or seven years. Earlier, more people than now made it, but even then not everybody. The very poor did not want or could not afford it. It is believed that when there are calamities like war, famine or epidemics, Pien Hung must be called at once. The ceremony is called "Turning it [i.e. a pig] to lie sideways" (*Waêng kûng kǎng*). For the smallest variety, a competent "minor ritualist" (*miên sib mién*) is enough, and the master of the house may perform. For the greater varieties the assistance of "grand masters" (*tûm sai kûng*) are required and the owner of the house must not perform as ritualist. The ceremony is made in front of the spirit shelf (household altar) and the ritualist must not use any other language than Mien when addressing Pien Hung. He must whisper in order to show special respect. Usually, more than ten persons are invited by the owner of the house to help in the preparations: to slaughter the pigs, to cut up and imprint paper to make spirit money, and to stamp horse figures on pieces of paper for the offering of horses to Pien Hung and to the ancestors of the family. Later, many more people arrive to eat and to drink. The usual variety is performed in one day. The greater ones require three days. Both need a minimum of two large pigs and some chickens. Women do not actively participate, except for one who cooks the rice. For this must be done by a woman. The pork that is not eaten is given to guests to take home. The two forelegs belong to the ritualist, who also receives silver.

The following extracts from my field notes are dated approximately one year later and relate to participant observation of "Turning it to lie sideways."

Date: 6th January (1966)
The ceremony will be performed to show gratitude and respect to Pien Hung, because everything is in good order and the family is prospering, and also to mark the fact that I shall soon leave the house after harmonious cooperation. It was particularly insisted upon by Yang Mui

Faam Kiem, the 87-year-old widowed mother of the owner of the house, Lei Tsan Kuei.

10 a.m.: An alien, a Shan by the name of Achan, who was temporarily hired for various chores, is sent away from the house.

11 a.m.: Spirit money and "horses" are prepared, and some "spirit gold" is produced, i.e. some of the sheets of home-made bamboo paper are colored yellow and hung up to dry in front of the house.

7 p.m.: The grand master Lei Fu Kwang arrives. The written ancestor list of the family is temporarily not available and the owner of the house recites from memory the names of the ancestors to be invited. The ritualist offers to the ancestors chicken, alcohol, and spirit money and invites them to the ceremony.

Date: 7th January

9 a.m.: Six men from the house owner's clan arrive to slaughter the two pigs. One of the pigs, especially raised for Pien Hung, is placed on a table, its back turned to the spirit shelf and is slaughtered in the usual manner, i.e. legs and snout are tied, and the carotid artery is perforated with a large knife. The blood is collected in bowls and the body is carried to the kitchen half of the house. The bristles are scraped off and the entrails are removed through a small incision in the belly. The meat is not cut up. The carcass is wrapped in paper and placed on a high bench in front of the spirit shelf, its right flank parallel with and close to the wall behind which the house owner has his sleeping quarters. Its hindquarters are turned towards the spirit shelf. The second pig, especially raised for the family ancestors, is slaughtered on the kitchen side and dressed in the usual manner. The meat is cut up, but the pieces are not dislocated. The carcass is then placed on a low bench (it is not wrapped in paper) with the snout pointing to the corner of the spirit shelf. In the empty space between the two benches, the directions of the long sides of which converge at right angles under the spirit platform, is placed a low stool for the ritualist.

10 a.m.: The spirit money that was prepared yesterday is divided into bundles which are carefully controlled by the ritualist. They will be offered to three different gods (brothers): Pien Hung, Lin Tsiu, and Tong Hung. They cooperated in the creation of the world and on various occasions when the Mien were rescued from imminent destruction. Some of the spirit money is tied by me to a bar that is suspended horizontally over the pig belonging to Pien Hung. This is my contribution to the ceremony. None of the participant males is permitted to remain idle. In marked contrast to all the other ceremonies at which I have assisted I am not allowed to use camera or to make tape recordings ("Pien Hung would not like it").

Noon: The grand master, carrying traditional Mien dress, sits down on the stool and begins to talk (in Mien). He addresses first (loudly) the family ancestors. These arrive first and eat first in accordance with the rule of etiquette according to which the less important guests arrive earlier but leave later than the more important ones.

1 p.m.: The ritualist puts on a black silk upper garment (belonging to the family) that is also carried by the grooms of the household in wedding ceremonies. He then addresses Pien Hung, whispering (in Mien).

Plate 1. Yao bride on the second day of her wedding. The man sitting is the bride's father-in-law addressing ancestral spirits.

Plate 2. *Kua Tang*: The initiates sitting.

An essential part of the ritualist's performance is to present himself and to explain to the gods the reasons why the ceremony is performed. The presentation involves not only personal data concerning the ritualist's background but also the ethnic identity of the Mien, the main features of which are contained in the *Book of the marriage custom*. The same principles for the definition of the situation appear in the ceremonies that are addressed to the Taoist "big spirits" (*tûm mién*), conceived as a celestial government.

Celestial Government

The ceremonies that are of interest for the present paper are social, economic, and artistic/dramatic structures of relatively short duration. On the other hand, they gather into particular houses considerable numbers of guests who may represent important sections of society through identification with specific households, villages, clans, and sometimes even with different ethnic groups and languages. A salient feature of the merit-making ceremonies, which are addressed to the Taoist gods, is their public character. The principle of exclusion of outsiders, which is prominent in ritual communications with the ethnic progenitor, is not emphasized.

The explicit purpose of the Mien feasts of merit is to increase the viability of the sponsors. For example, the *rite de passage* of *kwǎa tang* (illuminating lamp of *kua*[7]), that marks the entrance of the male initiate—and of his wife or future spouse—into social adulthood, is, according to grand master Lei Tsan Kuei "to improve their vigour so that they may be successful in their lives, that they may become great leaders, that evil spirits may not see them . . ." (see Plate 2). But the ceremony involves more than delegation of magical power. One of its central purposes is to teach basic human decency. For the initiates, it can be a profound psychological experience. It is also sociologically highly significant in the sense that it crucially involves some dyadic relationships of the authority structure of domestic situations, viz., father-son, husband-wife, older brother-younger brother, in that order.

In terms of supernatural reinforcement—delegation of supernatural power in the form of the "*yin* and *yang* principle soldiers"

---

[7] The term *kua* relates to the symbols, the trigrams, and the hexagrams of the *Book of changes* (*I Ching*), which in the traditional Chinese world view, are supposed to mirror the processes of nature (Needham 1956:304ff.).

13

(*yem paeng/yaang paena*)—the positions of father, elder brother and husband are associated with the position of donator, in the sense of being intermediary between the higher authority and the receptor. The pattern in the ceremony coincides with the emphasis on male dominance in the ideal Mien household (Kandra and Lei 1965). It is a fundamental rule that one of the "teachers" is always the father, but an elder brother can also occupy this position. In this particular initiation, the teacher-disciple relationship is quite formal. It is mainly a matter of delegating of magical power from the Taoist gods through the intermediation of grand masters. It does not necessarily involve actually teaching principles or precepts, which in the ceremonial context is the responsibility of the grand master.

The initiate shares the magical power thus obtained with his wife (or future spouse if he is unmarried), representing her in the ceremony by carrying the traditional upper garment for females. He keeps, however, for himself a majority of the "spirit soldiers." The proportion is three to two, which, as I understand, is a viable relationship between the *yang* and the *yin* elements according to Chinese metaphysics. Females are closely identified with their male counterparts in marriage.

Thus, among the Mien, the domestic dyads are interrelated, ordered, and ranked in the minds of people, not only in terms of the proper sentiments of filial piety, but also in terms of effective authority derived from magical Taoism, so that there is no doubt which of the dyads is the dominant one. The subsystems of kinship and supernatural "universalism" are mutually supportive, creating multibonded domestic relationships.

This does not, however, solve the problem of the function of Mien language. As we remember, in the sphere of ceremonialism addressed to the ethnic progenitor, the use of Mien is prescribed for the ritualist (to the exclusion of other languages) when he communicates with Pien Hung.

The Function of the Domestic Language

Language can be viewed as the repository of sentiments and values that obtain in the social context in which it is used and has developed. Prescription of a particular language in a particular social situation also implies the elimination from this context of those sentiments and meanings that are communicated through other languages:

What you say raises the threshold against most of the language of your companion, and leaves only a limited opening for a certain likely range of responses. This sort of thing is an aspect of what I have called contextual elimination (Firth 1964:69).

The Confucian notion of ceremonies (*li*), which is also quite obvious in the structure and content of Mien ceremonies, is one of orderly expression of sentiments appropriate to a particular social situation. As we have seen for the communications to the believed-in ethnic progenitor, only Mien language is considered appropriate. We can conclude that only the sentiments and meanings that relate to the use of this language are tolerated. And, obviously, the sentiments that are appropriate with regard to the "Father of the Mien" are the sentiments of the filial piety, which are communicated in the Mien domestic context in Mien.

Supernatural Constraints

But explanations of ceremonial structure in terms of appropriateness of symbolic expressions of sentiments must not lead us to underestimate the social significance of the quasisubstantive aspect of ceremonialism. Turning on the culturally determined belief that ceremonies are vital for the group's biological survival and material prosperity, they provide a means to effectively manipulate the universe.

The world view that determines the internal logic of the ceremonial operations (i.e. the arguments for the timing, choice of specific actions, paraphernalia and qualifications in the personnel) stresses quite neatly the fundamental importance of power structures as constraints for human choice and action. The universe is viewed in terms of hierarchies of power which continuously guide and correct processes of reproduction and destruction. The control is implemented through a system of sanctions. In this traditional Chinese supernaturalism, a powerful mechanism of social control, "guidance by the Way of the Gods" (Yang 1961:144–145), the supreme sources of authority are Heaven and Earth, whose wills are variously expressed and mediated by a "central government of the spirit world." The latter is viewed as a hierarchy of traditional Chinese immortals or divinities with specialized political functions for coordination, execution, reward, coercion, and education. The spirit government is headed by Nyud Hung [the Jade Emperor].

Ritual Expertise

Ritual expertise and leadership is validated among the Mien through a variety of roles: e.g. spirit medium, diviner, geomancer, healer, genealogist. The effective coordination of such minor practitioners is managed by high level nonmonastic Taoist priests, or grand masters (*tûm sai kûng*). These perform as leaders of ceremonies, drawing on authority that has been delegated to them by senior generations of grand masters. Presently, in the Upper Mekong, the network of teacher-pupil dyads is confined to intraethnic (Mien) relationships. But if viewed in a deeper historical perspective, Mien priesthood relates to the general supernaturalistic tradition of China. Certain ethnographic data suggest awareness by Mien priests of a connection with the Heavenly Leader of the Tiger and Dragon Mountain, the traditional and official head of the Taoist priesthood in China.

Effective performance in the role of a grand master of ceremonies requires competence (practical and theoretical) in the traditional Chinese technology of ceremony building,[8] some aspects of which are documented in the works of J. J. M. de Groot (1892–1910). These techniques involve handling liturgical texts, which presupposes a certain familiarity with literary Chinese, the special language of merit making. The formulas for communicating with Taoist divinities are codified in Chinese script, and the divinities to which the communications are addressed are believed to accept and understand only Chinese.

The participants' definition of proper behavior in situations of ceremonial merit making relates to the characteristic norms and values of the traditional (Imperial) Chinese ruler-subject dyad. These values establish the language of Confucius (the creator, according to Mien legendary tradition, of rulers, books and schools) as the appropriate language of the quasipolitical/quasijural discourse between the priestly mediator and the celestial government. The domestic language is contextually eliminated from this particular channel

---

[8]   My Mien informants are, for example, able to explain the principles of the Dragon Boat Racing of central China as reported by Yang Ssu-ch'ang (1588–1641) and partly analyzed by Chao Wei-pang (1943).

but not from the ceremony as a whole. Thus, in communication with family ancestors who always assist at merit making, Mien is used.

CULTURAL ECOLOGY OF THE UPPER MEKONG

No reliable history has been established concerning the migrations of the various ethnic elements in the Upper Mekong region, although, as far as we know, this region has continuously served as a reservoir for free-floating ethnic elements. Complex, frequent, and sometimes drastic population movements have been noted as a conspicuous characteristic of this frontier area, which has been exposed to many wars and population raids. The term "stable adaptation" when used, must therefore not necessarily be understood to mean uninterrupted residential continuity, not even with reference to sendentary paddy farmers. Sections of the Tai-Lue population were, for example, dislocated from their old state in southeast Yunnan (Sip Song Panna) and brought to Chiengkham in Thailand in the second half of the last century. This period was locally referred to as "the age of gathering vegetables to put into baskets; of gathering captives to put into settlements" (Moerman 1968:12). But population raiding was not the exclusive preoccupation of valley princes. Mien informants have mentioned that their ancestors sometimes raided other hill groups for children.

There is no evidence to show when the first representatives of the Yao-Meo category arrived in the Upper Mekong. Genealogies that note ancestral grave sites and oral family traditions suggest that the Mien definitely established their presence after 1850, moving in from adjacent parts of Yunnan. This is the period when the Tai Ping rebellion (1850–1864) and the Muslim insurrection in Yunnan (1855–1873) spread political unrest into adjacent areas of Tonking, Laos, and Burma. When the Mien arrived, not, it seems, in compact groups, but in a steady flow of households and combinations of households, they had to comply to the previously established political structures that involved Tai, Tibeto-Burman, and Mon-Khmer speakers.

Human adaptations in the culturally complex and politically anarchic situation in the Upper Mekong involve characteristic short-term and long-term relationships of linkage and segregation between different constellations of ethnic categories, exploiting different types of niches in the total environment. Sometimes, simple live-and-let-live, or peaceful symbiotic, relationships are sustained, but more often they are suspended and replaced, through influences emanating from the wider political setting, by strife, opposition, and even armed conflicts.

Inhabitants stably adapted to local conditions comprise two main subcategories, which are distinguished by different modes of exploitation of the natural environment. The alluvial valleys are inhabited by sendentary paddy farmers, who support traditional rulers, modern political entrepreneurs, Buddhist monks, artisans, and traders. The sparsely populated hills accommodate mobile agrarians, who use slash-and-burn shifting cultivation, growing mainly unirrigated rice and maize for subsistence and opium-poppy for cash.[9]

The valley peoples use various Tai dialects as domestic languages. Among these groups, the Lue and the Yuan have been particularly important for Mien adaptations. The hill Iu Mien and the Lantien [Indigo] Yao, together with mainly white Meo, represent the Miao-Yao linguistic family; the Tibeto-Burman family is represented mainly by the Akha, Lahu and Lisu, and the Mon-Khmer family by the Khmu and the Lamet. (The Lantien have now, however, largely established themselves in the lowlands.) Tai speakers use alphabets of Indian origin, while the Yao speakers exhibit, on a semiliterate level, much influence from the civilization of China. The cultural traditions of the other hill groups, however, are nonliterate. The *linguae francae* are Lahu, Yunnanese Mandarin and Tai.

A kind of symbiosis with the above groups has been achieved by a number of Yunnanese muleteer-traders and farmers (locally called Haw), among whom a significant element of Chinese Muslims can be found.[10]

---

[9]   The generalities of the cultural-ecological distinctions between hill people and valley people have been concisely established by Fortune (1939: 343–346) with reference to southern China and by Leach (1960) with particular reference to Burma.

[10]   There is a growing literature about the previously poorly documented Upper Mekong. The following works may provide, directly or indirectly, some basic elements of local ethnography. The list is in no way exhaustive:

Ethnographical overviews: Scott and Hardiman (1900: 576–620); Leach (1960); Young (1961); Kunstadter (1967).
Religion: Archaimbault (1964; 1972); Tambiah (1968); Spiro (1967).
Tai (especially *Lue*): Moerman (1967; 1968).
Akha: Feingold (this volume).
Lahu: Spielmann (1969); Walker (1972).
Lisu: Dessaint (1972).
Lamet (and *Khmu*): Izikowitz (1951).
Meo: Lemoine (1972).
Yunnanese Chinese (*Haw*): Mote (1967).

The various paramilitary groups that are found in the area, are, for the local population, a capricious, incalculable element in the environment. They are the main contributors to local insecurity and population movement. It is true that runners from wider political perimeters have been conspicuously present in the area as far back as the oral and literary evidence goes. But, on the whole, such groupings do not provide long-term identities. Some of their members marry local women, particularly from among the hill peoples, but the offspring are often assimilated into the wives' groups of origin. These patriots, adventurers, opium addicts, or businessmen represent a culturally mixed constellation of languages, religions, political ideologies, and commercial interests. Their presence in the area is largely an epiphenomenon of civic unrest in adjacent states.

The sendentary paddy farmers have been organized into small states. To these, the hill peoples have been affiliated through relatively impermanent semifeudal arrangements, traditionally involving oaths of allegiance to, and delegation of, supernatural authority from local Tai landlords. Politics have been combined with trade and channelled through valley centers. There, periodical markets have provided important opportunities for interethnic transfers (through purchase-adoptions) of children from dissolved or bankrupt families, particularly into the Mien ethnic category.

While a number of Mien women—often naturalized aliens or daughters of very poor families—are married to ethnic Chinese, I have not recorded a single adequately documented case of a regular Mien type of marriage between a Mien male and an alien female (if the term "alien" is used for a person that has not been previously socialized in the Mien domestic context).

Not only persons who lack offspring, but also the Mein in general, are usually eager to acquire children from other ethnic groups. As a result of continuous assimilation of people from a polyethnic environment, the Mien society in the Upper Mekong presently contains a minimum of 10 percent naturalized aliens among its married members. Marriage suggests full ethnic assimilation. Alien origins figure even more prominently among the unmarried. This discrepancy does not necessarily imply an increasing frequency of alien adoptions in recent times, since, in the initial period of "transplantation," mortality rates are considerably higher among alien children than among the corresponding age groups of native Mien children. Moreover, particularly in the cases of adopted males, adoptees tend to abandon their Mien homes upon reaching adulthood. Those who get married in Mien society, however, remain with the Mien.

The Mien multiclan and multisurname village (*laăng*) involve a single compact cluster of houses or a cluster of hamlets linked to water sources by bamboo aquaflumes. Preferably, the settlement is located in the proximity of some commercially important trail. Territorial boundaries are usually transitory and vague because land rights relate to usufruct and not to permanent ownership. Approximately 40 houses (250–350 persons) constitute the critical upper limit for demographic expansion in times of relative peace, i.e. when the settlements draw their sustenance from shifting cultivation and carry on commerce, unaided and undisturbed by external forces. Under conditions of civic unrest, and in commercially viable niches, more important aggregates tend to occur (compare Leach 1954: 24–28). It should be emphasized that Mien adaptations in the Upper Mekong usually do not involve long-term balancing of the ecosystems of swiddening, in marked contrast, for example, to the Lamet adaptations as reported by Izikowitz (1951).

Mien villages may admit "guests," e.g. Chinese. It is, however, expected that these will submit to the authority of the village "owners." When, as it sometimes happens, the guests become dominant, the Yao usually abandon the village site. Domination or defeat in such cases is explained in terms of the actions, both of ancestor spirits and of local spirits, which are themselves subject to the supernaturalism of local topography, the geomancy of "wind and waters" (*fung shui*).

THE STRUCTURE OF THE SITUATION

The valley peoples (Tai speakers) are Hinayana Buddhists. Their kinship systems are predominantly bilateral. Preoccupation with ancestors and related ideas of reciprocity seem to be confined— except in ruling families—to parent-child or grandparent-grandchild dyads. The hill peoples, on the other hand, are practically never Buddhists, although they may entertain certain notions borrowed from Buddhist metaphysics (e.g. concerning transmigration, retribution in hell). In spite of some Christian missionary influence, the majority of them still practice a vigorous animism. This usually involves, apart from a variety of elements that seem to be borrowed from popular Taoism and Buddhism, multigenerational ancestor worship. The latter closely relates to the principle of unilineal descent, prominent in their obviously Chinese influenced kinship system. The Lahu seem to occupy, in this respect, an intermediary position between the Tai and such groups as Mien, Akha, Lisu, Meo.

Cultural contrasts are not precise but rather involve complex phenomena of overlapping and interpenetration, particularly on the level of political culture. Thus, the political linkages between the ethnic constellations of hills and valleys have traditionally had, and continue to have to some extent, counterparts in shared quasipolitical supernaturalism, oriented to spirits of past rulers of specific domains. The cults of supernatural landlords, usually of alien ethnic origins (in some cases, they relate to past Mien chiefs or titled native leaders of other hill groups) are a regular feature of the Mien annual cycle of ceremonies, organized according to the principles of the traditional Chinese calendar.

Ethnic identity and mobilization is locally important, but in the political field it variously combines with ethnically cross-cutting connections. Thus, while the Mien, as an ethnic community, draw on what they conceive as their exclusive source of supernatural power—viz. the ultimate ancestor Pien Hung and his tutelary spirits, "Flag Soldiers"—certain individuals have access to personal Flag Soldiers. These are inherited patrilineally from chiefs who have usually acquired power and legitimacy from alien authorities (Tai or Chinese). The villages or polyethnic clusters of villages have been variously affiliated through headmen (*tao miên*) or chiefs (*tûm tao miên* [Mien: big headmen]) with the centralized political systems of Laos, Thailand, and Burma.

Mien villagers in the Upper Mekong combine relative mobility with notions of local spirit dominance that reflect the political history of the area. They view past political authority as a persistent attribute of the particular locality. An element of continuity, sustained by supernaturalism, transcends opportunistic short-term arrangements for the exploitation of natural and political environments. These ideas about the stability power distribution between persons and groups may be referred to, following Firth (1951:39–40) and Leach (1954:4), as the structure of the social situation in the Upper Mekong, as it is understood by the Mien.

The supernaturalistic element which promotes continuity has overridden even *de facto* military dominance. For, as Archaimbault points out, according to the Laotian tradition which has been continuously validated in royal ceremonialism, the principle of anterior right was recognized by conquerors:

Thus when the Laotian chief, according to the divine plan, came to set up the kingdom of Luang Prabang, he came into conflict with the Kha [Slave Peoples] who already occupied the land. These he had to evict. Recognizing their anterior right to land—and here is an important fact that the ritual emphasizes—he gave to his oldest son the name of the Kha chieftain whom he had just dispossessed (Archaimbault 1964:50).

PURITY AND POLLUTION

A study of the interrelationships between supernaturalism, language, and ethnicity among the Mien would be empirically incomplete and theoretically unsatisfactory if proper attention were not paid to certain characteristic concepts of supernatural pollution prominent in the Mien self-identification. The culturally determined phenomenon of supernatural pollution seems to be cross-culturally relevant for ethnic boundary maintenance in large areas of mainland Southeast Asia. Symbolic incorporation with Shan (Tai) civilization, according to Maran, is polluting for the upland Kachin:

"Members of the lowland *gumsa* society have been exposed to Shan influence and witchcraft and have stopped being real Kachins" (Maran 1967: 139). In order to be reassimilated among the "pure" Kachin they must be ritually purified (Maran 1967: 139).

The term "Mien" or "Iu Mien" is used in contradistinction to *kjăn* [alien], as in the Chinese *kjăn kae* [alien guests], and Meo *kjăn meo* [alien Meo]. The generic term for alien occurs also in the terms for "robber," "bandit" (*kjăn tsa?*), and "dead person" (*kjăn tài*). Both carry undertones of pollution. The latter term is never used for the ancestors of a family, the "family immortals" (*kjaa fin*), which are human souls extricated by Taoist priests from the polluting company of the homeless "murderous spirits." Informants characterize the latter as the bandits of the spirit world. These supernatural criminals mostly dwell in forests, attacking humans through disease and violent death. It has been maintained that the shortness of human life is largely due to such supernatural aggression. This contrasts with the postulate that "Mien do not aggress against Mien," implying that they constitute instead a community of harmonious complementarity for the prolongation of life and happiness. This postulate is closely related to the poetical expression, "one-house people living together in harmony" (Kandre and Lei 1965).

The foremost symbol of ethnic purity among the Mien is the small bamboo water container for the ethnic progenitor. Thus, in the ceremonialism addressed to Pien Hung, the prescription of domestic language (the language of filial piety) is combined with a concept of purity, validated in ritual action. One important theoretical conclusion to be drawn from this has been cogently suggested by Douglas:

The general processes by which language structure changes and resists change have their analogues at the higher level of cultural structure. The response to ambiguity is generally to encourage clearer discrimination of difference . . . Pollution rules can thus be seen as extension of the perpetual process: insofar as they impose order on experience, they support clarification of forms and thus reduce dissonance (Douglas 1968:339).

CONCLUSION

Evidence from the Upper Mekong attests to the critical function of affinity for ethnic solidarity among the Mien which is culturally defined through idioms that, along with the concept of a common source of supernatural power with its attendant purity, emphasize complementary relationships (organic solidarity) between parents-in-law.

To make analytical sense out of the native informants' assertions that language is not a criterion for being Mein, it is necessary to distinguish clearly between identity/status and role performance. Becoming a Mien and performing as a Mien are subject to different sets of rules and substantive constraints. Among the Mien, linguistic skill is irrelevant for an individual's incorporation, which is what determines whether he is classified as Mien or not. For adequate performance in the roles included in the Mien way of life, linguistic knowledge is crucial.

The social functions of the Mien and Chinese languages in the Mien context can be explained by combining the Confucian notion of a ceremony as the correct expression of sentiments appropriate to a particular social situation, with the concept of contextual elimination, which has been developed in sociological linguistics. The Mien language is appropriate in the domestic context for the validation of the values of filial piety. Chinese ritual is appropriate in the quasipolitical context of magical Taoism.

The functions of Mien ceremonialism for ethnic maintenance (integration and boundary maintenance) can be adequately analyzed as an ongoing dialectic of the presentation and avoidance rituals of deference behavior. This dialectic can again be viewed as part of a perpetual process of clarification of forms and reduction of cognitive dissonance.

To analyze the complex adaptations of the Mien in concrete situations of complex cultural and residential interpenetration, it is, however, not sufficient to view ceremonialism as straightforward symbolic communication between social actors oriented towards certain goals. It is equally essential to relate their cultural assumptions concerning supernatural constraints (both internal and external to the ethnic community), and including concepts of supernatural pollution, to the maintenance (largely unintended by individual actors) of authority structures, which are essential for the viability (in terms of mobilization and leadership) of operational groups.

REFERENCES

ARCHAIMBAULT, C.
  1964 Religious structures in Laos. *Journal of the Siam Society* 52 (1): 57–74.
  1972 *La course de pirogues au Laos: un complexe culturel.* Ascona: Artibus Asiae.

BONIFACY, A.
  1908 Monographie des Man Dai-Ban ou Sung (I). *Revue Indo-Chinoise* 9 (84).

CHAO WEI-PANG
  1943 The dragon boat race in Wu-Ling, Hunan. *Folklore* 2 (1):1–18.

CUSHMAN, R.
  1970 "Rebel haunts and lotus huts: problems in the ethnohistory of the Yao." Ph.D. dissertation, University Microfilms. Ann Arbor: University of Michigan.

DE GROOT, J. J. M.
  1892–1910 *The religious system of China*, six volumes. Leiden: Brill.

DESSAINT, A. Y.
  1972 Lisu settlement patterns. *Journal of the Siam Society* 60 (1): 195–204.

DOUGLAS, M.
  1968 "Pollution," in *International encyclopedia of the social sciences.*

DOWNER, G.
1961   Phonology of the word in highland Yao. *Journal of the School of Oriental and African Studies* 24 (3):532–541.
1973   Strata of Chinese loanwords in the Mien dialect of Yao. *Asia Major* 18 (1):1–33.

FIRTH, J. R.
1951   *Elements of social organization.* London: Watts.
1964   [1935] "On sociological linguistics," in *Language in culture and society*, 66–70. Edited by Dell Hymes. New York: Harper and Row.

FORTUNE, R.
1939   Yao society. *Lignan Science Journal* 18.

GOFFMAN, E.
1956   The nature of deference and demeanour. *American Anthropologist* 58:473–502.

HSU, F. L. K.
1969   *The study of literate civilizations.* New York: Holt, Rinehart and Winston.

IZIKOWITZ, K. G.
1951   *Lamet: hill peasants in French Indochina.* Göteborg: Etnografiska Muséet.

KANDRE, P. K.
1967   "Autonomy and integration of social systems: the Iu Mien ('Yao' or 'man') mountain population and their neighbors,' in *Southeast Asian tribes, minorities, and nations.* Edited by P. Kunstadter, 583–638. Princeton: Princeton University Press.
1970   "Custom, grouping and career among the Taa-Paan Yao of upper Mekong." Unpublished academic dissertation, University of Uppsala.
1971   Alternative modes of recruitment of viable households among the Yao of Mae Chan. *Southeast Asian Journal of Sociology* 4:43–52.

KANDRE, P. K., LEI TSAN KUEI
1965   "Aspects of wealth accumulation, ancestor worship and household stability among the Iu-Mien Yao," in *Felicitation volumes of Southeast Asian studies presented to H. H. Prince Dhaninivat* 1:129–148.

KUNSTADTER, P., editor
1967   *Southeast Asian tribes, minorities, and nations.* Princeton: Princeton University Press.

LEACH, E. R.
1954   *Political systems of highland Burma: a study of Kachin social structure.* London: Bell and Sons.
1960   The frontiers of Burma. *Comparative Studies in Society and History* 3 (1):49–68.

LEHMAN, F. K.
1970　On Chin and Kachin marriage regulations. *Man* 5:118–125.

LEMOINE, J.
1972　*Un village Hmong vert du haut Laos*. Paris: Éditions du Centre National de la Recherche Scientifique.

LOMBARD, S. J., H. C. PURNELL, JR.
1968　*Yao-English dictionary*. Ithaca: Cornell University Southeast Asia Program.

MARAN, LA RAW
1967　"Toward a basis for understanding the minorities in Burma: the Kachin example," in *Southeast Asian tribes, minorities, and nations*. Edited by P. Kunstadter, 125–146. Princeton: Princeton University Press.

MERTON, R.
1957　*Social theory and social structure*. Glencoe, Ill.: Free Press.

MOERMAN, M.
1967　Being Lue: uses and abuses of ethnic identification. *American Ethnological Society. Proceedings of the 1967 Spring Meeting*.
1968　*Agricultural change and peasant choice in a Thai village*. Berkeley: University of California Press.

MOTE, F.
1967　"The rural 'Haw' (Yunnanese Chinese) of northern Thailand," in *Southeast Asian tribes, minorities, and nations*. Edited by P. Kunstadter, 487–523. Princeton: Princeton University Press.

NEEDHAM, J.
1956　*Science and civilization in China*, volume two. History of Scientific Thought. Cambridge: Cambridge University Press.

SCOTT, J. C., J. P. HARDIMAN
1900　*The gazetteer of upper Burma and the Shan states*, Part one, volumes one and two. Rangoon.

SPIELMANN, H. J.
1969　A note on the literature on the Lahu Sheleh and Lahu Na of northern Thailand. *Journal of the Siam Society* 57 (2):321–332.

SPIRO, M. E.
1967　*Burmese supernaturalism*, Englewood Cliffs New Jersey: Prentice-Hall.

TAMBIAH, S. J.
1968　"The ideology of merit and the social correlates of Buddhism in a Thai village," in *Dialectic in practical religion*. Edited by E. Leach, 41–121. Cambridge: Cambridge University Press.

WALKER, A. R.
1972　Blessing feasts and ancestor propitiation among the Lahu Nyi (Red Lahu). *Journal of the Siam Society* 60 (1):345–373.

WIST, H.
1938　Die Yao in Südchina. *Baessler-Archiv*, Band 21:73–135.

YANG, C. K.
  1961   *Religion in Chinese society.* Berkeley: University of California Press.
YOUNG, G.
  1961   *The hill tribes of northern Thailand.* Bangkok: The Siam Society.

Malay Migration to Kuala Lumpur City: Individual Adaptation to the City

T. G. MCGEE

> If there is something specific and peculiar to the Marxist approach to the study of man, it is in its stubborn effort to combine into a unified whole the multifarious and divergent images of man as seen from different points of observation. To use the modern technical terminology we can say that Marxist social science aims at a 'hologram' of man instead of series of photographs.
>
> ZYGMUNT BAUMAN[1]

Few urbanologists would deny the complexity of the city. Many would assert a simplicity in their assessment of the reactions of an individual who shifts his place of residence from the country to the city. In the analysis of the rural-urban movement of populations in developed societies, most notably the United States, the focus of sociological research has been largely on the maladjustment of the migrant in the urban milieu.[2] Of course, much of this work has been carried out in "capitalist" or "capitalist-penetrated" societies, but there is also some evidence of problems of adjustment to the urban environment occurring within socialist societies (Turski 1967:17). To some extent problems of adaptation are to be expected in situations

---

[1] In: "Modern times, modern Marxism," page 399.
[2] The most comprehensive review of prewar studies in Europe and the United States is found in Thomas (1938). Since World War II migration studies have proliferated in both the developed and underdeveloped world. Useful summaries of the literature can be found in Bogue (1959) and the Milbank Memorial Fund (1958). Reviews of the literature pertaining to rural-urban migration can be found in Epstein (1967); Mitchell (1966); Turner (1962); McGee (1964); Hauser (1957, 1961); Eames (1954); and Pryor (1971). The seminal theoretical papers on the subject still remain Simmel (1957: 635–646) and Wirth (1957:46–63).

14

where people move from peasant and tribal worlds into the different socioeconomic structures of the city, for there will be new situations relating to work patterns and to relations with work partners and neighbors.

However, in the postwar period, research focusing on the problems of migrants in the cities of the Third World, while indicating severe economic problems, has not always supported the assertion that the migrants suffer grave problems of social adaptation. For instance, Lewis' study in Mexico was one of the first to highlight this point when he said:

The preliminary findings of the present study of urbanization in Mexico City indicate quite different trends, and suggest the possibility of urbanization without breakdown. They also show that some of the hitherto unquestioned sociological generalizations about urbanization may be culture-bound and in need of reexamination in the light of comparative studies of urbanization in other areas (1952:31).

Work by Bruner among the Toba Batak of Medan led him to a similar conclusion: "It is clear that the social concomitants of the transition from rural to urban life are not the same in Southeast Asia as in Western society" (1961: 508).

Janet Abu-Lughod has made a similar point with respect to absorption of migrants into Cairo City (Abu-Lughod 1961:22–32). The work of Mayer among the Bantu in East London provides additional evidence that there are many migrants who never become committed to urban society no matter how long they live in the city (Mayer 1962). During the sixties the work of Mangin and others has further strengthened the conclusions of these earlier researchers (Mangin 1970), so much so that the cohesive aspects of the migrants' adaptative process to the city—associations, etc.—are being held up by planners as concrete elements which can aid the urbanization process (Turner 1967). An important research thrust among political scientists has found migrants more conservative and satisfied with their conditions than the Western-based theories predicted (Nelson 1970).

Thus all these studies, despite the diversity of the cultural milieux in which they have been carried out, reach much the same conclusion —migrants to the cities of the Third World are not experiencing severe problems of social adaption. Many reasons are produced to explain this phenomenon, but few researchers contest the original hypothesis that cities are places where social maladjustments occur.

They simply state that the hypothesis is not valid in their field area. It is the writer's view that this original hypothesis, framed as it was within the context of the rural-urban continuum, was quite false, for the constructed model of rural and urban behavior which was elaborated was inaccurate. I have already discussed this point at some length elsewhere (McGee 1971). It is sufficient to point out here that the assumption of a unilinear shift from rural to urban behavior associated with the shift from country to town was severely criticized.

I will try to show here that the level of individual adaptation indicates that the majority of migrants retain attitudes which may be regarded as both urban and rural at the same time. Perhaps these attitudes will change after long periods of residence and work in the city, but it is dangerous to argue that they will necessarily change because of the influence of the city. We do tend to underestimate the considerable capacity of the individual to hold seemingly antithetical attitudes at the same time and the range of choice that individuals have in deciding these questions. The following study of Malay migrants in Kuala Lumpur City is an attempt to test these assumptions.

MALAY MOVEMENT TO KUALA LUMPUR[3]

Malaysia is a multiracial society in which Malays, Chinese, Indians, and other ethnic groups form what has been labelled a "plural society." Today it consists of three distinct geographic territories—the Malayan peninsula, Sabah, and Sarawak—but historically the development of Malaya and Singapore has been inseparable.[4]

This plural society grew up as a consequence of the extension of British control over the Malayan peninsula and Singapore during the nineteenth and twentieth centuries. The indigenous Malay population remained primarily in the countryside while the Chinese and Indians who arrived during the extension of British control tended to occupy the commercial sectors of the cities and the plantation labor forces. This created a situation in which the Malays were largely encapsulated within the peasant sector outside the cities. Only in some of the towns—in the predominantly Malay areas of the east coast and Kedah—did the Malay populations assume any dominance.

---

[3] This section is a considerably abridged version of McGee (1968, 1971).
[4] Despite the fact that today these are two separate states it is unrealistic to analyze them separately.

In the majority of the large towns of the west coast the Malays were historically a minority, a small community dominated by the Chinese. The capital of the present Malaysian Federation is Kuala Lumpur, founded in the 1840's, first as a raw and rambunctious Chinese mining camp. Later, in the 1890's, it became a major administrative center for the British as well as an important commercial center for the west coast as the rubber plantation industry expanded. Accompanying the expansion of these functions was a considerable increase of city population from 18,000 in 1891 to 175,000 in 1947. Throughout this period the city remained essentially an administrative and commercial center—a colonial city ruled by Europeans, dominated numerically by the immigrant Chinese and Indians, while the indigenous Malays remained marginal participants except for the Malay aristocrats who cooperated with the European rulers (Gullick 1956).

The period of the Japanese invasion in the early 1940's disrupted the structure of political power but did little to change the ethnic composition of the city or its functions. The reassertion of British control, the failure of the attempt to set up the Malayan Union, and the creation of the Federation of Malaya in 1948 with Kuala Lumpur as its capital led to a further concentration of administrative and commercial activities in that city. There was also a period of rapid devolution towards independence and of political instability associated with the communist revolt.

The 1955 elections saw the victory of the Malay-dominated Alliance Party in the newly-created House of Representatives in Kuala Lumpur, continuing the trend to centralize political control in that city. The rapid onset of independence precipitated the movement of civil servants, police, and army personnel to Kuala Lumpur. Many of the Malays from other states came to the capital so that for the first time in over a century the proportion of Malays in the total city population increased from 12.4 to 15 percent. The period since 1957 has seen an even more rapid growth of the city's population to almost half a million, increasing the proportion of Malays to 25 percent (Provencher 1971; Chander 1972).

The accelerated migration of Malays in this period appears to have comprised two broad streams. One stream of older married migrants moved with their families on transfer to take up government posts; a second stream of younger single males moved to Kuala Lumpur from the countryside in an effort to find jobs or for advanced education. On the whole, Malays have tended to occupy government jobs rather than commercial jobs which have been dominated by the Chinese.

In this movement of the Malays to the cities, there was, of course, a potential danger, for if the Malays did not find jobs in the Chinese-dominated city, they would put pressure on the Malay political parties to achieve this end. Thus the Alliance government encouraged programs of rural development and improved educational facilities to keep the Malays in the countryside. In this they were not markedly successful, and the communal riots of May 1969 between Malays and Chinese, while sparked by immediate political tensions, were fueled by this underlying failure.

INDIVIDUAL ANALYSIS: A HOLISTIC PICTURE

It is against this background of accelerating Malay movement to Kuala Lumpur and other cities along with the associated increase in Malay political power that the researcher has to assess the features of the Malay migrants in Kuala Lumpur. In 1962 and 1963 the author carried out a survey of 560 Malay households in Kuala Lumpur designed to obtain basic socioeconomic information and to assess their degree of adaptation to the urban setting. This was organized on a quota sample basis which represented a 5 percent sample of the estimated Malay population at that time. The following analysis is based on the data collected in that survey and during follow-up interviews and is an attempt to see the individual Malay in this city in his "totality."

I have not chosen to present the data in terms of a series of statistics categorizing a group—by date of arrival, for example—for this inevitably leads the researcher to argue that the group will act in the same manner, make demands in the same way or relate to the "urban situation" similarly. For as Bauman says, this group type of analysis is but a series of photographs departing from "man as such, pursuing the process of living through and by his social and cultural environment" (1967:399). Thus I have developed here an attempt to see each individual in the context of his urban situation. Twenty-eight indices have been chosen to measure each individual's urban adaptation to the "urban situation" of Kuala Lumpur.

It is at this individual level that the influence of *situational change*, to use Mitchell's term, seems most appropriate (1966:37–68). The forces of limited *structural change* have already allotted the individual to a broad socioeconomic position within the total society, but within that position the individual has certain possibilities of adaptation. The Malay in the city is encouraged to *accommodate* at a group level and *adapt* at an individual level. In this situation, the role of government is obtrusive and the preeminence of the non-Malay groups prohibiting. It is within this framework that individual adaptation occurs.

In choosing these indices, I have made certain assumptions that are generally in line with what we may label Western assertions concerning the urbanization process. Thus, for instance, I assume that the longer a person has resided in Kuala Lumpur, the more capable he is of adapting to the urban situation. I assume that if an individual is well educated, he will be more adaptable to the urban situation than the individual who had no education. I assume, too, that traditional stereotypes with respect to the city, for instance, the assertion that people are less friendly in the city than in rural areas, is a more traditional and less urban assertion than the claim that Malays in the city are more friendly. It must be emphasized that I do not claim that these assertions are necessarily a reflection of reality, simply that they are a reflection of a manner in which reality has been interpreted.

The twenty-eight indices which have been chosen are divided into seven main sectors:

1. Background situation
2. Respondent's socioeconomic background
3. Urban commitment
4. Respondent's present socioeconomic characteristics
5. Urban-rural ties
6. Communications and contact in the city
7. Urban attitudes

Within each of these sectors, a varied number of indices have been ranked according to a scale from 1 to 4. In every case, it is assumed that level 4 is the most urbanized, 1 is the least urbanized, while 2 and 3 represent points on a continuum between these two extremes. These are referred to as levels of urban adaptation throughout the remainder of the study and are equated with the four circles of the hologram. The outermost circle is thus level 4; the innermost circle, level 0.

Each individual household head was then assessed according to these twenty-eight indices grouped in seven broad sectors, and these

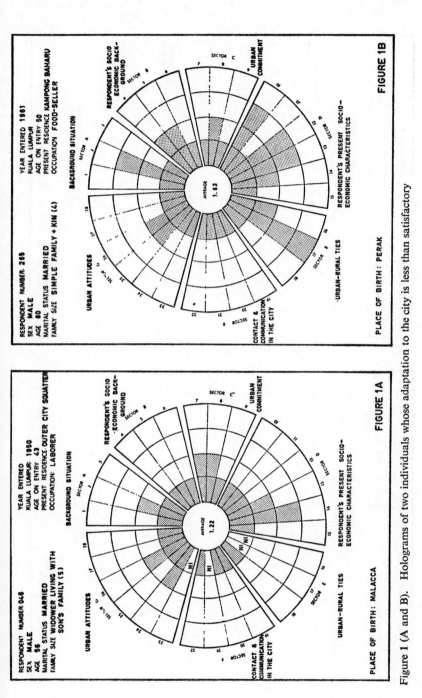

Figure 1 (A and B). Holograms of two individuals whose adaptation to the city is less than satisfactory

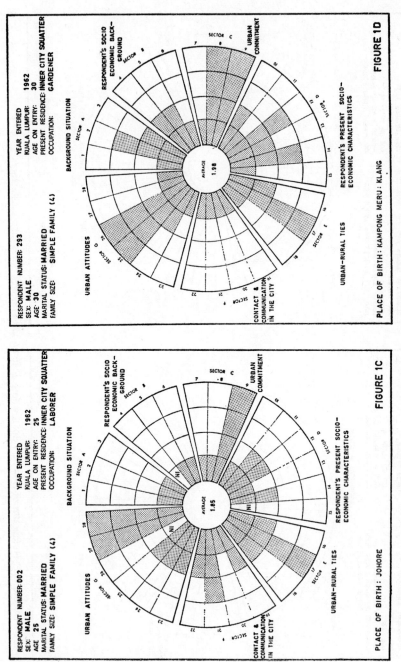

Figure 1 (C and D). Holograms of two individuals whose adaptation to the city is less than satisfactory

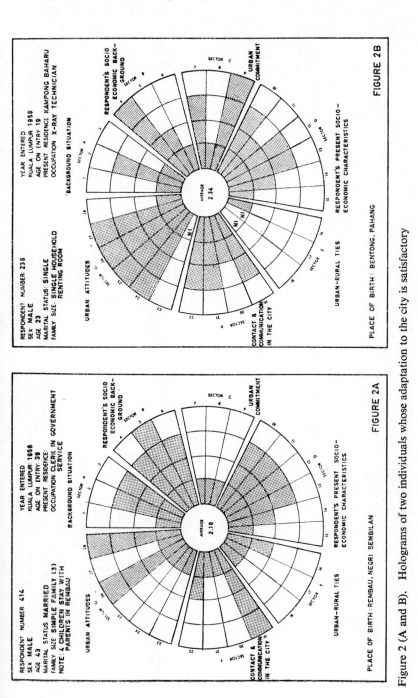

Figure 2 (A and B). Holograms of two individuals whose adaptation to the city is satisfactory

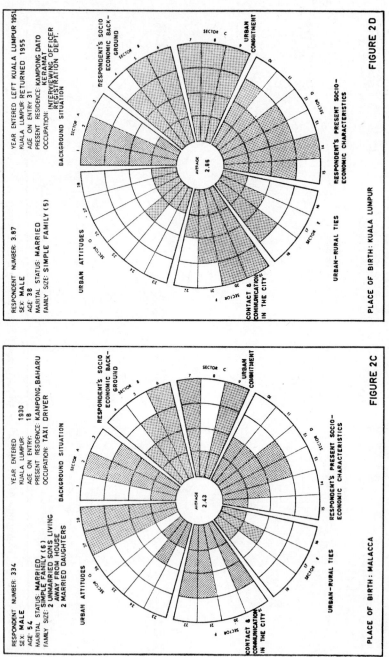

Figure 2 (C and D). Holograms of two individuals whose adaptation to the city is satisfactory

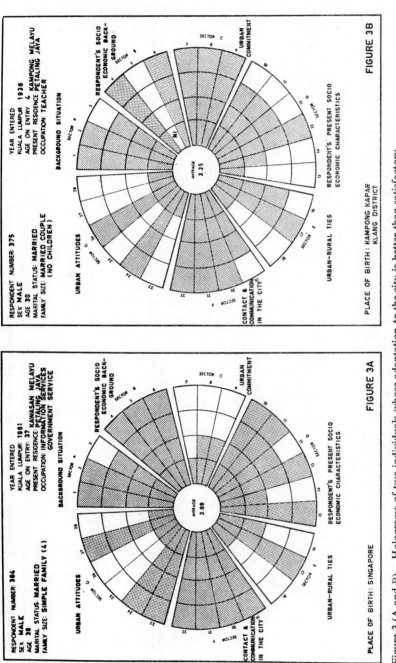

Figure 3 (A and B). Holograms of two individuals whose adaptation to the city is better than satisfactory

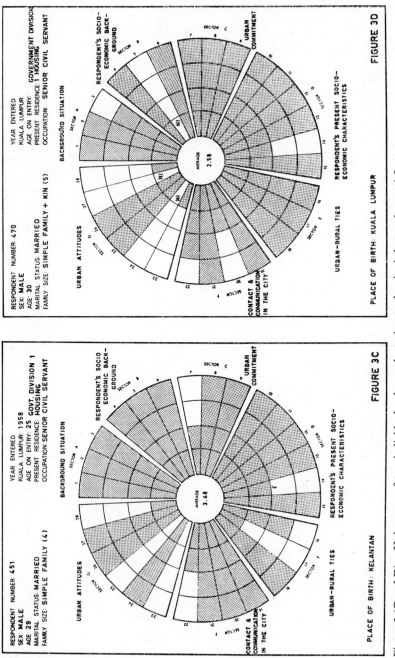

Figure 3 (C and D).   Holograms of two individuals whose adaptation to the city is better than satisfactory

were diagramatically shown on the holograms (see Figures 1–3 and Appendix). The numbers in the center of the hologram indicate the average score obtained by each individual on the four-point scale for the twenty-eight indices. Thus those individuals whose average score fell between 1 and 1.99 were least urbanized; those with scores between 2 and 2.99 more urbanized and those with scores of 3 and above the most urbanized.

The advantage of the hologram[5] is simply stated: it enables a quick, visual assessment of the structure of each individual's position to be ascertained, and in addition, allows a comparison at the individual level (not the group level) to be carried out. In the next section, I shall analyze each of these sectors of the urban indices.

It should be stressed that in presenting the data concerning each household head in this form, my aim is to illustrate the varied and often contradictory positions that an individual may assume when he or she lives in a city. Ness, writing about his interviews with government officials in Malaya, says:

Especially in an interview that stretches over more than an hour, and then continues over a "stengah" at the rest house or over cocktails at a party, people contradict themselves directly and indirectly, often more than once on the same subject. It is not that they lie or attempt to deceive the questioner, though this does happen. It is merely a reflection of the great human capacity for holding conflicting ideas with little strain (1967:x).

Indeed, it is clear that this great "human capacity for holding conflicting ideas" can be extended to an even broader capacity to adopt seemingly antithetical positions or postures. The advantage of the hologram is that it allows a more complex and holistic picture of the individual in the urban situation to emerge. He is not some passive adapter to an urban environment he cannot control. Thus we see an individual of complexity—there are no fewer images of the man who lives in a city than of the man who is a rural dweller. They are men—not urban men or rural men.

Some comment must be made about the limitations of the survey instrument as a means of collecting information for the ensuing holograms. The survey, to continue Bauman's analogy, is itself a photograph. Each questionnaire is delivered at a point in time and it records only a momentary slice of an individual's life. The reaction of the respondent may be distorted by the questioner's appearance; by his own immediate needs (at the end of a long tropical day: the

[5] These holograms are used to show a wide variety of socioeconomic data by place in Centre National Française de la Recherche Scientifique (1959).

need for food and sleep); by as many factors as one may conjure up. The photo may underexpose or overexpose—it is only a distorted moment of the individual's life. And these distorted moments we blow up into the reality of the total individual. The conclusion is obvious. The hologram, based on the survey, is only of limited value; and the author would have preferred to pursue the greater depth of the family studies as did Lewis in his significant work on Latin American families (1959).

INDIVIDUAL ANALYSIS: A HOLISTIC PICTURE

Despite these limitations the hologram does at least indicate that individuals do hold a complex and often conflicting set of *levels* (positions) on a theoretical rural-urban continuum. What is more, it is the argument here that no single variable, least of all the single fact of residence in the city, will act as an adequate explanation of the individual's behavior in the city. Rather, each action (in Western theory characteristically described as an "urban-influenced" action) will depend on a whole constellation of variables, as well as the position of each individual within his total society.

Thus it is the constellation which counts, not the single influencing variable. For instance, even a comparatively simple decision such as sending remittances to a relative in the countryside may be influenced by many other factors than the mere possession of money. The danger of seeking an independent variable in human behavior is the tendency to oversimplify man's actions. And this, of course, is the greatest weakness of the body of Western urban theory which has grown up, postulating the city as an independent variable.

In this section I have chosen twelve Malays from Kuala Lumpur City and constructed holograms to illustrate this point. The method of selection is not random; rather it is an attempt to indicate the spread of type rather than to be representative. The procedure was as follows: the 560 means were ranked from the lowest to the highest mean and four means selected for each level, aiming at as wide a spread as possible. On this basis twelve individuals were chosen and holograms constructed.

Level One: Marginal Urban Adaptation: Four Case Studies

RESPONDENT 046 (HOLOGRAM I): MEAN 1.22. Respondent 046 (see

Figure 1A) was ranked lowest of the completed holograms. A male of fifty-five, born in Malacca, he had been resident in Kuala Lumpur for twelve years; had been educated at Malay primary and worked as a farmer until the age of forty-three. In 1950 he left his farm in Malacca at the invitation of his son to join him in Kuala Lumpur. At the time he left for Kuala Lumpur he was unemployed, living on help from his nephew, and separated from his wife. In the twelve years since he arrived in Kuala Lumpur he has had three jobs. After four months of searching for a job, he found one as a laborer with a European firm. After that he was employed by the Central Electricity Board (again as a laborer). Finally, he took his present job as a laborer for the railway.

His lack of skills, Malay primary education, and low income did not help him in his general adaptation to the city. But he has taken some steps, notably purchasing a squatter house of fairly good quality in Kampong Haji Abdullah Hukum, which may lead him to settle more permanently in the city. Unfortunately, there is only limited information on his rural contacts but he has married again, a wife selected for him from his own district. He no longer owns any land in that district. (He comes from the Minangkabau area, where custom would prohibit his inheriting the land of his wife.)

Generally he seems undecided about Kuala Lumpur. He is uncertain as to whether he will stay there all his life for he prefers to work in his home area. In addition, he seems to take little advantage of the improved facilities of the city. He does not read newspapers or go to the cinema and knows very little about other areas of Malay settlement in Kuala Lumpur.

His attitudes toward such issues as traditional medicine versus Western medicine and the decline of religion in the city suggest no realization of the city as a breaking-down influence. He thinks that the *bomoh* [medicine man] (Winstedt 1951) is unquestionably best for illness of the mind or the heart (in the romantic sense), or *kena sumpah* [spells], while Western medicine is more suitable for physical injury. His attendance at mosque has not declined through residence in the city. He is no more interested in politics since he moved to the city. His only positive assertion concerned the lack of friendliness of Kuala Lumpur Malays.

This respondent shows the lowest level of urban adaptation on our scale but (as this analysis shows) he has by no means totally resisted the city. It would appear that kin ties are probably one of the most important forces holding him in the city, just as they drew him there.

As long as his son lives there, so will he. Meanwhile he has managed to coexist with the city, if not fully participate in it.

RESPONDENT 265 (HOLOGRAM II): MEAN 1.63. Respondent 265 (see Figure 1B) was the third lowest individual in terms of level of urban adaptation. Born in Parit Buntar in 1902, he had been living in a kampong four miles from Taiping for fifty-eight years, working a rubber "small holding." He had Malay primary education but no English education. Only recently arrived, he had come to Kuala Lumpur at the insistence of his brother-in-law in February 1961. At the time he left for Kuala Lumpur he still worked his own small holding, but felt he was growing too old to continue his work effectively.

In view of his recent arrival in Kuala Lumpur, it is perhaps not surprising that he is undecided how long he will stay. Certainly he is not enthusiastic to establish permanent residence, preferring to work in his home area. He still retains his land and home in his kampong, and presumably this offers some security if he desires to return.

He purchased a food-selling business in the Sunday Market three months after his arrival and is operating it with his brother-in-law. He claimed that his income was only $60 (Malayan) a month, but the interviewer commented this was very likely an underestimate. He travelled to Kuala Lumpur with his family, a daughter of eighteen at present teaching in a Malay school and a grandson of fourteen who is attending Secondary Continuation School (English) at Pasar Road. He rents a house for $36 a month, located behind the stalls, which is not elaborate but has adequate space and the basic amenities of electricity and water.

Relatively close ties are maintained with the rural home area. In the year that he has been in Kuala Lumpur he has returned to his home kampong three times for periods of up to twenty days, primarily to visit relatives and check on the condition of his rubber small holding. These trips back to the rural kampong are greatly facilitated by his self-employment. As his own boss, he can leave the business when he desires in his brother-in-law's hands. The example of this migrant shows the relative ease of circulatory migration between peasant and bazaar sectors of the economy. He does not remit any money to relatives in the countryside.

This migrant claims to have no time to read newspapers or attend the cinema. Instead, he must prepare food and sell it which takes all his spare moments.

His attitudes toward the urban environment seem to indicate a clear acceptance of what may be labelled the prevailing "rural" stereotypes. Yet the difference between attitude and action is quite marked. He is quite convinced that the people who live in the city are less religious, yet he attends mosque more frequently than he did in his rural kampong. However, he finds no marked differences between Malays in Kuala Lumpur and those of the kampong in terms of friendliness. The short period he has been in the city has neither increased his interest in politics nor changed his personality.

Like Respondent 046, he has entered the city at a much later age than most of the migrants—largely, it would appear, at the insistence of a relative. (But relatives' insistence aside, he still desires to return to his home.) His reaction to the city is on the whole not favorable. It is a place of work offering certain advantages for the education of his grandson and his own employment. His is a temporary and marginal adaptation.

RESPONDENT 002 (HOLOGRAM III): MEAN 1.85. Unlike the two earlier migrants, Respondent 002 (see Figure 1 C) arrived at the much younger age of twenty-five. He arrived in Kuala Lumpur almost a year ago with his wife and one child. Since his arrival a son, now three months old, was born. He rented a squatter hut for $20 a month in Kampong Sector almost immediately on arrival and was fortunate enough to acquire a job as a laborer in a sawmill within a few days.

His background is completely rural. He had worked as a farmer (rubber tapper) in his home kampong close to Bandar Maharani (MUAR) in the same occupation as his father. No information was gained about his education, but it may be assumed he had Malay primary education for he occasionally reads the Malay paper, *Berita Harian*. He claims that at the time he left for Kuala Lumpur he was temporarily unemployed but still suggests that his main reason for coming to Kuala Lumpur was more for curiosity (to see Kuala Lumpur) than his desire to find a job. There was no mention of relatives in the city.

While this respondent prefers working in Kuala Lumpur (in part because of the "broader outlook"), he still intends to return to his home kampong. The location and general condition of his house is poor. The roof is thatched and there is no piped water, sewerage or electricity. His income of $165 per month does, however, provide him with enough money to purchase adequate meals and clothing for his family. He has bought a bicycle to travel to work.

He maintains close contact with his home kampong (where his wife's parents also live), having returned four times since his move to Kuala Lumpur. These were all short visits (duration three days) except for Hari Raya when he and his family stayed for one week. He does not remit money to his relatives largely because he says there is not enough for his own family.

He does not make great use of the improved communications media of the city, reads *Berita Harian* occasionally, but he never attends the cinema. His closest friend is a driver from the same kampong, but his knowledge of other Malay areas in Kuala Lumpur is limited to the two adjacent kampongs—Kampong Semerang and Kampong Baharu. He finds little difference in attitudes; for instance, religious behavior and friendliness are the same in countryside or city: "We are all Malays."

He does, however, feel that residence in the city has changed his attitudes. He is far more interested in politics than before he came to the city. ("The Alliance Party is best for the country," he says.) In addition he claims his personality has changed since he arrived in the city. He now says he has a "broader outlook on things."

This migrant, while spending only a short period of time in the city has adapted very quickly. He wanted to move to the city for the very reasons (to see and experience) which allow him more flexibility in his adaptation. The fact that he feels he has changed in the city does not, however, affect his commitment to reside there. He still will *balak-ka-kampong* [return to the kampong]. His case stresses the many levels of adaptation which each migrant assumes.

RESPONDENT 293 (HOLOGRAM IV): MEAN 1.98. Respondent 293 (see Figure 1D) was born in Kampong Meru some five miles from Klang, twenty-five miles from Kuala Lumpur. He was one of a large number of migrants from Meru (of Javanese ancestry) who moved backward and forward between Kampong Meru and Kuala Lumpur in what is almost a classic form of circulatory migration.

He had only recently arrived in Kuala Lumpur (eight months' residence at the time of the survey). He had moved there partly at the invitation of his brother, and partly in search of a job. At the time of leaving for Kuala Lumpur he was unemployed, having lost his job as an attendant on a lorry running between Kuala Lumpur and Port Swettenham.

His earlier years had been spent in Kampong Meru, living with his mother and her family. His father generally visited on weekends from

Kuala Lumpur, where he worked as a *tukang kebun* [gardener] for a European family. The migrant had been educated in Malay and left school at twelve to work at home. Since that date he had worked around home and as a lorry attendant for a Chinese firm. Thus while he had been working in Klang, an urban area, he had continued to reside in his rural kampong. When he first came to Kuala Lumpur to seek a job he did not bring his family, but once he had found a job as a gardener with a European family he acquired a house in a squatter area of Kampong Baharu and moved his family to Kuala Lumpur. Despite his short residence in the city, he prefers Kuala Lumpur to Kampong Meru and intends to stay in the city all his life.

His occupation as a gardener earns him an income below $100 (Malayan) a month, but as he has to pay no rent for his house (which he owns) nor for amenities, he claims the amount is enough to keep his family although he has received temporary financial aid from his brother. It is hardly surprising in view of the closeness of Meru to Kuala Lumpur (and its relatively easy access) that he and his family have returned home five times to see his parents since his arrival in Kuala Lumpur. The visits, however, are brief and rarely last more than a day. His wife comes from the same area so that it is possible for her to visit her relatives as well.

Although he has Malay primary education, the respondent does not read Malay newspapers or attend the cinema. He knows only one other area of Malay settlement and claims no Malay friends. His attitudes generally reflect the rural stereotypes apart from the fact that he believes Malays in Kuala Lumpur are more friendly and recognizes that the increased demands of the city and cost of food prevent his saving as much as he would desire.

Level Two: Satisfactory Coexistence: Four Case Studies

Most of the Malays interviewed in the study fell into this second level of adjustment to Kuala Lumpur (75 percent), a level which (it can be suggested) showed a satisfactory capacity to fit into the city's structure. Indeed, most of the city dwellers can be said to exist in this balance between the rural and urban poles.

RESPONDENT 414 (HOLOGRAM V): MEAN 2.10. Respondent 414 (see Figure 2A) is very similar to those migrants on Level One in that he has spent only a short time in Kuala Lumpur and entered at an older age than most of the migrants. Born in 1919, he spent his early years in Rembau, despite the fact that his father, employed as a policeman, was away from home frequently.

This respondent has a history of ample experience with the urban situation. He was educated in a Malay primary school as well as English and continued with English at the secondary level. Immediately after he left school he joined the police force and later became a clerk working for the British Military Administration. Later he joined the administrative department of the Malayan Army where he was employed as a clerk.

It was in this position that he was transferred to Kuala Lumpur in 1958. During these earlier periods, he spent much of his time at Port Dickson Army Encampment and at Raub, which are small urban centers. Certainly in terms of the degree of "occupational urbanization" he was well equipped before his entry into Kuala Lumpur. Despite his five years' residence in Kuala Lumpur, he is by no means committed to the city. He intends to return to his home kampong as soon as he finishes working in Kuala Lumpur and prefers to work elsewhere. This view is almost certainly backed by the fact that his wife's parents and his own parents own land in the kampong to which he would like to return and work as a farmer.

His present socioeconomic position is comparatively secure. He earns an income of $310 a month working as a clerk on a Division-2 scale, which is quite a high-status occupation in government service. He rents an entire house for the comparatively low sum of $41 (Malayan) per month but has made little effort to build up a supply of status amenities, such as a refrigerator, which many other individuals in the same income scale have made efforts to acquire. The majority of his children still live in his home kampong and it is hardly surprising that he keeps very close contact with his home area. He remits $50 a month to his parents for the education and upkeep of his children and attempts to visit the family in Rembau as often as possible. Last year he managed four visits, the longest of which was one week. These visits are conditioned by the availability of leave.

As part of his job he says he reads the *Straits Times*, *Berita Harian*, and the *Utusan Melayu* every day. He does not attend the cinema and has not, as yet, acquired any close friend in the city. He has made no effort in his five years of residence to establish the spatial dimensions of the Malay community in Kuala Lumpur. Clearly he dislikes the urban environment, feeling that in terms of most forces—a decline in religious values and the unfriendliness of the Kuala Lumpur Malays —it has been a bad influence. As he says, the Malays in Kuala Lumpur are "less friendly." "People in town mind their own business." Nevertheless, he feels that Kuala Lumpur has changed him in terms of his personality for he has widened his social contacts and made contact with other ethnic groups.

This migrant, then, represents a classic example of the individual who regards the city purely as a workplace, and not as a place of commitment. To him it is a place to live because that is where the job has taken him, but not a place to remain, and as soon as he finishes his government career he will return to his home kampong and take up the life of a farmer which he clearly prefers.

RESPONDENT 236 (HOLOGRAM VI): MEAN 2.34. Respondent 236 (see Figure 2B) represents a comparative rarity among the individuals interviewed in the survey—a bachelor living by himself. Born in a kampong close to Bentong, Pahang State, he spent most of his early years in his parents' home where he helped his father on the small holding when he was not in school. After he left school he came to Kuala Lumpur to search for a job (unsuccessfully) with the intention of continuing his schooling. He did, in fact, spend one year improving his English at secondary level. During this time he stayed with his brother, a government servant who lived in government-provided accommodation, close to the Stadium Merdeka. However, when his brother was shifted from Kuala Lumpur, he had to vacate this accommodation and he moved to the present room he rents in Kampong Baharu.

Apart from the desire to continue his education, he left his home kampong because he wanted to join his friends in Kuala Lumpur who had left the kampong already and to register at the employment exchange in the hope of finding an occupation. After one year's schooling he did find a job as a salesman, which he continued for nine months. He then took a job as a technician in the X-ray department of the General Hospital at Kuala Lumpur. This he has held for the past three years and three months.

Considering his comparative youth and short period in the city, he has managed to progress well. Still, as he comments, he finds it hard to save, and his expenses are quite high, particularly the $40 a month he pays for renting one room in the house where he stays. When that is compared with the $20 which families pay for an entire house in some of the squatter areas, it is clear why the out-movement of Malays from the crowded Kampong Baharu to newer squatter areas has occurred.

As yet he has not concerned himself with the purchase of many consumer durables. He does own a bicycle which was given to him by his father, and this is his main asset, apart from clothes. There was no information on whether he remitted money to his parents in his home kampong, but he did return up to four times a year, generally staying for about a week in order to see his parents and visit former friends. He took considerable advantage of the improved communications—mass media of the city—reading the English newspapers and weekly newspapers, but attended Malay films only irregularly.

He had a large number of friends, mostly residents in Kampong Baharu, many of whom he had known in his own kampong before he came to Kuala Lumpur. In general, his attitudes were the most clearly urban of any of the individuals so far discussed. While he did not comment on the effect of the city on the general degree of religious attendance, he felt that in his case he attended mosque less frequently than he had before.

It was harder to save in Kuala Lumpur because of the additional expenses. For instance, he mentioned that one used firewood in the kampong; in the city one generally used kerosene. In addition there were more amusements, hence more costs. Generally he felt that the Malays in the city were more friendly and that he had become much more interested in politics since he lived in the city. These characteristics all add up to the complex picture of an individual who, while he is in no way committed to permanent residence in the city, manages to get as full a life as his comparatively low income will allow him.

RESPONDENT 334 (HOLOGRAM VII): MEAN 2.43. Respondent 334 (see Figure 2C) represents an exceptionally interesting example of geographical mobility. Now fifty-four, he first entered Kuala Lumpur at age eighteen, but during the Japanese invasion returned to his home kampong in Malacca and came back to Kuala Lumpur at the end of the Second World War. He has been married twice, having divorced his first wife. He has had eight children by the two marriages—four of whom are still living with him and four who are living elsewhere. Of the latter, two of the boys are unmarried and working at the Malayan Teachers' College, where they have accommodation provided. Two of his daughters are married and living with their husbands in other parts of Malaya. Of the children still living with him, ranging in age from ten to seventeen, all are attending school. Three are girls attending English secondary school, and the youngest boy, aged ten, attends the Malay school in Princess Road.

The respondent was born in a kampong on the outskirts of Malacca where his father was engaged in the state government as a clerk. He was married young—before eighteen—to a girl from Singapore and went to Singapore first to work with his father-in-law who was a seller of *songkoks* [hats]. However, he held this job for only one and a half years before he came to Seremban and began work as a chauffeur for a European family. This job lasted for a short time only before he came to Kuala Lumpur and went to work as a chauffeur for other European families. Later he joined the Sri Jaya Transport Company (a Malay taxi and bus service) as a taxi driver and has been working in that occupation for the last twenty years.

Although he lives in a peri-urban kampong, his father had an urban job so that his experience with urban areas was considerable before he took his first city job. Yet despite the long period in Kuala Lumpur, he still does not intend to stay there all his life but hopes to return to Malacca where he has inherited a few acres of rubber land. It is interesting to note that his wife owns a quarter-acre of land in Kampong Baharu on which they eventually intend to build a house for their children if the latter choose to stay in the city. If not, he will rent it when he returns to Malacca.

Generally, his socioeconomic status is better than many of the Malays in Kuala Lumpur. He earns over $200 a month and pays $48 per month rent. But the cost of his children's education and other expenses, particularly those related to his children, do not permit him to save. He has very close contact with his parents who are in the rural area, especially his mother, who is not well. He visits his ailing parents in his home kampong more than twice a month, bringing them medicine or food, and sometimes money.

In general, while in the city he has, considering his lack of English, taken good advantage of the availability of improved communications. He has made many friends, both at his work and in Kampong Baharu. His attitudes, however, remain persistently rural in that he views the city as a "disruptive" influence on religion and friendliness, although clearly he also regards it as a "positive" influence. He has become more interested in politics and feels that the city has changed him personally—not, it must be emphasized, in a particularly beneficial way. Thus, he argues that the large number of dependents and increasing number of expenses in the city are causing him excessive worry which he is sure he would not experience in his home kampong.

Nevertheless, he is very positive that his children will have as good an education as he can give them in the terms of his ambitions for them. He is thinking that his son should be educated enough to pursue a professional career in engineering. He hopes, too, that his daughters may take up teaching as a career.

Thus, except for the period of the Japanese invasion, this migrant has been resident in Kuala Lumpur for almost thirty years, yet he still looks forward to returning to the countryside and keeps very close contacts with his parents there. His problems are certainly sizable and have been exacerbated by his second marriage—additional expenses have been incurred because of the increased size of his family—and his realization of the need to provide his children with the best education possible. But, despite this awareness of the advantages of the city, he waits only to return to the countryside and his home kampong. For him the city is a workplace to which he has adapted, but in no sense has he committed himself for his entire life.

RESPONDENT 387 (HOLOGRAM VIII): MEAN 2.86. Since the indices measuring the levels of urban adaptation are heavily weighted in favor of urban residents, it is hardly surprising that the Kuala Lumpur-born are prominent in Level Three. However, as we pointed out in the text, the mere fact of birth within Kuala Lumpur does not automatically provide an individual with advantages for adaptation to the urban situation, nor does it necessarily mean that his contact with the rural areas is lacking.

This is well illustrated by Respondent 387 (see Figure 2D), a Kuala Lumpur-born resident who has seldom been out of a city and yet retains close contact with his wife's rural kinfolk who reside in the country. This individual, born in 1924, lived in a kampong on the northern fringes of the city near Sentul Pasar. He spent the first twenty-three years of his life there with his father, helping on their rubber small holding.

But for the Japanese invasion he probably would not have remained so long with his parents. He did not leave them until he joined the police force at twenty-three. He was employed in the police force as a wireless operator four years before he was transferred out of Kuala Lumpur to Kuala Lipis and later to Banting in Kuala Langat District, Selangor State. He returned to Kuala Lumpur in 1955 where he took a position with the Statistics Department and later moved to the Registration Department as an interviewing officer. At the age of thirty-eight he is married to a woman from a district adjacent to Kuala Lumpur (Ulu Langat) and has raised a family of four.

He is firmly committed to remaining in Kuala Lumpur all his life but still maintains close links with his wife's relatives in the district of Ulu Langat, visiting them approximately once a month for periods of up to two days, and if possible, longer. Money is sent to his wife's parents regularly, though this is not a great amount. He is committed to permanent residence in Kuala Lumpur in other ways as well. For example, he has purchased a house in Kampong Dato Keramat on a fifteen-year repayment plan, at a rate of approximately $32 a month to the municipality.

He has also managed to acquire more status amenities than the majority of the other individuals interviewed. He owns a 1950 Morris which he uses to visit in Ulu Langat and for travel around Kuala Lumpur. He takes full advantage of communications available in Kuala Lumpur, reading both English and Malay newspapers (having studied both English and Malay at primary level), and he has a number of friends living in Kampong Dato Keramat. His attitudes are surprisingly imitative of the traditional rural viewpoints (as can be seen from Hologram VIII) mainly with respect to the friendliness of Malays, for he considers that there is much the same attitude between Kuala Lumpur Malays and those living outside. However, despite the fact that he is permanently stabilized in Kuala Lumpur, the web of kinship involves him in continuing contacts with rural areas, as does his occupational history. Thus he is well aware of the urban-rural differences that may exist in Malay attitudes, and clearly believes them to be of some importance.

Level Three: Urban Men? Four Case Studies

Finally, we will consider four case studies of Malays who fall into the upper level of adaptation.

RESPONDENT 384 (HOLOGRAM IX): MEAN 3.09. Respondent 384 (see Figure 3A) represents the Malay who has an excellent urban background which has given him ample experience with the urban situation. Born in Kampong Melayu, Singapore, he was educated at an English secondary school, and passed his senior Cambridge examination. He was employed as a journalist by the *Straits Times* while in Singapore and as an information officer with an oil company in Brunei. Presently he is working with the Information Services of the Malayan government in an upper civil service position. He is, however, a recent arrival in Kuala Lumpur, having spent just over a year there after being transferred from government employment in Singapore. His socioeconomic status is high. He earns over $500 a month in an upper civil service position and possesses a majority of the status symbols of the new elite—motor car, refrigerator, and radio-phonograph. In the last year he has visited relatives in Singapore four times but does not remit money to them. He reads all newspapers, attends the cinema regularly, and claims to have friends of all races, though his closest friend is a Malay, the editor of the *Berita Harian*. His attitudes generally reflect his urban background although he considers the Malays in Kuala Lumpur less friendly than those in Singapore.

Hologram IX shows clearly that he is not committed to permanent residence in Kuala Lumpur. He still owns land in Singapore and quite probably will return there, but at the moment he is undecided. This migrant, then, does not fit into any category of a rural migrant moving to the city. Rather, he is an interurban migrant, for he still retains his property and some of his personal friendships and kinship ties in the city of Singapore. He is a case of interurban loyalty with the web of kinship rather than one of preference for a rural or urban environment.

RESPONDENT 375 (HOLOGRAM X): MEAN 3.25. Respondent 375 (see Figure 3B) should more correctly be regarded as Kuala Lumpur-born since he has lived in Kuala Lumpur since the age of four. His father was engaged in selling clothes and during his early years he lived in the family home at Kampong Baharu. Later they moved to a house on Klang Road (now the old Klang Road) not far from the present area of Kampong Petaling Bahagia. He was educated at English secondary school and later at the Malay Teachers' Training College and is presently a teacher.

He is firmly committed to future residence in Kuala Lumpur even though his wife comes from Kampong Kapar, Klang, the same area to which his parents have returned. At present he is earning an income in excess of $300 and living in a rented house for $60 a month in Kawasan Melayu (the Malay area of Petaling Java). He does not keep very close contact with his family, visiting them only two times a year, despite the fact that they are relatively accessible in terms of public transport. He does not remit money to them, and, in fact, generally seems to have limited his contacts to a minimum.

He makes full use of the communications and other facets of the city, has a large number of friends, and is well aware of the many and diverse settlements of Malays in the city. His attitudes are a mixture —generally he is inclined to regard the city as a force that does change people (affecting religion, attitudes, and friendliness), but he is of the opinion that it has effected little change in him. This may be because, having been resident there for so long, he sees the changes in his personality as principally a result of his general maturation.

RESPONDENT 451 (HOLOGRAM XI): MEAN 3.48. Social scientists doing research in the non-Western world make much of the concept of Westernization, often using it synonymously with "modernization" to mean an individual or group of individuals that has adopted the mores and value judgments of the supposedly advanced individuals of capitalist societies.[6] While the author thinks it is exceptionally hazardous to use this concept in the context of the non-Western world, if the concept is going to be utilized it might be applied to Respondent 451 (see Figure 3C).

Born the son of a doctor, he has had the classic education of the Malay elite—studying first at the Malay College at Kuala Kungsar and then moving to the United Kingdom, obtaining university degrees from Cambridge and Oxford. As the accompanying hologram shows, his whole background is one of constant experience with urban areas. He joined the Malayan civil service in 1958 after completing his degrees overseas, and since then has held an important post in a top government department.

For a Malay he has accomplished the rare feat of marrying a girl from another ethnic group whom he met when he was studying overseas. They have two children, both born in Kuala Lumpur, and employ two Chinese servants. He is, of course, in the top socio-economic grade, earning an income in excess of $500 and his wife is working also, giving them a combined income of almost $1,600 per month. His contacts with his relatives in areas outside Kuala Lumpur are irregular, rarely exceeding two visits a year though he continues to send money regularly to his parents.

Not surprisingly, he makes considerable use of the media, and his friendships in the city are wide, though he knows only a few areas of Malay settlement. Most of his friends, he claims, come from mixed ethnic groups. His attitudes, as well as his honesty, reflect his urban background, for he felt he could not comment on questions concerning religious attitudes in the city or for that matter, friendship, as he

[6] For a discussion of some aspects of this concept see Hagen (1964); Hoselitz (1960); and Moore and Feldman (1960).

is not well enough acquainted with these two phenomena in Kuala Lumpur City.

This individual probably represents the most well educated of any in the sample, as well as being a Malay who clearly understands the wider values and need for mixed ethnic harmony in the city and in the total society. He is firmly committed to residence in Kuala Lumpur as is indicated by the overall configuration of his hologram.

RESPONDENT 470 (HOLOGRAM XII): MEAN 3.58. This Kuala Lumpur-born Malay (see Figure 3D), employed in a senior government post, represents (as measured by the indices) a thoroughly urbanized individual. He came from a comparatively poor family in which his father was engaged as a chauffeur with only a limited education, but he has a remarkable education record, having studied at universities in China, Taiwan, and the United States for four years. He presently resides in government housing in Kuala Lumpur but he had made a substantial number of moves within Kuala Lumpur during his early years with his family. His father, when employed as a chauffeur for Europeans, generally lived in housing provided by them.

He is firmly committed to Kuala Lumpur and has no relatives living in the countryside or elsewhere. Although his attitudes are not completely urban he represents an urban individual who has had the maximum opportunity to achieve his present high post in government service. It is interesting that among the top-status individuals in the sample there are only two Kuala Lumpur-born, the majority of the others coming from other parts of Malaya. This, then, is an urban individual, totally committed to residence in Kuala Lumpar and to his future in the city.

CONCLUSION

In a way, this study represents a reversion to the older model of the rural-urban dichotomy criticized earlier. But there is a specific reason for this regression, namely, to point out that, allowing for the design of the analysis which utilizes the continuum between the "rural person" and the "urban person," the end result indicates that the majority of Malays (in terms of the continuum) are "rural persons" and "urban persons" at the same time. Some may have more urban characteristics than others, but this is in itself no surety that they will adopt "supposed" urban attitudes. In other words, the capacity of the individual to hold these seemingly antithetical positions, as assessed by the rural-urban continuum, invalidates its predictive qualities. The individual, even the most marginally provided for, is far more flexible in taking what he wants out of the urban situation than the model would allow, accepting the fact that this flexibility will be limited by the position of the individual within the broader structure of his society. Ultimately, the individual is the product of his society, not of his city.

APPENDIX: URBANIZATION INDICES

(Note: Each of the scores in these indices was expressed in quartiles and transferred to the appropriate ring of the hologram.)

Sector A: Background Situation

Sector A consists of three indices which give an indication of the individual's early influences and experience of the urban situation:

Index 1 URBAN RESIDENCE IN EARLY YEARS is measured as follows:

$$\frac{\text{Years spent in towns over 2,000 up to fifteenth birthday}}{\text{Number of years (14)}} \times 100$$

It was hypothesized that the greater number of years spent in the towns, the more likely it was that the individual would be able to adapt to the city.

Index 2 THE DISTANCE OF THE MAJOR PLACE OF RESIDENCE FROM THE LARGEST URBAN AREA IN THE STATE BEFORE THE INDIVIDUAL'S FIFTEENTH BIRTHDAY was considered to be important. It was hypothesized that the closer the resident to the larger urban center, the more likely the individual would be able to adapt to the city.

Index 3 FATHER'S OCCUPATION was measured to give an indication of the individual's likely entry into urban-centered occupations. It was hypothesized that the higher the status of father measured by income and occupation, the more likely that the individual would be able to adapt to the city.

Sector B: Respondent's Socioeconomic Background

Sector B is an attempt to measure the individual's socioeconomic background. Once again, ranked from "1" in ascending order to "4" in terms of what are considered to be the most advantageous individual assets to enable the individual to play a full and active role in the city. Three indices are used to measure these factors:

Index 4 RESPONDENT'S EDUCATION was ranked from higher education, level 4 (i.e. English secondary and attendance at higher-education institutions) to no education, level 1. Malay primary only was 2. Malay and English primary was 3.

Index 5 OCCUPATIONAL BACKGROUND was classified by levels as follows:
1. No previous employment apart from family labor on peasant farms
2. Unemployed or in daily employment possessing no skills (i.e. no occupational training)
3. Employed with some skills (generally with some training needed, such as chauffeurs)
4. Employed and possessing distinct occupational skills (e.g. civil servant, Division 1).

Index 6 URBAN EXPERIENCE BEFORE ENTERING KUALA LUMPAR was figured as follows:

$$\frac{\text{Years spent in towns over 2,000 up to fifteenth birthday}}{\text{Years after fifteenth birthday before entry to Kuala Lumpur}} \times 100$$

The ranking was from level 4 (75 to 100) to level 1 (0–24–9). It should be noted that Index 6 is not applicable to Kuala Lumpur-born with the exception of those who have been working outside Kuala Lumpur and returned.

Sector C: Urban Commitment

Sector C measures urban commitment. The importance of this index to much of the sociological work carried out in the underdeveloped world, particularly in Africa, should be noted. Three indices have been utilized:

Index 7 THE STABILIZATION INDEX measures the years in Kuala Lumpur since fifteen. The results were ranked as before.

$$\frac{\text{Years in Kuala Lumpur (metropolitan and peri-urban)}}{\text{Years since fifteen}} \times 100$$

Residence in Kuala Lumpur was defined broadly to include residence in the peri-urban fringes such as Kampong Pantai Halt.

Index 8 THE COMMITMENT OF THE INDIVIDUAL was measured in terms of his answer to question 128 which consisted of two parts:
Do you intend to stay in Kuala Lumpur all your life?
Yes/No/Don't know.
When you have finished working in Kuala Lumpur, will you go back to your home district?
Yes/No/Don't know.

The answers were based largely on the first part of the question. Thus "yes" was ranked as level 4; "no" as 1; and "don't know" as 2. In cases where there was doubt about the validity of the answer, the second question was used to clarify it.

Index 9 PREFERENCE FOR KUALA LUMPUR AS A LIVING PLACE was measured by question 123:

Do you prefer living in Kuala Lumpur more than your home district? Yes/No/Don't know.

Sector D: Respondent's Present Socioeconomic Characteristics

Sector D is designed to measure the individual's socioeconomic characteristics. In terms of ranking the results, the assumption has been made that higher status occupations, higher incomes, house ownership, etc. provide the individual with advantages with respect to his capacity to cope with the city.

This is, of course, a debatable assumption, since individuals of many different socioeconomic grades may adapt well to the city; but in terms of their capacity to cope with the city and improve their position, their opportunities may be limited. Six indices were used in this sector:

Index 10 OCCUPATION was ranked into four categories following the ranking of Index 3.

Index 11 INCOME was subjectively ranked as follows, after an evaluation of the household incomes:

1. $99
2. $100 to $249
3. $290 to $499
4. $500 and over

Index 12 ECOLOGICAL SITUATION was defined as follows:

1. Fringe squatters
2. Inner-city squatters
3. Legal Malay settlements
4. Government housing (middle and upper grade) and private housing

Index 13 HOUSEHOLD AMENITIES were defined as follows:

1. Poor quality (no electricity, water or piped sanitation)
2. Better quality (piped water/no electricity or piped sanitation)
3. Legal Malay settlement amenities (water and electricity/no sanitation in some cases).
4. High quality (all amenities)

Index 14 HOUSE OWNERSHIP was classified as follows:

1. Staying with relatives
2. Tenant
3. Own house but not land on which situated
4. Own house and land

Index 15   POSSESSION OF STATUS AMENITIES was classified as follows:

1. None
2. Possess motor scooter or motorbike
3. Car or refrigerator
4. Car and refrigerator

Sector E: Urban Rural Ties

Sector E is designed to measure urban-rural ties. Three indices were chosen:

Index 16   NUMBER OF VISITS TO RURAL AREA PER YEAR:

1. Nine or more
2. Three to eight visits
3. Three visits
4. None

Index 17   REMITTANCE OF MONEY:

1. Regular
2. Irregular
3. Level 3 omitted
4. Do not remit

Index 18   MARITAL TIES:

1. Wife from home district; marriage arranged
2. Wife from home district; marriage not arranged
3. Wife from elsewhere; marriage arranged
4. Wife from elsewhere; marriage not arranged

It should be noted that this index is designed to measure the degree of social pressure operating. The interviewers were asked to clarify the meaning of "arrangement" (since few Malay ceremonies are not arranged) as meaning the selection of a mate by parents or kinfolk.

It is assumed that the man who chooses his wife from other areas (not on parental advice) is more emancipated than those who do not.

In all these indices, it is assumed that the closer the link with rural areas, the more likely this is to inhibit urban adaptation.

Sector F: Communications and Contact in the City

One of the most frequent assertions concerning urban residence is that it exposes the individual to new ideas and attitudes through increased availability of newspapers, films, association, etc. On the face of it, there seems little to debate with such an assertion, but does the undeniable existence of these aids mean that the individual will take advantage of them?

Sector F attempts to measure some of the broader indications of the individual's utilization of these communications media and the friendship patterns which grow up among the urban residents. Here some attempt was made to measure the role of work as a place in which friendships are made. Finally, an effort was made to measure the degree of community awareness by the knowledge of other Malay areas. (This was only of limited value.)

The following indices were devised:

Index 19 REGULARITY AND TYPE OF NEWSPAPER READING:
1. Do not read newspapers
2. Malay or English irregularly (i.e. not daily)
3. Malay or English regularly (daily)
4. English and Malay regularly (daily)

Index 20 REGULARITY AND TYPE OF CINEMA ATTENDANCE:
1. Do not attend
2. Malay or English irregularly
3. Malay or English regularly
4. English and Malay regularly (more than once a month)

The reason for the distinction between the "Malay OR English" and "Malay AND English" communication types is simply to indicate the breadth of contact with the communications media. Those who have contact with the two streams of language are assumed to have broader contact than those who do not.

Index 21 FRIENDSHIP PATTERNS was based on question 116, designed to ascertain the respondent's closest friend (assumed to be mentioned first on the list). It is divided as follows:
1. None
2. Kin
3. Neighbors/other
4. Workmate

Index 22 KNOWLEDGE OF OTHER MALAY AREAS IN KUALA LUMPUR:
1. Do not know any
2. Three or less
3. Four to eight
4. Nine or more

It might be argued that the ranking of this category could be reversed, based on the assertion that a greater knowledge of Malay areas represents some form of community awareness (ethnic strengthening) with regard to the supposed breakdown of ethnic identity often said to occur in the urban setting.

I do not hold to this position, arguing that the knowledge of a greater number of Malay areas shows greater awareness of the urban situation and hence should be ranked above the other indices.

16

Sector G: Urban Attitudes

Sector G is devoted to urban attitudes. In general, it attempts to measure the degree of acceptance of what may be regarded as rural stereotypes concerning the urban milieu. The assumption in ranking is that the more closely the individual conforms to the stereotype, the less urbanized he tends to be. Six indices were chosen:

Index 23   ATTITUDES TOWARDS RELIGION IN THE CITY were calculated from response to question 106:
Do you think that people who live in the city are less religious than those who live in the country?
True/Not true/Same/Don't know.

The above query was ranked as follows:

1. True
2. Same
3. Level 3 omitted
4. Not true

Index 24   RELIGIOUS ATTENDANCE IN THE CITY was based on question 108:
Do you attend mosque more frequently, less frequently or the same as you did in the kampong?
The question was addressed only to the migrants and did not apply to the Kuala Lumpur-born except when they had been away from the city and had returned. It was ranked as follows on the assumption that the urban residence tended to break down religious adherence—a stereotype assumption:

1. More
2. Same
3. Level 3 omitted
4. Less frequently

Index 25   MALAYS' FRIENDLINESS IN KUALA LUMPUR was based on question 115:
Are Malays in Kuala Lumpur more friendly or less friendly than kampong Malays?
More/Less/Same/Don't know.
It was ranked in the following manner:

1. Less
2. Same
3. Level 3 omitted
4. More

Index 26   SAVING IN THE CITY was based on question 109:
Do you think that it is easier to save money, or harder to save money in Kuala Lumpur than in the kampong?
Easier/Harder/Same/Don't know.

It was assumed that the rural stereotype was that money was easy to acquire and save in the city. In fact, as the evidence shows, most residents felt it was much harder.

The ranking was as follows:

1. Easier
2. Same
3. Level 3 omitted
4. Harder

Index 27 INTEREST IN POLITICS IN THE CITY based on question 120:
Do you find you are more interested in Kuala Lumpur than you were before?
Yes/No/Don't know.

It was ranked as follows:

1. No
2. Undecided
3. Level 3 omitted
4. Yes

Index 28 INDIVIDUAL CHANGE IN THE CITY based on question 121:
Since you came to Kuala Lumpur have you as a person changed?
Yes/No/Don't know.

The answers were ranked as follows:

1. No
2. Don't know
3. Level 3 omitted
4. Yes

Again, the question was not applicable to the Kuala Lumpur-born except when they had been away from the city.

REFERENCES

ABU-LUGHOD, JANET
    1961   Migrant adjustment to city life: the Egyptian case. *American Journal of Sociology* 67:22–32.

BAUMAN, ZYGMUNT
    1967   Modern times, modern Marxism. *Social Research* 34:399–415.

BOGUE, DONALD J.
    1959   "Internal migration," in *The study of population: an inventory and appraisal*. Edited by Philip M. Hauser and Otis Dudley Duncan, 486–509. Chicago: University of Chicago Press.

BRUNER, EDWARD M.
1961   Urbanization and ethnic identity in north Sumatra. *American Anthropologist* 63:508–521.

CHANDER, R.
1972   *1970 population and housing census of Malaysia-community groups.* Kuala Lumpur: Jabatan Perangkaan Malaysia.

CENTRE NATIONAL FRANÇAISE DE LA RECHERCHE SCIENTIFIQUE
1959   *Étude sur les conditions de vie et les besoins de la population de Viet-Nam.* Paris.

EAMES, E.
1954   Some aspects of urban migration from a village in north Central India. *Eastern Anthropologist* 8:13–26.

EPSTEIN, A. L.
1967   Urbanization and social change in Africa. *Current Anthropology* 8:275–312.

GULLICK, J. M.
1956   *The story of early Kuala Lumpur.* Singapore: Donald Moore.

HAGEN, EVERETT E.
1964   *On the theory of social change.* London: Tavistock.

HAUSER, PHILIP M., editor
1957   *Urbanization in Asia and the Far East.* Calcutta: UNESCO.
1961   *Urbanization in Latin America.* Paris: UNESCO.

HOSELITZ, BERT F.
1960   *Sociological aspects of economic growth.* Glencoe, Illinois: The Free Press.

LEWIS, OSCAR
1952   Urbanization without breakdown: a case study. *Scientific Monthly* 75:31–41.
1959   *Five families: Mexican case studies in the culture of poverty.* New York: Random House.

MANGIN, WILLIAM, editor
1970   *Peasants in cities: readings in the anthropology of urbanization.* Boston: Houghton Mifflin.

MAYER, P.
1962   *Townsmen or tribesmen: conservatism and the process of urbanization.* Capetown: Oxford University Press.

MC GEE, T. G.
1964   The rural-urban continuum debate, the pre-industrial city and rural-urban migration. *Pacific Viewpoint* 5:159–181.
1968   "Malays in Kuala Lumpur city." Unpublished doctoral dissertation. University of Wellington, Wellington, Victoria.
1971   *The urbanization process in the Third World.* London: G. Bell and Son.

MILBANK MEMORIAL FUND
1958   *Selected studies of migration since World War II.* New York: Milbank Memorial Fund.

MITCHELL, J. CLYDE
1966   "Theoretical orientations in African urban studies," in *The social anthropology of complex societies.* Edited by Michael Banton, 37–68. London: Tavistock.

MOORE, WILBERT E., ARNOLD S. FELDMAN, *editors*
1960   *Labor commitment and social change in developing areas.* New York: Social Science Research Council.

NELSON, JOAN
1970   The urban poor: disruption or political integration in Third-World cities. *World Politics* 22:393–413.

NESS, GAYL D.
1967   *Bureaucracy and rural development in Malaysia.* Berkeley and Los Angeles: University of California Press.

PROVENCHER, RONALD
1971   *Two Malay worlds: interaction in urban and rural settings.* Berkeley: Center for South and Southeast Asia Studies, University of California.

PRYOR, ROBIN J.
1971   *Internal migration and urbanization: an introduction and bibliography.* Townsville: James Cook University of North Queensland.

SIMMEL, GEORG
1957   "The metropolis and mental life," in *Cities and society.* Edited by Paul K. Hatt and A. J. Reiss. Glencoe, Illinois: The Free Press. (Article originally published in 1900.)

THOMAS, D. S.
1938   *Research memorandum on migration differentials.* New York.

TURNER, JOHN F. C.
1967   Barriers and channels for housing development in modernizing countries. *Journal of the American Institute of Planners* 33:167–181.

TURNER, ROY, *editor*
1962   *India's urban future.* Berkeley and Los Angeles: University of California Press.

TURSKI, RYSZURD
1967   Town-country relations. *Polish Perspectives* 10:12–21.

WINSTEDT, RICHARD
1951   *The Malay magician being shaman, saiva and sufi.* London: Routledge and Kegan Paul.

WIRTH, LOUIS
1957   "Urbanism as a way of life," in *Cities and society.* Edited by Paul K. Hatt and A. J. Reiss. Glencoe, Illinois: The Free Press. (Article originally published in 1938.)

Tourism, Culture Change, and Culture Conservation in Bali

PHILIP FRICK MCKEAN

The process of culture change has often been viewed by ethnologists as the result of contact between "dominant" and "submissive" social groups, with indigenous culture weakened when brought into contact with those of superior military, technological, or organizational development. This view is most clearly seen in the studies of American Indians by anthropologists in the early years of this century (cf. Redfield, Linton, and Herskovits 1936; Walker 1972). While there has been an expansion of the technologically advanced societies into areas inhabited by "native" or indigenous ethnic groups during the colonial period, there has also been curiosity about these tribal groups. Ethnologists have studied customs and kinship, ecological adaptation and social structure, aesthetic expression and cosmological beliefs, and have been fascinated by what they found. This curiosity has also been shared, to varying degrees, by less scholarly travellers, now called tourists. This paper examines some of the interaction between the international tourists and one indigenous group, the Balinese of Indonesia.

Tourism is a contemporary phenomenon which can be studied

Research conducted during 1970–1971 under the auspices of the Department of Anthropology, Brown University, Providence, Rhode Island, U.S.A.; it was supported by a National Institute of Mental Health Fellowship No. 3 FO1 MH 47221 – 0151 CUAN, U.S. Department of Health, Education and Welfare. For encouragement and guidance I am grateful to many, especially my nuclear and extended families; Robert Jay, Philip Leis, George Hicks, Edward Bruner, Gregory Bateson; I Gusti Ngurah Bagus, his staff and colleagues at the Bali Museum and Udayana University.

empirically and analyzed conceptually: what technology and organization accompanies tourism? Who are the groups visiting, and who among the hosts have what roles, with what rewards, and at what cost? What kind of interaction takes place, with what frequency, and with what effects on traditional institutions? Yet the literature describing or theorizing about this vast movement of people and its effects on the areas visited, whether in European Alpine villages, New England coastal towns, or Caribbean islands, is meager. Most of the studies have concentrated on the social characteristics of the tourists, rather than the persons being visited (Kaplan 1960; Knebel 1960; Boorstin 1962; Waters 1966; Dumazedier 1967; Cohen 1972). These studies agree that the history of tourism is a recent one. Technological developments in transportation have been a *sine qua non* for the increase in mass tourism, with its emphasis on comfort, safety, and well-staged "pseudo-events" representing local ethnic or area peoples. The institutionalized tourists can be distinguished from the non institutional, so that the explorer and drifter-hippie types are included in the taxonomy. Cohen (1972:179) posits that the extent and variety of social contacts between the tourist and members of the host society is a factor of the types he describes. He states, however, that the impact of large-scale tourism on a culture, a style of life, and a world view, is presumably enormous, but that "the problem has not yet been systematically studied."

Several essays do exist which suggest dimensions of the effect of tourism on local populations. A pioneering piece by Nunez (1963) documents the interaction between Mexican villagers and urban tourists. Indigenous economic and political structures were affected by the "weekendismo" visitors, as residents in the rural locale had new models of wealth and power in their midst. Bodine (1964) describes the relationship between Taos Pueblo Indians and the white "Anglos" who both profit from the tourists. They have come to be allied in a "cultural symbiosis," with the Anglo motel and shop operators recognizing the importance of the Indians in attracting the tourists, and the Indians knowing that the whites operate necessary tourist services that enable them both to profit. If either of the groups finds alternate sources of income, or the ethnic distinctiveness of the Indians disappears, thus failing to attract tourists, then the symbiosis, based on mutual exploitation of the tourist industry, is likely to diminish.

Forster (1964) has suggested some hypotheses about the expected sociological consequences of tourism in developing nations, especially Polynesia. He notes that there is a change in the standard of living and style of life of the local community, with increased cash, new occupations, secularization of indigenous celebrations, a "phony folk culture," and conflicting attitudes about tourism, with attendant liabilities and advantages. Sutton (1967) has examined some of the factors which produce tension or harmony in the encounters between tourist and host, including such inherent characteristics as the transitory and nonrepetitive nature of interaction, an orientation toward immediate gratification, the ignorance of the traveller as opposed to the knowledge of the native, cross-cultural failure to communicate or understand messages, and economic differentials which lead to a mixture of conflict and cooperation between the tourist and his host.

Common to the above studies of cultural changes wrought by tourists are the theoretical assumptions that the changes (1) are brought about by the intrusion of an external, usually superordinate sociocultural system into a weaker, receiving culture; (2) are generally destructive to the indigenous traditions; and (3) are leading to a homogenization of cultures, in which ethnic or local identity is subsumed under the aegis of a technocratic bureacracy, postindustrial economy, and jet-age life-style. There is, in short, little analysis of any mechanisms available as indigenous populations resist change, of efforts to retain and revitalize their traditional social fabric, or of attempts to conserve culture. It is to this problem which we turn in analyzing contemporary Bali.

The Balinese have a special place in ethnological research because of the efforts of many prominent scholars who have analyzed them, including Korn (1932), McPhee (1936), Covarrubias (1937), Goris and Dronkers (1953), Bateson and Mead (1942), Belo (1949, 1953, 1969, 1970), Geertz (1959, 1963), Swellengrebel (1960), Sugriwa (1952, 1957), Raka (1955), J. Hooykaas (1960, 1963), C. Hooykaas (1960, 1964), and Ngurah Bagus (1968, 1969, 1970). Bali has been celebrated for its elaborate traditions in music, dance, architecture, drama, and social organization. In part because of the films and publications about Bali by these and other authors, it has become an attractive stop for tourists. According to the figures of the National Tourist Development Office in Bali, more than 25,000 international tourists arrived in 1969 when a jetport was opened; more than 40,000 arrived in 1970; and about 65,000 arrived in 1971. Predictions based on a rate of growth of 15 percent to 20 percent would lead to over a quarter of a million tourists by the late seventies, and a half million annually in another decade. International hotels are going up, tourist bureaus and airlines have increased publicity and personnel, while a master plan for Bali, with directives for land utilization, capital investment, infrastructure development, and profit margins has been prepared by the World Bank and the United Nations Development Program.

The tourists, who began to visit Bali on cruise ships operated by the Dutch colonial authorities in the 1930's, are offered elaborate programs of music, dance, and drama. They may purchase a wide range of handicrafts, carvings, and paintings, drive through spectacular scenery from irrigated wet-rice terraces (*sawah*) to active volcanoes, then return to air-conditioned hotels. Between arrival and departure in jets taking them to yet another destination—Sydney or Hong Kong, Singapore or Banghok—the tourists will have "experienced Bali" for an average of three-and-a-half days. What does this mean to the social organization and cultural values of the Balinese?

It is fruitful to frame the interaction between islanders and visitors in terms of the model of "performances," and to propose a taxonomy of "culture performances." This includes a variety of activities which may be analytically separated into three categories, depending on the audience attending the performances.

Singer (1972:71) has proposed such a typology, writing about his research in Madras:

As I observed the range of cultural performances . . . it seemed to me that my Indian friends—perhaps all peoples—thought of their culture as encapsulated in these discrete performances which they could exhibit to visitors and to themselves. The performances became for me the elementary constituents of the culture and the ultimate units of observation.

The concept of "cultural performances" was first suggested by Singer in correspondence with Redfield (1956:56), and has been applied to Bali in an effort to conceptualize the total culture as "performance" (McKean 1971:1-7). Culture performances in Bali could include the whole range of activities, cognitions, and contemplations used to communicate knowledge and express emotion, but they may be separated for the purposes of analysis into three categories—divine, local, and tourist—depending on the dominant audience for whom the performance is staged:

1. *The divine audience*: the unseen realm of demons, gods, nymphs, ghosts, witches and ancestors is a "spirit audience" believed to be present by the Balinese. It is this spiritual realm (*suargan* or *dunia halus*) which justifies, for Balinese, the elaborate offerings, costumes, dances and musical activities which are ubiquitously present on the island. The presence of the divine, in all his (or her) manifestations, is prepared for, invited, expected, and experienced at most Balinese performances, but pre-eminently at the recurring temple ceremonies (*odalan*). These rituals honor benevolent spirits and propitiate evil ones, frequently accompanied by trance (*kesurupan*), during which a divine spirit (*batara*) is said to enter the human world, making known its otherwise invisible presence. Temple ceremonies are staged for the benefit of these divine spirits by each of the social groups which cross-cut each other in Bali, including the clan (*dadia*), hamlet (*bandjar*), village (*desa*), and irrigation society (*subak*) (Geertz 1959).

The main themes in the temple ceremonies have a multitude of variations, but generally consist of the preparatory stage, the celebrative events, and a cleaning-up stage. Offerings and decorations are made, costumes and instruments are dusted off, rehearsals are conducted, and then the group begins to assemble, usually parading to the site while carrying the necessary paraphernalia. Ceremonies at the temples are presided over by local priests (*pemangku*) who lead chants, sacrifice fowl, and distribute holy water (*air tirta*) to the worshippers. A *gamelan* orchestra accompanies the rituals and plays for the dancers who welcome the divine visitors. The presentation of these offerings, which include flowers, fruits, cooked fowl, eggs, rice, incense, as well as the dances and music, is intended to delight the unseen divine audience, so that the ancestors and spirits will be honored with the best performances. The temple performances, at once expressing and creating religious belief, are the major vehicles for perpetuating the ancient and exquisite culture of Bali.

2. *The local audience*: a highly visible audience of villagers is present at many of the rituals, particularly if the dancing, music, drama, or entertainment is thought to be worthy of attention. They crowd around the perimeter of the dance or drama stage, peer over

walls, or relax outside the arena near the refreshment stands (*warung*), which spring up when performances begin. The more crowded (*ramai*) with spectators and worshippers, the more a ceremony is valued. Elders and priests of both sexes are up front, just below the altars, while an adjacent *gamelan* orchestra beats out its powerful rhythm. Watching from a slightly elevated or more central position are village officials, persons of high status, and honored guests. All are clothed in the appropriate ritual garb (*pakaian adat*).

In precolonial times the most resplendent stages for music, dance, and drama were in the great family temples (*pura*), or in the residential compounds of the nobility (*puri*). In postrevolutionary Bali, the high-caste families (Brahmin and Ksatria) have officially lost their power. But there remains a residual mutual respect and authority, so these noblemen regularly feel obliged to invite outstanding artists to perform, marking a rite of passage or other formal occasion. Neighbors and bilateral kin are invited to witness the spectacle, and offerings are made to the divinities. Spectators may be critical of the performers, greeting a graceless misstep with laughter and ridicule, nodding approval of a refined and delicate artist. In short, sponsors and participants in public ceremonies seek to please both divine and human audiences.

3. *The tourist audience*: from the compressed descriptions above of the two kinds of audiences, it should be clear that the Balinese, unlike other ethnic groups such as the Pueblo Indians (Dozier 1970:184), celebrate all their religious rituals publicly and are not secretive about them. Children not yet formally initiated into adult status may observe the ceremonies. Visitors are tolerated and accepted, so long as they show proper respect by their decorum and dress. When guests, whether from another village or another country, appear, the Balinese are not visibly troubled by the presence of additional, unknown members in the audience. On the other hand, they do not make a special effort to please or accommodate guests unless they have special status, and go on about the business—or pleasure—at hand. This attitude is not found in those performances, now becoming numerous and regular, especially staged for tourists.

The "tourist shows" which have gained popularity have been edited from indigenous productions and are shortened versions of the originals: Barong and Rangda, Legong, Ketjak (Monkey Dance), and Ramajana. There is almost no direct interaction between tourist and performer. The tourist arrives on the local site of the performance, usually a temple courtyard, conducted by a guide accompanying his taxi or bus. A ticket is purchased (generally U.S. $1.50 or $2.00), half of which goes to the local performing group and half of which goes to the tourist agency. The tourist is given a libretto, explaining something of the plot, and sits in a chair facing the stage. Musicians and dancers appear from backstage, then leave without meeting the spectators, who have rushed off to tour more of Bali, having seen a narrow range of the rich variety Balinese can perform.

These shows are staged on a regular basis at villages on the tourist trek, and they are done in order to bring more cash into the hands of local community organizations. Income is used to pay for necessary expenses, such as decorations, flowers, offerings, refurbishing costumes and buildings. Any profits are disposed of by the leaders of the sponsoring group. This frequently means that there is money available to pay for massive ceremonials, including the temple ceremonies (*odalan*), and rites of passage such as cremation and purification.

In one case, the sponsoring residential unit is slowly acquiring a bicycle for each of the 110 participating family groups. If no tourists were to appear on a given day, no performance would be held. Since the intended audience is not present, neither the divine nor the local audience would be substituted, though offerings to the divine audience would have been made, and villagers may have gathered. In exchange for his money, a tourist is allowed to enter the mythic realm of the Balinese cosmos, and to be a welcomed spectator at a well-staged aesthetic event.

The effect of tourists on contemporary Bali is indeed profound, for several thousand outsiders are daily roaming the island, having contact with Balinese. The interactions are, for the most part, formalized and well-structured, through the staff of the hotels, tourist agencies, and guides who serve as "culture brokers." But the economic impact of tourism is considerable. If the not unreasonable figure of U.S. $5.00 per day per tourist (65,000) times the average stay (three-and-a-half days) is used to estimate the currency reaching the hands of Balinese (apart from the hotels and travel agents), the total for 1971 would be U.S. $1,137,500. The majority of these funds are at the disposal of corporate groups who are organized to create and sell art objects—dances, dramas, music, carvings, paintings, and other souvenirs.

These corporate groups use their new wealth in traditional ways, for the most part: erecting new and more elaborate temples or meeting halls (*balé bandjar*), adding more exquisite dance costumes or masks, preparing for larger community rituals, arranging for better *gamelan* instruments or more skilful instruction. The Balinese, in short, are finding a source of income by doing what they enjoy doing traditionally—performing their culture. Rather than substituting new patterns or roles for the ancient ones, they have added another repertoire, suitable to another valued audience. The tourist audience is appreciated for the economic assets it can bring a corporate group, but its presence has not diminished the importance of performing competently for the other two audiences, the villagers and the divine realm. Rather, the funds, as well as the increased skills and equipment available, have enriched the possibility that the indigenous performances will be done with more elegance, in effect conserving culture.

The studies which suggest that tourism inexorably and automatically "ruins" or "destroys" an indigenous cultural tradition need to be reconsidered in light of evidence from Bali—and the hypothesis concerning Bali will need reanalysis in the future, of course. A number of questions may lead to a deeper understanding of the cross-cultural relationship between tourism and indigenous traditions:

1. Is the sociocultural tradition which is presented to tourists a reflection of an existing folk tradition, as in Bali, or the re-invention of discontinued traditions, as in Tahiti?

2. Is the economic opportunity from tourism as great or greater than that offered by alternative employment, such as manufacturing, mining, or agriculture? What factors affect vocational choices?

3. Is tourism an industry operated by local or national businessmen, so that ties of kin, tribe, or friendship significantly affect its organization?

4. What are the salient characteristics of the tourist clientele, in terms of national origin, economic level, duration of stay, interests in recreation, history, culture, etc.?

5. What, if any, autonomous political authorities have control over taxes, land use, licenses, and other sanctions which may control the expansion and extent of tourism?

6. What organizational, cultural, or interactional factors preserve and revitalize ethnic identity *vis-à-vis* tourists? Is the identity of certain or all ethnic groups strengthened internally by the presence of "outsiders" or "foreigners" who are so obviously strangers?

Further research on these and other questions may enable

ethnologists to chart the variety of interaction between tourists and a local population, deepening our comprehension of this important emerging phenomena.

REFERENCES

BATESON, GREGORY, MARGARET MEAD
1942 *Balinese character: a photographic analysis*. Special Publications of the New York Academy of Sciences 2. New York.

BELO, JANE
1949 *Bali: Rangda and Barong*. New York: J. J. Augustin.
1953 *Bali: temple festival*. New York: J. J. Augustin.
1969 *Trance in Bali*. New York: Columbia University Press.
1970 *Traditional Balinese culture*. New York: Columbia University Press.

BODINE, JAMES
1964 "Symbiosis at Taos and the impact of tourism on the Pueblo: a case of 'unplanned' economic development." Manuscript read at symposium of the Central States Anthropological Society.

BOORSTIN, DANIEL
1962 *The image*. New York: Atheneum.

COHEN, ERIK
1972 Toward a sociology of international tourism. *Social Research* 39:164–182.

COVARRUBIAS, MIGUEL
1937 *Island of Bali*. New York: Knopf.

DOZIER, EDWARD P.
1970 *The Pueblo Indians of North America*. New York: Holt, Rinehart and Winston.

DUMAZEDIER, J.
1967 *Towards a society of leisure*. New York: Free Press.

FORSTER, JOHN
1964 The sociological consequences of tourism. *International Journal of Comparative Sociology* 5:217–227.

GEERTZ, CLIFFORD
1959 Form and variation in a Balinese village. *American Anthropologist* 61:991–1011.
1963 *Agricultural involution: the process of ecological change in Indonesia*. Berkeley: University of California Press.

GORIS, R., P. L. DRONKERS
1953 *Bali: cults and customs*. Djakarta: Government of Indonesia, Department of Information.

HOOYKAAS, C.
1960   Two exorcists in Bali. *Man* 60:231.
1964   *Agama tirta: five studies in Hindu-Balinese religion.* Amsterdam: Noord-Hollandsche Uitgevers.

HOOYKAAS, J.
1960   *A ritual purification of a Balinese temple.* Amsterdam: Noord-Hollandische Uitgevers.
1963   *Märchen aus Bali.* Zurich: Die Waage.

KAPLAN, M.
1960   *Leisure in America: a social inquiry.* New York: John Wiley and Sons.

KNEBEL, H. J.
1960   *Soziologische Strukturwandlungen im modernen Tourismus.* Stuttgart: F. Enke.

KORN, V. E.
1932   *Het adatrecht van Bali.* The Hague: Martinus Nijhoff.

MC KEAN, PHILIP FRICK
1971   *A preliminary analysis of the inter-action between Balinese and tourists: the "little," "great," and "modern" traditions of a culture.* Denpasar: Museum Bali, Department of Education and Culture, Government of Indonesia.

MC PHEE, COLIN
1936   The Balinese wajang kulit and its music. *Djawa* 16:1–50.

NGURAH BAGUS, I GUSTI
1968   *Arti Dongeng Bali.* Singaradja: Department of Education and Culture, Government of Indonesia.
1969   *Mutu Pewajangan Bali.* Denpasar: Museum Bali, Department of Education and Culture, Government of Indonesia.
1970   *A short note on the modern Hindu movements in Balinese society.* Denpasar: Department of Anthropology, Udayana University.

NUNEZ, THERON A.
1963   Tourism, tradition, and acculturation: weekendismo in a Mexican village. *Ethnology* 2:3:347–352.

RAKA, I GUSTI GEDE
1955   *Monographi pulau Bali.* Djakarta: Central Bureau for Rural Agriculture, Government of Indonesia.

REDFIELD, ROBERT
1956   *Peasant society and culture.* Chicago: University of Chicago Press.

REDFIELD, ROBERT, RALPH LINTON, MELVILLE S. HERSKOVITS
1936   Memorandum on the study of acculturation. *American Anthropologist.* 38:149–152.

SINGER, MILTON
1972   *When a great tradition modernizes.* New York: Praeger.

SUGRIWA, I GUSTI BAGUS
1952 *Hari raja Bali Hindu*. Denpasar: Balimas.
1957 *Babad pasek*. Denpasar: Balimas.

SUTTON, WILLIS A., JR.
1967 Travel and understanding: notes on the social structure of touring. *International Journal of Comparative Sociology* 8: 218–223.

SWELLENGREBEL, JAN L.
1960 *Bali: studies in life, thought, and ritual*. The Hague: W. van Hoeve.

WALKER, DEWARD E., JR., *editor*
1972 *The emergent native Americans*. Boston: Little, Brown.

WATERS, S. K.
1966 The American tourist. *The Annals of the American Academy of Social Science* 368:109–118.

Matrilineal Societies in Southeast Asia: Examples from Highland Vietnam

NEIL H. OLSEN

The genesis of this paper derives from comparative studies of main-land Southeast Asia by K. G. Izikowitz (1951), who undertook field-work among the Lamet, a Mon-Khmer-speaking swidden[1] culture in north Laos. In his study he contrasted Lamet culture with lowland wet-rice (paddy) groups by attempting to discern what differences and similarities were reflected in the respective socioeconomic systems of the two technologies.

In examining data on the descent systems and social structures of the various cultures in mainland Southeast Asia (Lebar et al. 1964; Murdock 1967), several overall trends emerge. Most of the lowland wet-rice civilizations, such as the Burmese, Mon, Thai, Lao, and Khmer, exhibit bilateral social organization, with the exception of the patrilineal Vietnamese. The majority of the highland groups have unilineal descent systems (predominantly patrilinial) with a few bilateral systems. The only anomaly to this schema is a wide scatter-ing of matrilineal societies which can be grouped into two tentative geographic clusters. The first cluster includes all of the Austronesian-speaking peoples (Chàm, Ro˙glai, Rhadé, Jarai) extant on the Indo-chinese Peninsula, along with several Mon-Khmer groups adjacent to them (Chrau, Mnong, Sre); the second cluster comprises the Garo and Khasi in Assam. We will concern ourselves here primarily with the former group. Two questions are raised upon examination of the data: (1) what factors determine matrilineal descent, and (2) after

---

[1] Swidden is another term for slash-and-burn, or shifting, cultivation (French *brûisl*, Vietnamese *rẫy*, Koho *mir*, Rhadé *hma*).

these factors are known, how can the existing matrilineal societies be accounted for in a region of predominantly patrilineal descent systems?

As studies on the origins and characteristics of matrilineal systems are abundant in the literature,[2] the emphasis here is on its occurrence among highland groups in Vietnam. The results of an inquiry into matrilineal society are covered in Schneider and Gough's definitive work (1962) in which Aberle concluded:

The origins of matrilineal systems are probably to be sought in technology, division of labor, types of subsistence activities, and the ecological niches in which these activities occur. In general, matriliny is associated with horticulture, in the absence of major activities carried on and coordinated by males, of the type of cattle raising or extensive public works. It tends to disappear with plough cultivation and vanishes with industrialization. In plough cultivation areas, it is often found in "refuge areas," where a horticultural group exists in an environment marginal for plough cultivation or in geographical isolation from plough cultivation. Where it is found in hunting and gathering groups, it is often associated with stable fishing resources . . . (1962:725).

Among most highland peoples in Southeast Asia, swidden cultivation is an extensive agricultural system. The majority of the societies of highland Vietnam practice this form of agriculture either exclusively or semi-exclusively while a few groups such as the Sre concentrate their efforts primarily on paddy cultivation. In the rugged upland regions, the type of cultivation is dictated by harsh geographic and environmental realities.

Fait remarquable, presque partout où la topographie et la pédologie l'ont permis, les montagnards ont créé des rizières dans les pays *Hré*, pays *Sré*, pays *Mnong Rlam*, *Churu* ou des champs permanents (dans le pays *Mdhur*): si la grande majorité des montagnards reste toujours fidèle au ray, c'est, semble-t-il, parce que les réalités locales le lui imposent (Lafont 1967a: 42–43).

In other words, the Sre practice swidden cultivation to supplement their paddy fields only because they have no additional area available to utilize as paddies. The Sre are a subgroup of the Ko·ho people[3]

---

[2]   Lingat (1952), Nakane (1967); Ner (1930); Schneider and Gough (1962).
[3]   Ko·ho [ka'hɔ] is a Chàm word that previously designated all the highland peoples other than the Chàm proper, but is presently utilized as an ethnolinguistic appellation collectively denoting several Mon-Khmer groups speaking mutually intelligible south Bahnaric dialects, including the Mà, Sre, Cil, Làc (Lat), Nõp, etc. The Ko·ho number approximately 100,000 people and inhabit Lâm-Đồng and Tuyên-Đức provinces (former Haut-Donnai) in southern central Vietnam.

who have been cited by W. A. Smalley (1955:659) as offering a potential control group for comparative study of the highland/ lowland dichotomy to which I have added a patrilineal/matrilineal dimension. According to Smalley:

In the Sre as compared with some of their neighbours such as the Cil, such a study should be immensely rewarding, for in this case the language is close to the point of easy mutual intelligibility, speaking for a non-distant common origin for the two groups. What difference of social and economic structure accompanies the difference in agriculture, and what are the possible cause-and-effect factors involved? (Smalley 1955).

As both the Cil and Sre are matrilineal, we must look to the Mà subgroups—one of the few patrilineal societies (along with the Stieng) among the southern Bahnaric peoples—for a possible independent variable. The Ko·ho are the only Mon-Khmer tribe known to date that encompass both matrilineal and patrilineal subgroups. Both the closely related Mnong (Condominas 1957, 1960, 1965; Lafont 1967b) and Chrau (Thomas 1971:26) are entirely matrilineal.[4] In order for this method of inquiry to have any utility, several assumptions are implicit in a conceptual model of a prototypical Mon-Khmer society (i.e. a society whose subsistence is primarily dependent on swidden agriculture, with patrilineal descent groups often found with long houses). The Mà as described by Boulbet (1957, 1964, 1966, 1967) typify this hypothetical model. The dependent variable is represented by the Sre subgroup, which is matrilineal, including clans associated with long houses and deriving subsistence mainly from paddy cultivation (Dournes 1948).

Historically, the Ko·ho, with the exception of the Mà subgroups, were subject to intensive influence from Austronesian peoples, especially in the guise of Chàm economic and political domination.[5] This influence is reflected in the residual dialect area of Chamic languages which divide the Bahnaric languages into northern and

---

[4] These peoples are matrilineal in the sense of the ethnographic present, which is used here as a term of reference since most of the societies concerned in this study have been either decimated, relocated, or assimilated as a result of the Indo-Chinese wars.
  Several other Mon-Khmer groups are suspected as having been matrilineal, such as the Brũ, Puộc, and Xà-Câu or Khang in North Vietnam (Phan-Huu-Dat 1962, 1964), and some Bahnar subgroups in central Vietnam (Le-Thi-An 1969). All of these groups could have been influenced by the Chàm prior to Vietnamese displacement in the fifteenth century.
[5] The upper Donnai River region (Vietnamese *Đồng-Nai*, Koho *Dà Dơng*) did not come under Vietnamese domination until after 1698.

southern entities. The cultural traits associated with the Austronesian superstratum are: (1) paddy cultivation; (2) rice ceremonies;
(3) long houses (associated with clans); and (4) matrilineal descent
systems (Loeb and Broek 1947:421). On the periphery of this region
are Mon-Khmer-speaking groups which reflect this influence in
varying degrees (Bourotte 1955:31, 40–41).

According to Murdock, only the direct transition from patrilineal
to matrilineal descent is impossible (1949:190), but: "Under matrilocal pressures, patrilineal societies can become bilateral, and thence
perhaps eventually matrilineal. They cannot, however, undergo direct
transition to a matrilineal form of organization" (1949:218). The
Bahnar, who have bilateral descent and matrilocal residence patterns
(Guilleminet 1952:468–498), seem to exhibit the above criteria,
although some observers feel that they are in transition from matri-
lineality to patrilineality (Le-Thi-An 1969:50–55). Assuming that
the prototypical Mon-Khmer peoples were indeed patrilineal, one
could explain the Bahnar as in the process of losing their Chamic-
influenced matrilineal system and acquiring patrilineal characteristics
due to more recent and intensive Vietnamese influence. An example
of this phenomena may be found in the Chrau (Thomas 1971:26).

The Mnong appear to have been influenced by the highland
Austronesians rather than the Chàm proper and thus have adopted
sociocultural traits common to the Rhadé. All matrilineal Mon-
Khmer groups for which there are sufficient data exhibit a clan
system (or vestiges thereof) and some variation of Hawaiian cousin
terminology. In their cousin terminology, the Mnong Gar incorporate both the Chàm Hawaiian terms and the Crow system of the
Rhadé.[6] This unique system is discussed in detail by Lounsbury
(1964). The Sre employ a different variation, where the terms of
address are Hawaiian but the terms of reference are Eskimo (Evans
1962:48–50). This is similar to the Khmer (Lebar et al. 1964:102),
who are presently bilateral, but were probably matrilineal within
historical times. From the available evidence, it appears that the Mà
possess identical kinship terms as the Sre, with slight dialectical
differences so Mà cousin terminology appears to be Hawaiian (at
least for terms of reference) (Boulbet 1967:132–137). However, Tax
points out that "... methods of classification often differ considerably not only in tribes of the same linguistic stock but even in those
which are so closely related that the actual terms are practically

[6] For Chàm kinship terminology, see Lafont (1964); for Mnong Gar,
Condominas (1960); for Mnong Ro'lo'm, Lafont (1967b).

identical" (1937:6). The Mà have been isolated historically and are considered more resistant to cultural change than the other Ko·ho groups. These people did not absorb Chàm traits, repulsed the Vietnamese for centuries, and were not pacified by the French until the first quarter of this century (Bourotte 1955:40–41). Among the Mà of northwestern Lâm-Đồng province, the term *mpŏl* is used in the sense of the extended family (Boulbet 1937:136), whereas both the Mnong and the Sre use *mpŏl* to indicate more precisely the clan (or matri-sib) (Condominas 1972:203; Dournes 1948:102).

Despite the lack of adequate ethnographic material from some groups, the continuing examination of social structure, settlement patterns, linguistic, and ethnohistorical evidence provides a preliminary basis for explaining the occurrence of matriliny in highland Vietnam. It appears that the Austronesian intrusion from along the coast and into the central highlands coupled with ecological factors favoring a degree of dependence upon paddy cultivation could account for matrilineal societies in this region. In their study of the relationship of long houses to social organization, Loeb and Broek state that matriliny and long houses are traits not original to Mon-Khmer-speaking peoples and were diffused from the Chamic tribes of Darlac plateau (1947:418–419). All of the matrilineal Mon-Khmer groups have some type of unilineal descent group, either in the form of a presently functioning clan, or vestiges of such a system within historic times, and almost always closely associated with long houses. These matrilineal societies also have a Hawaiian cousin terminology or a variant thereof.[7] It is, therefore, premature to attribute categorically the appearance of matriliny in Southeast Asia as a random occurrence of a particular trait of social organization, as some observers have indicated (Murdock 1949:192).

REFERENCES

BOULBET, J.
  1957 Quelques aspects du coutimer (N'dri) des Cau Maa. *Bulletin de la Société des Études Indochinoises* 32:108–178.
  1964 Modes et techniques du pays Ma. *Bulletin de la Société des Études Indochinoises* 39:169–300.

[7] Except the Khasi of Assam, who have an Iroquois cousin terminology and clans, but no long houses (Nakane 1967).

1966   Le miir—culture itinérante avec jachère forestière en pays maa'. *Bulletin de l'École Française d'Extrême-Orient* 53:77–98.

1967   *Pays des Maa' domaine des génies.* Publications de l'École Française d'Extrême-Orient 62. Paris.

BOUROTTE, B.
1955   Essai d'histoire des populations montagnardes du Sud-Indochinois jusqu'à 1945. *Bulletin de la Société des Études Indochinoises* 30:1–133.

CONDOMINAS, G.
1957   *Nous avons mangé la forêt.* Paris: Mercure.

1960   "Les Mnong Gar du Centre Viêt-Nam," in *Social structure in Southeast Asia.* Edited by G. P. Murdock, 15–23. Viking Fund Publications in Anthropology 29. New York.

1965   *L'exotique est quotidien.* Paris: Plon.

1972   Aspects of economics among the Mnong Gar of Vietnam: multiple money and the middleman. *Ethnology* 11:202–219.

DOURNES, J.
1948   Structure sociale des montagnardes du Haut-Donnai: tribu des rizculteurs. *Bulletin de la Société des Études Indochinoises* 23:101–106.

EVANS, H.
1962   *Ko'ho language course,* two volumes. Dàlat: Christian and Missionary Alliance.

GUILLEMINET, P.
1952   La tribu Bahnar du Kontum. *Bulletin de l'École Française d'Extrême-Orient* 45:393–561.

IZIKOWITZ, K.
1951   *Lamet: hill peasants in French Indochina.* Etnografiska Museet Studier 17. Göteburg, Sweden.

LAFONT, P. B.
1964   Contributions à l'étude des structures sociales des Cham du Viêt-Nam. *Bulletin de l'École Française d'Extrême-Orient* 52:157–171.

1967a L'agriculture sur brûlis chez les Proto-Indochinois des Hauts Plateaux du Centre Viêt-Nam. *Les Cahiers d'Outre-Mer* 20:37–48.

1967b Notes sur les structures sociales des Mnong-Rlam du Centre Viêt-Nam. *Bulletin de l'École Française d'Extrême-Orient* 53:675–683.

LE-THI-AN
1969   Some features of Bahnar society described (in Vietnamese). *Nghiên-Cúu Lich-Su* 121:50–55.

LEBAR, F. M., G. C. HICKEY, J. K. MUSGRAVE
1964   *Ethnic groups of mainland Southeast Asia.* New Haven: Human Relations Area Files.

LINGAT, R.
1952   *Les régimes matrimoniaux du sud-est de l'Asie.* Hanoi.

LOEB, E. M., J. O. M. BROEK
1947   Social organization and the long house in Southeast Asia. *American Anthropologist* 49:414–425.

LOUNSBURY, F. G.
1964   "The formal analysis of Crow- and Omaha-type kinship terminologies," in *Explorations in anthropology.* Edited by W. H. Goodenough. New York: McGraw-Hill.

MURDOCK, G. P.
1949   *Social structure.* New York: Macmillan.
1967   *Ethnographic atlas.* New Haven: Human Relations Area Files.

NAKANE, C.
1967   *Garo and Khasi:—a comparative study in matrilineal systems.* The Hague: Mouton.

NER, M.
1930   Au pays du droit maternel: compte rendu de missions. *Bulletin de l'École Française d'Extrême-Orient* 30:533–576.

PHAN-HUU-DAT
1962   Materials on the social and family organization of the Puoc people of northwest Vietnam (in Russian). *Sovetskaia Etnografia* 5:48–56.
1964   Nationalities belonging to the Mon-Khmer language family in North Vietnam (in Vietnamese). *Tín-Túc Hoạt-Dong Khoa-Học* 57:24–27.

SCHNEIDER, D., K. GOUGH
1962   *Matrilineal kinship.* Berkeley and Los Angeles: University of California Press.

SMALLEY, W.
1955   Review of *Nri: recueil des coutumes Srê du Haut-Donnai,* by J. Dournes. (Sàigòn: Éditions France-Asie, 1951). *Bulletin de l'École Française d'Extrême-Orient* 47: 653–661.

THOMAS, D. D.
1971   *Chrau grammar.* Honolulu: University of Hawaii.

TAX, S.
1937   "Some problems of social organization," in *Social anthropology of North American tribes.* Edited by F. Eggan, 3–34. Chicago: University of Chicago Press.

Some Filipino (Cebuano) Social Values and Attitudes Viewed in Relation to Development (A Cebuano Looks at Utang-Na-Loob and Hiyâ)

LOURDES R. QUISUMBING

Modernization studies now draw from all social sciences because of the way in which economic, political, and social forces interact in development and modernization. Economists recognize the mutual interaction of economic and noneconomic forces over long periods of time as comprising the essence of development (Dalton 1971). Empirical studies revealing unusual success or unusual failure pinpoint both cultural heredity and economic and physical environment as factors inducing success or failure (Dalton 1971:13). It is increasingly apparent that sociocultural dimensions are often instrumental in the success or failure of development programs (Rogers and Svenning 1969:361); and yet much of the research in less developed nations has been strictly economic in nature, ignoring sociopsychological variables and cultural aspects of the development problem (Inkeles 1967:v). Much more is known about gross national products and per capita income in less developed countries than about perceptions, attitudes, and beliefs of the people (Rogers and Svenning 1969:361).

Social psychologists and other behavioral scientists maintain that while the process of modernization involves change in technology, in social systems, in political and economic institutions, it also involves change in the attitudes, values, and behavior of people. Whether such changes in people are the cause or effect of technological modernization, it remains a fact that they are important because the beliefs and attitudes of a people play a significant part in determining how readily modernizing trends will spread (Guthrie et al. 1970:1).

Smith and Inkeles (1966), in presenting the thesis that individual members of a modern society have a certain set of attitudes, values, and beliefs, have offered an overall modernity (OM) scale designed to measure the sociopsychological characteristics of modern man. McClelland (1966) and other authors emphasize the role of individual attitudes and behavior in modernization, claiming that need achievement (n Ach) is a precondition to development.

Most social scientists are concerned with national and macro-development, or with impersonal problems and sectors, such as foreign trade and capital formation; and while it is readily admitted that some of the most intractable problems met in modernization exist on the rural community level, less focus is placed on development from below (Dalton 1971:3). The culture-bound research methodology of social scientists from more developed countries hinders social research in less developed countries because there are important sociocultural differences between these countries, and researchers often squeeze less developed countries into their methodological models instead of making new moulds to fit the new research situation (Rogers and Svenning 1969:361–362). The role of the anthropologist in development and the planning of change is imperative, especially at the village level (Sinha 1968).

That development can take place within the cultural context of the people, utilizing their own behavior patterns and value orientations, is compatible with the theory that it is traditionalism, not tradition, which is a barrier to modernization (Weiner 1966). Traditions are constantly subject to reinterpretation and modification, and as such constitute no barrier (Weiner 1966). This writer adopts the view that development programers would do well to utilize local models and cultural patterns. It is better to explore their positive features, and to introduce innovation by directing, as well as adapting change to existing local value and belief systems avoiding incompatibility with the people's norms and practices. There is no doubt, of course, that rational-empirical approaches, like first-hand knowledge of alternative ways of doing and producing things and reduction of the high risks of adopting innovation, as well as power-coercive strategies can effect faster change (Bennis et al. 1962), but innovation requires new attitudes and skills, and adjustment to existing social structures and cultural expectations creates problems. Understanding and respect for the client's own values and attitudes facilitates the change-agent's choice of appropriate techniques and strategies for effecting change and increases the acceptability of the innovator himself. In personalistic societies like the Philippines, social acceptance of the person must oftentimes precede acceptance of his views and ideas.

That the Philippines is a traditional society undergoing modernization is obvious, but the process is taking place in different regions of the country in varying tempo. Metropolitan Manila, some major cities and their near suburbs manifest clear evidences of urbanization and industrialization. The increasing network of communication and transportation facilities, the building of more roads and bridges, accelerate the rate of change. Notwithstanding this, the great majority of the country depends on an agricultural economy, is rural in orientation and predominantly traditional in outlook. Values cluster around personalism, particularism, and nonrationalism. The explanation of events tends to be personalistic rather than mechanistic, intuitive rather than scientific, subjective rather than objective. The cultural ethos sustains close personal ties, harmony with nature, not control; smooth interpersonal relations and reciprocity, rather than independence and achievement.

This paper is focused on the analysis of two major themes in Philippine value orientation; *utang-na-loob* and *hiyâ* in a Cebuano context,[1] on the premise that these themes, because they play a dominant role in Philippine behavior and social organization, can be utilized for development and, therefore, should be better understood. Recent studies by social scientists and psychologists have shown the prevalence of these two values among many peoples of the Philippines and their importance as conceptual tools for the analysis and understanding of social interaction (Pal 1958; Lynch 1959, 1970; Kaut 1961; Bulatao 1964, 1970; Guthrie and Jimenez-Jacobs 1966; Landa Jocano 1966; Barnett 1966; Lawless 1966; Kiefer 1968; Hollnsteiner 1970). The existence of equivalents to the terms *utang-na-loob* and *hiyâ* in the different Philippine languages further proves their presence as a Filipino cultural universal.[2]

---

[1] The island of Cebu is located in the central Visayas region of the Philippines. Due to its strategic location, Cebu City is the second largest commercial center in the country. Cebuano-Visayan is spoken by the majority of the people in the Visayas and Mindanao.

[2] Some other equivalents to *utang-na-loob* and *hiyâ* are: *utang-nga-naimbag-a-nakem* and *mabain* (Ilocano); *otang-nalub* and *nababainan* (Pangasinan); *utang-lub* and *marinê* (Pampango); *utang-na-buot* and *supog* (Bicolano); *utang-nga-kaburut-on* and *awud* (Waray); *kabalaslan-sa-lawas* [debt of one's self] and *huyâ* (Hiligaynon); *buddhi* or *panumtuman* [a remembrance] both meaning a debt which is not to be demanded; *pangdagdag* [the sentiment in the creditor upon the failure of a friend to repay], *way sipug* (*hiyâ*) [that on the part of the debtor who fails to repay] (Tausug).

This study attempts to give further elucidation to *utang-na-loob* as the dominant principle in Philippine behavior and *hiyâ* as the strongest sanction ensuring it. Analysis of Cebuano conversational patterns among the rural folk, especially household helpers, vendors, and small landholders; interviews and group discussions with the writer's students in cultural anthropology on the graduate and undergraduate levels, supported by the writer's actual observation and personal experience, provide the bases of the conclusions drawn and herein presented. This writer contends that the viewpoint of the participant-in-the-culture provides a deeper insight and adds valuable understanding to such an area as values and attitudes, cultural realities which are difficult to observe, describe, or measure, and are at best *felt* and *experienced*. The time has come when the behavioral scientist, especially the anthropologist, should join hands with the trained native to arrive at more reliable conclusions on any aspect of the latter's culture.

Reciprocity or *utang-na-loob* (*utang-kabubut-on* in Cebuano) and *hiyâ* (*kaulaw, ka-ikog, katahâ* in Cebuano), as they operate in Cebuano society, offer fine distinctions and different shades of meaning, an analysis of which reveals their importance as premises and sanctions of social behavior. While reciprocity is accepted as a universal norm, its emphasis and importance in Philippine social life are dramatically manifest and institutionalized in highly specific and patterned ways. *Utang-na-loob*, translated by Hollnsteiner as a "debt inside oneself" and by Kaut as a "debt of prime obligation," is described as a special type of reciprocity which stems from a good or favor received, or a service rendered and which allows no quantification in terms of payment, nor termination (Hollnsteiner 1970; Kaut 1961). This is distinct from *utang*, a simple debt of contractual nature, where terms of payment are specified and exact, and the obligation is terminated upon payment with no emotions involved. *Utang-na-loob* is a unique Philippine pattern of reciprocity, which exists with some interesting, significant, and logically related variations in different parts of the country, in Luzon, in the Visayas, and Mindanao (Kiefer 1968). Kiefer refers to the exchange of gifts and services as conjunctive reciprocity or *buddhi* among the Tausugs of Sulu; and to blood debts or revenge on the other hand, as disjunctive reciprocity.

Every Filipino is expected to possess a fine sense of *utang-na-loob*, to be keenly aware of his indebtedness and obligations to those from whom he has received favors, by being grateful and by repaying

them when possible and at an appropriate moment. Among Cebuanos, an individual possessing *utang-kabubut-on* is admired for his
concern and thoughtfulness, his solicitude and consideration for
another's needs and feelings. He is a *maayong tawo* [good man],
maantigo mo balus sa iyang mga utang-kabubut-on [knows how to
repay his indebtedness to others]. The Tagalogs say he has a *magan-
dang utang-na-loob* [a beautiful sense of gratitude]. *Utang-na-loob* is
never uttered or referred to in a trivial manner. It reflects a "system
of social sentiments," of a deep and strong affective nature and
expressively symbolizes a whole configuration of reciprocal obligations (Kaut 1961). Similarly, in Cebuano, the concept of *utang-
kabubut-on* implies a complicated network of reciprocal relationships
that reflect deep and strong affective sentiments.

Emotions accompanying such indebtedness do not cease upon repayment, since such a debt is never completely repaid. As Cebuanos
say it, "*Ang utang-kabubut-on dili kabayran ug salapi hangtud sa
kamatayon; hangtud sa kahangturan*" [A debt of gratitude cannot be
paid with money; it lasts until death or forever]. This is truly so, for
utang-kabubut-on is passed on to one's family and kin, and repayment
can be made to any member of the benefactor's reference group, even
after his death. Reciprocity takes on different forms and degrees
depending on the varying social contexts in which it occurs, the
circumstance and the nature of the gift, and the relationship between
the giver and the receiver. The degree of indebtedness increases with
the intensity of the need of the receiver, the generosity and goodwill
of the giver, and the closeness of the relationship between them.

The notion that *utang-kabubut-on* is created only when the presentation of goods and services is *unsolicited* fails to account for reciprocity
in the case of intimate alliances where mutual requesting and accepting can be taken for granted. A favor, good, or service *solicited* from
someone with whom one has close relationships, usually a kin or a
friend, also creates a great sense of indebtedness. Here the Cebuano
does not speak of a mere *pañgayo* [asking] but a *hangyo* [request]
which he expects to be granted. Refusal of a serious *hangyo* hurts the
amor propio [personal dignity] of the person requesting. An *unsolicited*
offer, however, because it is tendered by a person sensitive enough to
see the other's needs, is highly appreciated, and elicits a touching
utang-kabubut-on. The unsolicited gesture comes from one with
whom the receiver has a pre-existing relationship. It is a symbol of
affinity which the receiver can accept with confidence.

The assertion that the gift activates a unilateral relationship of indebtedness reversible only by means of a properly offered return gift (Kaut 1961) does not seem very precise in the Cebuano case. While it is true that there is an implied expectation of return, the giver-receiver relationship becomes mutual upon acceptance and the primary concern is not to have the gift repaid but to maintain or strengthen existing ties. The acceptance of the *kabubut-on* [gift of oneself] further implies that the receiver is willing and eager to help the giver when the latter's need for help arises. The receiver may now give something better or more than the original gift; or whatever lies within his means, not as interest on an investment, but as an acknowledgment of goodwill and generosity and a means of reinforcing relationships.

Emphasis on the feeling of uneasiness and the burden imposed on the receiver in the never-ending "see-saw kind of reciprocity" referred to by Kaut and Hollnsteiner certainly misses that sense of self-satisfaction and fulfilment which the receiver experiences when, as he becomes a giver, he is able to repay a socially expected obligation which he has embraced wholeheartedly. As soon as an individual becomes the recipient of a favor, he willingly takes upon himself not only the obligation to repay but also the duty of seeking opportunities which will allow him to show his gratitude. Repayment is not made at any time. There are proper occasions and necessary circumstances when it is expected, foremost among them being the time when the donor is in need and when the receiver is in a position to repay.

Utang-kabubut-on, translated as "debt of one's volition," expresses this willingness to assume the obligation, the payment of which not only enables one to fulfil a duty but also to form, renew, or strengthen social ties and relationships. *Utang-kabubut-on* is not a mere exchange of gifts or services, but a reciprocal interaction, creating or strengthening social bonds not only between the giver and the receiver, but between their families as well, a process by which the individual can place himself in a secure network of mutual obligation extending even beyond kinship lines.

Because the Cebuano is aware of the social and personal meaning of a gift, he is careful in choosing the person to whom he gives or from whom he accepts a gift. A girl who does not intend to accept a suitor is not expected to accept his gift, especially if it is an expensive one. As Kaut says, acceptance (*pagtanggap*) institutes a virtual contract, but to say that this signifies that the donor can then expect a greater type of return at a later time is to overstate the investment aspect. In fact, when a receiver has the slightest suspicion that this is the motive behind the gesture, he is careful not to accept the favor, and his *amor propio* [sense of personal worth] is hurt.

Care in accepting a gift, *ang pagdawat*, because of its deep significance, carries with it the delicate task of knowing when and how to refuse a gift, *ang pagbalibad*. Rejection of a gift or voluntary aid which is equivalent to rejection of the person of the giver could be an extremely serious act, affecting both the giver and the potential receiver with the unpleasant or bitter consequences of *hiyâ* [shame] or revenge (Kaut 1961). The Cebuano usually feels *kaulaw* [hurt, embarrassment, shame] when his offer is rejected, and *ka-ikog* [complex feelings of consideration, respect, and fear to displease] when he has to refuse a gift.

Intrafamilial reciprocity partakes of a deeper meaning and more intense emotionality. *Utang-kabubut-on* to one's parents is permanent and can never be adequately or completely repaid. One owes one's very life and existence to the care and loving solicitude of one's parents, to whom deep and lifetime loyalty is rightfully due. In return, grown-up children, whether married or unmarried, consider it a serious and sacred obligation to take care of their aged, disabled, or needy parents in their own households, where they continue to be respected and consulted. Growing old in Cebu, as well as in almost all parts of the Philippines, is usually much less of a problem than it is in other countries. A Cebuano saying expressing this filial obligation goes this way: one never completely repays or understands one's debt to one's parents until he himself becomes a parent, *"dili gayud kita makabalus sa utang-kabubut-on sa atong guinikanan, hangtud nga kita usab mahimong guinikanan."* Among siblings and other close kin, reciprocal exchanges are frequent and to be expected. These deepen their interaction and relationship.

Failure to observe the norms of *utang-na-loob* is identified with disloyalty, lack of consideration, negligence. *Walay ulaw, walay ka-ikog, walay ikagbalus*, and *walay batasan* are very strong terms referring to ingratitude.[3] They operate as powerful sanctions.

Utang-kabubut-on to one of a superior status is accompanied by feelings of *ka-ikog* or *katahâ*, a sense of awe and respect. Repayment is not expected in equivalent terms, since one is usually not in a position to make that kind of payment. Thus, personal services are tendered instead. These would consist in assisting at household chores, such as laundry and kitchen work, housecleaning or gardening, in attending to a sick member of the family, or attending to visitors

---

[3] Cebuano terms expressing lack of respect for traditional values and customs.

18

during a *fiesta*, wedding, baptism, burial, and other family social gatherings. Willingness and availability to serve, when needed, count most. Thus, the value of the reciprocation does not lie so much in the material or monetary amount of the gift or in the economic equivalent of the service, but in the timeliness of the help, the goodwill and intention behind the gesture, and the feelings of friendship or loyalty that go with it. Cebuanos do not use the term *bayad* [payment] which suggests a cash amount but *balus*, which is a mutual exchange or personal reciprocation, the giving of self. This explains why the non-reciprocation of *utang-kabubut-on* when the benefactor is in need or when there is an event of significance to celebrate like a departure, an arrival, a birthday, an anniversary, the wedding of a family member and other similar situations, is looked upon as negligence or default. The same applies to nonacceptance or refusal to receive a favor or gift. The refusal amounts to personal rejection.

The norm of reciprocity has been the subject of considerable study and has been established as a universal principle at work in the social order. The *utang-na-loob* manifestations in different Philippine groups possess features characteristically similar to those exhibited in tribal societies and peasant economies, where exchanges are reciprocal gestures conceived as "noneconomic," governed and often instigated by direct social relations, and constrained always by the kinship and community standing of the parties concerned (Dalton 1971:51).

Each sector implies appropriate norms of reciprocity, which is not always a one-for-one exchange, but a complex continuum of variations in the directness and equivalence of exchange . . . Observable at one end of the spectrum is assistance freely given, the small currency of everyday kinship, friendship, and neighborly relations, the "pure gift" Malinowski called it, regarding which an explicit demand for reciprocation would be as unthinkable as it is unsociable—although it would be equally bad form not to bestow similar casual favors in return, if and when it is possible. Toward the middle of the continuum stand balanced exchanges, in which a fair and immediate trade is right behavior, as for example when kinsmen come from a distance seeking food and bearing gifts. And at the far end of the spectrum self-interested seizure, . . . (Dalton 1971:51–52).

The end points of the continuum are referred to as "generalized" and "negative" reciprocities; the midpoint, "balanced" reciprocity (Service 1966).

At this point it may be stated that as the Philippines shifts from traditional to cash economy, it may be expected that *utang-na-loob* as an operating principle of interrelationships and redistribution of surplus goods may decline (Hollnsteiner). Ambivalent attitudes among the Filipinos themselves regard *utang-na-loob* as both an incentive and a deterrent to progress. While Filipino effort continues to be motivated by gratitude to the significant persons in one's life and community projects may still hinge on loyalty to people one is indebted to, there are definite trends towards preference for cash and stipulated payment of goods and services rather than goodwill and smooth relations, reliance on merit rather than on personal influence and connections. Original resistance to such modern institutional practices like insurance, hospitalization, banking transactions, co-operatives, and credit unions is lessening; traditional values, attitudes, and beliefs are undergoing many adaptations to changing conditions. Technological, economic, and political changes penetrate through the whole Philippine social and cultural fabric, even though discontinuities and lags still exist.

Modernization brings about profound changes in traditional settings and social relationships, as kinship units lose their pervasiveness and values become less personalistic and particularistic. But this is not to say that *utang-na-loob* and all the other Filipino personalistic traits will completely disappear, nor to expect that the people will relinquish their traditional way of life in favor of highly impersonal modern attitudes, for as Anderson aptly puts it in his study of Philippine entrepreneurship,

...despite the obvious and oft-cited maladaptiveness of personalism for development (such as red tape, erosion of bureaucratic honesty, encouragement of corruption, undermining of public morality), personalism may on balance provide functions without which development could not take place (without a rather complete structural and ideological revolution). The advantages of Filipino economic personalism constitute another challenge to the ethnocentric fallacy that only Western social forms and psychological conditions give rise to incipient and more advanced economic development (Anderson 1969).

Claude Lévi-Strauss further underscores this writer's viewpoint:

...Societies which are at present engaged in the processes of economic development and industrialization may with the help of their own specific cultural wealth build up their own systems of motivations and incentives; and before these are criticized by reference to criteria peculiar to the industrial societies of the West, they must be subjected to minute examination. They also offer us a rewarding field of study (Lévi-Strauss 1954).

Finally, in discussing the modernization of social relations, Smelser (1966) expresses the danger developing nations face when they conceive speed of economic development to be the only criterion of growth—the too rapid destruction of various forms of social integration taking place at the very high cost of social unrest and political instability that may in the end defeat the very effort to develop (Weiner 1966:111). In the last analysis, development is for the people, and their choice of priorities should be respected.

REFERENCES

ANDERSON, JAMES N.
  1969   Buy-and-sell and economic personalism: foundations for Philippine entrepreneurship. *Asian Survey* 9(9).

BARNETT, MILTON L.
  1966   *Hiyâ*, shame and guilt: a preliminary consideration of the concepts as analytical tools for Philippine social science. *Philippine Sociological Review* 14(4):276–282.

BENNIS, WARREN G., *et al.*
  1962   *The planning of change: readings in the applied behavioral sciences.* New York: Holt, Rinehart and Winston.

BULATAO, JAIME
  1964   *Hiyâ. Philippine Studies* 12:424–428.
  1970   "Manileño's mainsprings," in *Four readings on Philippine values.* IPC 2. Edited by Frank Lynch and Alfonso de Guzman II, 89–114. Quezon City: Ateneo de Manila University Press.

DALTON, GEORGE
  1971   *Economic development and social change.* New York: The Natural History Press.

GUTHRIE, GEORGE M., PEPITA JIMENEZ-JACOBS
  1966   *Child rearing and personality development in the Philippines.* University Park: Pennsylvania State University Press.

GUTHRIE, GEORGE M., *et al.*
  1970   *The psychology of modernization in the rural Philippines.* IPC Papers 8. Quezon City: Ateneo de Manila University Press.

HOLLNSTEINER, MARY
  1970   "Reciprocity in the lowland Philippines," in *Four readings on Philippine values.* IPC 2. Edited by Frank Lynch and Alfonso de Guzman II. Quezon City: Ateneo de Manila University Press.

INKELES, ALEX
1967 "Forward," in *Economic development and individual change: a social-psychological study of the Camilla experiment in Pakistan.* Edited by Howard Schuman. Harvard University, Occasional Papers in International Affairs 15. Cambridge, Massachusetts.

KAUT, CHARLES
1961 *Utang na loob:* a system of contractual obligation among Tagalogs. *Southwestern Journal of Anthropology* 17.

KIEFER, THOMAS M.
1968 Reciprocity and revenge in the Philippines: some preliminary remarks about the Tausug of Jolo. *Philippine Sociological Review* 16(3–4): 124–131.

LANDA JOCANO, F.
1966 Rethinking "smooth interpersonal relations." *Philippine Sociological Review* 14(4):282–291.

LAWLESS, ROBERT
1966 A comparative analysis of two studies on *utang na loob. Philippine Sociological Review* 14(3):168–172.

LÉVI-STRAUSS, CLAUDE
1954 Economic motivation and structure in underdeveloped countries. *The International Social Science Bulletin* 6(3).

LYNCH, FRANK
1959 *Social class in a Bikol town.* Philippine Studies Program, University of Chicago, Series 1.
1970 "Social acceptance reconsidered," in *Four readings on Philippine values*, IPC 2. Edited by Frank Lynch and Alfonso de Guzman II. Quezon City: Ateneo de Manila University Press.

MC CLELLAND, DAVID C.
1966 "The impulse to modernization," in *Modernization: dynamics of growth.* Edited by Myron Weiner, 28–39. New York: Basic Books.

PAL, AGATON
1958 A Philippine barrio. *Journal of East Asian Studies.* University of Manila.

ROGERS, EVERETT M., LYNNE SVENNING
1969 *Modernization among peasants: the impact of communication.* New York: Holt, Rinehart and Winston.

SERVICE, ELMAN
1966 *The hunters.* Englewood Cliffs New Jersey: Prentice-Hall.

SINHA, D. P.
1968 *Planned socio-cultural change: myth, possibility or reality.* Proceedings VIIIth International Congress of Anthropological and Ethnological Sciences, Tokyo and Kyoto, volume three.

SMELSER, NEIL J.
   1966   "The modernization of social relations," in *Modernization: dynamics of growth*. Edited by Myron Weiner. New York: Basic Books.

SMITH, DICK HORTON, ALEX INKELES
   1966   The OM scale: a comparative socio-psychological measure of individual modernity. *Sociometry* 29:353–377.

WEINER, MYRON, *editor*
   1966   "Introduction," in *Modernization: dynamics of growth*. New York: Basic Books.

The Economic Importance of Children in a Javanese Villa⁻e

BENJAMIN WHITE

While there has been comparatively little research in Java on fertility attitudes and practices, there are several quantitative and qualitative studies which indicate the prevalence among both rural and urban couples of the desire for large numbers of children, matched in practice by a high level of marital fertility (see, for example, Gille and Pardoko 1965; IPPA 1969a, 1969b; Geertz 1961; Koentjaraningrat n.d.). These studies on the whole confirm Jay's impression that "The value that Javanese society places upon a family full of children can scarcely be exaggerated. . . . Across the entire social spectrum . . . children are desired in abundance" (Jay 1969:97).

In view of the acuteness of the population problem in Java, one's first impulse perhaps is to regard the desire for children "in abundance" as totally out of step with the reality of Javanese economic life, as a prime example of the "irrationality" that social scientists so frequently describe in peasant life. In the aggregate or statistical sense —that is, from the point of view of the Javanese economy as a whole

Field research (beginning in August 1972 and still in progress at the time of writing) was carried out in a village in Kabupaten Kulon Progo, special district of Jogjakarta, as part of a project on "The economic cost and value of children in four agricultural societies" under the general direction of Dr. Moni Nag, Columbia University. The project was funded by the National Institutes of Health—National Institute of Child Health and Development, under Contract Number NIH—NICHD-71-2209. I am very grateful to Moni Nag and Anne Stoler for advice and encouragement at all stages of the research; also to Drs. Masri Singarimbun, Hanna Papanek and Mely G. Tan for the opportunity to present earlier versions of this paper in seminars at Gadjah Mada University, Jogjakarta and University of Indonesia, Jakarta.

—there is ample justification for the view that high fertility will in the foreseeable future mean only more mouths to feed in that crowded island and more children to educ~te, who when they reach potentially productive age, will add themse.ves to an already overcrowded and underproductive labor force. Population growth certainly implies for the large majority of the children born each year, increasingly bleak economic prospects. However, because the basic unit of demographic behavior (and likewise, in Java, of economic behavior) is the family, if we wish to examine the economic rationality or otherwise of demographic behavior, we must transfer our attention from large-scale statistics to individual couples in their individual economic environments. In doing so, we should not assume that the Javanese family economy merely replicates in miniature the Javanese economy as a whole. In this paper, I hope to question the view that rural overpopulation implies that prospective Javanese parents have no economic justification for producing large families of potential child laborers.

Such a view, I think, is based on dubious assumptions concerning the implications of overpopulation in terms of labor opportunities and the value of children's labor within the family. Overpopulation and the existence of a labor surplus in the Javanese rural context does not mean that large numbers of people are reduced to complete idleness for long periods of time ("idleness" in the sense of having no opportunity to work at all, is perhaps a peculiar characteristic of the unemployed in industrial economies, as depicted in the cry of America's depression years, "How can I work when there's no work to do?"). On the contrary, people are forced by population pressure into increasingly marginal and *under*productive activities (that is, activities with increasingly low returns to labor) and must therefore work increasingly *longer* hours to achieve the required minimal returns. Labor is abundant, and cheap in the market, but since it is the only resource available to so many Javanese families, it is still for them a valuable resource. Under these conditions, rather than assuming *a priori* that the economic costs of children to their parents outweigh the economic benefits, we should consider carefully the extent to which Javanese parents may derive benefit (although their children, and the economy as a whole, do not) from the production of large numbers of children as a potential source of labor. In what follows, with the aid of preliminary results from field research in a Javanese village, I shall attempt to outline some of the economic benefits arising from high fertility, considered from the parents' point of view.

No systematic research on this topic has yet been done in Java, or in other agricultural societies so far as I know; but there are some studies which, though not specifically concerned with the cost and value of children, give us some general information about the ages at which Javanese children begin participating in production and the kinds of tasks they engage in. Slamet, for instance, estimates (1965: 173) that by the age of eight children in Java have begun to join in all the subsistence activities and daily work of their parents. Koentjaraningrat (n.d.:146ff.) notes that in Tjelapar (South Central Java) regular school attendance is rare; instead, girls are engaged in household tasks, cooking, pounding paddy, or caring for younger sibs, while boys are sent by their parents to collect branches and leaves from the woods (for use as wrappers or for weaving), to help in garden cultivation, etc. A majority of boys and girls also earn wages herding water buffalo, cows, goats, or ducks. The conflict between children's education and the need for their labor is mentioned also by Budi Prasadja (1972:46), who notes that in Gegesik (West Java) economic pressures often force small farmers and landless laborers to neglect their children's education, because they need their labor, especially in the case of male children. Gille and Pardoko note that "As soon as he reaches school age [six or seven years] every child born into a farmer's family is put to work on the land during the peak periods of planting and harvesting, when all available labour is used" (Gille and Pardoko 1965:503–504). In rural Modjokuto (East Java) Jay wrote that he

... observed children to be industrious, even at an early age, in picking up small piecework jobs such as hulling peanuts or sorting and bundling onions. ... As the children move into adolescence, their labour of course becomes more valuable. A daughter in particular is able to carry much of the load of housework and also to work with the mother in the fields for cash wages when there are opportunities. Sons are helpful not so much for the work they may do with the father, which in my observation was minimal, but for the exchange labour they can perform as a young male of the household (1969:69).

In small-town Modjokuto, "little girls [i.e. preadolescent] ... soon learn to do the whole family shopping alone, and—if the mother sells in the market—may take over the mother's stand for short periods." During adolescence, boys may start to earn money by

... occasional farm-work, as a labourer in a shop making cigarettes, as a ticket-collector on one of the many jitneys [or] as apprentice to a tailor or carpenter. Girls rarely work except in the mother's business . . . they usually remain at home, occupied with a continual round of domestic duties (Geertz 1961:116, 118ff).

While these observations are of interest, much more quantitative research is necessary if we wish, for instance, to compare the Javanese case with Clark's estimate that children in Asian peasant societies may become "net producers" (i.e. produce more than they consume) at ages as low as seven years (Clark 1970:226). Indeed, the question turns out to be a very complex one on closer examination.[1] In order to compare the "economic cost" with the "economic value" of children, we require a substantial amount of data from families of various sizes and economic levels on at least the following points. With regard to the *costs* of children, we would need to know as a minimum: (1) the economic costs of pregnancy and childbirth; (2) the cost of feeding, clothing, educating, and otherwise caring for a child at various ages; (3) the cost of all the social and ritual obligations incurred from the time of the mother's pregnancy until the child reaches adulthood (in Java these costs are considerable); and (4) the opportunity costs involved in the production and rearing of an extra child, e.g. the time lost by the mother in pregnancy, childbirth, and nursing when she might otherwise be productively employed. In addition, we should determine from current mortality levels (5) the probability that a child will survive to a given age, and thus the costs "lost" on children who fail to reach productive age. Turning to the economic *value* of children, two kinds of values should be considered: (6) the value of children as sources of security for parents in old age (a factor whose resistance to quantification does not negate its importance in the shaping of reproductive decisions); and (7) the value of children as a source of productive or useful labor in the household economy. Since it is clearly impossible to deal with all of these questions here, I shall confine myself almost entirely to the last one. This question itself requires data on the following points: (1) At what ages do children of either sex become *capable* of performing various productive or useful activities? (2) How does their output at various ages compare with that of an adult? (3) Granted a given level of *potential* of children in productive or useful activities, what is the *actual* extent of their involvement in the household economy?—in other words, to what extent does the overpopulated, "labor-surplus" economy still allow room for the participation of children.

[1] Various approaches to the study of the economic value of children in agricultural societies, and some relevant ethnographic data, are discussed in Nag (1972)

It is important to remember that while the *potential* of children, for various kinds of economic activity depends largely on physiological factors (levels of health and nutrition, etc.), the extent of their actual participation in the economy depends upon a number of additional factors specific to the particular economy and society in question. Thus, before providing any data on children's economic activities, I shall attempt to put the material in an economic framework with a brief description of the economy of the village sample studied and the available opportunities for productive activity.

Economic Characteristics of the Population Studied

The population studied consists of several hamlets in a village complex approximately twenty-five kilometers northwest of the city of Jogjakarta. Basic demographic and economic data were obtained from about 500 households, but I shall deal here with only forty households which were selected for detailed research on the participation of children in the household economy. This small sample (which at a later stage of research was increased to 100 households) consisted of small farmers and landless laborers, and the households selected contained at least one child of potentially working age (over six years) so that the average household size (6.3) was considerably larger than the average for the village as a whole (4.5). Average landholdings per household and per capita are shown in Table 1.

Table 1. Average landholdings in the forty household sample (in hectares)

	Per capita	Per household
Sawah (irrigated rice fields)	0.0170 hectares	0.1066 hectares
Pekarangan and *tegalan* (house compounds and dry fields)	0.0289 hectares	0.1811 hectares
Total:	0.0459 hectares	0.2877 hectares

In the region in question, the varying quality of *sawah* (mostly rather low) and an uncertain water supply make for equally uncertain yields, so that it is not easy to estimate how much *sawah* is necessary to supply the average household's rice needs. However, taking 125 kilograms of hulled rice as the average per capita requirement per year (see Penny and Singarimbun 1972:83) and thus almost eight quintals as the annual requirement of a household of average size in our sample, we can be certain that, at the very least, all households with less than one-tenth hectare (that is, almost three-quarters of the forty-household sample) fall in the category of those unable to meet their rice requirement from their own land in normal years. Garden crops are also sold for cash or in exchange for rice, but there are no households in our sample whose primary source of income or subsistence is garden cultivation. The large majority of our sample, then, are compelled to rely on activities outside the "family farm" for a major part of their basic subsistence. I shall briefly describe the most important of these other subsistence activities.

Sharecropping.   With this system, the landowner usually provides none of the inputs (cost of seeds, fertilizer, cultivation, etc.) although he usually pays the land tax, and receives as rent one-half of the total yield. It can thus be said that from the sharecropper's point of view, the returns to his inputs of cash and labor are approximately one-half what they would be were he cultivating his own land. There are nine sharecroppers in our forty-household sample.

Agricultural wage-labor.   Irrigated rice, besides requiring almost continual attention, demands large amounts of labor over short periods of time at three stages in the cycle (hoeing, planting, and harvesting); even small holders can rarely provide this labor from their own families, and must therefore seek outside labor. Some small farmers enter reciprocal (*gotong-royong*) labor exchange arrangements for this purpose, but the large majority engage hired labor. At the time of my research, wages for these tasks were as follows:

Male labor (ground preparation): thirty to forty rupiah for three to four hours

Female labor (planting): fifteen to twenty-five rupiah for three to four hours; (harvesting): one-sixth to one-tenth of the total rice she harvests.

A day's harvesting yields more in rice than other kinds of wage labor (Anne Stoler's research in the same village showed the average share or *bawon* received by harvesters to be 3.5 kilograms of unhulled rice), and this partly explains why planting wages are so low; those who have participated in the planting expect later to be invited, or at least allowed, to join in the harvest. Some do not even ask for planting wages, in the hopes that their *bawon* at harvesting will be increased.

Wages are quoted for half-day periods of three to four hours because labor is normally engaged by the half-day, and only at peak periods can laborers obtain an occasional full day's paid labour.

Handicrafts for cash sale. The main handicrafts for cash sale are *tikar* [pandanus sleeping-mats], woven by women, and *kepang* [split-bamboo mats], used often for drying rice, and usually woven by men. Almost all the households studied engage in mat weaving as a part-time occupation. Some also gather, cut, boil, and soften pandanus-leaves for sale to *tikar* weavers. Most of the *tikar* weavers produce on an average one *tikar* each five days, weaving for about four hours each day; the cost of materials is thirty-five rupiah, while the finished product sells for sixty to 120 rupiah depending on size, quality and on the season. Thus the weaver makes only one to four rupiah per hour; returns to labor for a *kepang* weaver are only slightly higher.

Small trading. In the forty households, a large number of women and a few men are engaged in small-scale trade as a permanent or seasonal source of income; carrying loads of goods or produce, usually on foot and occasionally by bicycle, from home to market, from market to town, or from market to market over a range of up to thirty kilometers, for very small profits. Given the distances covered, this is a very time-consuming occupation (a minimum of four hours daily, and a maximum of twenty-four hours in the case of the distant markets). Most of these small traders or *bakuls*, with a working capital of 500–1000 rupiah, earn perhaps fifty to a hundred rupiah on their selling days.

Animal husbandry. The forty households own and care for a large number of animals: altogether 298 chickens, 61 ducks, 46 goats or sheep, 32 cows, and 4 water buffalos. Chickens generally find their own food, apart from being fed kitchen scraps, but all other animals require a considerable amount of labor to care for and feed. Ducks must be fed and taken to water for extended periods each day; goats, sheep, cows, and water buffalos all require fodder which is generally cut and brought to them from gardens, roadsides, river banks, irrigation channels and the edges of rice fields. In addition, cows and water buffalos must be taken to water. For those households with enough labor to care for them, these animals provide an important means of storing wealth, besides a regular source of income in the case of laying chickens and ducks, and a seasonal source of income in the case of working cows and water buffalos. An idea of the value of the larger beasts is given by two common practices. First, a household with enough labor to care for a beast but not enough capital to purchase one will often undertake to care for animals belonging to a richer household. The animals remain the property of the original owner, but half of their offspring become the property of the "sharecropping" household. Second, a cow or water buffalo requires at least one large basket of green fodder each day, mixed with another of paddy stalks; an owner who cannot provide the labor from his own household will pay from thirty to fifty rupiah per day (compare this with the wages quoted above) for that amount of fodder. It should be noted that here, as elsewhere in rural Java, animal husbandry does not provide a significant source of meat or eggs for home consumption; 95 percent of the eggs, and virtually all the animals, are sold. The major source of protein is the much cheaper *tempe* [fermented soybean cakes].

Production of food for sale. Twelve of the forty households are engaged in the production of various food items for cash sale, mostly in the collection of coconut palm sap and the process of boiling it down to produce *gula Djawa* [palm sugar]. A man will climb the trees twice daily (about two hours in all) to collect the sap [*nderes*], while his wife will boil the sugar (*nites*) for about four hours. Also, up to two hours daily will be necessary to provide sufficient firewood. These labor inputs (figures are for a household tapping four trees) produce a daily yield of sixty to eighty rupiah. Other items produced for sale are *tempe* (the fermented soybean cakes mentioned above) and *dawet* [boiled drink made from rice or arrowroot flour, coconut milk, and *gula Djawa*]. Both of these require comparable amounts of labor in preparation, as well as firewood. To these labor inputs should be added the hours spent in selling the finished product—a whole morning at the market, unless the product is bought in the house, at a lower price, by neighbors or small traders.

The above summary indicates some important characteristics of household economy in rural Java. If we compare wages or returns to labor from the activities described above with an individual's rice needs (about ⅓ kilogram daily) and with the local price of rice (which rose gradually throughout the research period, from forty to seventy-five rupiah per kilogram), it is clear that though the returns from those activities may meet or even sometimes surpass the rice requirement of one adult, they definitely fail even to nearly meet the requirements of a whole household of four to six people; even more so if we include a household's other daily expenditures on kerosene for lamps, tobacco, tea, etc. In such conditions, *all* family members in addition to the household head must take whatever labor opportunities there are in order to meet the household's needs. For those households with insufficient land resources and without enough capital to engage in large-scale trade, the most profitable activity in terms of returns per hour is agricultural wage labor, particularly harvesting with the *bawon* system. This is confirmed by the common practice of stopping or reducing all other activities during the busy agricultural seasons in order to avail oneself of the more profitable opportunity. But because of the strictly limited nature of such opportunities, all family members must usually spend a large majority of their time in the less productive sectors mentioned above, however low the returns may be, or in other words, *whatever their cost in labor time* to produce the necessary minimal return. The question we now turn to is to what extent under such conditions a married couple may expect to derive economic benefit from the accumulation of large numbers of children as sources of labor.

The Value of Children in the Household Economy

Age of beginning various economic activities.   First we need some idea of the ages at which children are capable of performing various economic activities, and the ages at which they begin regularly performing them. A total of 146 household heads were asked at what age their children had begun performing ten types of activity: fetching water, care of chickens or ducks, care of goats or cattle, cutting green fodder, hoeing irrigated rice fields, hoeing dry fields, transplanting rice, harvesting rice, care of younger siblings, and wage-labor of any kind. I have included such activities as fetching water and child care under the heading of "economic activity" (and later shall include others, such as cooking and other housework) because, while not strictly productive, these tasks are necessary for the maintenance of the household, and may frequently be indirectly productive when performed by young children through the freeing of an older household member for more productive labor. The results are summarized in Table 2. From the table it can be seen that while there are isolated cases of children beginning various tasks at five or six years of age, most children begin them at a somewhat later age. This is confirmed by more detailed observations described below. Thus for the sake of simplification I have omitted children below the age of seven years from further consideration in this paper, because the majority of them cannot be considered significantly productive or useful to their parents before that age. But from ages seven to nine, it appears, children of both ages will have begun regular performance of such tasks as water carrying, animal care, fodder collection and (in the case of the girls) rice planting and harvesting; while the heavier tasks of hoeing a wet or dry field (boys) and all kinds of wage labor (both sexes) are not generally begun until thirteen years. An exception to this last is harvesting for a *bawon*-wage, which as we shall see is often performed by very young girls.

Table 2.   Numbers of children engaged regularly in various productive or useful tasks, age of beginning (youngest case) and average age of beginning (from a sample of 146 households)

Activity	Number of children Boys	Girls	Age of beginning (youngest case)	Average age of beginning
Fetch water	29	66	5 years	8.8 years
Care of chickens/ducks	38	18	5	7.9
Care of goats/cattle	58	9	6	9.3
Cut fodder	80	4	6	9.5
Hoe *sawah*	41	—	8	13.0
Hoe dry field	39	—	10	13.1
Transplant rice	—	50	5	9.9
Harvest rice	8	61	7	9.7
Care of younger sibs	36	35	5	8.0
Wage labor	12	8	8	12.9

Productivity of children's labor. With this information as a beginning, we next need to know how the productivity per hour of children at various ages compares with that of adults in various tasks. Relative productivity, in all kinds of manual occupations, depends on a combination of skill and strength (in the forty households there was only one man, a teacher, engaged in nonmanual work). So far as skill is concerned, very few of the tasks commonly performed by members of our sample can be classed as skills which take great lengths of time to acquire (the exceptions are tasks performed almost exclusively by adults, such as plowing and perhaps certain kinds of trading). In agriculture, for example, a boy can do all the tasks involved in preparing a rice field (apart from plowing) with as much skill as an adult after about one season's experience. This does not mean, of course, that farming is not a highly skilled occupation, demanding years of experience of differing weather conditions, crop varieties, pests, market conditions, and many other variables. The point is that these skills lie largely in deciding what is to be done and when to do it, rather than in the actual performance of the tasks once the crucial decisions have been made.

From detailed observation of daily activities in the forty-household sample (the methods used are described below), some interesting facts emerged with regard to the productivity of children's labor, if the level of wages received can be taken as an indication of productivity. In the case of wage labor by boys aged thirteen to fifteen years (hoeing *sawah* or *pekarangan*, and weeding), the wage was in every case the same as that received by adults; for girls of thirteen to fifteen, from a much larger number of observed cases, the wages for planting were in all cases the same as the adult wage. There were also two cases where a girl of eight years received the same wage as her mother, for the same hours of work, in the same field. In the case of harvesting with *bawon*-payment, Anne Stoler's research shows that the *bawon* received by girls below ten years and in the eleven to fifteen age group averaged 3.0 kilograms of unhulled rice, while that of the over-fifteen age group was 3.5 kilograms. These data indicate that the productivity per hour of children's agricultural labor of the most common kinds, at least from the early teens, is not much lower than that of adults. The same appears to be true of nonagricultural wage labor, from the few cases that we observed. Boys of fourteen years regularly received an adult wage for a full day's labor in construction projects, and girls of fifteen weaving on handlooms in a small local factory, though paid at piecework rates, took home the same wages as their adult counterparts.

For other tasks, particularly those in which younger children are engaged, it is much more difficult and in some cases impossible to estimate absolute or relative productivity per hour. In the case of cutting fodder (the most common of all male children's tasks), it frequently occurred that an adult male would one day cut grass for two hours to feed the household's animals, while a few days later a boy in the ten to twelve or thirteen to fifteen age group would spend the same amount of time to feed the same number of animals. For those below the age of ten, productivity in this task may be somewhat lower, because the basket in which they carry the cut grass is usually smaller than that which adults and older children use. Girls of thirteen and above seem to be able to weave *tikar* with the same speed as their mothers, although the quality may be somewhat lower if they have only recently begun weaving, and may thus fetch a lower price. But what of the productivity of young children in such tasks as taking

19

cattle to bathe, herding goats or ducks, scaring birds from a field of ripe paddy awaiting harvest, or staying at home cooking, caring for younger children and keeping chickens from a *kepang* full of rice drying in the sun, while the mother is working in the fields or trading at the market? The most that can be said is that these tasks are very frequently performed by extremely young children; that they involve long periods of time but little physical effort; that although these tasks in themselves may not be productive, they are all *necessary* in the sense that they must be done if the household in question wishes to keep animals, to save its rice from depredation, or to free an older household member for more productive labor. Furthermore, there is nothing in my observations to suggest that an adult could perform these tasks any better or faster than a small child, although, on the other hand, there are many other tasks in which an adult can be more productive than a small child, if he or she is freed from these "necessary but unproductive" tasks. The same would be true of many other tasks such as fishing in streams and irrigation channels to supplement the family's diet, collecting firewood, fetching water (an extremely time-consuming task in the dry season, when water must be scooped in coconut shells from a seep hole by the water's edge, the river water not being clean enough for household use without this filtering). It is thus interesting, though not surprising, to see that small children spend large amounts of time every day in these "adult-freeing" tasks (Table 3).

Many other cases concerning other tasks could be mentioned if space allowed, each of them suggesting the same conclusions. First, there are a large number of economically useful, sometimes necessary, but not very productive tasks—both in household maintenance and in the productive effort itself—in which small boys and girls from ages as low as six in some cases, and generally by the age of nine, can be virtually as productive or efficient as their adult counterparts could be. However, they remain largely children's tasks because adults and older children can be more productively occupied in other ways. Second, most of the more productive tasks (such as mat weaving, cutting fodder, planting, harvesting, hoeing) can be performed by children thirteen to fifteen years old with a productivity virtually equal to that of adults.

Extent of children's participation in household economy. Given this *potential* for the participation of children in household economy and production, we turn to the question of their *actual* contribution to

the total production of the household. In other words, having estimated their relative productivity per hour in various kinds of work,
we must discover how many hours per day they actually spend in
these tasks compared with adults, because a given potential of children, however great, is of no practical significance unless the household economy, and the larger framework of the "labor-surplus"
village economy surrounding it, still leaves room for the actual exercise of that potential. In order to ascertain the average number of
hours spent daily by children and adults of various ages in various
kinds of activity, a regular series of visits was made to each of the
forty selected households in order to ask each family member how
he or she had spent the twenty-four hour period immediately preceding the interview, and the time of beginning and ending each activity.
The households were each visited every six days over a period of
several months (although I am using here only the data from the first
two months, because the remainder were not yet processed at the
time of writing). The six-day interval was chosen so that visits should
not coincide either with the Javanese five-day market week or with
the seven-day week which might have affected the pattern of daily
activities, for instance, in trading and school attendance respectively.

Because the writer could not attend each interview, a majority of
the interviews was delegated to a team of local secondary school
children or secondary school graduates, who came from the same
hamlets as the small group of households they interviewed and thus
were already well acquainted with their subjects.

A number of questions may be raised concerning the accuracy of
data collected in this way, particularly in regard to the extent to which
the household members, possessing no clocks or watches, will have
known with any accuracy the duration of each of their activities. So
far as it has been possible to check independently the accuracy of the
information recorded, it seems that while there have undoubtedly
been omissions and inaccuracies, the general level of accuracy is much
higher than I had expected. Omissions that could be easily checked
(involving activities that must be done every day, such as cooking,
cutting fodder, etc.) were very rare, while irregular or unusual activities (such as *gotong-royong* labor) are of course much more easily
recalled. With regard to the accuracy of the times recorded, I found
to my surprise that the majority of people whom I asked could
correctly estimate the time of day to within a quarter of an hour. It is
interesting to note that several features of everyday Javanese village
life combine to give both old and young a considerable awareness of

the time of day. One might mention the relatively invariable time of sunrise and sunset in a region close to the equator; the practice of gong beating by hamlet heads at various relatively fixed times of day and night to announce that all is well; the close attention to how many hours are spent in agricultural labor, since the pay varies in accordance with the time spent; the presence in the middle of crowded hamlets of primary schools whose classes begin and end at specific times; and finally the five obligatory daily Moslem prayers, which although performed by only a few of our sample, at least were performed by some of their neighbors. What inaccuracies there are will probably have occurred throughout the whole sample, so that the material, whatever its absolute errors, can be used with some confidence for internal comparisons.

It should be noted that the two months of data used here (from mid-October to mid-December 1972), covering the end of the dry season harvest and the beginning of the rainy season, are from a relatively peak period of labor inputs in agriculture. Subsequent data will determine how much the levels of productive activity are decreased, or channeled into different types of activity, at other times of year.

In order to present the results simply, all economic activities have been grouped into eight broad categories as follows:

A1. *Care of small children.*
A2. *Household* (includes fetching water, house cleaning, washing clothes and kitchen implements, drying paddy and other crops, all kinds of food preparation).
A3. *Collect firewood.*
B. *Production outside agriculture* (weaving and all other handicrafts, food preparation for sale, trading, fishing).
C. *Animal care and feeding* (cutting fodder, collecting other food for chickens, ducks, cattle etc., herding and bathing of animals).
D. *Nonagricultural wage-labor* (weaving in a small factory, carpentry, construction, carrying goods for a wealthy trader, etc.).
E. *Exchange or communal labor* (unpaid labor building or repairing a neighbor's house etc.; does NOT include reciprocal agricultural labor—see category F—and does NOT include nonproductive labor such as serving guests at a neighbor's ceremonial).

F.   *Agriculture* (all agricultural labor, on one's own or an-
     other's land, whether unpaid, paid in cash or with *bawon*,
     etc.)

Taking the data from a series of eight days and ordering them in
the above eight categories, I have divided the totals by eight to give a
picture of the average number of hours spent *daily* by individuals
according to age group, sex, and type of activity. The results are
presented in Table 3. From this table it can be seen that the average
time spent by adults in "work" each day is nine hours (men) and
twelve hours (women), or if we exclude care of small children, nine
hours (men) and eleven hours (women).[2] Girls of age thirteen to
fifteen and sixteen to eighteen almost equal the adult contribution,
while children in the other groups contribute about one-half as much,
with the exception of boys of seven to nine who contribute only one-
fourth of the adult working hours. Looking more closely, we see that
children exceed the adult contribution in some important tasks both
in the "useful" (A1 - A3) and "productive" (B - F) categories. Children of *all* age groups spend more time on the average than adults in
child care, with the result that only a little of the adults' time is spent
in this way; an example of the function of children in freeing adults
for more productive labor. The collection of firewood and animal
care are clearly in large part the responsibility of children rather than
adults. In all kinds of "productive" activity (categories B, C, D, and
F) boys and girls of sixteen to eighteen years almost equal, and in
some cases exceed, the contribution of adults, so that if all these
activities are counted together we find that the totals of productive
activity almost equal those of adults in the case of girls, and exceed
them in the case of boys. Recalling the observation of Jay (1969) that
male children frequently replace the adult in fulfilling *gotong-royong*
(communal or reciprocal labor) obligations, it appears that boys in
the ten to twelve and thirteen to fifteen age groups regularly engage
in *gotong-royong* labor, but that their contribution is small compared to that of the sixteen to eighteen age group, who slightly
surpass the adult contribution in this activity. The table also shows
that during the two months covered, girls of thirteen and over spend
as much time as adult women in agriculture, but that girls of seven
to nine and ten to twelve spend only one-third of that time; there is,

---

[2]   These figures confirm the view of Koentjaraningrat (n.d.: 355) that Javanese
villagers "need no enticement or encouragement to work hard." Rather, they
need help that can increase the productivity of their work.

Table 3. Average hours per day per person devoted to various tasks, according to age, sex and type of activity (N = forty households, eight days of observation per household)*

Age group, sex, and number in the sample: Activity:	7-9		10-12		13-15		16-18		19-29		30+	
	M (N = 18)	F (10)	M (14)	F (10)	M (18)	F (11)	M (9)	F (12)	M (6)	F (12)	M (39)	F (42)
A1 Care of small children	0.2	1.2	0.5	1.7	0.5	1.5	0.3	0.1	—	0.6	0.4	1.2
A2 Household	0.1	1.2	0.3	1.1	0.2	2.3	0.2	2.8	0.1	3.1	0.3	4.3
A3 Collect firewood	0.7	0.2	0.6	0.3	0.7	0.5	0.2	0.1	0.1	0.1	0.3	0.1
B Production outside agriculture	0.2	1.3	0.4	0.2	0.8	1.9	0.2	4.9	3.2	4.8	1.8	4.9
C Animal care and feeding	1.2	1.0	2.7	0.5	2.2	0.1	1.6	0.1	0.8	—	0.8	0.1
D Nonagricultural wage labor	—	0.1	—	—	0.1	0.4	1.7	0.3	2.1	1.3	1.1	—
E Exchange or communal labor	—	—	0.2	—	0.2	0.1	0.7	0.2	0.4	0.3	0.6	0.1
F Agriculture	0.1	0.8	0.7	0.7	1.1	2.1	3.2	2.3	2.6	2.3	3.7	1.6
Total hours of "work" per day	2.5	5.8	5.4	4.5	5.8	8.9	8.1	10.6	9.3	12.5	9.0	12.3

* Because these per-person, per-day averages are derived from a sample of at least nine individuals in each group, and from a total of eight days of observations, they do NOT give a realistic picture of one day in the life of one individual. In reality, each member of the sample spends a greater amount of time in a small number of activities each day.

however, a possibility that when the period is extended to cover the whole of a harvest season, the contribution of small girls will be much greater. Anne Stoler's research during the 1973 wet season harvest, with the same forty households, found that the number of days spent harvesting according to age group was as follows: up to ten years of age, 12.6 days on the average per person (N = 12); eleven to fifteen years, 21.1 days (N = 11); sixteen years and over, 14.5 days (N = 56).

Having compared the contributions of the various age groups and sexes, it is interesting to see if there are any significant differences to be found *within* those groups; for example, it is important to know whether children from large families do more or less work, and what kinds of work, compared with children from small families. This question is very closely related to that of the "cost and value" of high versus low fertility. In the economic environment of "labor-surplus," it might easily be supposed that the larger the family size, the smaller the productive contribution of each child in the family must be, because the household can only provide strictly limited labor opportunities for them. Or possibly we might find that although children in large families work for long periods, the greater the family size, the greater the likelihood that children's work will be less productive. In this case even the elder children would be engaged in the less productive activities in large families, simply because the household cannot provide them with the chance to be more productive, although they are potentially capable of being so. If this were the case (i.e. if the number of children in the family varied inversely with their productivity), we would have to conclude that increasing the number of one's children results in economic "loss" to the parents, because of the effect hypothesized above. In order to examine the validity of such an argument, the sample was divided into two further groups of children: (1) children with only one, or no sibs in the potentially productive age group seven to eighteen years, i.e. "children from small families" and (2) children with two or more sibs in that age group (i.e. "children from large families"). Dividing these new categories into only two age groups (so as to retain a sufficiently large sample in each group), and calculating per-person averages in the same manner as previously, some interesting results emerge which are presented in Table 4.

Taking the children of seven to twelve years first, it can be seen that children from the larger families (those with many sibs) do *more* work in *all* types of activity (excepting "nonagricultural production") than

Table 4. Average hours per day devoted to various tasks by children according to age, type of activity, and number of siblings (N = 102 children in forty households, eight days of observation per household)*

Age, number of sibs in that age group, and number in the sample: Activity:	7–12 years		13–18 years	
	0–1 sibs N = 15	2 or more sibs N = 37	0–1 sibs N = 15	2 or more sibs N = 35
A1 Care of small children	0.5	0.9	0.8	0.5
A2 Household	0.4	0.6	1.3	1.2
A3 Collect firewood	0.5	0.5	0.3	0.5
B Production outside agriculture	1.9	1.1	1.9	2.4
C Animal care and feeding	0.7	1.2	1.4	1.0
D Nonagricultural wage labor	—	0.1	0.5	0.5
E Exchange or communal labor	—	0.1	—	0.4
F Agriculture	0.3	0.6	1.3	2.2
Total hours of "work" per day	4.3	5.1	7.5	8.7

* Those in the left-hand column of each age group have one or no sibs in the potentially productive seven to eighteen age group, and are referred to in the text as "children from small families"; those in the right-hand columns, with two or more sibs in that age group, are referred to as "children from large families."

do their counterparts from the smaller families. In the case of the older children of thirteen to eighteen years, the children from large families also do more work (comparing the total work hours daily), and that difference is due to the fact that children from large families work more in the directly productive categories of B - F, while those from small families work more in the useful but nonproductive categories of A1 - A3 (with the exception of animal care and feeding). If these differences can be taken to indicate a significant trend (which can be subsequently tested by the calculation of similar totals from a total of a hundred households over a period of several months), then they clearly tend to refute the argument examined above, leading us instead to the conclusion that *children from large families tend to be not less, but more productive than those who come from small families.* Perhaps the reasons for this might be as follows: first, that children with many sibs are encouraged by the presence of elder sibs to participate in all kinds of work and, using their elder sibs as examples, begin performing each task at an earlier age than usual; and second, that children with many sibs, precisely because of their younger sibs' earlier participation in the useful but unproductive chores, are themselves liberated from those chores and free to engage in more productive activity.

In any case, there seems to be a strong possibility that in the village studied, high fertility does not reduce the productivity of children in the family economy, but rather tends to raise it. For the majority of households whose land and capital resources are severely limited— for whom the large part of their income must be sought in the application of their labor in whatever opportunities are available outside the household's own resources—the productivity of labor is determined by the population-resources ratio of the larger economic environment, over which they themselves have no significant control. In other words, productivity depends on the general demographic and economic conditions obtaining *outside* the individual family, not on the size of that particular family. Certainly, the situation might improve if *every* family were to limit the number of its children, but in the absence of this it is possible that individual parents may derive relative economic benefit from producing large numbers of children, in direct conflict with the needs of the economy as a whole, whose difficulties stem in large part precisely from a century and a half of steady and continuing population growth.[3]

A great deal more research is necessary before the question of costs and benefits of high versus low fertility to Javanese parents can be resolved, particularly in the area of costs of children, which I have not attempted to cover here. However, I hope at least to have suggested the value of further research along these lines, both in rural and urban communities. For example, one imagines that urban children in Java are considerably less productive than their rural counterparts, but there are certainly no data to prove this. The streets of Jakarta and other cities teem with small boys, collecting bags full of cigarette ends for "recycling," selling old magazines, shining shoes, or simply begging; how does their "productivity" compare with the cost of their keep and with that of their rural cousins, cutting grass and bird-watching in the *sawah*? Finally, we should consider whether there are any practical conclusions to be drawn from the data and preliminary conclusions presented above,

---

[3] For those readers interested in population history, I have suggested a basically similar hypothesis to account for Java's demographic growth under colonial rule in White (1973).

from the point of view of the effort to reduce fertility in Java through the Indonesian National Family Planning Program. Suppose it were confirmed in further research that high fertility does tend to result in net economic gain from the parents' point of view. Such a conclusion does not necessarily imply bleak prospects of success for the family planning program; for, although I have been narrowly considering the economic consequences of high fertility from the parents' point of view in this article, it is not at all the case that these are the only factors entering into reproductive decisions. Even casual research shows that Javanese parents are extremely anxious for their children's future economic welfare as well as for their own, and that they are acutely aware that, whatever the consequences of high fertility for themselves, the consequences for the welfare of their children are disastrous. In this case, perhaps the argument for family planning most likely to succeed is not so much "limiting the number of your children will benefit *you*" (an argument which may not be valid), but rather "limiting the number of your children will benefit your children"—an argument which is known to be true, and therefore might be easily received by the generation of prospective Javanese parents who must make the crucial reproductive decisions.

REFERENCES

BUDI PRASADJA, A.
 1972   "Pembangunan desa dan masalah kepemimpinannja." Unpublished thesis, University of Indonesia.

CLARK, COLIN
 1970   "Economic and social implications of population control," in *Population control*. Edited by A. Allison, 222–237. London: Penguin.

GEERTZ, HILDRED
 1961   *The Javanese family*. Glencoe: Free Press.

GILLE, H., R. H. PARDOKO
 1965   "A family life study in East Java: preliminary findings," in *Family planning and population programs*. Edited by Bernard Berelson et al., 503–523. Chicago: University of Chicago Press.

IPPA
 1969a "KAP survey, knowledge, attitude and practice of family planning, Djakarta, Indonesia, 1968." Draft Report of the Preliminary Findings. Indonesian Planned Parenthood Association, Jakarta.

1969b "Hasi 12 Penelitian Pengetahuan-Sikap-Praktek Keluarga Berentjana, Kabupaten Bekasi 1967." Indonesian Planned Parenthood Association, Jakarta.

JAY, ROBERT
1969 *Javanese villagers.* Cambridge: MIT Press.

KOENTJARANINGRAT
n.d. "Tjelapar: sebuah desa di Djawa Tengah Bagian Selatan," in *Masjarakat Desa di Indonesia Masa Ini.* Edited by Koentjaraningrat, chapter eight. Jakarta, Yayasan Penerbit Fakultas Ekonomi, University of Indonesia.

NAG, MONI
1972 "Economic value of children in agricultural societies: evaluation of existing knowledge and an anthropological approach," in *The satisfactions and costs of children: theories, concepts, methods.* Edited by James T. Fawcett. Honolulu: East-West Center.

PENNY, D. H., MASRI SINGARIMBUN
1972 *A case study in rural poverty.* Bulletin of Indonesian Economic Studies 8(2): 79–88.

SLAMET, INA A.,
1965 *Pokok: Pembangunan Masjarakat Desa.* Jakarta: Bhratara.

WHITE, BENJAMIN
1973 Demand for labour and population growth in colonial Java. *Human Ecology* 1(3): 217–236.

Problems in Comparison of Kinship Systems in Island Southeast Asia

WILLIAM D. WILDER

I. That there is a determinate, and determinable, relation between social classification and residence patterns in any given social system has been one of the more venerable hypotheses in anthropological research over the years. This has been so at least since 1889, when Tylor referred to residence practices and patterns as "the fundamental fact" in explaining modes of customary behavior. Fifty years later Kroeber (1938) spoke of "basic" as against "secondary" patterns of social structure in the same broad context. And that the hypothesis is a fruitful one has more recently been amply demonstrated in the work of Lévi-Strauss, Leach, and Geertz, to name only three examples.

The attempt here is to seek clarification of some problematic features of kinship systems, or "social structure" as it is sometimes called, in island Southeast Asia, by reference to this hypothesis. In the course of the discussion I will cite representative ethnographic data, including my own materials on Malay villagers of Pahang State in the Malay Peninsula (West Malaysia). I do not claim to provide an entirely convincing, or even necessarily adequate, verification of the hypothesis, but it seems to me that the results are

The fieldwork which supplied the data on Pahang Malay villagers was supported by the London-Cornell Project for East and Southeast Asian Studies; the Project was financed by the Carnegie Corporation of New York and the Nuffield Foundation. My thanks are due chiefly to the London Committee of the Project. I would also like to acknowledge helpful comments on parts of the argument in the present paper by Professors P. E. de Josselin de Jong and Sir Raymond Firth of Leiden and London respectively.

encouraging enough to warrant calling them to the attention of other workers in the field of Southeast Asian social structure.

In his review of ethnoscience (1964), Sturtevant noted that one of the relatively unexplored problems of that field of research was that concerning multiple or complementary naming systems specifically characteristic of Southeast Asia. Some of these naming systems, or social classifications, have not even been satisfactorily labelled as yet, as Lévi-Strauss (1962) observes; and in consequence, formalization in the study of these category systems has barely begun. An encouraging start has been made by Bernot (1965).

One reason for the relatively scant work on nomenclatures by anthropologists may stem from the simple fact that names, in many cultures, are taken so much for granted; they are almost like the force of gravity. This may be particularly so in cultures where *anonymity* is a threat. Thus any objective approach to names would seem like a careless meddling with reality itself, and anthropologists themselves are subject to this limitation of perspective. The ego-center in kinship analysis is another very prominent example of such a limitation. The idea that kinship is "ego-centered" is a survival of Morgan (1877), rather than Rivers (1914); as with other of Morgan's ideas, modification has been slow. The ego-focus is an obstacle in the study of kinship because it precludes an understanding of a number of kinship usages, to be discussed in this paper, that are not ego-centered. Some examples are: (1) address to nonspeakers, such as babies (pet names) (cf. Wilder 1970:256); (2) teknonyms; (3) necronyms; (4) birth-order names (versus relative-age categories); and (5) self-reciprocal terms of address. These are some of the forms of "indirect" naming and personal address found in Southeast Asia but not readily accounted for in the orthodox styles of kinship analysis.

I suggest, therefore, that the distinctive nature and distribution of such forms of person classification in Southeast Asia requires that we take into account their noticeably self-exclusive, or *soi autre*, character (Lévi-Strauss 1962:254–255), an approach which would go far beyond the usual egocentric assumptions of "kinship" analysis. The same characteristic appears also, for example, in the pronominal forms of many Southeast Asian languages (e.g. Malay *kita* versus *kami*, the inclusive "we" as against the "editorial we"). Leach has recently shown how fruitful a sociolinguistic examination, without prejudice towards kinship or nonkinship categories, can be (Leach 1971; cf. Wilder 1973).

I shall therefore attempt to show that the mobility and developmental patterns in residence groups typical of a number of Southeast Asian societies are associated in regular ways with person classification. First of all, however, I shall try to outline the different naming features that exist in the related cultures of the island region and within which the diverse elaborations to be discussed have received emphasis. Three system features in particular seem to be closely connected in the kinship classifications of island Southeast Asia. These are: (1) self-reciprocal terms; (2) birth-order names; and (3) teknonyms.

Let us look first at a comparatively simple case. Here it is a question of only two coexisting vocabularies, rather similar to each other in part, but also differing in their principles of classification. These two systems are the Pahang Malay reference and address nomenclatures that I recorded in 1965. The terms are listed in a somewhat simplified form in Tables 1 and 2. In cases where the relationship

Table 1.   Pahang Malay reference terms

Generations difference	Senior	Junior
0	Abang (eB)	Adek (ySibl)
	Kakak (eZ)	
	Pupu (Cous)	
	Abangpupu (eCous, male)	Adekpupu (yCous)
	Kakakpupu (eCous, female)	
	Ipar (SpSibl, SiblSp)	
	Abangipar (SpSibl, SiblSp, older, male)	Adekipar
	Kakakipar (” ” ” , female)	(SpSibl, SiblSp, younger)
	Biras (WZH, HBW)	
	Besan (CSpP)	
	Laki (H)	Bini (W)
1	Ayah (F)	Anak (C)
	Mak (M)	
	Bapaksaudara (PB)	Anaksaudara (SiblC)
	Maksaudara (PZ)	
	Bapakmentua (SpF)	Anakmenantu (CSP)
	Makmentua (SpM)	
2	Tokaki (GF)	Chuchu (GC)
	Wan (GM)	
3	Moyang (GGP)	Chichit (GGC)
4	Moyet (GGGP, GGGC)	

Abbreviations: F=father, M=mother, P=parent, B=brother, Z=sister, Sibl= sibling, C=child, H=husband, W=wife, Sp=spouse, Cous=cousin, G=grand- or great-, e=elder, y=younger.
Key to pronunciation: -k in final position=q (silent), i.e. for words in noncompounded form (such as mak or tok); e is short (silent) before -n, otherwise it is long; a in final position is=ö (ø).

expressed is self-reciprocal (symmetrical), only one term is given between the columns (Table 1). In Table 2 the reciprocals are in all instances personal names.

. What I have tried to stress through these tables is the striking difference between the two vocabularies, not in basic "type," but in emphasis. Among Malay villagers, address terms appear to exist not only as contextually distinct from reference terms, but also as systematically distinct. Whereas the reference terms are, as it were, "square" and self-contained, the address terms are lopsided and truncated; the address terms lack any distinctive terms for junior categories but have an extreme development of terms for senior relatives (birth-order names in the parental generation). We are prompted to ask what *local* peculiarity is responsible for this difference of nomenclatures. It is one which is not, as far as I know, reproduced to this extent in other parts of the Malay Peninsula (that

Table 2. Pahang Malay address terms

Generations difference	Senior			
0	Abang (Any older, male consanguine or affine, own generation)			
	Kakak (" " , female " " " , " ")			
1	Ayah	(F)		
	Mak	(M)		
	Pakwa	(PB, SpF,	1st	born)
	Pakngah	(" "	2nd	")
	Pakda	(" "	3rd	")
	Pakteh	(" "	4th	")
	Pakendak	(" "	5th	")
	Piktan	(" "	6th	")
	Paklang	(" "	7th	")
	Pakchik	(" "	8th	")
	Pakchu	(" "	9th	")
	Makwa	(PZ, SpM,	1st	born)
	Makngah	(" "	2nd	")
	Makda	(" "	3rd	")
	Makteh	(" "	4th	")
	Makendak	(" "	5th	")
	Miktan	(" "	6th	")
	Maklang	(" "	7th	")
	Makchik	(" "	8th	")
	Makchu	(" "	9th	")
2	Tokaki	(GF)		
	Wan	(GM)		
3	Moyang	(GGP)		
4	Moyet	(GGGP)		

Note: Junior relatives are addressed by name.

is, outside of Malay and Malay influenced groups of the center of the Peninsula). Yet an almost identical development of birth-order names *is* found in association with other types of nomenclature as far afield as Borneo, among the linguistically-related Penan, and highland Burma among the linguistically-unrelated Kachin (Lévi-Strauss 1967:302–305).

What accounts for this distribution of similar features within otherwise dissimilar systems? It would clearly be an evasion of the question to say, as Hildred Geertz has done of the Javanese kinship system (1961), that the Pahang Malays simply have two different kinship nomenclatures. It would be equally mistaken, it seems to me, to adopt the avowedly "comparative" approach of Murdock (1960). In Murdock's view, reference terms give the fuller account of the "the" kinship system and, accordingly, the other impoverished forms of usage may be discarded. I think it is easy to see how arbitrary such procedures are; the result can only be, as Needham (1962) has shown, a crude typology that actually precludes an understanding of the systems and thus rules out genuine comparison altogether. It is to treat kinship as a thing in itself, which it is not. In the approach I am advocating, naming systems are considered to be multiple, differing chiefly in variety or stress, but always working, as it were, from a similar cultural "base." It is the facts of the case, not the scheme, that decide what kind of naming is prior.

There are, then, a number of modes of social classification in island Southeast Asia other than the bare reference terms of kinship; all these modes of naming apparently constitute a sort of reservoir of cultural possibilities available to each community, and so I contend that if we are to do any useful comparison in studying the kinship systems of this region, these several other modes of classification cannot be neglected. In order to arrive at a better understanding of social classification as such in island Southeast Asia, we must avoid trying to treat kinship as a thing in itself, a tendency which until now has led to the setting up of typologies (as for example Murdock 1960) rather than the search for significant variations.

I have already summarized the kinship terminologies as used among Pahang Malay villagers, that is, the reference terms and address terms (as they are usually known in anthropology). One particular feature within the set of address terms used by Pahang Malays is a lengthy series of birth-order names. There also occur in the island area of Southeast Asia two other comparably elaborated instances of kin classification: teknonyms (among the Balinese)

20

and self-reciprocal terms (among the Hanunoo). In each of these cases, a principle of categorization has been extended so that in a real sense it dominates the system. On the face of it these are "type cases" if ever there were any. What I seek to show, however, is that, despite some tendencies toward "classic" proportions, these systems are actually neither isolated nor anomalous. Nor can they be fully understood simply on the grounds of possessing one feature to the exclusion of others. They, and some other systems, can indeed be said to express the "fullest possible development" of an institution (Needham 1959:86; Geertz 1964:104)[1] but such institutions, I suggest, are already hinted at in many other, more "plain" looking communities in island Southeast Asia. It is our task to look at some of these communities and, if possible, to discover the causes of variations in the basic set of institutions.

II. The Balinese and Hanunoo systems have been well (if briefly) described quite recently (Geertz 1964; Conklin 1964), and it will only be necessary to highlight the points relevant to our discussion here. Teknonymy is highly developed among the Balinese. As is well known, teknonymy (a term introduced into anthropology by Tylor in his article of 1889, already cited) is the social recognition of a person (by some one party or body of persons who use the term) by means of a two-word phrase $(a+b)$ made up of (a) his relationship to (b) one of his successors who is named; not (as in European or Arab usage) by means of (c) his predecessor(s), who is (are) named (the "surname") and (d) himself (his "given" name), a usage which takes the general form $(d+c)$. In patronymy, the man is (rather implicitly) a child, but in teknonymy the man is a father. The social repercussions of the widespread use of one or the other type of naming are considerable, not least of all in the Balinese case.

In a typical Balinese hamlet (usually less than 500 persons) an unmarried commoner is addressed by a birth name, with or without the addition of his personal name, by all the other members of the hamlet. But married persons, by the time they have children, become recognized in address by teknonyms; that is, their own or their birth name is now lost to them. In societies where teknonymy expresses *only* parenthood, there are but two relationship terms constituting

---

[1]   Cf. Jakobson and Halle (1956: 6), who stress that "when analyzing the pattern of phonemes and distinctive features composing them, one must resort to *the fullest, optimal code* at the command of the given speaker" (emphasis added).

the system, one for father/husband, one for mother/wife; in Bali, however, five forms are in use: the two for parent status (*Nang* or *Pan*, and *Men*), plus two more for grandparent status (*Kaki* or *Pekak*, and *Tjutjun*) and one for great-grandparent status (*Kumpi*) (Geertz 1964:107). In other words, the Balinese have extended the institution of teknonymy to make it cover much more than just parenthood. The result of this great elaboration of the teknonymous principle is, as the Geertzes make clear, a far-reaching suppression of personal names, or birth names; that is, with the birth of a child, a persons' own name usually disappears not only from himself but also from his parents' teknonym (if it ever appeared there at all, for we must remember that there is room for only one child/sibling's name in a teknonym). This institutionalized "amnesia" concerning persons is a social fact of considerable importance because it carries to the farthest reaches of the community.

Thus, in Balinese villages birth (or personal) names can usually only be heard in any way, shape, or form, when they indicate the very young or the unmarried, who in reality are the smallest and most insignificant members of the community. Children and the childless, then, form the ballast, the bottom grade, of the Balinese commoner community; only they have not been totally subjected to the classification of persons by means of teknonymy. All other modes of address (among the commoners, that is) virtually force the Balinese into a single, exclusive form of age-grading or procreational stratification (Geertz 1966:25). The Geertzes point out that the teknonymous institution in Bali is a formalization, in effect, of an isolated four-generation, direct-line "family." I will say more about this later, when I consider the group correlates.

Teknonymy in Bali constitutes the all-important reference and address system of relationship for the Balinese commoners (90 percent of a hamlet). How important and how total it is can be gauged from Geertz's (1966: Note 16) observation that even a man's own children address him by teknonym!

The third of the name-classification devices that I shall consider is self-reciprocal terms, that is, the "exchange" of identical names. In Southeast Asian systems there are two especially distinctive uses of this category-principle, in coparent terms and in the equating of members of different generations. Both are exemplified in the Pahang Malay reference-terminology, given above; *besan* and *moyet* respectively. The self-reciprocal feature, in these two forms, is fairly common among the terminologies of the class of Indonesian systems

called "central" by Berthe (1970)—Javanese; Baduj (Badui); Balinese; Pahang Malay, for example. But in the Hanunoo system
(Mindoro in the central Philippines) the principle is most unusually
prominent. Hanunoo kinship possesses no fewer than seven terms
which are symmetrical, or self-reciprocal, for relatives of generations other than Ego's own. As I interpret Conklin's account (1964:
36–37, Figure 2), they are:

1. *Bapaq*   (parent's sibling, male; sibling's child, male speaking)
2. *Bayih*   (parent's sibling, female; sibling's child, female speak-
             ing)
3. *Lakih*   (grandparent, male; grandchild, male speaking)
4. *Qiduh*   (grandparent, female; grandchild, female speaking)
5. *Qumput* (great-grandparent; great-grandchild)
6. *Pupuh*   (great-great-grandparent; great-great-grandchild)
7. *Qapuh*   (remote ancestor, remote descendant)

The really notable feature, not found in the other terminologies
discussed so far, is the classification given as 1 and 2 above: *Bapaq*:
uncle + nibling (sibling's child), and *Bayih*: aunt + nibling; that is,
self-reciprocal terms linking two *adjacent* generations. Again, we
must ask what factors have yielded this particular logical elaboration
in Hanunoo society of a type of category principle which, in more
basic form, is common to a number of societies in island Southeast
Asia.[2]

We have looked so far at three terminological features of social
classification, all of which find some sort of expression in a great
number of Southeast Asian communities but which are more fully
and logically developed in only a few. Thus, *teknonymy* receives an
intensive and possibly unique expression in Balinese commoner
society; *self-reciprocal terms* are carried to their fullest extent among
the Hanunoo; and *birth-order names*, no less distinctively, are

---

[2]   Incidentally, I am quite certain that this very feature of Hanunoo kinship is
really the thing responsible for Conklin's claim concerning the precision and
economy of his Stage 3 ("Abstract principles" 1964: 41ff), and does not result, as
he claims, from his own rigorous procedures in data organization (see especially
1964: 43). Conklin's interpretative omission here, proves, I think, the point that
I am trying to make in this paper—namely, the importance of broadening our
comparative perspective to encompass as much of the ethnographic reality as
may ultimately prove to be relevant. In short, as Leach has often insisted, we
must make the generalizations first, not last. (To be fair, though, Conklin, in
contrast with some componential analysts, does attempt to relate the terminology
to real life, in this case, to the marriage rules.)

systematically developed to the greatest degree among some groups of Peninsular Malay (or Malay-type) peoples, as well as in Borneo and in the Burma Hills on the mainland proper. It is clear, I think, that the regular variation that prevails in the social organization of the region under consideration cannot be explained by means of some one-dimensional taxonomy or even by the aid of indiscriminate collection of further facts about these many different societies. Much more important is to treat the kinship systems of this region as parts of more all-embracing sociolinguistic systems of classification proper to each society, as Geertz (1966) and Leach (1967, 1971) have shown so splendidly for three Southeast Asian societies (Balinese, Sinhalese, Kachin).

III. Before attempting to set out a scheme for the broader universe of social classification in the systems so far considered, it is necessary to enter in the lists one further example of a system in one respect possibly unique, as is the Balinese already outlined: namely, that of the Penan of Borneo, reported by Needham (1954), in the form of "death names." Alongside the kinship system, there is among the Penan a system of death names, or necronyms, which in everyday intercourse works in such a way as to displace the kinship system entirely; that is, the linguistic expression of social categories (or, as Radcliffe-Brown would have had it, type relations) is virtually the same as that of the kinship system and hence can and does serve in its stead. Only the words, it seems, and the occasions make the two systems really distinguishable. The context in which necronyms are used is decidedly unusual: except in a few cases, they are "entered," as the Penan say, at the death, not during the life, of the specified types of relatives.

There are some twenty-six of these names in use among the western Penan. In addition, the Penan use a simple form of tek-nonym, embracing two terms. The Penan case is of special interest because these two nomenclatures seem to form a system, and the necronyms happen to include an extensive series of birth-order names (nine separate words for as many siblings, i.e. up to "ninth child dead"). In actual practice, these two types of name seem to alternate in their application to what must be a substantial majority of the mature Penan population (the parents); almost by definition it seems they must do so, for as long as a Penan wife bears children.

I shall not attempt to explain why the Penan rely on the circumstance of death to give expression to their system of classification (although I can see that this is in perfect complementarity with birth, and as such is surely significant for constituting a larger whole, as suggested here). For present purposes, the important features are the apparently regular linkage, or "periodicity" of teknonyms and necronyms among the Penan (Lévi-Strauss 1962:254), and the associated fact that the teknonyms alternate almost entirely with respect to the same type relationship (parent-child, and in each case by reference to a specified child, either named or birth-ordered, and *not* to the speaker). In practice, both institutions reflect the same concern —recruitment to Penan society of teknonyms instigated by the birth of children and necronyms instigated for the most part by the death of children in advance of their parent(s) rather than in connection with any other type of relative. We could say, therefore, that parents are "named after" their children in Penan society because this completes a wider set of institutions (including death names) whose concern is also with children in relation to their parents, but in which the children are, as it were, "un-named" when they precede their parents in death. (The necronyms are pure relationship terms and unlike teknonyms they do not include a personal name.) Even more important than this functional association of necronyms and teknonyms, however, is the incorporation of a fully-developed child-sibling series into the death name system of the Penan. (To a small degree, as Needham notes, the teknonyms can also reflect birth-order, giving perhaps a further link between the types of naming.) That the Penan birth-order series refers to a generation of *children*, while the Pahang Malay series refers to a generation of *parents* may well be significant, as I shall suggest when I consider residence patterns. The Penan case, then, despite its anomalous appearance, fits in well with the hypothesis I am offering.

I must now answer the question of why these three features of social classification—self-reciprocal terms, teknonyms, and birth-order names—seemed, to me at least, to have special significance for the social organization of the groups under consideration here. Do they form a universe? I consider that they do because, as may be seen from the descriptions given thus far, they all seem to have certain semantic traits in common. It may be argued chiefly that they all suppress the possessive "tense" of the social situation in which they occur. The speaker, or Ego-center, is not directly part of the relationship he refers to by using the terms. In the case of birth-order names, in whichever position in the system they may happen to occur, the sense of "relatedness" is diminished by the tendency of these terms toward personal names. In the case of teknonyms, the "relatedness" is outside the speaker; the teknonym is, in a way, used on behalf of a dyad of which the speaker is not a member. Penan necronyms are like teknonyms in this sense because, although they express only relationship, this relationship is strictly external to the speaker(s).

Self-reciprocal terms, I admit, fall in somewhat lesser measure under this formulation. They go only as far as suppressing the *asymmetry* of a relationship. Yet I would argue that this is clearly a step towards suppressing the possessiveness of which I spoke above; that is, the relatedness of persons *across* generations, which can even be said to obtain in coparent terms, is deliberately weakened by linguistic identification or equality. So while there is no tendency toward introducing personal names or something like them, as with birth-order names or teknonyms, there is a tendency with self-reciprocal terms (which also occurs with the other two principles of nomenclature) to deny or reduce the complexity of relationships. This is done in the use of self-reciprocal terms by levelling the speaker and the spoken-of. In the other instances it is done by excluding the speaker altogether and at the same time adding personal names to the situation (teknonymy) or simply suggesting a trend toward individual names (birth names). All of these usages, then, imply a semantic midpoint between a completely "individualized" classification (with members possessing only personal names) and a completely relational classification (restricted to kin terms). For this reason, these three terminological features of island Southeast Asian societies seem to me to "hang together," and deserve to be treated accordingly.

IV. To summarize so far: I have argued that there are three particularly distinctive terminological features of classification systems occurring in a number of widely differing, or at least distantly separated, Southeast Asian societies. The terminological features have one powerful semantic feature in common which sets them off, namely an "objective" reference or implication. They impose on a situation this one particular detached way of expressing certain types of social relations; these relations are usually lineal or sibling relations but are always exclusive of the speaker in the sense described above. My concern, however, is not with their inherent semantic style nor with their place in whichever wider system they happen to be found. Rather, I am concerned with the reasons for their differential elaboration and their distribution over the entire region, or at least in some of its widely separated islands. In short, if it is correct to say that at one significant level the features are analogous (as shown schematically in Table 3), how can we then account for the very strongly marked differences of emphasis from place to place on one or more of the three features in question?

Table 3.   Types of person-classification in island Southeast Asia

	Self-reciprocal terms	
	=	
—		+
Teknonyms		Birth-order names

It may be important to note that despite their distancing effect semantically, these terminological features occur in direct address ("face-to-face") situations. While this is hardly a necessary theoretical requirement for their use, the suggestion of propinquity or terminological adaptation to residence patterns is quite strong. To conclude this argument, I have set up a parallel scheme of corresponding residence patterns (Table 4).

Table 4.   Types of local community in island Southeast Asia

	Intergroup/translocal networks and alliances (Hanunoo, Javanese)	
	=	
—		+
Extreme localization (centripetal) (Bali)		Segmentary (centrifugal) (Pahang Malay)

As I see it, there is an association between classification and residence patterns. This has already been demonstrated in previous analyses of specific cases, by the Geertzes for the Balinese for example. I think the case can be strengthened, however, by showing continuity and variation, Tables 3 and 4 are meant to set up the framework for this expansion of the argument.

The Geertzes have noted that commoners among the Balinese (the great majority of villagers), as distinct from the gentry, do not build extra-village social ties and that, equally distinct from the gentry, they use the teknonymy system. The effect of teknonymy, they say, is that it "actively prevent[s] . . . translocal descent ties . . . from developing" (Geertz 1964:105). Commoner descent in Bali is a truncated, localized, and reversed line of patrifiliation resulting largely if not entirely from the cultural paradigm (as they refer to it) of tek-nonymy; all this is reinforced by a high degree of village endogamy. In Bali, the teknonymous limits are so close that beyond them lies, not other groups identified as such, but rather sheer social anonymity.

For the Hanunoo and many Javanese communities the social situation is the opposite of that on Bali: the marriage rules demand a high degree of kin and local exogamy. In such communities also, there is an especially high development of self-reciprocal terms applied across generations. How can this be explained? It is Berthe's view (1970) that the self-reciprocal feature in the terminology of Javanese communities is an historically-developed level of the Javanese systems reflecting super-ordinate political-legal control imposed by the Javanese kingdoms. Berthe concludes that the intro-duction and grafting-on of self-reciprocal terms in Javanese local communities, used both within a generation and across generations, was a consequence of the introduction of wet rice cultivation and highly centralized authority that went with that type of economy; the function of these terms was to bring into the same circle of kin [*parentèle*] a large mass of persons, but without allowing the forma-tion of permanent groups which might in turn make themselves into autonomous circles resistant to the central power which, in theory, was absolute.

Berthe calls systems such as the Javanese "central" with delimina-tive terminologies. The Hanunoo do not appear to fit so well into his interpretation, but Conklin's description of local group charac-teristics among the Hanunoo makes at least one strong point in favor of a Javanese-type local organization: in Conklin's view, the gradations of collateral relationship and marriage prohibitions (as measured by fines for infraction) are strictly correlated with genera-tion depth, and as we have seen the Hanunoo system in effect marks out generation depth by a series of self-reciprocal terms. In its most important features, then, the Hanunoo residence pattern would seem to be like that of Javanese communities.

The segmentary or centrifugal communities, such as the Malay village I studied in 1965, constitute in many ways an intermediate example between the extremes just mentioned. Here are com-munities which tend to throw out daughter villages or groups in a kind of suburban sprawl. The question of community endogamy is no longer in the forefront; instead of the affinal links within or between groups, more dynamic wave formations extend from parent to daughter village. In such communities, a number of sibling groups tend to stay together at the center. In the Pahang Malay village where I worked, the geographical center of the settlement (which was the original one in the subdistrict) was also the center of power, politically, economically, and in terms of prestige (educational advancement). This power was carried by members of large sibling groups ("large" meaning four and usually more siblings who lived to marry and have children). In other words, the maintenance of numerical superiority usually indicated social success too. In a sense, the village grew like a volcano, with concentrated expansion at the center and more of a centrifugal expansion at the peripheries.

It might be thought that local group organization among the Penan is so different from that of Pahang Malays that the association between birth-order names and community growth must be immediately disconfirmed by the Penan case. I have noted above, however, an apparently significant shift in the *position* of birth-order series within the respective terminologies. Could we interpret this shift of position of otherwise practically identical sets of terms as one from the image of *assured expansion* to one of *feared contraction*? This seems to fit the Penan case where, as Needham has indicated, the viability of local groups, because of fewness of numbers is precarious.

A fluid marriage and residence pattern such as that of the Pahang Malay villages, or of the Penan nomads, is not easy to characterize, synchronically at least. Yet in each case there remains, in association with the community, the striking and virtually identical elaboration of a terminological feature, birth-order names. The series is an expression, in the most exhaustive fashion, of the smallest kinship unit possible—the sibling group. The principle of classification results from one of the simplest of criteria, that of precedence or clock-time. It is therefore possible that in the formalization of sequential order among siblings we can also see a kind of metaphor for community growth and expansion or the lack of it (as in the Penan terminology of death). A number of other processes, such as the tendency to form marriage alliances, or corporations within the village, seem to be suppressed.

V. I realize that the third of the associations I have suggested is likely to be the least convincing of all. A generalization meant to include utterly distant populations of Malay villagers, Kachin rebel tribesmen, and Penan forest hunters, whose sole common feature is a nine-position sequence of birth-order names will need more than the brief argument I have given to reach an acceptability perhaps comparable to that of the Geertzes' for the Balinese or Berthe's for the Javanese. Nevertheless, I believe the wider triad of features I have drawn above could well have substance considered in its entirety, and that with further refinement these formulations can be made to yield firmer correlations. Even as far as I have taken it, the argument seems to me to make more intelligible the general proposition (here restated with regard to primitive thought), which is this:

> Although there is undoubtedly a dialectical relation between the social structure and systems of categories, the latter are not an effect or result of the former: each, at the cost of laborious mutual adjustments, translates *certain historical and local modalities* of the relations between man and the world, which form *their common substratum* (Lévi-Strauss 1966:214; emphasis added).

Finally, I will conclude by indicating how the scope and postulates of the present paper can be brought to bear even more generally on the study of kinship and social structure in Southeast Asia. The questions out of which my argument grew were originally simple ones concerning various features of the terminologies I had myself collected among Pahang Malays, such as the difference between the two sets of kinship nomenclatures, the birth names, which are especially characteristic of one set of terms, and the question of self-reciprocal terms (found in the other).

Gradually I began to see that the diversity of category systems was more than this alone; it also extended *within* the given functional set or institution. Needham had recently reminded us of Lowie's admonition: that "a given nomenclature is molded by disparate principles" (Needham 1971:17, quoting Lowie's *Culture and ethnology* 1917). The question, then, became one of accounting for disparateness of principles, not sameness of—or reduction to—a type. So I developed my comparison of Southeast Asian kinship systems from another angle. In Southeast Asia kinship and naming systems are especially close, so close that they overlap and it is frequently, indeed usually, a waste of time to try to distinguish them as one or the other. It was necessary, in other words, to reduce the bias in favor of "kinship" and to talk in more dynamic terms.

Kinship systems, it appears, are not *necessarily* distinguished by the way their components (or categories) are assembled as wholes or by one or two arbitrarily-selected category principles (such as collaterality); rather, they are distinguished in the working of their parts, by the development, to a greater or lesser extent of some of their features. In the island Southeast Asia region, such an extreme development as teknonymy in the Balinese system (as against self-reciprocal terms and birth names, which are also present), contrasts with the birth-order names of the Pahang Malays or Penan. In other ways of course the Balinese and Malay systems, at least, are virtually identical.

Dumont has recently written (1971:119) of the difficulty in social anthropology of passing from moderately general theories, which are all too commonly developed from a few kinship systems of a particular region of the world, to an all-embracing theory. This difficulty seems to arise from attempts to fit the materials into a *typology* of whole systems, a form of the frequently deplored habit of butterfly collecting. The implicit notion behind such attempts seems to be that, since the cultures of the region are probably related, there must be an *original* system or systems which give us the basic type. This notion would have us looking at historically subsequent varieties of the basic type. My contention is that it avoids the question of comparison. The puzzles of the homeland of Malayo-Polynesian speakers, and of rice and other ecological features such as pile houses (found also, for example, in Japan); as well as the strikingly uniform tendency to sex equality in formal kinship in island Southeast Asia, are enough to make any reconstructions difficult. But that is a separate question, one of explaining similarities, whereas the real question, as far as comparison of kinship systems goes, is to account for the differences. The typologist Murdock, for instance, has failed here.

To put the case more simply: the terminological developments in island Southeast Asian societies (teknonyms and the rest) are parts of the kinship systems, or whatever we wish to call the classificatory mechanisms of these societies. The underlying, abstract principles of the different features are strikingly similar when the features are looked at in isolation; but these do not constitute "the system." It is the organization of groups that harnesses capricious logic and helps us to understand the arbitrary (in the sense of "optional") developments of actual societies. I have argued in this paper, though not as completely as I would have liked, that the variety of developments can and should be *explained*, not just exhibited, as curiosities or inessentials. I am sure that similar models can be developed to account for this sort of cultural detailing in other parts of the world. As for island Southeast Asia, in order to improve and extend in the meantime what seems to be a promising comparison, much more work will be needed on the types and distribution of terminologies in Southeast Asia and on the composition and dynamics of its local groups.

REFERENCES

BERNOT, L.
1965   Levirat et sororat en Asie du Sud-est. *L'homme: revue française d'anthropologie* 5:101–112.

BERTHE, L.
1970   "Parenté, pouvoir et mode de production: éléments pour une typologie des sociétés agricoles de l'Indonésie," in *Échanges et communications,* two volumes. Edited by P. Maranda, 707–738. Paris and The Hague: Mouton.

CONKLIN, H. C.
1964   "Ethnogenealogical method," in *Explorations in cultural anthropology.* Edited by W. H. Goodenough, 25–55. New York: McGraw-Hill.

DUMONT, L.
1971   *Introduction à deux théories d'anthropologie sociale: groupes de filiation et alliance de mariage.* Les textes sociologiques 6. Paris and The Hague: Mouton.

GEERTZ, C.
1966   *Person, time, and conduct in Bali: an essay in cultural analysis.* Southeast Asia Studies, Cultural Report Series 14. New Haven: Yale University Press.

GEERTZ, H.
1961   *The Javanese family.* New York: Free Press.

GEERTZ, H., C. GEERTZ
1964   Teknonymy in Bali: parenthood, age-grading and genealogical amnesia. *Journal of the Royal Anthropological Institute* 94 (2): 94–108.

JAKOBSON, R., M. HALLE
1956   *Fundamentals of language.* Paris and The Hague: Mouton.

KROEBER, A. L.
1938   Basic and secondary patterns of social structure. *Journal of the Royal Anthropological Institute* 68:299–309.

LEACH, E. R.
1967   "The language of Kachin kinship: reflections on a Tikopia model," in *Social organization: essays presented to Raymond Firth*. Edited by M. Freedman, 125–152. London: Cass.
1971   "More about 'Mama' and 'Papa'," in *Rethinking kinship and marriage*. Edited by R. Needham, 75–98. Association for Social Anthropology Monographs 11. London: Tavistock.

LÉVI-STRAUSS, C.
1962   *La pensée sauvage*. Paris: Plon.
1966   *The savage mind*. London: Weidenfeld and Nicolson.
1967   *Les structures élémentaires de la parenté* (second edition). Paris and The Hague: Mouton.

MORGAN, L. H.
1877   *Ancient society*. New York: Henry Holt.

MURDOCK, G. P.
1960   "Cognatic forms of social organization," in *Social structure in Southeast Asia*. Edited by G. P. Murdock, 1–14. Viking Fund Publications in Anthropology 29. Chicago: Quadrangle Publications.

NEEDHAM, R.
1954   The system of teknonyms and death-names of the Penan. *Southwestern Journal of Anthropology* 10:416–431.
1959   Mourning terms. *Bijdragen tot de Taal- Land- en Volkenkunde* 115:58–59.
1962   Notes on comparative method and prescriptive alliance. *Bijdragen tot de Taal- Land- en Volkenkunde* 118:160–182.
1971   "Remarks on the analysis of kinship and marriage," in *Rethinking kinship and marriage*. Edited by R. Needham, 1–34. Association for Social Anthropology Monographs 11. London: Tavistock.

RIVERS, W. H. R.
1914   *Kinship and social organisation*. London: Constable. (Reprinted 1968 as *Kinship and social organization*, with commentaries by Raymond Firth and David M. Schneider. London School of Economics Monographs on Social Anthropology 34. London: Athlone.)

STURTEVANT, W. C.
1964   "Studies in ethno-science," in *Transcultural studies in cognition*. Edited by A. K. Romney and R. B. D'Andrade, 91–131. *American Anthropologist* 66 (3,2).

TYLOR, E. B.
1889   On a method of investigating the development of institutions; applied to laws of marriage and descent. *Journal of the Anthropological Institute* 18:245–269.

WILDER, W. D.
1970   "Socialization and social structure in a Malay village," in *Socialization: the approach from social anthropology.* Edited by P. Mayer, 215–268. Association for Social Anthropology Monographs 8. London: Tavistock.
1973   The culture of kinship studies. *Bijdragen tot de Taal- Land- en Volkenkunde* 129:124–143. (Anthropologica.)

Cultural Anthropology in the Philippines—1900–1983: Perspectives, Problems, and Prospects

MARIO D. ZAMORA

This paper offers a fresh and critical assessment of the history, problems, and possibilities of a subdiscipline of cultural anthropology in the Philippine Republic from the point of view of a native Filipino anthropologist who has been directly and seriously involved in the growth and development of that subdiscipline for the past decade (1963–1973) as an academic administrator, author, researcher, and teacher of cultural anthropology in the Philippines. Specifically, I will present an objective-subjective historical context of the development of cultural anthropology based on four periods chosen more or less arbitrarily:[1] (1) the United States colonial period: 1900–

This paper was informally discussed in a colloquium presented before the anthropology and sociology faculty and selected graduate students of the University of Montana, Missoula on May 12, 1973. I am grateful to the participants led by Dr. Floyd W. Sharrock, professor and chairman, for making the arrangements and for his kind help and criticism. I thank George W. Rollins and Bulah Manning of Eastern Montana College as well as Larry Moser and Ducella Norma Zamora for their help in various ways. These individuals are not responsible for statements made in this paper; I own all its faults. President Stanley J. Heywood's visiting foreign professorship program enabled me to write this paper in the quiet halls of Eastern Montana College, an opportunity for which I am most grateful.

[1] Explanation of time categories: the period categories are indeed highly arbitrary and even subjective. I did not cover the pre-1900 in view of time limitations in writing this paper. However, the works of Dr. Jose P. Rizal (the Filipino national hero who was in professional contact with German and other European scholars like Bastian), as well as the writings of Blumentritt (see Brinton 1899 for an excellent discussion of Blumentritt's significant works on the Philippines) are often cited by Filipinists as pioneers before the American colonial period. 1946 is the year of Philippine Independence from the United States, and 1963 is the year of graduation of the first two Filipino Ph.D. holders in anthropology from the University of Chicago and from Cornell University.

1945; (2) Independence and after: 1946–1962; (3) the contemporary period: 1963–1972; and finally, (4) the next decade: 1973–1983. I will also attempt to summarize, synthesize, and project into the future the dominant issues (innovations), organizations (institutionalization), and training (indigenization) related to cultural anthropological development, and to offer significant information on the current practitioners in the field in the Philippines.

Definition of Terms

INNOVATION. The process by which new ideas, personnel, techniques, and other behavior and values are introduced into another society. In this context, innovations refer to theoretical, methodological, and applied concerns in cultural anthropology as well as the introduction of new personnel (anthropologists) who later became innovators or carriers of change from the outside to Philippine society.

INSTITUTIONALIZATION. The process by which institutions, organizations, and other units or entities for anthropological training, research, and public service are established and take root in the society. Anthropological institutes, departments, and programs in the Philippines and abroad are examples of the institutionalization process.

INDIGENIZATION. The process by which the native Filipinos are trained in the discipline of anthropology and obtain positions of power, influence, and leadership in Philippine anthropological teaching, research, and administration of native anthropology departments. The training of native Filipino anthropologists by Filipino and foreign scholars and institutions is embraced by the indigenization process.

Scope of the Study

This paper has several limitations. First, the scope is limited only to cultural anthropology in the Philippines, 1900–1983. I have not included physical anthropology,[2] archaeology,[3] and linguistics.[4] In addition, my review is focused mainly on the three operationally-defined processual categories of innovation, institutionalization and indigenization. Second, there were a number of papers and documents unavailable to me while writing this paper which could perhaps have enriched my discussion. Third, this paper is to a large extent both subjective and objective. I have made, for example, relative judgments on the role of dominant figures and innovators (e.g. Beyer versus Eggan). On the other hand, I have tried to be as factual as the evidence permits. I have relied heavily on the very scanty and scattered publications on the cultural anthropological history of the Philippines (e.g. Tangco 1940; Beyer 1954; Casiño 1967; Lynch and Hollnsteiner 1961; and Davis and Hollnsteiner 1969), and on my own past participant, observer, and even interventionist, roles during the last decade (1963–1973). Fourth, this paper is necessarily tentative and preliminary, and a more comprehensive and definitive work on the subject is forthcoming.

THE COLONIAL PERIOD: 1900–1945

The main trends during this period under colonial rule in Philippine anthropology include the arrival of American anthropological innovations and innovators, the organization of institutions to disseminate and propagate the innovations, and, to some extent, the effort to utilize Filipino talents to assist in research, teaching, and public service in cultural anthropology by the colonial innovators. The key figure and innovator during this period was H. Otley Beyer.[5]

[2]   For an excellent review of the state of physical anthropology and a modest bibliography, the reader is referred to Jerome B. Bailen's article (in Zamora 1967). Bailen is a pioneer Filipino physical anthropologist and is on the faculty of the Department of Anthropology, University of the Philippines, Diliman, Quezon City, Philippines.

[3]   For archaeology, see the reports of Alfredo E. Evangelista in *Asian Perspectives* (1960, 1961, 1962, 1963) as well as the Zamora and Arcellana bibliography (1971). See also the works of Robert B. Fox, Wilhelm Solheim III, and Daniel J. Scheans for archaeology.

[4]   See the summary reviews and bibliographic data by Ward (1971), Lande (1964), Welsh (1950), Zamora and Arcellana (1971), and by the Summer Institute of Linguistics of the Philippines. Bibliographies by Shiro Saito (1972) and Zamora and Arcellana (1971) also offer rich documentation in the field of ethnography and other subdisciplines of cultural anthropology. Manuel's folklore bibliography (1965) is significant and useful.

[5]   For a broad and comprehensive evaluation of H. Otley Beyer's contribution to Philippine anthropology, see his Festschrift, *Studies in Philippine anthropology* (*in honor of H. Otley Beyer*) (Zamora 1967).

Innovations

The discipline of anthropology was an innovation of considerable importance to the early American military and civil governments in the islands. The innovators' main objective was to conduct research among the many ethnic minority groups in the islands, the knowledge of which was useful to the early colonial military and civil administrators. To this end, some American scholars made gigantic trail-blazing efforts. Otto Scheerer (1900) conducted research in linguistics and wrote on the Benguet Igorots. He was later followed by H. Otley Beyer (1901), David Barrows (1903), Reed (1904), Saleeby (1905), Jenks (1905), Gardner (1906), Cole (1908), and Christie (1909). The other outstanding American scholars who published extensively on the mountain peoples of the northern Philippines were R. F. Barton, Felix Keesing, Francis Lambrecht, and Morice Vanoververgh, among others. However, the most outstanding figure among this crop of colonial anthropological pioneers was H. Otley Beyer. All these scholars focused their studies and investigations primarily on the tribal minorities, not only for purely academic reasons, but also for applied anthropological purposes. Davis and Hollnsteiner (1969:60), on this score, wrote:

The first four decades of Philippine anthropology are characterized by a nearly exclusive concern for two primary interests, culture history and non-Christian peoples. . . . It is not surprising that these should be the dominant interests of Philippine anthropologists for the first quarter of this century, since these were also the prime concerns of American anthropology in general.

This research focus on cultural minorities or non-Christian peoples preoccupied Beyer till his death in 1965. His life to some extent reflects the objectives and basic character of anthropology itself during this period. For despite Beyer's limited formal academic training in anthropology, he nevertheless forged ahead in research, in teaching, and in applied anthropology in the Philippines. It is appropriate at this juncture to review briefly his life and career. Beyer arrived in the Philippines in 1905. He worked for some time at the Bureau of Education and later at the Bureau of Science of the Philippine government. He was then recruited as a faculty member of the University of the Philippines in 1914. Beyer retired in 1954 as professor and chairman of the Department of Anthropology at the University of the Philippines, a department he founded. He became professor emeritus and was curator of the Institute and Museum of Ethnology and Archaeology of the University of the Philippines (Zamora 1967). The account of Hartendorp (1967), a contemporary and friend of H. Otley Beyer, is highly instructive:

Born in Edgewood, Iowa, of an old American family, he was graduated from the University of Denver where he obtained the degrees of A.B. and A.M. Later he did special work at Harvard University as a Winthrop scholar. For his contributions in the field of Philippine archaeology, anthropology, and history, he was conferred honorary doctorate degrees by Silliman University, the Ateneo de Manila and the University of the Philippines.

His interest in the Philippines was aroused by the Philippine exhibits at the Louisiana Purchase Centennial Exposition held at St. Louis, Missouri in 1904, and it was Dr. Albert Ernest Jenks, who directed the Philippine exhibit through whom Beyer got his appointment to come here. He was first stationed in Ifugao, and his ethnological work started there, as did also his work in Philippine language, mythology, folklore, and custom law, these studies broadening out into research in the prehistory of the Philippines. In 1926, with the building of the Novaliches Dam, he came upon ancient Philippine stone implements—also later pottery and porcelains, and extended his search for such artifacts to various parts of the country. Simultaneously, he discovered quantities of the so-called tektites, dark, glassy objects of outer-space origin, of which he has amassed the greatest collection in the world, now of special interest in space research.

While in Ifugao, early in his career, he married the daughter of a prominent Banaue chief and has one son by her, William Beyer, who has given him 16 grandchildren.

H. Otley Beyer wrote many books and several papers in ethnology, archaeology, and history (Zamora 1967); however, many of his papers are still unpublished.[6]

Institutionalization

During the colonial period, three vital anthropological institutions were organized to advance the cause of anthropology—and directly or indirectly the cause of colonial rule: (1) the Department of Anthropology of the University of the Philippines; (2) the Institute and Museum of Ethnology and Archaeology, University of the Philippines; and (3) the Bureau of Non-Christian Tribes of the government. During this period, the University of Chicago, through

[6] H. Otley Beyer's only son, William Beyer, is in possession of almost all of the late Beyer's collection and significant papers.

Professor Fay Cooper-Cole, also showed research interest in the Philippines.

DEPARTMENT OF ANTHROPOLOGY. H. Otley Beyer had the honor of founding the Department of Anthropology of the University of the Philippines in 1914. Lynch and Hollnsteiner (1961:1) cited the University of the Philippines as "the first institution in the Far East —and one of the earliest in the world, for that matter—to have a department of anthropology . . ." (Zamora 1967:6). Ricardo Galang (1957:532) affirms the Lynch–Hollnsteiner observation thus: "the establishment of the Department of Anthropology of the University of the Philippines has aided a great deal the anthropological work in the islands" (Zamora 1967:6). According to Melendez and Caccam (1967:7), "The beginnings of the Department of Anthropology are intimately connected with the person of H. Otley Beyer, who was to be its chairman for almost four decades."

INSTITUTE AND MUSEUM. The second important institution founded by H. Otley Beyer in the Philippines was the Institute and Museum of Ethnology and Archaeology, University of the Philippines. This institution gained fame through Beyer's efforts to make it a center for research, artifact collection, study, and even teaching purposes. Though never formally recognized by the University of the Philippines, the Institute became one of the popular and professional centers of curiosity and interest by Filipinos and foreigners.

BUREAU OF NON-CHRISTIAN TRIBES. This Bureau was formally organized during the early part of the present century by the American civil administration in order to enhance the well-being of the cultural minorities of the islands through research, education, and welfare. After Philippine Independence in 1946, this Bureau became known as the Commission on National Integration (CNI). Anthropologists like H. Otley Beyer at one time or another helped in the research program of the Bureau of Non-Christian Tribes.

These three institutions were highly instrumental in propagating anthropology as a useful discipline during the colonial regime.[7]

That the role played by Fay Cooper-Cole of the University of Chicago in the advancement of Philippine anthropology was very

[7]   See Rudolf Rahmann's very informative and useful article (Zamora 1967). Dr. Rudolf Rahmann, an anthropologist, became president of San Carlos University, Cebu City, Philippines.

significant was confirmed by Eggan (1963) in his obituary of Cole. Cole not only conducted researches himself among the Tinguians of Mindanao, but he also encouraged his students and colleagues to go into Philippine studies.[8] It is important to note that Eggan restudied the Tinguians later on and founded the Philippine Studies Program of the University of Chicago, which in turn trained the next generation of American and Filipino anthropologists. These anthropologists have played a decisive and crucial role in the development of research, teaching, and public service in anthropology, as I will explain in the succeeding section of this paper.

Indigenization

The period under review can be characterized as almost unproductive in terms of training Filipino anthropologists, because of Beyer's main preoccupation with research and with teaching general courses in anthropology at the University of the Philippines. For example, from 1914 (founding date of the anthropology department) up to 1954 (Beyer's year of retirement), the Department of Anthropology graduated only six Masters of Arts, and, of the six candidates, only two were Filipinos: Generoso Maceda, who wrote a thesis on *The Dumagats of Famy* in 1932 and E. Arsenio Manuel, who wrote *A lexicographic study of Tayabas Tagalog* in 1954. Beyer's record of indigenization is indeed poor compared to Fred Eggan's efforts in the succeeding period of Philippine cultural anthropological history. Also under Beyer, a number of lecturers and instructors had at one time or another taught anthropology courses in the anthropology department. Among them were Marcelo Tangco, Eduardo Palma, Cecilio Lim, Engracio Guazon, Mariano Abogon, and Benicio Catapusan (Melendez and Caccam 1967). Many of these Beyer assistants never became professional anthropologists for one reason or another. Only Marcelo Tangco and later E. Arsenio Manuel became full-fledged anthropologists.

This period covering the 45 years of Beyer's academic reign, however, was a time devoted mainly to imparting knowledge of anthropology to undergraduate students at the University of the Philippines. A number of students who later became eminent in their own lines of specialization were taught anthropology by Beyer

[8] See the enlightening obituary of Fay Cooper-Cole in *American Anthropologist* (Eggan 1963).

and later by Marcelo Tangco. Among the former Beyer students are General Carlos P. Romulo (first Asian President of the United Nations General Assembly), President Ferdinand E. Marcos of the Philippines, and a long list of senators, congressmen, industrialists, educators, and professionals from every major part of the Philippines.

As far as anthropology is concerned, two of the more successful students and assistants of Beyer were Marcelo Tangco and E. Arsenio Manuel. Tangco became the first Filipino Ph.D. candidate at Harvard University and later at the University of California in Berkeley. At present (1973) an emeritus professor of anthropology at the University of the Philippines, Tangco carried the burden of teaching in the university for many years until his retirement in 1957–1958. He also published several papers and a significant monograph on *The Christian peoples of the Philippines* (1951). E. Arsenio Manuel, who joined the anthropology department later than Tangco, conducted researches in folklore and in social anthropology. He published two volumes of *A dictionary of Philippine biography* which promise to be basic standard references for years to come. Manuel earned his Ph.D. in 1965 at the University of Chicago under Eggan's supervision.

Problems

The main problems encountered during the colonial period, from a native viewpoint, were the following: (1) American dominance of cultural anthropology;[9] (2) lack of theoretical and methodological sophistication in cultural anthropology, and (3) lack of trained personnel, funds, equipment, etc.

INDEPENDENCE AND AFTER: 1946–1962

Innovations

The most prominent innovations in cultural anthropology during

[9] The phrase "American dominance of cultural anthropology" is moot. This brief study reveals the many positive significant contributions of American anthropologists in the Philippines, and on balance there are also negative contributions. For an initial reading on this, see Casiño (1967). This is one "hot" topic which American and Filipino anthropologists should assess together in an atmosphere of academic and scientific detachment and not in the spirit of myopic chauvinism.

the Independence and after (1946–1962) were studies in (1) social anthropology, (2) ethnoscience, and (3) applied anthropology. The key dominant figure and innovator in Philippine anthropology during this period was Fred Eggan, professor of anthropology and director of the Philippine Studies Program of the University of Chicago.

Fred Eggan, better trained in anthropology than H. Otley Beyer and undoubtedly better known professionally abroad, deserves the distinction of being the first American anthropologist to introduce systematic social anthropology in the Philippines. Davis and Hollnsteiner (1969:61) shared this view:

Modern sociologically oriented studies . . . did not really get under way until Fred Eggan's (1941) pioneering attempt to synthesize data on social process in the Mountain Province and the appearance of Keesing's (1949) Bontoc study.

Eggan has continued his significant research on social organization and change since his initial research thrusts in 1941. On this aspect of Eggan's research, Davis and Hollnsteiner (1969:62) wrote:

On the synthetic side, Eggan (1963) has amplified his earlier article (1941) dealing with culture change in northern Luzon, and has incorporated data on the Kalinga which were not available for the earlier work. He is again concerned with an explanation for the increasing social and cultural complexity which is encountered as one goes from the Cordillera to the lowlands and suggests that this is essentially a process of adaptation to wet rice cultivation.

Eggan graduated from the University of Chicago with a Ph.D. degree in anthropology in 1933. He studied under A. R. Radcliffe-Brown, an eminent British social anthropologist who was then a visiting professor at the University of Chicago. A Viking Fund medalist and former president of the American Anthropological Association, Eggan is author of *The social organization of the western Pueblos* (1950), *The American Indian* (1966), and editor and co-author of *The social organization of North American tribes* (1955). These three books, for which Eggan earned world fame, are considered by many professional anthropologists as classics in American Indian scholarship. He delivered the Lewis Henry Morgan Lectures at the University of Rochester and was a Fellow of the Center for Advanced Study in the Behavioral Sciences at Palo Alto,

California. At present (1973), Eggan is Harold Swift Distinguished Service Professor at the University of Chicago.

Eggan's enduring contribution to Philippine anthropology lies not only in his own fieldwork but also in the institutionalization and indigenization processes shown in the succeeding discussion. Eggan's Chicago-trained students broadened and enriched the literature on social anthropology in the Philippines. Among these scholars are Charles R. Kaut (Tagalog society), Willis E. Sibley (Ilongo), Robert Fox (Tagbanua and Tagalog), Frank X. Lynch (Bicol), Melvin Mednick (Maranao), David Baradas (Maranao), F. Landa Jocano (Sulod), E. Arsenio Manuel (Manuvu), Jules DeRaedt (Kalinga), among others. Alexander Spoehr, professor at the University of Pittsburgh and an eminent Eggan student, is one of the latest Filipinists doing research in Zamboanga, Philippines. Alfredo Pacyaya of the northern Philippines and Timoteo Oracion of Silliman University also studied for their master's degrees in anthropology under Eggan in Chicago.

Another leading innovator in Philippine anthropology was Harold C. Conklin, professor and former chairman of the Department of Anthropology, Yale University. Conklin, who was for many years closely associated with H. Otley Beyer, systematically introduced ethnoscience in this country. Davis and Hollnsteiner (1969:73) describe ethnoscience as ". . . a call for more sound ethnographic description . . . it also takes the theoretical position that culture is best understood by the use of techniques which render it intelligible to informants themselves." Conklin's publications (1954, 1955, 1957, among others) demonstrate the significance and applicability of ethnoscience to the Philippine environment. Charles O. Frake (1955, 1961) reinforced Conklin's earlier efforts to apply ethnoscience to Philippine shifting cultivation.

Institutionalization

The most significant events in the institutionalization process in Philippine cultural anthropology were the establishment of (1) the Philippine Studies Program (PSP) of the University of Chicago in 1952, (2) the Community Development Research Council (CDRC) of the University of the Philippines in 1957, and (3) the Departments of Anthropology and Sociology in Ateneo, Silliman University and San Carlos University, Cebu.

PHILIPPINE STUDIES PROGRAM. The Philippine Studies Program published significant handbooks and monographs that have enriched the growing body of anthropological literature on the Philippines. One massive project undertaken in cooperation with the Human Relations Area Files of Yale University was the 1956 Area Handbook of the Philippines supervised by Fred Eggan himself. In addition, many of the doctoral dissertations of Eggan's students were published in preliminary form.

THE COMMUNITY DEVELOPMENT RESEARCH COUNCIL. The second important landmark, in my view, in the institutionalization process was the organization of the Community Development Research Council (CDRC) of the University of the Philippines in 1957. The CDRC is the research evaluation department of the office of the Presidential Arm on Community Development (PACD) of the Philippine government. About twelve or more Filipino scholars representing various disciplines (e.g. anthropology, sociology, education, agricultural economics, political science, social work, agriculture, statistics, psychology) meet weekly to review and recommend proposals for action research geared toward directed community development and social change. They also administer research grants and extend public service in the form of seminars and symposia on matters related to development and change. Since its inception, the CDRC has published quality monographs in many fields of the social sciences, including anthropology. Among the anthropologists whose research findings saw publication are E. Arsenio Manuel on Manuvu society, Moises C. Bello on Kankanay social organization and change, F. Landa Jocano on controlled comparison in Panay, Eric Casiño on Jama Mapun culture, Mary Hollnsteiner on political sociology and anthropology in a Tagalog municipality, Prospero Covar on innovations in planting rice and the traditional responses, Natividad V. Garcia on economic change, Leticia Lagmay on culture and personality, Marcelino N. Maceda on economic anthropology in the Visayas, and Esteban Magannon on religion and economic development in Kalinga society. The CDRC is still an active entity to date and in my view it will continue to function for the coming decades [10]

---

[10] To obtain at cost CDRC publications, write the Executive Secretary, Community Development Research Council, College of Education Building, University of the Philippines, Diliman, Quezon City, Philippines.

DEPARTMENTS OF SOCIOLOGY AND ANTHROPOLOGY. The third development in this institutionalization process was the founding of sociology-anthropology departments in Ateneo, San Carlos, and Silliman Universities, the three leading private institutions of higher learning in the country. The rise of these departments reinforced the research, teaching, and public service functions of the public and private anthropological institutions already in existence.

Indigenization

The events of crucial significance in the indigenization process during this period were (1) the Filipinization of the headship of the University of the Philippines anthropology department, (2) the graduation of the first Filipino Ph.D. in anthropology from Freiburg University in Europe and the training of Filipinos in the United States and other foreign universities, and (3) the beginnings of increased research by Filipino-managed institutes and departments which partly include training.

DEPARTMENTAL LEADERSHIP FILIPINIZATION. The retirement of H. Otley Beyer in 1954 from the University of the Philippines anthropology department headship signalled the faster acceleration of the indigenization process not only in the state university but also in other universities with anthropology-sociology departments. Marcelo Tangco, the first Filipino Ph.D. candidate in anthropology[11] and a long-time teacher under Beyer, succeeded the latter as head of the department. From then on, the leadership and staff of the department have been in Filipino hands and this trend is also true in San Carlos, Silliman, and Ateneo de Manila Universities.

MACEDA: FIRST FILIPINO PH.D. During the period under review, the first Ph.D. degree in anthropology was awarded by Freiburg University to Marcelino N. Maceda, currently professor of anthropology at San Carlos University, Cebu City. Maceda was a student of Rudolf Rahmann, former editor of *Anthropos*, president of San Carlos University, and an anthropologist himself. Maceda finished his bachelor's and master's degrees at San Carlos University. He

---

[11] Tangco never finished the Ph.D. degree in anthropology because, according to him, his Ph.D. dissertation rough drafts were burned.

has since then researched and published on the Mamanuas of the Philippines. He also conducted archaeological and ethnological researches in the Visayas and Mindanao. During this period, several anthropology graduate students were taking their degrees abroad, notably at Chicago and Cornell Universities.

FILIPINO INSTITUTE RESEARCH. Another significant event in the indigenization process was the beginning of increased research output by Filipino-managed institutes and departments in the country, which partly include the training of Filipino students in social research. As already discussed, the CDRC of the University of the Philippines is the best example of this Filipino-managed institute that encouraged research training for all its workers.

Problems

From a native point of view, the problems in cultural anthropology during this period were: (1) lack of Filipino organization, system, and direction in research, teaching, and public service; (2) lack of adequate native personnel, funds, and equipment; (3) lack of adequate recognition of the discipline as an academic subject; (4) American dominance of research activities, and (5) lack of native involvement in anthropological international concerns.

THE CONTEMPORARY PERIOD: 1963–1972

The most fundamental feature of this period under review was the improvement in quantity and quality of the processes of innovation, institutionalization, and indigenization. The indigenization process especially has undergone a rapid transition which, if pursued for the next decade, will undoubtedly alter the content, rate, and direction of the history of cultural anthropology in the Philippines.

Innovations

During this period, the following innovations have been pursued with greater precision and vigor than before: (1) value studies;

(2) urban anthropology; (3) applied anthropology; and (4) lowland Christian peasant studies, among others.[12]

The study of values was initially started and later continued by the Ateneo de Manila University anthropologists and other social scientists, especially the Institute of Philippine Culture. Among the leading proponents of value studies are Frank X. Lynch (Ph.D., Chicago), Mary Hollnsteiner (M.A., University of the Philippines), John J. Carroll (Ph.D., Cornell), and Jaime Bulatao (Ph.D., Fordham).[13] Another leading anthropologist from the University of Virginia who has also done work on values is Charles R. Kaut (Ph.D., Chicago). These scholars were pioneers in extracting the so-called Philippine cultural values, based on their research on Filipino society and culture. Three of the leading critics of the value studies conducted by the Ateneo group are F. Landa Jocano (1966: 282–291) of the University of the Philippines, Robert Lawless (1966, 1967:101–136) of the New School for Social Research in New York, and Milton L. Barnett (1966:276–282) of the Agricultural Development Council in Malaysia and formerly of the University of Wisconsin. Their burden of criticism lies in the methodology employed by the Ateneo group involved in the serious study of cultural values.

Urban anthropology is another form of innovation in the Philippines during the contemporary period. The two leading institutions involved in this type of innovation are the University of the Philippines and the Ateneo de Manila University. The Departments of Sociology and Anthropology, in cooperation with the Asian Center and the Institute of Mass Communications of the University of the Philippines and supported financially by the University Social Science Research Council, have been conducting a long-range program of research on "The Manila Complex." This involves a series of interdisciplinary researches of urban Manila and surrounding areas which will hopefully result in significant findings regarding urban behavior and values in time and space. The leading workers in this study are Ofelia Angangco (chairman, sociology department, University of the Philippines), Gloria D. Feliciano (director, Institute of Mass Communication), Ruben D.

[12]   There are of course other concerns during this period but those cited in my view are of too far-reaching consequences to Philippine scholarship to escape notice.
[13]   For more information on the Ateneo scholars' ideas on values, see Frank X. Lynch's compilation *Four readings on Philippine values* and other works cited in the references.

Santos-Cuyugan (director, Asian Center), and Mario D. Zamora (chairman, Department of Anthropology). Ricardo Zarco, Belen T. Medina, Fe Arcinas, Manuel Bonifacio, M. Valencia, and Rodolfo Bulatao, all University of the Philippines' sociologists, are involved in this study. The results of these investigations will be known in the coming years.[14]

The Institute of Philippine Culture, Ateneo de Manila University, has also been actively involved in the study of urban Manila. Mary Hollnsteiner's studies on Tondo, as well as the research conducted by Wilfredo Arce (Ph.D., Cornell) and Helga Jacobson (Ph.D., Cornell), have complemented the University of the Philippines' group. Another crucial institutional research in urban problems is being done by St. Louis University in Baguio City; this supplements the excellent performance of Baguio City Mayor Luis L. Lardizabal's and the City Planning Board's research program of urban Baguio in cooperation with the Asia Foundation and the Agency for International Department. San Carlos University, Silliman University, Xavier University, and even Mindanao State University have likewise conducted some studies in the areas of urban anthropology and sociology, especially in cooperation with the Institute of Planning of the University of the Philippines. These research efforts will bear fruit in the next decade.

Applied anthropology initiated among the cultural minorities during the colonial period (e.g. Zamora 1967) has also flourished during this time, especially in the University of the Philippines, Silliman University, and among private and public organizations like the Presidential Arm on National Minorities (PANAMIN) and other units. In the University of the Philippines, the most active agent is the Community Development Research Council. The sociologists of the University's College of Agriculture led by Gelia T. Castillo (Ph.D., Cornell) have made significant breakthroughs in social research in the Tagalog region. Silliman University, under the leadership of another Cornell sociologist, Agaton Palen Pal, and with the collaboration of a distinguished group of workers such as Timoteo Oracion, Robert Polson, Hubert and Harriet Reynolds, Alexander Grant, Richard Lieban, Donn V. Hart, and Peter Gowing, has contributed to applied social science research in anthropology and sociology.

[14] Some articles, based on this research, recently appeared in the journal on mass communications sponsored by the Institute of Mass Communications of the University of the Philippines led by Director Gloria D. Feliciano, a respected colleague and friend.

PANAMIN headed by Manuel Elizalde, Jr., a wealthy industrialist widely known as the "champion" of the minorities, has also involved a number of anthropologists in the study and betterment of the lives of our ethnic minorities, especially those from Mindanao, Sulu, and Palawan. Elizalde has had the benefit of the experience and expertise of Robert B. Fox (Ph.D., Chicago), the chief anthropologist of the National Museum of the Philippines, "discoverer" of the famous Tabon caves in Palawan, and presidential adviser on national minorities. Fox has been involved also in training students in archaeological field methods as well as in ethnology and applied anthropology. Applied anthropology has been carried on in Cotabato and among the Tasadays in Mindanao, a tribe discovered by Elizalde in his world-famous wanderings among the tribal minorities in the Mindanao forests.

The study of social anthropology and peasant Christian lowland society has been pursued vigorously during this period by almost every anthropologist trained by Fred Eggan and by the Cornell anthropologists (e.g. Arce, Hollnsteiner, Zamora). Among Eggan's students who conducted research during this period are Charles Kaut (Laguna), Melvin Mednick (Lanao del Sur), Willis E. Sibley (Iloilo), F. Landa Jocano (Panay), Frank Lynch (Tagalog, Sulu), David Baradas (Lanao), E. Arsenio Manuel (Davao), Aram Yengoyan (Mindanao), Robert B. Fox (Palawan). There has also been a shift from the study of mountain peoples and cultural minorities to the study of peasant lowland Christian societies. The outstanding work of Donn V. Hart of Syracuse and northern Illinois and that of Agaton Pal should not be ignored. Hart has made many significant contributions in lowland Bisayan research as well as in the indigenization process. Donn V. Hart, for example, initiated Mario D. Zamora, Mary Hollnsteiner, Aleli Alvarez, Natividad V. Garcia, and Prospero Covar into cultural anthropological research in a Bulacan village.

Applied anthropology in education has not been neglected during this period. The College of Education of the University of the Philippines under Alfredo T. Morales is one of the early pioneers. Priscila Manalang (1971) finished her Ph.D. at the University of Pittsburgh under Alexander Spoehr with education and anthropology as a major focus of her research. Patricia Snyder, another student of Donn V. Hart at Syracuse University, also did a doctoral dissertation in educational anthropology in the Bisayan region. F. Landa Jocano's significant monograph, *Growing up in a Philippine barrio* (1969) reflects this growing interest in educational anthropology. Zamora and Alicia P. Magos of the University of the Philippines have coauthored an annotated bibliography on education and anthropology, which is forthcoming.

Institutionalization

During this contemporary period, two agencies of the Philippine government concerned with the development of research, training native Filipinos in anthropology, and the uplift of ethnic minorities were organized. The Commission on National Integration (CNI), headed by Mamintal Tamano of Lanao del Sur, initiated and organized the Tribal Research Center on the pattern of a similar unit established in Chiengmai, Thailand. The first Director General of the Center is Mario D. Zamora. The Center (later renamed National Research Center for the Integration of Filipino Society and Culture) published a modest bibliography on minorities in 1967, the history of CNI known as *They are also Filipinos: ten years with the cultural minorities* by Leothiny Clavel, and the *Journal on National Integration*. The Center also printed the policy statements of the Commissioner on National Integration and sponsored several national and regional conferences on the problems of national minorities.

The other governmental agency is the Presidential Arm on National Minorities headed by Elizalde. PANAMIN was originally a private organization called Private Association for National Minorities (also called PANAMIN), designed to espouse the cause of minority groups. PANAMIN has encouraged research and publication on the minorities, the latest of which deals with the newly-discovered Mindanao tribe, the Tasaday. Elizalde enlisted the support of anthropologists Robert Fox, Frank Lynch, David Baradas, and Carlos Fernandez for this purpose.[15] Teodoro Llamzon, an eminent Filipino linguist, is also with the anthropology group in PANAMIN. Several undergraduate and graduate students have been involved at one time or another in PANAMIN's research, publication, and public service programs. The students come from the anthropology departments of the University of the Philippines

---

[15] Carlos Fernandez and Frank X. Lynch recently came out with a publication on this world-famous Tasaday tribe. For more information, write to Frank Lynch, Ateneo de Manila University, Quezon City, Philippines.

22

National Museum, San Carlos, Silliman, and Ateneo, among others.

The Institute of Philippine Culture has expanded its teaching, research, and public service functions. Contacts and contracts with institutions such as the University of Hawaii, the Peace Corps, the Research Foundation for Anthropology and Archaeology, the United States Department of the Navy, and the Philippine Sociological Society have been made. A systematic publication program has been launched, including their celebrated *Modernization Series*. The leading figures are Frank Lynch, Mary Hollnsteiner, John J. Carroll, Jaime Bulatao, Wilfredo Arce, Mary Gonzales. Horacio dela Costa, an eminent historian, also contributed to some extent to the program.

The Department of Anthropology in the University of the Philippines also organized the first Anthropological Society in 1963–1964. The first advisers were Mario D. Zamora and Milton L. Barnett. The Society has since been active in the enhancement of anthropology in the Philippines. Another significant institution in the field of folklore studies was established at Xavier University and was headed by a Filipino Jesuit, Francisco Demetrio (Ph.D., University of California at Los Angeles). This unit complements the Research Institute for Mindanao Culture under the leadership of another eminent Jesuit sociologist Francis C. Madigan, the well-known author of a CDRC-funded monograph, *The farmer said no*.

Indigenization

The indigenization process takes the form of (1) the transfer of leadership from American to Filipino hands among the leading anthropology departments and centers, (2) the graduation of the first two Filipino Ph.D.'s in anthropology from American universities in 1963 and the first French-trained Ph.D., (3) the accelerated training of undergraduate and graduate Filipino students in Philippine and foreign universities, (4) the emergence of research institutions and foundations designed to help in the indigenization process, and (5) the increasing involvement of Filipino anthropologists in international professional affairs.

LEADERSHIP INDIGENIZATION. The retirement of H. Otley Beyer in 1954 after more than four decades of colonial leadership of the

University of the Philippines anthropology department saw the leadership fall into Filipino hands. Marcelo Tangco, Beyer's heir apparent, became the first Filipino head of the Beyer-controlled department, but he also retired at the end of 1957–1958. E. Arsenio Manuel, a leading Filipino anthropologist, folklorist, and bibliographer, assumed the chairmanship in an acting capacity. Manuel was succeeded by Mario D. Zamora as chairman (1963–1969). F. Landa Jocano, one of the most eminent Filipino anthropologists, succeeded Zamora upon the latter's appointment as dean of the University of the Philippines at Baguio City. In Ateneo de Manila University's Department of Sociology and Anthropology, three Filipinos were at one time or another chairman of the department: Mary Hollnsteiner, Mary Gonzales, and Wilfredo Arce. At San Carlos University's Department of Anthropology and Economics, Marcelino N. Maceda was for many years the head of his department while in Silliman University, and Agaton Pal and Timoteo Oracion assumed leadership at one time or another. In the National Museum of the Philippines, Robert B. Fox, for many years the chief anthropologist of the National Museum, gave way to Alfredo Evangelista and later to Eric Casiño, a Ph.D. candidate in anthropology from Sydney University, Australia.

FIRST AMERICAN-TRAINED FILIPINO PH.D.'S. The first two Filipino Ph.D.'s in anthropology to graduate in America in 1963 were F. Landa Jocano, trained by Fred Eggan at the University of Chicago and Mario D. Zamora, trained by Morris E. Opler at Cornell University.[16] The first Sorbonne-trained ethnologist, Zeus A. Salazar of the University of the Philippines also graduated during this period. Immediately after graduation, Jocano became a senior anthropologist of the National Museum while Mario D. Zamora was appointed chairman of the University of the Philippines anthropology department. Salazar rejoined the University of the Philippines faculty.

TRAINING ACCELERATION. From 1963 onwards, the training of Filipinos, both graduate and undergraduate in the Philippines and abroad, was accelerated. In the Philippines, the University of the

---

[16] It is interesting to note that Fred Eggan and Morris E. Opler were 1933 Ph.D. graduates of the University of Chicago. For more information about Opler's life and career as well as his theoretical contributions to world anthropology, see Zamora, Mahar, and Orenstein (1971).

Philippines has considerably increased its anthropology enrollments from 17 students in 1914 to 474 in 1964–1965 (Melendez and Caccam 1967). The Department graduated Filipino M.A.'s; Ateneo and Silliman enrollments also increased, while San Carlos inaugurated its Ph.D. program in anthropology. In the United States, the University of Chicago, Cornell University, University of Colorado, University of Arizona, University of California at Berkeley and at Santa Barbara, Harvard University, Yale University, University of Washington, University of Hawaii, University of Indiana, the Catholic University of America, University of Pittsburgh, University of Pennsylvania, the University of Illinois at Urbana, among others, are at the forefront of the indigenization process. In Europe, the University of Sorbonne; in Australia, Sydney University; and in India, Madras University are also involved in this indigenization process.

RESEARCH INSTITUTES. The establishment of some research institutes and foundations also contributed to the indigenization process. The Philippine Studies Program at Chicago, the CDRC at the University of the Philippines, the Institute of Philippine Culture, the Asian Center of the University of the Philippines, Xavier University's Mindanao Institute of Philippine Culture as well as the Philippine Sociological Society, the Research Foundation for Anthropology and Archaeology, the National Science Development Board, the National Research Council of the Philippines, the Ford and Rockefeller Foundations, and the Fulbright/Smith-Mundt Program of Educational Exchange have contributed immensely to the training of Filipinos in instruction, research, and applied anthropology.

INTERNATIONAL INVOLVEMENTS. The final trend during this period is the increasing involvement of Filipino anthropologists in international professional activities. For example, many of the leading Filipino anthropologists are associates of *Current Anthropology* (the world journal of the sciences of man edited by Sol Tax of the University of Chicago). F. Landa Jocano, well known for his *Growing up in a Philippine barrio* (1969) and *Sulod society* (1968), attended conferences and workshops in the United States, France, India, and Malaysia. Marcelino N. Maceda was a Fulbright professor at the University of Arkansas and authored several papers published in the European journal *Anthropos*. E. Arsenio Manuel published significant papers in the United States and Japan. Alfredo Evangelista

was the Philippine representative in the *Asian Perspectives*, while
Enya Flores Meiser became a fellow of the American Anthropological
Association and attended several national and international con-
ferences. Albert Bacdayan coauthored papers with scholars (e.g. in
Ethnology) and received a Cornell–London Fellowship and lately the
Andrew Mellon Fellowship from the University of Pittsburgh.
Patricia Afable, the first Filipino Ph.D. from Yale trained by Harold
Conklin, is currently teaching in Malaysia. Mario D. Zamora
conducted research in India and the United States and became a
Fellow of the American Anthropological Association, the Royal
Anthropological Institute of Great Britain and Ireland, and the
Canadian Sociology and Anthropology Association. A life member
of the Indian Anthropological Association, Zamora likewise edited
three books (1967, 1969, 1971) involving international authorship.

Problems

The problems during this contemporary period of cultural anthropological history are more or less similar to the problems encountered
during the Independence period. Because of the accelerated training
of graduates, professional placement has become a problem. There
has also been serious rethinking on the part of native Filipino
anthropologists on the theoretical, methodological, and applied
work done by foreign scholars. The problems of lack of central
orientation and direction brought about by the absence of a Filipino-
organized and managed Philippine Anthropological Association, the
lack of personnel and material resources for research, training, and
public service still persist.

THE NEXT DECADE: 1973–1983

The next decade will depend to some extent on the outcome of
President Ferdinand E. Marcos's martial law regime proclaimed last
September 23, 1972. Other factors that will determine the shape of
the next decade will be funds, equipment, and many other imponder-
ables within the nation and abroad. My discussion of the next
decade should be taken as projections and even perhaps as
conjectures.

Innovations

Filipino, American, and European scholars will continue their research on various facets of Filipino culture: ethnoscience (e.g. Conklin, Frake, et al.), urban anthropology (Hollnsteiner, Arce, Jacobson), ecological anthropology (Lewis, Lawless, among others), economic anthropology (e.g. Davis, Mednick), social anthropology (almost all of the Eggan students) and folklore (e.g. Manuel, Demetrio, Jocano). Educational anthropology will be pursued more vigorously (Manalang, Snyder, Zamora) while studies on Filipinos in America will be a new venture (Jocano for Hawaiian Filipinos and Zamora for mainland Filipinos). Applied anthropology will be a prime concern by many anthropologists in the field.

Institutionalization

This decade will see the continuation of already existing research/ teaching/public service anthropological institutions in the Philippines and the establishment of new ones. The different anthropology departments in the University of the Philippines, Ateneo de Manila, Silliman, San Carlos, Xavier, St. Louis, Notre Dame College in Jolo, Ateneo de Davao, among others, will continue their functions of teaching, research, and public service. Other private and public institutions in the Philippines show embryonic signs of establishing anthropological units, if not anthropology curricula: for example, the University of Santo Tomas, Mindanao State University, Philippine Normal College, Centro Escolar University, Philippine Women's University, Central Luzon State University, Central Philippine University, Angeles University, the University of Baguio, the Baguio Colleges Foundation, and the Lyceum of Baguio are among the many institutions that show indications of joining the established anthropologically-oriented units in encouraging research and training in the field of cultural anthropology. Anthropological courses have been introduced and are being taught; plans are being made to supplement already existing staff and curricula. Another trend is the introduction of anthropology courses in professional schools (e.g. in colleges of medicine, nursing, commerce, and public administration).

Abroad, the emerging units for anthropological advancement include the Center for Southeast Asian Studies at the Northern

Illinois University under anthropologist Donn V. Hart, the University of Colorado's program of research in Mindanao under Robert Hackenberg, the Center for Southeast Asian Studies at Singapore and at Hull, England, and the Cornell and University of California at Berkeley Southeast Asia Programs. I also foresee the ultimate organization of the long-delayed Philippine Anthropological Association.

Indigenization

The training of Filipinos for higher degrees in anthropology, especially the Ph.D. degree, will be continued and even pursued perhaps more vigorously by local and foreign institutions. The University of the Philippines is at the forefront of this training, particularly on the bachelor and master's levels. The Ph.D. will be introduced in the University of the Philippines following San Carlos University's lead. Abroad, other universities will join in the intensified training of Filipino students for the Ph.D degree program: the University of Chicago, University of California, University of Illinois at Urbana, the New School for Social Research, University of Hawaii, and Cornell University, among others. The other institutes of research actively involved in the training and support of Filipino anthropologists are the Institute of Philippine Culture, the Community Development Research Council, and the National Museum of the Philippines.

SUMMARY AND CONCLUDING REMARKS

1. This paper discusses briefly the perspective, development and trend in Philippine cultural anthropology from 1900 to 1983, divided into time periods as follows: the colonial period—1900–1945; Independence and after—1946–1962; the contemporary period—1963–1972; and the next decade—1973–1983.

2. The historical review is based on three operationally-defined processual categories of innovation, institutionalization, and indigenization.

3. Innovations during the colonial period were focused on ethnography and applied anthropology of tribal minorities for effective United States colonial rule. Three units were established: the

Department of Anthropology at the University of the Philippines, the Institute and Museum of Ethnology and Archaeology, and the Bureau of Non-Christian Tribes of the Philippine government. Training of Filipinos was confined to assisting the colonial anthropologists in research, teaching, and public service. H. Otley Beyer was the key figure and innovator.

4. During the Independence period (1946–1962), innovations were in social anthropology, ethnoscience, and applied anthropology. The Philippine Studies Program of the University of Chicago and the sociology-anthropology departments of Ateneo de Manila University, San Carlos University, Silliman University, and the Community Development Research Council of the University of the Philippines were organized. The key figure during this era was Fred Eggan of the University of Chicago. The first Filipino Ph.D. in anthropology was graduated from Freiburg University in Europe during this period; indigenization in the leadership of the University of the Philippines' anthropology department took place.

5. During the contemporary period (1963–1972), studies related to values, urban and educational anthropology, as well as applied anthropology and lowland Christian peasant studies, were introduced. The Tribal Research Center of the Commission on National Integration and the Presidential Arm on National Minorities were established. The first two Filipino Ph.D.'s in anthropology from Chicago and Cornell Universities were graduated in 1963. Indigenization of sociology-anthropology departments have been accelerated during this decade.

6. During the next decade (1973–1983), anthropological developments will depend on the political climate generated by President of the Philippines Ferdinand E. Marcos' martial law regime.

7. Philippine cultural anthropology has been conceived, shaped and directed, for the most part, by American anthropologists during the 83-year period under review. This fact is substantiated by Donald Tugby (1968:186) when he wrote:

... United States workers account for 68.2% of all field visits to the Philippines (compared with Indonesia 33.3%, Malaysia 48.9% and Thailand 43.8%) substantiating the European impression that the United States dominates research in that country.

8. The native Filipino anthropologists, however, are gradually doing serious study and research on their own societies and other cultures (e.g. India, the United States, France). They are getting

increasingly involved in international professional activities and are slowly dominating positions of leadership and power in leading schools in the Philippines.

9. The Philippine Anthropological Association (PAA) will yet be organized to give form, substance, system, and direction to Philippine cultural anthropology and its future.

10. Scholars from other nations such as Japan, India, Denmark, Australia, and Canada have been doing research in cultural anthropology in the Philippines. This trend will continue for the next decade.

REFERENCES

BAILEN, JEROME B.
1967 "Studies in physical anthropology on the Philippines," in *Studies in Philippine anthropology (in honor of H. Otley Beyer)*. Edited by Mario D. Zamora, 527–558. Quezon City: Alemar-Phoenix.

BARNETT, MILTON L.
1966 *Hiya*, shame and guilt: preliminary consideration of the concepts as analytical tools for Philippine social science. *Philippine Sociological Review* 14:276–282.

BARROWS, DAVID P.
1903 *Population, census of the Philippine islands, 1903*. U.S. Government Printing Office.

BEYER, H. OTLEY
1954 Anthropology at the Manila congresses, 1953. *Polynesian Society Journal* 63:247–250.

BRINTON, DANIEL G.
1899 Professor Blumentritt's studies of the Philippines. *American Anthropologist* 1:122–125.

CASIÑO, ERIC S.
1967 The future of anthropology in the Philippines. *Solidarity* 2:16–23.

CHRISTIE, EMERSON B.
1909 *The Subanuns of Sindangan Bay*. Manila: Bureau of Science.
1914 Notes on irrigation and cooperative irrigation societies in Ilocos Norte. *Philippine Journal of Science* 9:117–120.

CONKLIN, HAROLD C.
1954 An ethnoecological approach to shifting agriculture. *Transactions of the New York Academy of Sciences* 17:133–142.

COOPER-COLE, FAY
1908 The Tinguian. *Philippine Journal of Science* 4:197–213.

1955 Hanunoo color categories. *Southwestern Journal of Anthropology* 11:339–344.

1957 *Hanunoo agriculture: a report on an integral system of shifting cultivation.* Rome: United Nations Food and Agriculture Organization.

1967 "Ifugao ethnobotany, 1905–1965," in *Studies in Philippine anthropology (in honor of H. Otley Beyer)*. Edited by Mario D. Zamora, 204–262. Quezon City: Alemar-Phoenix.

DAVIS, WILLIAM G., MARY R. HOLLNSTEINER
1969 Some recent trends in Philippine social anthropology. *Anthropologica* 11:59–84.

EGGAN, FRED
1941 Some aspects of culture change in the northern Philippines. *American Anthropologist* 43:11–18.

1950 *The social organization of the western pueblos.* Chicago: University of Chicago Press.

1963 Cultural drift and social change. *Current Anthropology* 4:347–355.

1963 Cooper-Cole, Fay: 1881–1961 (Obituary). *American Anthropologist* 65:641–648.

1966 *The American Indian; perspectives for the study of social change.* Chicago: Aldine.

1967 "Some aspects of bilateral social systems in the northern Philippines," in *Studies in Philippine anthropology (in honor of H. Otley Beyer)*. Edited by Mario D. Zamora, 186–203. Quezon City: Alemar-Phoenix.

EGGAN, FRED, *editor*
1955 *The social anthropology of North American tribes.* Chicago: University of Chicago Press.

EVANGELISTA, ALFREDO E.
1962 Philippine archaeology up to 1950. *Science Review* 3:17–22.

1960 Regional reports: Philippines. *Asian Perspectives* 4:85–88.

1961 Regional reports: Philippines. *Asian Perspectives* 5:67–70.

1962 Regional reports: Philippines. *Asian Perspectives* 6:46–47.

1963 Regional reports: Philippines. *Asian Perspectives* 7:52–56.

FRAKE, CHARLES O.
1955 "Social organization and shifting cultivation among the Sindangan Subanun." Unpublished Ph.D. dissertation, Yale University.

1961 The diagnosis of disease among the Subanun of Mindanao. *American Anthropologist* 63:113–132.

GALANG, RICARDO
1957 "Anthropological work in the Philippines," in *Encyclopedia of the Philippines*. Edited by Zoilo Galang, 529–535.

GARDNER, FLETCHER
1906 Philippine (Tagalog) superstitions. *Journal of American Folklore* 29:191–204.

HARTENDORP, A. V. H.
1967 "The Beyer symposium," in *Studies in Philippine anthropology* (*in honor of H. Otley Beyer*). Edited by Mario D. Zamora, 614–617. Quezon City: Alemar-Phoenix.

HOLLNSTEINER, MARY R.
1961 Reciprocity in the lowland Philippines. *Philippine Studies* 9:387–413.

JENKS, ALBERT ERNEST
1905 *The Bontoc Igorot.* Manila: Bureau of Public Printing.

JOCANO, F. LANDA
1966 Rethinking "smooth interpersonal relations." *Philippine Sociological Review* 14:282–291.
1968 *Sulod society: a study in the kinship and social organization of a mountain people of central Panay.* Quezon City: University of the Philippines Press.
1969 *Growing up in a Philippine barrio.* New York: Holt, Rinehart and Winston.

KAUT, CHARLES
1961 *Utang na loob:* a system of contractual obligation among Tagalogs. *Southwestern Journal of Anthropology* 17:256–272.

KEESING, FELIX M.
1949 Some notes on Bontok social organization, northern Philippines. *American Anthropologist* 51:578–601.

LANDE, NOBLEZA ASUNCION
1964 "Bibliography of Philippine linguistics." Mimeographed.

LAWLESS, ROBERT
1966 A comparative analysis of two studies on *utang na loob. Philippine Sociological Review* 14:168–172.
1967 The foundation for culture-and-personality research in the Philippines. *Asian Studies* 5:101–136.

LYNCH, FRANK
1962 Philippine values, II: social acceptance. *Philippine Studies* 10:82–99.

LYNCH, FRANK, *editor*
1964 *Four readings on Philippine values* (second revised edition). Quezon City: Ateneo de Manila University Press.

LYNCH, FRANK, MARY HOLLNSTEINER
1961 Sixty years of Philippine ethnology: a first glance at the years 1901–1961. *Science Review* 2:1–5.

MANALANG, PRISCILA S.
1971 "A Philippine rural school: its cultural dimension." University microfilms, University of Michigan.

MANUEL, E. ARSENIO
1965   *Philippine folklore bibliography; a preliminary survey.* Quezon City: Philippine Folklore Society.

MELENDEZ, PEDRO, JOSEPHINE CACCAM
1967   "The U.P. department of anthropology: 1914–1965," in *Studies in Philippine anthropology (in honor of H. Otley Beyer).* Edited by Mario D. Zamora, 6–22. Quezon City: Alemar-Phoenix.

REED, WILLIAM A.
1904   *Negritos of Zambales.* Dept. of Interior Ethnological Survey Publications 2.

SAITO, SHIRO
1972   *Philippine ethnography: a critically annotated and selected bibliography.* Honolulu: University Press.

SALEEBY, NAJEEB M.
1905   *Studies in Moro history, law, and religion.* Dept. of Interior, Ethnological Survey Publications 4.

SCHEERER, OTTO
1900   *Igorots of Benguet.* Taft Commission report. Washington, D.C.: U.S. Government Printing Office.

SNYDER, PATRICIA ANN
1971   "Education and the process of socio-cultural change in a Bisayan Filipino town: a study of conflict in the Siaton schools." University microfilms, University of Michigan.

TANGCO, MARCELO
1940   Anthropology and the Philippines. *Philippine Social Sciences and Humanities Review* 12:189–211.
1951   *The Christian peoples of the Philippines.* Natural and Applied Science Bulletin 11.

TUGBY, DONALD J.
1968   Ethnological and allied work on Southeast Asia, 1950–1966. *Current Anthropology* 9:185–206.

WARD, JACK H.
1971   *A bibliography of Philippine linguistics and minor languages* (with annotations and indices based on works in the library of Cornell University). Ithaca: Cornell Southeast Asia Program.

WELSH, DORIS V.
1950   *Checklist of Philippine linguistics in the Newberry library.* Chicago.

ZAMORA, MARIO D., *editor*
1967   *Studies in Philippine anthropology (in honor of H. Otley Beyer).* Quezon City: Alemar-Phoenix.

ZAMORA, MARIO D., JOSE Y. ARCELLANA, *editors*
1971   A bibliography of Philippine anthropology. *Verge, A Journal of Thought* 3:1–164.

ZAMORA, MARIO D., J. MICHAEL MAHAR, HENRY ORENSTEIN, *editors*
  1971 *Themes in culture (essays in honor of Morris E. Opler)*. Quezon
        City: Kayumanggi.

ZAMORA, MARIO D., ZEUS SALAZAR, *editors*
  1969 *Anthropology: range and relevance (a reader for non-anthropologists)*. Quezon City: Kayumanggi.

Biographical Notes

SYED HUSIN ALI (1936–   ) is Lecturer in Anthropology at the University of Malaya. He received his doctorate from the University of London and has published articles concerning social structure in Malaysia in the *Journal of the Royal Asiatic Society* (Malaysian Branch). He is author of *Social Stratification in Kampong Bagan* (1964) and *Malay peasants: society and leadership* (1973).

DAVID J. BANKS (1945–   ) is Associate Professor of Anthropology at the State University of New York at Buffalo. He received his doctorate in Anthropology from the University of Chicago, and has done fieldwork in West Malaysia. Among his publications are "Changing Kinship in North Malaya" in the *American Anthropologist* (1972), "Malay kinship terms and Morgan's Malayan terminology: the complexity of simplicity" in *Bijdragen Tot de Taal-, Land En Volkenkunde* (1974) and "Islam and inheritance in Malaya: culture conflict or Islamic revolution?" to appear in *American Ethnologist.*

GEOFFREY BENJAMIN (1940–   ) is Lecturer in the Department of Sociology at the University of Singapore. He received his doctorate in Anthropology from Cambridge University and did his fieldwork among the Temiar of West Malaysia. His articles include "Temiar kinship" (1967) and "Headmanship and leadership in Temiar society" (1968), published in the *Federation Museums Journal*, Kuala Lumpur, Malaysia.

ISKANDAR CAREY (1924–   ) is Lecturer in Anthropology at the University of Malaya. He completed his doctorate in Social Anthropology at the University of Edinburgh and served as Commissioner for

Aboriginal Affairs for the Malayan Government. He has written numerous articles concerning the languages and cultures of the Malayan aborigines as well as *Tenglek Kui Serok: a study of the Termiar language, with an ethnographical summary* (1961).

ROBERT K. DENTAN (1936–) is Associate Professor in the Departments of Anthropology and American Studies at the State University of New York at Buffalo. He received his doctorate in Anthropology from Yale University and has done fieldwork in East Africa, Malaysia, and Erie County, New York. He is author of a book, *The Semai, a nonviolent people of Malaya* (1968), and articles on Semai ethnography, ethnoscience, and ethnic identity.

DAVID A. FEINGOLD (1940–) is Director for Research and Planning for the Institute for the Study of Human Issues (I.S.H.I.). He directs the Institute's Center for Opium Research and is Senior Editor of *IROS: The International Review of Opium Studies*. He received his undergraduate education at Dartmouth College and graduate education in Southeast Asian Studies at Yale University and in Anthropology at Columbia University. His publications include articles and papers on Akha law, Shan political organization, face-to-face interaction, and the ecology of opium agriculture. He has recently co-edited a book with Karen Kerner: *Perspectives on the evasion of social responsibility*.

JAMES W. HAMILTON (1930–) is Associate Professor of Anthropology at the University of Missouri. He received his doctorate in Anthropology from the University of Michigan and has done fieldwork in Thailand, Tanzania, and Mexico. His works include "Effects of the Thai market on Karen life" in *Practical Anthropology* (1963) and "Problems in Government Anthropology" in *Anthropology Beyond the University* (1973).

RIAZ HASSAN (1937–) completed his graduate studies at Ohio State University and is currently Lecturer in the Department of Sociology at the University of Singapore.

MARILYN W. HOSKINS (1934–) studied family and child development and nutrition at Southern Illinois University. She received her M.S. in this field from Ohio State University and her M.A. in Anthropology from the Catholic University of America. She did research for the U.S. Department of Agriculture on goals and values of young Ohio farm families. In 1962–1965 she lived in Vietnam where she taught research methods in a UNESCO program at the University of Saigon, did research and wrote on goals and values of rural Vietnamese families, and prepared an ethnographic study of an urban area in Saigon. In 1965–1967 she was in Thailand where she wrote a series of articles on Thai women. Since 1967 she has served in Washington as a consultant to the U.S. Government on cultural values of Southeast Asian societies and has published on this subject.

KENJIRO ICHIKAWA (1925–) is Professor of History and Anthropology at the Tokyo University of Fisheries. He received his B.S. degree from the University of Tokyo. He has published "Japanese and Chinese societies in Bangkok" in the *Journal of Tokyo University of Fisheries* (1974).

MILADA KALAB (1924–) is Lecturer in the Department of Anthropology in the University of Durham. She received her education at Santiketan in West Bengal, The University of Bombay, and The University of London. She has done fieldwork in Thailand and Cambodia and in the frontier regions of Manipur and Nagaland in India. Her interests include education and the study of social mobility. She has published the "Study of a Cambodian village" in *The Geographical Journal* of the Royal Geographical Society of London (1968).

PETER K. KANDRE (1931–) is Research Associate in the Department of Social Anthropology at Uppsala University, Sweden. He has done fieldwork concerning the cultural geography of northern Thailand, western Laos, and Burma. His publications include "Alternative modes of recruitment of variable households among the Yao of Mae Chan" in *The South-East Asian Journal of Sociology* (1971) and "Autonomy and integration of social systems: the Iu Mien ('Yao' or 'Man') mountain population and their neighbors," in *Southeast Asian Tribes, Minorities and Nations* (1967).

T. G. MCGEE (1936–) received his B.A. from the University of New Zealand and his M.A. and Ph.D. degrees from the Victoria University of Wellington, New Zealand. He has taught at the Universities of Malaya, Hong Kong, and Wellington. He is at present Senior Fellow in the Department of Human Geography, Research

23

School of Pacific Studies, Institute of Advanced Studies, Australian National University. He is author of *The Southeast Asian city* (1967), *The urbanization process in the Third World* (1971), *Hawkers in Hong Kong* (1974), and numerous other publications. He is at present on the editorial boards of *Human Organization, Urban Anthropology, Pacific Viewpoint* and the *Journal of Urban History*.

PHILIP FRICK MCKEAN (1936–) is Associate Professor of Anthropology in the School of Social Science, Hampshire College, Amherst, Massachusetts. He studied Divinity at Brown University after completing a B.A. degree from Yale, and completed a doctorate in Anthropology at the same university. He has taught as Lecturer in the Department of Anthropology, Udayana University, Den Pasar, Bali. His writings include: "The trickster figure in Indonesian folklore: a translation, historical and structural analysis of *Kantjil* tales," in the *Journal of Asian Folklore* (1973) and "From purity to pollution? The Balinese *ketjak* as a symbolic form in transition," forthcoming from the Society for Asian Studies in a symposium on Space, Time, and Symbolic Forms in Southeast Asia.

NEIL H. OLSEN (1946–) is a Research Assistant affiliated with the Social Sciences and Linguistics Institute at the University of Hawaii. He received his education at the University of California, Northridge, and the University of Hawaii, Manoa, where he received his M.A. (1976) in Linguistics. His thesis title is: "An acoustic-phonetic study of a Sre idiolect". In addition, his publications include: *Basic Koho—grammar and conversation guide* (1968) and "Sre kinship terminology" to appear in *Mon-Khmer Studies*, Number 6. He is currently working on a computer-assisted compilation of a Trukese-English dictionary.

LOURDES R. QUISUMBING (1921–) is Dean of St. Theresa's College in Cebu City and Professor of Education and Anthropology at the University of San Carlos Graduate School, Cebu, the Philippines. Among her interests are culture-personality studies, the Filipino family, and child-rearing. Her researches and publications include "Marriage customs in rural Cebu," "Child-rearing practices in the rural environs of Cebu City," "Interlocking relationships in a mountain sitio," and "Paraliturgical elements in the Mango Harvest Festival."

BENJAMIN N. F. WHITE (1946–) was born in England. He studied at Oxford University (B.A. 1968) and is now at the Department of Anthropology, Columbia University, where he is writing a Ph.D. dissertation based on field research done in a Javanese village in 1972–1973. His interests include anthropological demography, economic anthropology, Southeast Asian ethnography, and contemporary development problems.

WILLIAM D. WILDER (1939–) is Lecturer in the Department of Anthropology at the University of Durham. Mr. Wilder received his B.A. degree from Harvard University and has pursued graduate studies at the London School of Economics. He is author of a number of papers on Malay culture and society including "Socialization and social structure in a Malay village," in *Socialization: the approach from social anthropology* (1970), and "Islam, other factors and Malay backwardness: comments on an argument," in *Readings on Malaysian economic development* (1975). He has also written papers concerning general theoretical issues in the study of kinship and social structure: "Purum descent groups: some vagaries of method" in *Rethinking kinship and marriage* (1971).

MARIO D. ZAMORA (1935–) is Professor of Anthropology at the College of William and Mary, Williamsburg, Virginia. He has been Chairman of the Department of Anthropology at the University of the Philippines and Dean of the University of the Philippines at Baguio. He is editor of *Studies in Third World Societies: An Interdisciplinary Journal on Asia, Africa and Latin America*. He has done fieldwork in the Philippines, India, and the United States and is the author of numerous scholarly publications. He is editor of *Themes in culture* (*essays in honor of Morris E. Opler*) (1971).

Index of Names

Index of Subjects

Akha, 72, 83–92
Akha-English dictionary (Lewis), 91
American Anthropological Association, 95, 319, 331; *Report of the Committee on Minorities and Anthropology*, 38
American Anthropologist (journal), 38
American Ethnologist (journal), 38
American Indian, The (Eggan), 319
Angeles University, Philippines, 332
Anthropos (journal), 330
Asia Foundation, 325
Asian Perspectives (journal), 313, 330–331
Assam, 249
Ateneo de Davao University, Philippines, 332
Ateneo de Manila University, Philippines, 320, 322, 324, 327–328, 329, 332, 334; Institute of Philippine Culture, 324, 325, 328, 330, 333
Austronesian, 249, 251–252, 253

Baduj, kinship systems among, 297–298
Baguio Colleges Foundation, Philippines, 332
Bahá'i, 63, 64, 66
Bahnar, 252
Bahnaric languages, 251–252
Bali, 25–29, 237–245; kinship systems in, 295–299, 303–305, 306; local

audience in, 241–242; National Tourist Development Office, 239–240; spirit audience in, 241; tourist audience in, 242–243
Bali Museum, 237
Bantu, 200
Benguet Igorots, 314
Berita Harian (Malay newspaper), 215, 216, 218, 224
Book of the marriage custom (Iu Mien document), 175–177, 183
Borneo, 74–75; kinship systems in, 295, 299–301
Brown University, 237
Buddhism, 155, 157–168, 190–191
Buddhist University, Cambodia, 167–168
Burma, 83, 86, 148, 187, 191, 249; Iu Mien in, 172–174, 180; kinship systems in, 295, 299

Cairo, 200
Cambodia: Buddhist monasteries in, 155–168; Khmer Peace Committee, 166; National Congress, 159
Cambodian News, 166
Canadian Sociology and Anthropology Association, 331
Carnegie Corporation, 291
"Castes, estates, classes and religion" (Weber), 24–25
Catholic University of America, 330
Census of India, 1911 (Webb), 83